# HANDBOOK OF RESEARCH ON SOCIAL ENTREPRENEURSHIP

# Handbook of Research on Social Entrepreneurship

*Edited by*

## Alain Fayolle

*Professor of Entrepreneurship, EMLYON Business School, France and Visiting Professor, Solvay Brussels School of Economics and Management, Belgium*

## Harry Matlay

*Professor of Small Business and Enterprise Development, Birmingham City Business School, Birmingham City University, UK*

**Edward Elgar**
Cheltenham, UK • Northampton, MA, USA

Published by
Edward Elgar Publishing Limited
The Lypiatts
15 Lansdown Road
Cheltenham
Glos GL50 2JA
UK

Edward Elgar Publishing, Inc.
William Pratt House
9 Dewey Court
Northampton
Massachusetts 01060
USA

A catalogue record for this book
is available from the British Library

Library of Congress Control Number: 2009941155

ISBN 978 1 84844 427 0 (hardback)
ISBN 978 0 85793 330 0 (paperback)

Typeset by Servis Filmsetting Ltd, Stockport, Cheshire
Printed and bound by CPI Group (UK) Ltd, Croydon, CR0 4YY

# Contents

# Contributors

**Terri F. Barr**, Miami University, USA

**Jerome Boncler**, Université Montesquieu Bordeaux IV, France

**François Brouard**, Sprott School of Business, Carleton University (Ottawa), Canada

**Giovany Cajaiba-Santana**, EMLYON Business School, France

**Jacques Defourny**, HEC-University of Liège, Belgium

**Alain Fayolle**, EMLYON Business School, France

**Mark D. Griffiths**, Stern School of Business, New York University, USA

**Lisa Gundry**, De Paul University (Chicago), USA

**Valerie Hackl**, University of St Gallen, Switzerland

**Chantal Hervieux**, Université du Québec à Montréal, Canada

**Daniel Hjorth**, Copenhagen Business School, Denmark

**Martine Hlady Rispal**, Université Montesquieu Bordeaux IV, France

**Jill Kickul**, Stern School of Business, New York University, USA

**Sophie Larivet**, École Supérieure du Commerce Extérieur (ESCE), Paris, France

**Gregg A. Lichtenstein**, Collaborative Strategies, LLC, USA

**Thomas S. Lyons**, Baruch College, City University of New York, Zicklin School of Business, USA

**Johanna Mair**, IESE Business School, Spain

**Harry Matlay**, Birmingham City Business School, UK

**Paul Myers**, Simmons School of Management, USA

**Teresa Nelson**, Simmons School of Management, USA and EUROMED Management, France

**Raymond Saner**, University of Basle and CSEND Geneva, Switzerland

**Brett R. Smith**, Miami University, USA

**Christopher E. Stevens**, Gonzaga University, USA

**Elisabeth Sundin**, School of Management, Linköping University, Sweden

**Malin Tillmar**, School of Management, Linköping University, Sweden

**Marie-France B. Turcotte**, Université du Québec à Montréal, Canada

**Patrick Valéau**, Université de la Réunion, France

**Thierry Volery**, University of St Gallen, Switzerland

**Lichia Yiu**, CSEND, Geneva, Switzerland

# 1 Social entrepreneurship: a multicultural and multidimensional perspective
*Alain Fayolle and Harry Matlay*

The current financial crisis and its global consequences have increased the need to position social questions at the heart of the economy. We believe that entrepreneurship can be an important way to restore a better balance between economic purposes and social well-being. Indeed, entrepreneurship can be a great source of economic value creation, but it can also be (or at least should be) a means to contribute to greater social justice. This concept seems to be gaining momentum, both in theory and practice, with the emergence of a new field of research: 'social entrepreneurship'.

Entrepreneurship is a multidimensional phenomenon and is shaped by the context in which it operates. The entrepreneurial process, generally defined as 'how, by whom and with what effects opportunities to create new goods and services are discovered, evaluated and exploited' (Shane and Venkataraman, 2000), is very much conditioned by the level of economic development and the cultural, political and social contexts in which it appears (Atamer and Torres, 2008). It is common knowledge, for example, that entrepreneurship in developing countries, or countries in transition, is quantitatively and qualitatively different from what we observe in most industrially developed countries.

The main vocation of social entrepreneurship – besides new venture creation with a social purpose – is to meet social and societal needs that have not yet been addressed by the state or the commercial sector (Alvord et al., 2004; Thompson, 2002). Unlike the commercial and capitalistic economy, which is narrowly concerned with meeting strictly financial objectives, social entrepreneurship promotes a logic of solidarity that favours social cohesion and welfare. Social entrepreneurship, and the place it occupies in contemporary society, makes us wonder about the return to the origins of a concept that first appeared in the nineteenth century, albeit in a different form. We postulate that this increased interest in social entrepreneurship is not totally alien to the radical changes that have affected nations since the first oil crisis, and that it supports entrepreneurial behaviour at every level of economic activity. The reassertion of social entrepreneurship seems to be linked to significant evolutions in the entrepreneurial phenomenon, which reflect a desire to restore the balance between its two structuring components: the economy and social well-being.

## ENTREPRENEURSHIP: AN EVOLVING PHENOMENON THAT IS HEADING TOWARDS . . . MORE SOCIAL ADDED VALUE

The nature of entrepreneurship is changing from a narrow, simplistic vision[1] (new venture creation) to a more sophisticated and complex perception. As the phenomenon gains impetus, we are witnessing a multiplication of its definitions and forms. Some authors evoke the emergence of an entrepreneurial economy in which knowledge, in particular, plays a key role (Audretsch and Thurik, 2004). Implicitly, they also talk of an entrepreneurial society and institutional or cultural norms, applied nationally or locally, that would contribute to shaping entrepreneurs by influencing individual behaviour (see, for example, Audretsch, 2007). For others, entrepreneurship is a method, a frame of mind, a way of thinking, of raising and solving problems. The systemic view is adopted by many practitioners and researchers (see, in particular, Bruyat, 1993) in this field of economic activity. The new firm is seen as an open system that evolves within its environment: it is not surprising, therefore, to see that great importance is granted to actor networks, social interactions and exchanges with the institutional environment. Whatever the context under consideration, the development of entrepreneurship seems largely conditioned by the implementation of a specific ecosystem. The entrepreneur is a component of this system, but he is far from playing the leading role, or at least his expertise and skills have evolved into a situational intelligence, that is to say a capacity to decode the contexts (political, economic, legal, social and cultural environments) with which he intends to interact.

Consequently, the environment in its broadest sense, entrepreneurial support systems and related stakeholders are becoming increasingly important. Researchers suggest, for example, the need to create an entrepreneurial ecosystem[2] in order to develop rural entrepreneurship (Lee and Phan, 2008) or to enable the environment to specialize and allocate structures and resources that will dynamically encourage the process of new venture creation (Venkataraman, 2004). Several authors argue that entrepreneurship and its benefits can only develop within a formal institutional framework designed to promote and support entrepreneurial activity. This suggests a rethinking of public policies, which are often founded on well established and tested ideas and/or assumptions.[3] As a result, most of the outcomes of entrepreneurial policies are disappointing and myths are maintained regarding entrepreneurs' contribution to economic and employment growth. Some believe that public policies target all and sundry, whereas many researchers attribute the inefficiency of support measures to the variety or complexity of entrepreneurial situations and contexts within which these are deployed. We suggest that there is a need, on the one hand, to find the most appropriate frameworks and methods to evaluate public policies and, on the other hand, to simplify and clarify entrepreneurial policies, measures and support initiatives.

The culmination of these developments in entrepreneurship, on both economic and social levels, seems to manifest in the emergence of new forms of entrepreneurship, such as social and rural entrepreneurship, not only in industrially developed countries such as France and Great Britain, but also developing countries and those in transition. These new forms of entrepreneurship appear to correspond to new social and economic needs and an increasing awareness of the limits of a liberal logic pushed to its extreme.

The social and solidarity-based economy, however, is not a new phenomenon: it is the result of nineteenth-century political policy in France that attempted to react and respond to the rampant capitalism of the time. Similarly, the cooperative movement is not a recent phenomenon, and cooperative enterprises are to a large extent already part of the social economy. The solidarity-based economy appeared more recently, notably in the 'alterglobalist' discourse. It appears as a set of initiatives in an action/reaction approach to compensate for shortcomings and social failures resulting from state and private organization interventions.

Social entrepreneurship aims to better accommodate a social dimension within the traditional economic behaviour, to take into consideration social problems, countries' and communities' contexts and situations, and the plight of socially challenged or disadvantaged individuals. Within this movement, we encounter the search for greater social justice and inclusion. It is in this way that entrepreneurs can contribute to the development of humanity and social progress – and social entrepreneurship appears to be a unique method that helps us rethink, reformulate and resolve human problems on the path to social progress.

The emergence of social entrepreneurship raises two important questions that will be addressed in this book: 1) what are the forms and manifestations of social entrepreneurship; and, 2) to what extent should current developments lead to a redefinition of stakeholders' strategies and roles in the quest for better consideration of the social dimension? The chapters that form Parts II and III set out to address these questions in some detail. Part III deals with social entrepreneurship from a multicultural perspective in order to highlight the diversity of social entrepreneurship forms and practices. From a strategic perspective, Part III investigates the essential role played by various factors and actors in the development of social entrepreneurship.

Social entrepreneurship encompasses a variety of meanings and perspectives, depending on authors and contexts (much like entrepreneurship in general), and this results in a great deal of conceptual confusion. In view of a vast array of related concepts and contexts, attempting to define social entrepreneurship is not a simple task. The definition put forward by Zahra and his colleagues, for example, is in line with the concept of entrepreneurship that we have given previously. It stipulates that social entrepreneurship 'encompasses the activities and processes undertaken to discover, define and exploit opportunities in order to enhance social wealth by creating new ventures or managing existing organizations in an innovative manner' (Zahra et al., 2009). It is important to note, however, that a multitude of other definitions or concepts of social entrepreneurship coexist in the specialist literature, as illustrated in the first part of the Handbook of Research on Social Entrepreneurship.

## PART I   A CONCEPTUAL AND DEFINITIONAL PERSPECTIVE OF SOCIAL ENTREPRENEURSHIP

In Chapter 2, 'Social entrepreneurship: taking stock and looking ahead', Johanna Mair raises essential questions about social entrepreneurship. She attempts to elucidate why social entrepreneurship exists in the first place, and what its implications are. She discusses the nature and the contents of social entrepreneurship. The author sets out to take stock of existing practices in order to conceptualize this phenomenon. She then goes on to illustrate its context-specific nature, and to draw implications for fostering social entrepreneurship as a positive force for social and economic development. The main objectives are twofold: first, to help stimulate a productive agenda for future research, one that goes beyond questions of 'who' and 'what' by pursuing the important considerations of 'where', 'why' and 'how'; and second, in so doing, to generate insights for advances in both social entrepreneurship theory and practice.

Chapter 3, the 'Essay of clarifications and definitions of the related concepts of social enterprise, social entrepreneur and social entrepreneurship', written by François Brouard and Sophie Larivet, throws light on three different, but related notions. Social entrepreneurship is an emergent concept gaining in popularity across industrially developed and developing economies. University courses have been developed on this aspect of entrepreneurship, relevant research has been disseminated in specialized journals, new associations were dedicated to the promotion of social entrepreneurship and numerous government initiatives were implemented to support it. The concept of social entrepreneurship, however, is not well defined or even understood. Concepts such as social enterprise, social entrepreneurs, and social entrepreneurship represent different meanings, yet are often used interchangeably in both the research and practitioner literature. Based on a literature review and an analysis of various definitions, the objective of the chapter is to distinguish between social enterprise, social entrepreneur and social entrepreneurship, to provide a definition for each concept, and clarify their relationships.

In Chapter 4, 'Concepts and realities of social enterprise: a European perspective', Jacques Defourny underlines the fact that the concept of 'social enterprise' can be used to designate two quite different phenomena: on the one hand, they refer to new ventures, created *ex nihilo* that may often be viewed as a sub-group of the third sector; on the other hand, they can also designate a process, a new entrepreneurial spirit influencing and reshaping older, third sector initiatives. The chapter begins with a discussion of the main approaches that, for more than a quarter century, have been developed to describe the realities of the third sector. From this perspective, the author then analyses the European approach to social entrepreneurship mainly through empirical work from the first 15 European Union members. The chapter provides valuable insights by analysing European theoretical potential in the light of the most recent developments in North American research.

In Chapter 5, 'Socially constructed opportunities in social entrepreneurship: a structuration model', Giovany Cajaiba-Santana proposes a theoretical framework for the study of social entrepreneurship. The research on social entrepreneurship has gained momentum over the last decade. Nevertheless, its theoretical frameworks have not yet been fully explored and there is considerable room for contributions to both theory and practice. To date, one important issue that researchers have neglected to explore is the concept of opportunity in a social entrepreneurship context. This chapter addresses the question of how best to study the phenomenon of social entrepreneurship as a socially constructed phenomenon. This implies that both the entrepreneur and the opportunity are intrinsically linked to the social context within which they are embedded, co-evolve with this social system and should not be studied independently from each other. Drawing upon structuration theory, a model is proposed in order to guide future inquiry and increase the empirical relevance of this emergent concept.

## PART II   A CONTEXTUAL PERSPECTIVE OF SOCIAL ENTREPRENEURSHIP

Chapter 6, 'Social entrepreneurship in France: organizational and relational issues' focuses specifically upon the French context. As stated by the authors, Martine Hlady Rispal and Jerome Boncler, French social entrepreneurship involves the community in meeting the demand that governments and markets no longer engage with. It pursues social aims that set it apart from mainstream, profit-driven entrepreneurs. Thus, social enterprises present specific challenges to set up as well as operate. The solutions proposed in this chapter are based on the French-language literature and a selection of relevant case studies. It identifies the prime distinctions from mainstream enterprise and relates the issues generated by adherence to the principles of social entrepreneurship.

In Chapter 7, 'Sustainable transborder business cooperation in the European regions: the importance of social entrepreneurship', Raymond Saner and Lichia Yiu highlight the importance of social entrepreneurship in promoting cross-border business cooperation and ensuring its sustainability. Three social roles are investigated and put forward as solutions that could facilitate transborder integration, namely those of Business Diplomats, Entrepreneurial Politicians and Cultural Ambassadors. These roles are proposed as complementary social competencies for businessmen, government officials and representatives of society, who play a leading role in transborder cooperation. The tri-national region of the Upper Rhine Valley is used to illustrate the potential usefulness of these new concepts. The area in question encompasses neighbouring provinces of Switzerland (Basle), France (Alsace) and Germany (Baden and Southern Palatine).

Chapter 8, 'The intertwining of social, commercial and public entrepreneurship' contributes empirical cases of social entrepreneurship in commercial and public sectors. In this chapter, Elisabeth Sundin and Malin Tillmar have drawn on Schumpeter and argue that entrepreneurship exists in all types of organizations (but not in all organizations) and apply this principle to the field of social entrepreneurship. Consequently, the authors suggest that social entrepreneurship is also to be found in the public sector, in what has been termed 'public entrepreneurship'. They propose a typology which implies a re-contextualization of social entrepreneurship. This typology aims to serve as a methodological and theoretical guideline for future research in social entrepreneurship.

In Chapter 9, 'The promise of social franchising as a model to achieve social goals', Thierry Volery and Valerie Hackl offer insights into the concept of social franchising. Social franchising is an adaptation of commercial franchising in which the developer of a successful social concept (franchisor) enables others (franchisees) to replicate the model by using a proven system and a brand name in order to pursue and achieve social benefits. Social franchising can be defined as a system of contractual relationships, which uses the structure of a commercial franchise to achieve social goals. As such, it is a new institutional arrangement in the field of social entrepreneurship and it represents a promising leverage tool to achieve social goals. The chapter aims to outline the potential of social franchising, as an organizational form, to grow and develop social ventures. The authors examine the relevance of two main theories – agency theory and social capital theory – as pertinent to social franchising. This leads to a description of the data collection and analysis procedure. Following an account of a multiple case study, the authors then consider the structure and coordination features of social franchising and distinguish them from the activities of commercial franchises.

In Chapter 10, 'Social entrepreneurs' actions in networks', Chantal Hervieux and Marie-France B. Turcotte use network theories to study relevant social entrepreneurship research questions. The authors argue that, to date, social entrepreneurship research has focused mainly on descriptive case studies or definitional aspects, with a marked lack of theory building. Based on previous case studies in social entrepreneurship, the authors propose to fill this gap. They offer conceptual insights based both on theory – Granovetter's theory on weak ties – and on observation from a case study of a Northern Fair Trade cooperative. Data for the case study was collected over a 10-month period, using multiple methods and data sources (interviews, observation, published articles on this organization, internal documents, and so on). Based on the grounded theory method, the authors alternated phases of data collection and analysis and used alternative inductive and deductive coding.

## PART III    A STRATEGIC PERSPECTIVE OF SOCIAL ENTREPRENEURSHIP

In Chapter 11, 'Social entrepreneurs in non-profit organizations: innovation and dilemmas', Patrick Valéau argues that entrepreneurship within the non-profit sector does not happen without difficulties and appears in many ways more complicated than traditional entrepreneurship in the for-profit sector. The main problem faced by these entrepreneurs lies in the fact that they combine a number of values and goals. They want their organizations to be sustainable, to develop and even grow and, at the same time, to respect values such as independence, equality and solidarity. Such entrepreneurs aim to professionalize their structure and also to remain spontaneous, collective and democratic. They set out to help others, but sometimes feel like giving up. As a result, these entrepreneurs cannot always seize simple and obvious opportunities. They often encounter situations that do not allow them to cater for their various values and goals simultaneously, often forcing them to arbitrate. These times of confrontation of their ideal vision with reality are, according to the author, turning points for the social entrepreneurs in non-profit organizations.

Chapter 12, 'Innovating for social impact: is bricolage the catalyst for change?' adopts Claude Lévi-Strauss's theoretical framework of bricolage to investigate socially oriented change. The authors, Jill Kickul, Mark D. Griffiths and Lisa Gundry, focus on the prosocial behaviour of entrepreneurs whose environments are typically resource constrained. In this empirically rigorous study of bricolage behaviour by social entrepreneurs, the authors used a three-equation mediational model and found that the growth rate of social impact is fully mediated by catalytic innovation. It emerges that catalytic innovation serves as an important link between bricolage behaviour and the growth rate of social impact. In impoverished environments, bricolage may explain key behaviours that social entrepreneurs adopt when they encounter institutional constraints and are without regulatory structure or support.

Chapter 13, 'A community-wide framework for encouraging social entrepreneurship using the pipeline of entrepreneurs and enterprises model', written by Thomas S. Lyons and Gregg A. Lichtenstein, proposes an original approach to social entrepreneurship. The field of social entrepreneurship is ripe for research that enables it to go beyond description toward the establishment of its own theory, testing of theory, and the creation of models for its successful effectuation. This chapter falls into this latter category and the authors modify the 'Pipeline of Entrepreneurs and Enterprises' model to make it a relevant tool for thinking about, and effectively managing, a community's social entrepreneurship assets. In this chapter, the authors briefly explore the current literature on social entrepreneurship and its impact upon practitioners, both social entrepreneurs and those who assist them to take effective action. They outline the theory, its relationship and utility to social entrepreneurship, and demonstrate how the pipeline could be used to manage the social assets of a community effectively. The chapter concludes by noting potential and related uses for the pipeline model in social entrepreneurship research.

In Chapter 14, 'Considering social capital in the context of social entrepreneurship', Paul Myers and Teresa Nelson use the experiences of information technology (IT) executive and social entrepreneur Radha Basu to examine key conceptual areas for the purpose of understanding how social enterprise goals narrow, broaden, challenge and/or otherwise change current understandings of social capital deployment. In this context, theoretical extensions of the process and content of social capital creation are suggested in regard to the practice of social entrepreneurship and, given its core objective, a radical innovation for social welfare enhancement. The authors perceive the complex use of social capital by social entrepreneurs as an informative general model for entrepreneurs and entrepreneurship researchers, as value creation is considered. The chapter begins by defining the concept of social capital and how it relates to social entrepreneurship. The authors then present the case of Basu's social venture, the Anudip Foundation for Social Welfare, to demonstrate the role that social capital can play in the formation and growth of ventures that embrace both social and commercial purposes. The chapter concludes with a discussion of the theoretical and research implications emerging from this exploratory analysis.

Chapter 15, 'Social entrepreneurs and earned income opportunities: the dilemma of earned income pursuit', by Brett R. Smith, Christopher E. Stevens and Terri F. Barr, returns to the concept of entrepreneurial opportunity (see Chapter 5). One common form of social entrepreneurship is the pursuit of earned income opportunities (EIOs) by non-profit organizations. In the pursuit of EIOs, social and economic value creation come into close proximity to one another and this raises questions about the tensions involved in such dual-value creation processes. Through exploratory qualitative evidence the authors identify three primary 'tensions' experienced by non-profit organizations: (1) organizational identity tensions; (2) institutional tensions; and (3) risk-related pressures. Collectively, these aspects provide a more nuanced understanding of the dilemmas often faced by social entrepreneurs in the evaluation and exploitation of EIOs and offer rich conceptual lenses for future empirical and theoretical research in social entrepreneurship.

## CONCLUDING REMARKS

In this introductory chapter we have tried, based on the richness and variety of contributions, to underline the multiculturalism and the multidimensionality of social entrepreneurship. It is widely acknowledged, for example, that North American and European approaches to social entrepreneurship can differ considerably. Furthermore, we can also see differences within the European approach to social entrepreneurship.

In here, we have introduced 14 chapters presented in three parts, but the book includes two additional chapters. One is our conclusion, focusing on recommendations for future research in social entrepreneurship (Chapter

17). The other is Chapter 16, 'Ending essay: sociality and economy in social entrepreneurship', written by Daniel Hjorth. This chapter could also be seen as a more general conclusion to this volume. Daniel Hjorth reaffirms a claim made in earlier publications that 'entrepreneurship is a social force creating society, and not only (or even primarily) an economic force creating companies and products'. Having been interested for a long time in analysing social entrepreneurship discourse, Daniel Hjorth criticizes the dominant Anglo-American discourse which sees social entrepreneurship as an extension of the market into new areas of society, in order to represent social problems as economic. He suggests 'the need to move into a discussion of the public and the role of the citizen therein, rather than to stay with the social (re-described in terms of the economic) and its central figure – the consumer'. Daniel Hjorth's conclusion is a call to refuse to limit the social entrepreneurship concept to the economic, managerial, strategic, or decisional nature of practices. Social entrepreneurship should also include the political and ethical sides of the field.

## NOTES

1. Which does not of course question its social and economic importance.
2. All the interconnected elements including individual risk takers, resource providers, intermediaries, needs and demand for goods and services, likely to act together in order to create a virtuous circle of wealth creation. (Source: Lee and Phan, 2008.)
3. See for example articles by Philippe Albert and Didier Chabaud in the first issue of *L'Expansion Entrepreneuriat* (January 2009), as well as the book by Scott Shane (2008).

## REFERENCES

Albert, P. (2009), 'Le high-tech, grande illusion de décideur', *L'Expansion Entrepreneuriat*, **1**, January, 14–19.
Alvord, S.H., L.D. Brown and C.W. Letts (2004), 'Social entrepreneurship and societal transformation: an explanatory study', *The Journal of Applied Behavioural Science*, **40**(3), 260–83.
Atamer, T. and O. Torres (2008), 'Modèles d'entrepreneuriat et mondialisation', in A. Fayolle (ed.), *L'Art d'Entreprendre*, Paris: Editions Village Mondiale, pp. 29–37.
Audretsch, D.B. (2007), *The Entrepreneurial Society*, Oxford: Oxford University Press.
Audretsch, D.B. and A.R. Thurik (2004), 'A model of the entrepreneurial economy', *International Journal of Entrepreneurship Education*, **2**, 143–66.
Bruyat, C. (1993), 'Creation d'entreprise: contributions épistémologiques et modélisation', unpublished doctoral dissertation in Management Science, Grenoble.
Chabaud, D. (2009), 'Pour sortir de la naïveté sur la création d'entreprise', *L'Expansion Entrepreneuriat*, **1**, January, 62–5.
Lee, S.H. and P.P. Phan (2008), 'Initial thoughts on a model of rural entrepreneurship in developing countries', working paper, World Entrepreneurship Forum 2008, EMLYON Business School.

Shane, S.A. (2008), *The Illusions of Entrepreneurship: The Costly Myths that Entrepreneurs, Investors and Policy Makers Live By*, New Haven, CT: Yale University Press.

Shane, S.A. and V. Venkataraman (2000), 'The promise of entrepreneurship as a field of research', *Academy of Management Review*, **25**(1), 217–26.

Thompson, J. (2002), 'The world of the social entrepreneur', *The International Journal of Public Sector Management*, **15**(4–5), 412–31.

Venkataraman, S. (2004), 'Regional transformation through technological entrepreneurship', *Journal of Business Venturing*, **19**, 153–60.

Zahra, S.A., E. Gedajlovic, D.O. Neubaum and J.M. Shulman (2009), 'A typology of social entrepreneurs: motives, search processes and ethical challenges', *Journal of Business Venturing*, **25**(4), 519–32.

# PART I

# A CONCEPTUAL
# AND DEFINITIONAL
# PERSPECTIVE OF SOCIAL
# ENTREPRENEURSHIP

# 2 Social entrepreneurship: taking stock and looking ahead
*Johanna Mair*

## SOCIAL ENTREPRENEURSHIP: A TREND OR MORE?

Social entrepreneurship is trendy! Every year in February social entrepreneurs mingle with the CEOs of the world's largest corporations and prominent politicians at the World Economic Forum in Davos. Social entrepreneurs are the VIPs at other global events such as the Clinton Global Initiative and they are the favourite investees of the 'new' philanthropists: the Jeff Skolls or Bill Gates of this world. Although the academic interest in social entrepreneurship is increasing – calls for special issues are launched; international academic conferences and workshops are organized – research and scholarly investigation into the phenomenon can hardly be regarded as the catalysing force behind the recent momentum on social entrepreneurship.

Instead one could argue that it has been elite endorsement of the phenomenon by the leaders of powerful communities – political, business, philanthropic and celebrity – that has stimulated the broad interest in and public exposure to social entrepreneurship as a defining trend of the twenty-first century.[1] What is special about social entrepreneurship as a trend is that its diffusion occurs in parallel within different domains, each with separate networks and agendas. Ideas associated with social entrepreneurship have permeated several different spheres of society and kick off development within these realms. In politics, for example, it has inspired proactive legislation for community and social enterprise and debates on the future of the welfare system under the UK's Blair administration (Grenier, 2009). In association with the label business at the 'base of the pyramid' (BOP) it has stimulated thinking and acting around new business models with and for low-income populations in the developing, and now increasingly in the developed world (Seelos and Mair, 2007). In finance the latest discussion reflecting social entrepreneurship centres around social stock markets, socially-responsible investing, and the creation of a new asset class (Emerson, 2003). Finally the field of philanthropy has witnessed a dramatic shift towards strategic and impact orientation (Letts and Ryan,

1997) inspired by the business acumen of successful social entrepreneurs. While at present these trends occur in their defined domains, the potential exists for social entrepreneurship to blur the long-established boundaries between the public, private and citizen sectors. This process could occur in two stages: the first involving a blending mainly at the discursive level; but in a second stage this blending might well occur at the level of behaviour, for example, by the exchange and alignment of practices and professional standards.

So is social entrepreneurship just hype, a fashion or something more? In fact, for researchers, whether it is a trend or indicative of something greater does not matter; it is more important to understand why social entrepreneurship exists in the first place, and what the implications are. This chapter sets out to take stock of existing endeavours to conceptualize around the phenomenon. It then goes on to illustrate its context-specific nature, and finally to derive implications for fostering social entrepreneurship as a positive force for social and economic development. The objectives of this chapter are twofold: first, to help stimulate a productive agenda for future research that goes beyond questions of 'who' and 'what' by pursuing the important considerations of 'where', 'why' and 'how'; and second, in so doing, to generate real insights for advances in both theory and practice.

## A VARIETY OF MEANINGS AND A VARIETY OF PERSPECTIVES

In parallel with the number of articles in the public press and journals, the number of definitions used to describe the phenomenon of social entrepreneurship has also notably increased. Social entrepreneurship means different things to different people. It also means different things to people in different places. Social venturing, non-profit organizations adopting commercial strategies, social cooperative enterprises, and community entrepreneurship are just some of the distinct phenomena discussed and analysed under the 'umbrella construct' of social entrepreneurship.[2] I deliberately emphasize 'distinct' phenomena, since the entrepreneur, the entrepreneurial process and the activities involved, as well as the environment that enables or triggers entrepreneurship, all differ substantially. Research and public discourse refer to a variety of actors and activities as social entrepreneurs and social entrepreneurship. Table 2.1 illustrates the diversity in both discourse and phenomena. Although all these phenomena embrace a social impact dimension, they differ substantially with respect to the actors, contexts and mechanisms at play, and theories of social change.

*Table 2.1*   *A snapshot of phenomena discussed under the umbrella construct of social entrepreneurship*

| Phenomenon under study | Description | Key author |
|---|---|---|
| Community entrepreneurship | The community is the entrepreneurial actor and beneficiary. E.g., a village engaging in fair trade coffee farming and selling. | (Peredo and Chrisman, 2006; Johannisson and Nilsson, 1989) |
| Social change agents | Individuals who alter public perceptions about (specific) social issues. Examples range from John Elkington, the founder of sustainability, to Bono, of the group U2. | (Waddock and Post, 1991; Drayton, 2002) |
| Institutional entrepreneurs | Individuals or organizations that alter social arrangements and the institutional fabric hampering development. | (Mair and Martí, 2009; Martí and Mair, 2009) |
| Social ventures | Business ventures that provide a product or service that creates social or environmental benefit, such as the production and distribution of biodegradable water bottles. | (Dorado, 2006; Sharir and Lerner, 2006) |
| Entrepreneurial non-profit organizations | Non-profit organizations that engage in commercial activities to create an income stream and enhance financial sustainability. | (Fowler, 2000; Frumkin, 2002) |
| Social enterprise | Organizational forms following principles of cooperatives. | (Borzaga and Defourny, 2001) |
| Social innovation | Innovation understood broadly and including processes and technology for the social good. | (Alvord et al. 2004; Phills et al., 2008) |

From a research perspective, social entrepreneurship is currently clearly enjoying an 'emerging excitement' (Hirsch and Levin, 1999) from various disciplines and theories, yet as a scholarly field of investigation it faces two major challenges. First, many of the perspectives and research fields it engages, such as entrepreneurship theory or the literature on non-profit organizations, largely lack theoretical consensus themselves and, therefore, it is not surprising that a consensus on how to define and operationalize social entrepreneurship has not been achieved. Second, social entrepreneurship research is caught in between seemingly conflicting demands for relevance and rigour. Hirsch and Levin (1999) elegantly label those who are concerned with relevance as 'umbrella advocates' because they promote broad views and emphasize the messy and complex nature of the phenomenon and social life in general. Conversely, they label researchers who emphasize methodological rigour 'validity police' as they call for narrow views built on stringency, validity and reliability.

Lifecycle assessments of umbrella constructs in various areas of research suggest that whether social entrepreneurship as an academic field will collapse or become permanent critically depends on its continued endorsement from practitioners (Hirsch and Levin, 1999). In the case of social entrepreneurship the continuing support by foundations that have been created with a clear mandate to foster social entrepreneurship (such as Ashoka, the Schwab Foundation, the Skoll Foundation or Echoing Green) might also be of importance. These organizations have been instrumental in mobilizing resources and awareness and have clearly contributed to the diffusion of the term 'social entrepreneurship' across political and economic realms. These organizations, however, are also heavily engaged in shaping the meaning of social entrepreneurship. Founders or managing directors provide their views on 'what social entrepreneurship is', 'what social entrepreneurs do' and 'who they are' (Drayton, 2002; Martin and Osberg, 2007; Elkington and Hartigan, 2008) and therefore critically shape identities at the field level and influence field boundaries. This chapter pays tribute to these effects and considers social entrepreneurship as a phenomenon in the making. Nevertheless it attempts to integrate and synthesize existing theoretical and practical perspectives on social entrepreneurship.

## A PERSPECTIVE: SOCIAL ENTREPRENEURSHIP AS A CONTEXT-SPECIFIC – LOCAL – PHENOMENON

An assessment of activity labelled as social entrepreneurship, for example, by examining the work of Ashoka or Schwab fellows, reveals that w*here* social entrepreneurs operate affects *what* they do and *how* they do it.

In too many places on this planet the economic, social and political institutions (such as markets, companies, charities and bureaucracies) that are designed to cater to the basic needs and rights of individuals in society are failing to serve large segments of the population. As a result millions of people remain marginalized, locked into an informal system that does not guarantee the right to be paid fairly, to be treated equally or to access education and health services, often leading to situations of chronic poverty. Even in so-called 'developed' countries, too many people are falling through the cracks. On the other hand, new problems are continually being created as a result of the very same institutions, organizations and individuals striving to satisfy other perceived needs or wants in society. In economic terms these are usually called externalities and have paradoxically resulted in the resurgence of a whole new set of unfulfilled basic human needs. For example, pollution caused by companies in their competitive race for growth and technological advances, leads to new basic needs for clean air and water. Rapid economic growth and radical transformation of social, economic and cultural life, often as a result of technological change, has led to increased inequalities both within and between countries across the globe.

Armartya Sen (1999) has argued that these basic human needs are also, in fact, basic human rights. Sen refers to them as 'instrumental freedoms' that enable development by fostering individual capabilities. Whether one takes a needs or a rights-based approach, few would argue that these ubiquitous fundamentals are not being delivered by society to all of its members. Building on this approach, I suggest that one way of 'making sense' of social entrepreneurship is to view it as individual and/ or collective actors addressing the opportunity spaces created by these failures. They may be fulfilling the role of delivering products, services or institutions that existing organizations in the public, private or voluntary sector do not provide. Or they may address needs newly created either by legitimate activities (for example market externalities created by pollution or climate change), or by illegitimate actions (such as child labour). As the latter example illustrates, needs may be created by social change as well as economic or political change.

Contrary to widely-held popular beliefs, unfulfilled basic needs are not only present in developing countries. A number of indices issued by national and international organizations, as well as barometers such as the Human Development Index and GDP indices, inform us regularly about the economic, social and political conditions in a country. Yet these reports reflect only the average performances and results of countries, and are poor proxies for the 'everyday states' and realities encountered at the local level.

Social entrepreneurship as viewed in this chapter refers to a process of catering to locally-existing basic needs that are not addressed by traditional organizations. Depending on the need addressed, the process usually involves the provision of goods or services and/or the creation of missing institutions or the reshaping of inadequate ones. However, the main objective is to change or modify the social and/or economic arrangements that create the situation of failure to satisfy basic needs. While financial sustainability through earned income represents an important pillar of social entrepreneurship, it is not a sufficient condition. In fact, in some situations the target group's ability to pay becomes an important hurdle towards financial sustainability, and social entrepreneurial organizations may also access resources through patrons.

The defining purpose of social entrepreneurship, regardless of the financial model, is to effect social change by altering the social, economic and political day-to-day realities at the local level. It is therefore the local context that shapes opportunities for social entrepreneurship and determines the strategies and tactics employed. These strategies and tactics reflect an entrepreneurial approach to action characterized first by resourcefulness (without necessarily having the resources in hand); second, by the ability to recombine resources into new value-creating configurations ('bricolage' of material, institutional and cultural resources); and finally by creative and innovative, that is, novel ways of doing things.

One of the most widely celebrated social-entrepreneurial innovations is microfinance. The current hype about microfinance suggests that giving the poor access to financial products is the recipe for social and economic development. This can be misleading, as microfinance alone, or better, standard banking activities alone, do not affect and thereby change the social structure that makes economic development so difficult in the first place. Very often it is the non-banking activities of organizations offering access to credit (such as training and education) which, when coupled with the banking activities, create social value and provide the lever for social change. From the perspective offered in this chapter, simply giving credit and loans without also empowering the women in Bangladesh, would hardly qualify as social entrepreneurship.

The key to social entrepreneurship is therefore an explicit or implicit theory of change. This theory of change is manifested in strategies, tactics and the (business) model, that is, the configuration of resources and activities. This perspective also invites a more agnostic view on *who* is the social entrepreneur. In other words, this perspective suggests that, depending on the needs addressed and the local conditions shaping the entrepreneurial approach, the actor can be an individual entrepreneur, an established organization or even a social movement (Mair and Martí, 2006). Also the choice of the organizational form is more a reflection of the particular problem at hand rather than a paradigm issue. For-profit and non-profit should not be seen as defining characteristics of social entrepreneurship but as a specific choice that is made to best suit the overall model and the local context. As mentioned above, certain needs in certain contexts lend themselves more easily to for-profit models when the willingness and ability to pay exists. In addition the legislative context and especially fiscal law implications are important decision criteria in the choice of for-profit or non-profit organizational set-up.

## HOW SOCIAL ENTREPRENEURSHIP VARIES ACROSS ECONOMIC AND CULTURAL CONTEXTS

If the opportunity space for social entrepreneurship is defined by the local social, economic and political arrangements, then it is not surprising that the social entrepreneurship phenomenon manifests itself differently in different contexts. As a result, researchers, policy makers or businesses have to situate the phenomenon (or the social entrepreneurial actor) in a specific context in order to understand it fully. The vast body of research undertaken on 'varieties of capitalism' (see Jackson and Deeg, 2008 for a recent review) provides a useful lens to understand entrepreneurship across economic and cultural contexts. Following this research tradition and applying a stylized classification to the contexts where social entrepreneurship takes place conform to three main types: 1) the liberal economy, in which the market mechanism is considered the best way to shape and maintain economic and social justice (the US economy is an example); 2) the cooperative economy, in which the state plays an important role in redistributing wealth, and markets are conditioned by regulative interventions (for example most European economies); and 3) the informal economy, in which neither the state nor the market can create wealth and maintain social justice but instead affiliation to social groups determines the local creation and distribution of wealth and justice (a good example is India, but many countries of Latin America and Asia also conform to this type).

In applying this typology to understand entrepreneurship in general, the main variables considered are the role and power of the government versus the role and power of markets. Is this typology also useful for 'making sense' of *social* entrepreneurship across contexts? I believe so. The typology allows us to identify macro-trends and/or make general statements about things, such as the likelihood of social entrepreneurship taking place in a particular context as well as the origin and/or type of needs addressed by the social entrepreneur. I argue that such an approach provides a fruitful avenue for much-needed empirical efforts to understand social entrepreneurship. Differentiating between these three contexts would allow us to develop theory and gain evidence on the *occurrence* of social entrepreneurship. For example, the following testable proposition comparing social entrepreneurship across these three contexts can be derived following the thrust of existing theory as applied to the phenomenon of social entrepreneurship.

*Proposition 1*   The likelihood of social entrepreneurship is higher in liberal economies than in cooperative economies.

Straightforward arguments to support this proposition include the following. In liberal economies many social needs are not taken care of by the state or the public sector and therefore the volume of needs not catered for is higher. Liberal economies are traditionally characterized by a more entrepreneurial mindset and activity in general; therefore an entrepreneurial approach represents a 'natural' way to address the problem or need.

The second important area in which existing knowledge and literature on varieties of capitalism could be beneficial for enhancing our understanding of social entrepreneurship is in the explanation of variance. That is, *how* do the ways social entrepreneurial initiatives address specific needs vary across different contexts? Potential propositions to be derived could include:

*Proposition 2a*   Social entrepreneurship in a liberal economy typically relies on market-based mechanisms to address a social need.

Or formulated in a comparative way:

*Proposition 2b*   Social entrepreneurship in liberal economies is characterized more by market mechanisms compared to social entrepreneurship in cooperative economies or informal economies.

While I view existing research on varieties of capitalism as hugely beneficial to inform emerging theorizing efforts and empirical endeavours, I argue in this chapter that the complexity involved in social entrepreneurship requires existing typologies to be paired with additional variables that capture the local economic, social, cultural and natural heritage characterizing the specific microcosm in which the social entrepreneurial initiatives are operating.

For example social entrepreneurship in India, Bangladesh and Pakistan is very much shaped by the political context or, more specifically, by the political problems in those countries since independence. In India, for example, many social entrepreneurs address the huge gap that exists between formal legislation (which recognizes no discrimination across social strata) and social reality (the prevalence of the caste system). In Bangladesh social entrepreneurial organizations such as BRAC or Grameen have assumed the role and activities of absent or ineffective government. In addition the opportunity space for and activities of social entrepreneurs in this part of the world is shaped significantly by the natural disasters occurring on a regular basis (flooding and hurricanes in Bangladesh and the Western part of India, as well as earthquakes in Pakistan). Social entrepreneurs have created organizations that complement and substitute for missing action by national and international relief activities.

In many Latin American countries the political heritage of weak and corrupt governments and public sectors has encouraged entrepreneurial solutions to social problems. An additional important factor to understand the entrepreneurial activity in this part of the world is the strong influence of the Church. Traditionally the churches have encouraged entrepreneurial – or informal – approaches to social issues. More recently the entrepreneurial spirit developed under such regimes has independently taken off. However, similar to South Asia, it is the specific political and socio-cultural context that has shaped social entrepreneurship.

In traditional liberal economies such as the US, local social and cultural aspects do affect social entrepreneurship. Specific target groups, such as Native Americans or inner city poor that have been to some extent ignored by public social systems are at the centre of social entrepreneurial activities. Another important opportunity space for social entrepreneurs in liberal economy countries such as the US is the weak execution of public responsibilities. For example the public education system is failing in a number of aspects and one of the biggest criticisms is that it fosters educational inequality. Social entrepreneurs such as Wendy Kopp, who set up Teach for America to address this failure, have come up with innovative ways to tackle this specific problem and to make sure that 'one day, all children in this nation will have the opportunity to attain an excellent education' (Teach for America, 2009).

Finally, in Europe new socio-demographic trends such as increased immigration from Africa and Eastern Europe pose important challenges to the portfolio of social services offered by the public sector. New needs are also emerging as traditional ways of doing things clash with modern practices and expectations. In Germany, for example, the traditional shared belief that women with children under four should stay at home to look after them clashes with new career models for women. The lack of social infrastructure to take care of babies and young children during working hours thus provides an opportunity space for social entrepreneurs.

An important point to note here is that the boundaries of these models are in flux. For example, we can see that the cooperative model present in many European countries is blurring and becoming infused with elements from the liberal economy model present in the US. At the same time we observe many countries with a long informal economy tradition, now building up a fast-track liberal economy-based sector. In other words we will, and already do have instances where principles from two or three models govern in parallel within one country. Conflict or tension between models might then provide additional opportunity spaces for social entrepreneurs, or at least affect the operating conditions, that is, the entrepreneurial environment.

These examples illustrate an important – probably the most important – role of social entrepreneurship. Social entrepreneurs and their models provide proof of concept. Many 'needs gaps' persist because existing businesses or public organizations fail to address them or address them inadequately. Filling one such gap is social entrepreneur David Green who, working with the Aravind Eye Hospitals in India, has been able to produce intraocular lenses at a fraction of the traditional cost while still making a profit. Companies often shy away from addressing basic needs as they do not see the business case, that is, the potential to make profits. Because of the strict rules of the game (such as quarterly earnings reports), as well as cognitive limitations (thinking out of the box is hard), businesses rely on someone else to provide the proof of concept. Similarly, governments often shy away from experimenting and engaging in new ways of addressing social problems, simply because their rules of the game are determined by a four to five-year run to re-election.

## WHERE TO GO FROM HERE . . . IMPLICATIONS FOR THEORY AND PRACTICE

Social entrepreneurship can supply a positive force not only to spur economic development directly but also, and especially, to provide fertile ground for such growth to take root and to ensure its sustainability. Social entrepreneurs contribute fertilizer in the form of social capabilities and address inequalities across different dimensions (social, economic and political) that can be a source of unbalanced progress making social and economic development vulnerable. Implications we can derive from the admittedly-limited systematic understanding of social entrepreneurship we have generated over the last decade can be summarized as follows.

### The Entrepreneurial Individual

In an ideal world, after they had developed the proof of concept, social entrepreneurs would be replaced by governments or businesses. However, in reality, new opportunity spaces for social entrepreneurship arise every day across the globe. How can we support social entrepreneurs? The recent momentum to include social entrepreneurship in the curriculum of business schools is important. It illustrates alternative career paths and/or opens the minds of future CEOs to envision opportunities for collaboration with social entrepreneurs. Enhanced social and environmental consciousness might even increase the chances that some future social needs never surface. However, educating future business leaders and/or educating a future generation of professional managers of social entrepreneurial organizations is only the tip of the iceberg. A promising avenue lies in integrating social entrepreneurship into high school education and undergraduate programmes. In addition to educating the next generation we could also place greater emphasis on the potential inherent in the 'older generation'. With increased life expectancy and enhanced living conditions, we can draw from a large pool of highly-educated and experienced retired people who represent a powerful resource for social change agents or supporting social change efforts. For example, the founder of the Aravind Eye Hospitals – Dr G. Venkataswamy (known as 'Dr V') – started his initiative only after he had officially retired from public service. It is now the largest eye hospital group in the world (Aravind Eye Hospitals, 2009).

As mentioned previously, support organizations such as Ashoka have been instrumental in mobilizing support structures across sector boundaries. Sustained efforts, not only by the financial, business, multilateral, and public sectors but also the academic sector, will be critical to maintaining the current momentum for social entrepreneurship.

**The Entrepreneurial Environment**

The momentum for social entrepreneurship is also dependent on favourable contextual conditions. These conditions refer to economic but also to social dimensions. The current momentum, for example, makes social entrepreneurs fashionable. All 'hype' reduces over time and loses momentum. Thus it will be critical to maintain an elevated social status for social entrepreneurs. Of course it matters to people whether being a social entrepreneur is 'cool' or not. The challenge in the coming years will be to find a good balance between attributing 'social hero' stories to social entrepreneurs and creating a solid role associated with status in our societies. The biggest task, that of sustaining the role of social entrepreneurs in economic and social life, is faced by governments. While some countries, such as the UK, have been proactive in drafting favourable legislation, others are lagging behind. Again, consolidating social entrepreneurship beyond the hype requires the provision of solid legislative frameworks ranging from organizational forms to taxation.

**Entrepreneurial Actions**

At the current stage we see experimentation, but more is needed. We have too few models to confidently talk about 'best practice'. The role of academia at this stage is important. Academics can follow and examine emerging practices; some of them will fail and some of them will succeed. What is important is to follow and document the process, and to capture both failures and successes along the way. In particular, academics could assume the role of watchdogs. As a reflection of the hype, we are currently observing a transposition of practices from the business world to social entrepreneurship that might have detrimental effects. The quest for growth, an imperative in the business world, has been adopted by the world of social entrepreneurship, which is not surprising if we consider the scale and magnitude of global social needs. Yet this trend leads to the application of consulting templates and performance measurement schemes designed for and used in very different contexts. How do we evaluate performance in the case of social entrepreneurship? While one of the obvious weaknesses of the social sector is limited accountability for results as well as inefficiencies, the solution is not to import performance benchmarks and practices. Social impact cannot be reduced to simple and measurable indicators; it reflects local realities and therefore comparing impact across needs and across contexts is difficult. Finally, academics should not shy away from documenting and theorizing about the 'dark side' of social entrepreneurship: inefficient use of resources as well as undermining opportunities for traditional business are just a few examples that require more empirical and conceptual examination to inform both theory and practice.

## TO CONCLUDE

The perspective on social entrepreneurship put forward in this chapter resonates with Salamon and Anheier's 'social origin' approach on the emergence of social sector organizations (Salamon and Anheier, 1996). Accordingly, social entrepreneurship is viewed, not as an isolated phenomenon but an integral part of a social system. Thus the role, nature and scale of social entrepreneurship cannot be discussed without taking into consideration the complex set of institutional, social, economic and political factors that make up this context. For research, social entrepreneurship represents an exciting opportunity to unpack mechanisms driving social and economic development. At this stage of the life cycle of social entrepreneurship research (Hirsch and Levin, 1999) we can be sceptical about efforts to generate 'grand' theories of social entrepreneurship. Rather we should see enormous potential in theoretical and empirical efforts that aim at building mid-range theories and unravelling the social mechanisms constituting the phenomenon (Hedstrom and Swedberg, 1998; Davis and Marquis, 2005). Finally we would like to emphasize the potential of social entrepreneurship research to bridge disciplinary divides and inspire the broader field of entrepreneurship to take advantage of building on theories from both sociology and economics (Sorenson and Stuart, 2008).

## NOTES

1.  See Williams (1999) for a similar argument in the area of entrepreneurship.
2.  Hirsch and Levin (1999) introduce the term 'umbrella construct' to describe emerging areas of research without clearly defined conceptual boundaries.

## REFERENCES

Alvord, S.H., L.D. Brown and C.W. Letts (2004), 'Social entrepreneurship and societal transformation', *The Journal of Applied Behavioural Science*, **40**(3), 260–82.

Aravind Eye Hospitals (2009), 'Homepage', available at: www.aravind.org/ (accessed 7 April 2009).

Borzaga, C. and J. Defourny (2001), *The Emergence of Social Enterprise*, London: Routledge.

Davis, G.F. and C. Marquis (2005), 'Prospects for organization theory in the early twenty-first century: institutional fields and mechanisms', *Organization Science*, **16**(4), 332–43.

Dorado, S. (2006), 'Social entrepreneurial ventures: different values so different process of creation, no?', *Journal of Developmental Entrepreneurship*, **11**(4), 319–43.

Drayton, W. (2002), 'The citizen sector: becoming as entrepreneurial and competitive as business', *California Management Review*, **44**(3), 120–32.

Elkington, J. and P. Hartigan (2008), *The Power of Unreasonable People: How Social Entrepreneurs Create Markets that Change the World*, Boston, MA: Harvard Business School Press.

Emerson, J. (2003), 'The blended value proposition: integrating social and financial returns', *California Management Review*, **45**(4), 35–51.

Fowler, A. (2000), 'NGDOs as a moment in history: beyond aid to social entrepreneurship or civic innovation?', *Third World Quarterly*, **21**(4), 637–54.

Frumkin, P. (2002), *On Being Nonprofit*, Cambridge, MA: Harvard University Press.

Grenier, P. (2009), 'Social entrepreneurship in the UK: from rhetoric to reality?', in R. Ziegler (ed.), *An Introduction to Social Entrepreneurship: Voices, Preconditions, Contexts*, Cheltenham, UK and Northampton, MA, USA: Edward Elgar, pp. 174–204.

Hedstrom, P. and R. Swedberg (1998), 'Social mechanisms: an introductory essay', in P. Hedstrom and R. Swedberg (eds), *Social Mechanisms: an Analytical Approach to Social Theory*, New York, USA and Cambridge, UK: Cambridge University Press, pp. 1–31.

Hirsch, P.M. and D.Z. Levin (1999), 'Umbrella advocates versus validity police: a life-cycle model', *Organization Science*, **10**(2), 199–212.

Jackson, G. and R. Deeg (2008), 'From comparing capitalisms to the politics of institutional change', *Review of International Political Economy*, **15**(4), 680–709.

Johannisson, B. and A. Nilsson (1989), 'Community entrepreneurs: networking for local development', *Entrepreneurship & Regional Development*, **1**(1), 3–19.

Letts, C.W. and W. Ryan (1997), 'Virtuous capital: what foundations can learn from venture capitalists', *Harvard Business Review*, **75**(2), 36–44.

Mair, J. and I. Martí (2006), 'Social entrepreneurship research: a source of explanation, prediction, and delight', *Journal of World Business*, **41**(1), 36–44.

Mair, J. and I. Martí (2009), 'Entrepreneurship in and around institutional voids: a case study from Bangladesh', *Journal of Business Venturing*, **24**(5), 419–35.

Martí, I. and J. Mair (2009), 'Bringing change into the lives of the poor: entrepreneurship outside traditional boundaries', in T. Lawrence, R. Suddaby and B. Leca (eds), *Institutional Work*, New York, USA and Cambridge, UK: Cambridge University Press, pp. 92–119.

Martin, R.L. and S. Osberg (2007), 'Social entrepreneurship: the case for definition', *Stanford Social Innovation Review*, **1**, 29–39.

Peredo, A.M. and J.J. Chrisman (2006), 'Toward a theory of community-based enterprise', *Academy of Management Review*, **31**(2), 309–28.

Phills, J.A., K. Deiglmeier and D.T. Miller (2008), 'Rediscovering social innovation', *Stanford Social Innovation Review*, **6**(4), 34–43.

Salamon, L.M. and H.K. Anheier (1996), 'Social origins of civil society. Explaining the non-profit sector cross-nationally', *Working Papers of the Johns Hopkins Comparative Nonprofit Sector Project*, Baltimore, MD, USA, The Johns Hopkins Institute for Policy Studies.

Seelos, C. and J. Mair (2007), 'Profitable business models and market creation in the context of deep poverty: a strategic view', *Academy of Management Perspectives*, **21**(4), 49–63.

Sen, A.K. (1999), *Development as Freedom*, Oxford, UK and New York, USA: Oxford University Press.

Sharir, M. and M. Lerner (2006), 'Gauging the success of social ventures initiated by individual social entrepreneurs', *Journal of World Business*, **41**(1), 6–20.

Sorenson, O. and T.E. Stuart (2008), 'Entrepreneurship: a field of dreams?', *The Academy of Management Annals*, **2**(1), 517–43.

Teach for America (2009), at http://www.teachforamerica.org (accessed 7 April 2009).

Waddock, S.A. and J.E. Post (1991), 'Social entrepreneurs and catalytic change', *Public Administration Review*, **51**(5), 393–401.

Williams, G. (1999), 'An entrepreneurial Odyssey: why the next century will belong to entrepreneurs', *Entrepreneur*, April, 106–13.

# 3 Essay of clarifications and definitions of the related concepts of social enterprise, social entrepreneur and social entrepreneurship

*François Brouard and Sophie Larivet*

## INTRODUCTION

Entrepreneurship is a relevant and important field of research (Shane and Venkataraman, 2000). Social entrepreneurship is a particular form of entrepreneurship (Henton et al., 1997). With the ever present or growing social problems and social needs over the last hundred years, it is easy to find a number of examples of social enterprise in different parts of the world (Christie and Honig, 2006; Fulton and Dees, 2006; Mair and Martí, 2004).

However, many concepts, such as *social enterprise, social entrepreneur* or *social entreneurship* are used to describe a field of research that has only recently come into official or common use (Borzaga and Defourny, 2001; Christie and Honig, 2006). A review of the rapidly expanding literature on those topics suggests that definitions of each of these terms are still being developed and are by no means agreed upon (Certo and Miller, 2008). Martin and Osberg (2007: 30) conclude that 'social entrepreneurship has become so inclusive that it now has an immense tent into which all manner of socially beneficial activities fit'. Fontan et al. (2007) and Defourny and Nyssens (2008a) underline the difference in the development of the terminology and its clarity. In the United States, it has its own identity and is influenced by large private foundations. In the United Kingdom, the state is at the forefront of its development and identity. In Europe, it is more about social economy and cooperatives.

Thus those terms are emerging, ill-defined (Barendsen and Gardner, 2004; Weerawardena and Sullivan Mort, 2006) and often used without any nuance on their specific meaning, probably because they are as yet not tidy concepts (Peredo and McLean, 2006). Even if 'a consensus over the boundaries of social entrepreneurship remains elusive' (Nicholls, 2006: 7), 'the need to draw boundaries so as to delimit scope and clarify whether it really is an independent field of research, and the need to identify the different level of analysis, disciplines and literatures' (Mair and Martí, 2006: 42) should be pursued. Being able to outline a consensus on the definition and key elements of the contruct is recognized as a valuable research exercice (Certo and Miller, 2008). Hopefully this research will contribute to the field: 'One of the biggest concerns in identifying a new field is the issue of definition' (Christie and Honig, 2006: 1); 'Establishing concrete definitions will help overcome the vagueness of the concept of social entrepreneurship, which places obstacles on research in the area' (Certo and Miller, 2008: 269).

Therefore, our main research objective is to establish a definition for each concept that encompasses the existing definitions. Based on a literature review and analysis of various existing definitions, the purpose of this chapter is to highlight characteristics of social enterprise, social entrepreneur, and social entrepreneurship, then to present a definition for each concept, and clarify their relationships. The chapter is organized as follows. The next section provides an overview of the positioning between related concepts. The next three sections provide analysis of existing definitions and characteristics of social enterprises, social entrepreneur, and social entrepreneurship. Each section will propose a definition for the concept under study. The last section gives more details about their relationships.

## POSITIONING OF THE CONCEPTS

To help set boundaries, we take, as an initial step, a wider and more global perspective on the related concepts, using sectors and types of organizations usually related to the concepts of social enterprise, entrepreneurs and entrepreneurship.

In addition to the three concepts we are interested in, social economy is another item found in the literature. The social entrepreneur occupies a privileged place in the social enterprise, which is part of the social economy. Inspired by Painter (2006), Figure 3.1 positions different types of social enterprises depending on the various sectors and organizational types. In Figure 3.1, it is possible to distinguish three main groupings (located on the left, in the centre and on the right) to understand the distinction better.

The left side of Figure 3.1 distinguishes four large sectors: public sector and private sector in the extreme, NGOs (non-governmental organizations) and social economy (Painter, 2006). The public sector refers to 'federal, provincial, territorial and local governments, government organizations, government partnerships, and school boards' (CICA, n.d., Introduction).

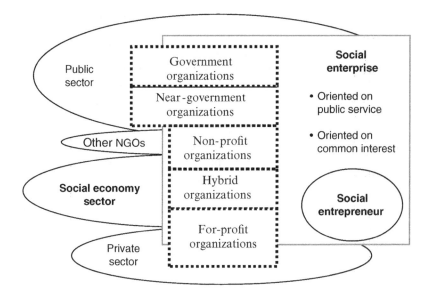

*Figure 3.1   Social economy, enterprise and entrepreneur*

From the nature of their activities, many public sector organizations have a social mission and could be considered social enterprises. The private sector includes organizations with a profit objective. Other NGOs could include, for example, organizations such as unions or churches. The social economy 'is a fairly new label for a diverse and evolving combination of non-governmental organizations (NGOs) that have been producing and delivering goods and services in communities across Canada and around the world for well over a century' (Painter, 2006: 30).

The left side of Figure 3.1 distinguishes social enterprises and social entrepreneurs. The social entrepreneur is the individual or group of individuals who act(s) as social change agent(s) using his (their) entrepreneurial skills for social value creation. In contrast with Nicholls' (2006) interpretation of the work of Dees (1998) and Alter (2006), we don't consider the social enterprises as a subset of social entrepreneurship, but social entrepreneurship as a subset of social enterprises. Our argument is that social enterprise doesn't necessarily include the entrepreneurship component. An example could be a recreational hockey club for children. In that regard, we agree with the conclusions of the EMES research network (Defourny and Nyssens, 2006). For social enterprises, their mission could be common interest or public service objectives (Painter, 2006). A soup kitchen or organizations providing training to individuals who need help securing employment are examples of public service. A local sports association for children and a forestry workers' cooperative are examples of organizations focused on common interest.

Favreau (2006) proposes a typology of three families of social economy organizations, such as associations, cooperatives and mutuals. For a better understanding of the diversity, we could examine the various types of organizations (in the centre of Figure 3.1). We find government organizations, such as state-owned firms and agencies, near-government organizations, such as hospitals, universities and colleges. For Smallbone et al. (2001: 15) 'the social economy is essentially a collection of social enterprises'. Within the social economy, non-profit organizations are seen as an important legal structure (Valéau et al., 2004). A non-profit organization (NPO) is 'an organization, usually formed for social, philanthropic or similar purposes, in which there is normally no transferable ownership interest and that does not carry on business with a view to distribution or use of any profits for the pecuniary gain of its members' (CICA, 1992: 143). A for-profit organization is the opposite of a non-profit organization. Hybrid organizations have characteristics of both non-profit and for-profit organizations. They could aim for philanthropic or commercial goals, like a cooperative selling food.

Figure 3.1 is a representation of sectors and actors, so it is difficult to position an abstract item such as social entrepreneurship on it. Nevertheless, Defourny and Nyssens (2008a: 4) provide the following comment: 'simplifying a little, one could say that social entrepreneurship was seen as the process through which social entrepreneurs created social enterprises'. Maybe it is too much simplification. Because each concept, *social enterprise, social entrepreneur* or *social entreneurship*, is often viewed in the literature as encompassing so many different sorts of organizations or individuals, it is essential to develop a definition for each concept that emphasizes the major characteristics recognized in the world today. Clarifying the relationships between the concepts would also be useful. This will help move the field of social entrepreneurship forward. The present study is a systematic attempt to map definitions with their characteristics (Mair and Martí, 2006).

Our methodology is to perform an extensive, but not exhaustive, literature review to find various definitions of the three concepts. It is similar to Bacq and Janssen's (2008a, 2008b) methodology. From the exact definitions of various authors for each concept (see Tables 3.1, 3.2, and 3.3), we examine them to be able to outline the primary and secondary characteristics of each concept and to come up with a definition for each. The difference between primary and secondary characteristics depends on the general agreement in the literature of the mandatory/non-mandatory character of a specific characteristic.

# ANALYSIS OF EXISTING DEFINITIONS AND CHARACTERISTICS OF SOCIAL ENTERPRISE

In this section, we analyse different definitions of social enterprise cited in the literature (see Table 3.1). Fontan et al. (2007) underline the presence of the social enterprise concept in Europe and America, without necessarily corresponding to the same reality but with similar aims. It is with those aims in mind that we will try to identify the main characteristics of social enterprise. From a cross-country perspective, it is possible to identify some economic and social elements that help understand some key characteristics of social enterprise (Babos et al., 2007; OECD – LEED Programme, n.d.). Social enterprises have developed over the years in response to social needs. Sometimes viewed as a compromise between the market, the state and civil society (Babos et al., 2007; Nicholls, 2006), social enterprises are associated with the social economy, the third sector, and the non-profit sector.

Even if the legal form is convenient and used in many countries to identify the social enterprise, it varies across different contexts and is arbitrary (Defourny and Nyssens, 2006). Therefore the legal form is not considered a primary characteristic for our definition.

Primary characteristics of social enterprises (SE_PRISE) are:

(A1) SE_PRISE are defined as enterprises, organizations or projects
(A2) SE_PRISE have a social mission which is central to addressing social needs/problems
(A3) SE_PRISE assets and wealth are used to create community benefit
(A4) SE_PRISE have varying degrees of positive social transformation
(A5) SE_PRISE have varying degrees of innovation
(A6) SE_PRISE have varying degrees of financial self-sufficiency
(A7) SE_PRISE take a wide variety of legal forms.

Secondary characteristics of social enterprises (SE_PRISE) are:

(A8) SE_PRISE may use business approaches, tools and techniques
(A9) SE_PRISE may rely on a diverse mix of resource streams
(A10) SE_PRISE may be engaged in goods and services in a market place (earned income strategies and economic business model)
(A11) SE_PRISE may be market driven and client driven
(A12) SE_PRISE may be a competitive business
(A13) SE_PRISE may have risk-taking behaviour
(A14) SE_PRISE may have a double or triple bottom line paradigm
(A15) SE_PRISE surplus is principally reinvested for the social purpose

*Table 3.1    Definitions of social enterprise*

| Author(s) | Year | Definitions of social enterprise |
| --- | --- | --- |
| REDF | 1996 | 'A revenue generating venture to create economic opportunities for very low income individuals, while simultaneously operating with reference to the financial bottom-line' (in Alter, 2006: 4) |
| OECD | 1999 | 'Any private activity conducted in the public interest, organised with an entrepreneurial strategy but whose purpose is not the maximisation of profit but attainment of certain economic and social goals, and which has a capacity of bringing innovative solutions to the problems of social exclusion and unemployment' (p. 10) |
| Bates et al. | 2001 | 'Put simply it is about trading with a social purpose, using business tools and techniques to achieve explicitly social aims. [. . .] A social enterprise is not defined by its legal status but by its nature: what it does that is social, the basis on which that social mission is embedded in a form of social ownership and governance and the way that it uses the profits it generated through its trading activities.' (p. 1) |
| CONSCISE Project | 2001 | 'Social enterprises are not-for-profit organisations, which seek to meet social aims by engaging in economic and trading activities. They have legal structure, which ensure that all assets and accumulated wealth are not in the ownership of individuals but are held in trust and for the benefit of those persons and/or areas who are the intended beneficiaries. They have organisational structures in which full participation of members is encouraged on a co-operative basis with equal rights accorded to all members. They also encourage mutual co-operation with other similar organisations.' (p. 34) |
| Smallbone et al. | 2001 | 'Competitive businesses, owned and trading for a social purpose' (p. 13) |
| Social Enterprise Knowledge Network – Harvard Business School | 2001 | 'A social enterprise is any kind of enterprise and undertaking, encompassed by nonprofit organization, for profit companies or public sector businesses engaged in activities of significant social value or in the production of goods and services with an embedded social purpose' (in Fontan et al., 2007: 23) |

*Table 3.1*   (continued)

| Author(s) | Year | Definitions of social enterprise |
| --- | --- | --- |
| Bibby | 2002 | 'Social enterprise – An organization that is equally committed to generating economic, social and environmental profit – known as "multiple bottom lines" – and is geared towards creating meaningful and lasting change within the community.' (p. 38) |
| DTI | 2002 | 'A social enterprise is a business with primarily social objectives whose surpluses are principally reinvested for that purpose in the business or in the community, rather than being driven by the need to maximise profit for shareholders and owners' (p. 13) |
| Gray et al. | 2003 | 'Social enterprise refers to a broad set of approaches that use business acumen to address social goals.' (p. 141) |
| Paton | 2003 | 'Most simply, an organisation where people have to be business-like, but are not in it for the money. Defined in this way, social enterprise is a generic term encompassing many very different sorts of organizations (just as private enterprise does).' (p. x) |
| Pearce | 2003 | 'Defines social enterprises as those which are: not-for-profit organisations; seek to meet social aims by engaging in economic and trading activities; have legal structures, which ensure that all assets and accumulated wealth are not in the ownership of individuals but are held in trust and for the benefit of those persons and/or the areas that are the intended beneficiaries of the enterprise's social aims; have organisational structures in which full participation of members is encouraged on a co-operative basis with equal rights accorded to all members.' (p. 32: also in Hare, Jones and Blackledge, 2007, p. 114) |
| Crossan et al. | 2004 | 'Social enterprises are organisations that are driven by a social mission, aims and objectives, that have adopted an economic business model to achieve their social aims' (p. 7) |
| Dart | 2004 | 'Social enterprise is considered synonymous with organizations becoming more market driven, client driven, self-sufficient, commercial, or businesslike.' (p. 414) |

*Table 3.1*   (continued)

| Author(s) | Year | Definitions of social enterprise |
|---|---|---|
| Harding | 2004 | 'Social enterprise potentially covers everything from not-for-profit organizations, through charities and foundations to cooperative and mutual societies' |
| Haugh and Tracey | 2004 | 'A business that trade [*sic*] for a social purpose' (in Defourny and Nyssens, 2008b: 13) |
| Fondation Muttart – Shelley Williams | 2005 | 'A venture/business activity within a non-profit organization providing financial and/or social benefits that further the mission' (in Fontan et al., 2007: 24) |
| Alter | 2006 | 'A social enterprise is any business venture created for a social purpose – mitigating/reducing a social problem or a market failure – and to generate social value while operating with the financial discipline, innovation and determination of a private sector business.' (p. 5) |
| Defourny and Nyssens – EMES Network | 2006 | 'Organizations with an explicit aim to benefit the community, initiated by a group of citizens and in which the material interest of capital investors is subject to limits. Social enterprises also place a high value on the autonomy and on economic risk-taking related to ongoing socio-economic activity.' (p. 5) |
| Desa and Kotha | 2006 | 'TSVs [technology social ventures] . . . develop and deploy technology-driven solutions to address social needs in a financially sustainable manner . . . TSVs address the twin cornerstones of social entrepreneurship – ownership (financial return) and mission (social impact) using advanced technology.' |
| Gould | 2006 | 'A social enterprise is a business dedicated to a social mission, or earning a profit for the financial furtherance of a social mission, although these are likely not the sole reasons for existence.' (p. 5) |
| Haugh | 2006 | 'Social enterprise is a collective term for a range of organizations that trade for a social purpose. They adopt one of a variety of different legal formats but have in common the principles of pursuing business-led solutions to achieve social aims, and the reinvestment of surplus for |

*Table 3.1*  (continued)

| Author(s) | Year | Definitions of social enterprise |
| --- | --- | --- |
| | | community benefit. Their objectives focus on socially desired, non financial goals and their outcomes are the non financial measures of the implied demand for and supply of services.' |
| Hockerts | 2006 | 'Social purpose business ventures are hybrid enterprises straddling the boundary between the for-profit business world and social mission-driven public and nonprofit organizations. Thus they do not fit completely in either sphere.' |
| Office of the Third Sector (UK) | 2006 | 'A social enterprise is a business with primarily social objectives whose surpluses are principally reinvested for that purpose in the business or in the community, rather than being driven by the need to maximise profit for shareholders and owners' (p. 10) |
| Thompson and Doherty | 2006 | 'Social enterprises – defined simply – are organisations seeking business solutions to social problems. They need to be distinguished from other socially-oriented organisations and initiatives that bring (sometimes significant) benefits to communities but which are not wanting or seeking to be "businesses".' (p. 362) |
| Babos et al. | 2007 | 'Social enterprises typically engage in delivery of social services and work integration services for disadvantaged groups, as well as community services, including in the educational, cultural and environmental fields, in both urban and rural areas.' (p. 5) |
| Cochran | 2007 | 'Social enterprises are enterprises devoted to solving social problems. The reason for their existence is not to maximize return to shareholders, but to make a positive social impact' (p. 451) |
| Office of the Third Sector (UK) | 2007 | 'Social enterprises are businesses with primarily social objectives whose surpluses are principally reinvested for that purpose in the business or in the community. Social enterprise is not just "business with a conscience". It is about actively delivering change, often tackling entrenched social and environmental challenges.' (p. 2) |

*Table 3.1*    (continued)

| Author(s) | Year | Definitions of social enterprise |
|---|---|---|
| Institute for Social Entrepreneurs | nd | 'Social enterprise: Any organization, in any sector, that uses earned income strategies to pursue a double or triple bottom line, either alone (as a social sector business) or as part of a mixed revenue stream that includes charitable contributions and public sector subsidies.' (p. 1) |
| OECD – LEED Programme | nd | 'Social enterprises are organizations that take different legal forms across OECD countries to pursue both social and economic goals with an entrepreneurial spirit. Social enterprises typically engage in delivery of social services and work integration services for disadvantaged groups and communities, whether in urban or rural area [*sic*]. In addition, social enterprises are also emerging in the provision of community services, including in the educational, cultural and environmental fields.' (p. 1) |
| Social Enterprise Alliance | nd | 'Social enterprise: An organization or venture that advances its social mission through entrepreneurial, earned income strategies.' (p. 1) |
| Social Enterprise London | nd | 'Social enterprises are competitive businesses that trade for a social purpose. They seek to succeed as businesses by establishing a market share and making a profit. They emphasise the long-term benefits for employees, consumers and the community. They bring people and communities together for economic development and social gain by combining excellence with action for change.' (p. 5) |

(A16)    SE_PRISE may have rules prohibiting or limiting distribution of surpluses among members

(A17)    SE_PRISE may be the result of an initiative by a community

(A18)    SE_PRISE may have complex and democratic governance arrangements

(A19)    SE_PRISE may be seen as accountable to both its members and a wider community.

Building upon these definitions for the purposes of this work, the authors define social enterprises as organizations which pursue social missions or purposes that operate to create community benefit regardless of ownership or legal structure and with varying degrees of financial self-sufficiency, innovation and social transformation.

## ANALYSIS OF EXISTING DEFINITIONS AND CHARACTERISTICS OF SOCIAL ENTREPRENEUR

In this section, we analyse different definitions of social entrepreneur cited in the literature (see Table 3.2). Social entrepreneurs could be associated with their traits (Henton et al., 1997) and with their actions. In other words, what is important is who they are and what they do.

Primary characteristics of the social entrepreneur (SE_NEUR) are:

(B1)   SE_ NEUR is defined as an individual
(B2)   SE_ NEUR is a change agent and a leader with a vision for change
(B3)   SE_ NEUR tackles social problems
(B4)   SE_ NEUR wants to achieve social value creation and sustainability
(B5)   SE_ NEUR is more concerned with caring and helping than making money
(B6)   SE_ NEUR possesses an entrepreneurial spirit and personality (passionate, dedicated, persuasive)
(B7)   SE_ NEUR sees and recognizes new opportunities
(B8)   SE_ NEUR displays innovativeness and proactiveness.

Secondary characteristics of the social entrepreneur (SE_NEUR) are:

(B9)   SE_ NEUR may provide a blend of business and social principles
(B10)  SE_ NEUR may gather together the necessary resources
(B11)  SE_ NEUR may want to put new ideas into concrete transformational solutions
(B12)  SE_ NEUR may connect the economy (market forces) and the community
(B13)  SE_ NEUR may weigh the social and financial return of each investment
(B14)  SE_ NEUR may display reasonable risk-taking propensity
(B15)  SE_ NEUR may be motivated by long-term interest
(B16)  SE_ NEUR may operate in all sectors.

*Table 3.2    Definitions of social entrepreneur*

| Author(s) | Year | Definitions of social entrepreneur |
|-----------|------|-------------------------------------|
| Waddock and Post | 1991 | 'Social entrepreneurs are private sector citizens who play critical roles in bringing about "catalytic changes" in the public sector agenda and the perception of certain social issues.' (p. 393) |
| Henton et al. | 1997 | 'Civic entrepreneurs are catalysts who help communities go through the change process. They build economic community – tight, resilient linkages between community and economic interests. [. . .] Civic entrepreneurs have five common traits. They: see opportunity in the new economy; possess an entrepreneurial personality; provide collaborative leadership to connect the economy and the community; are motivated by broad, enlightened, long-term interests; work in teams, playing complementary roles.' (p. 14) |
| Leadbeater | 1997 | 'Social entrepreneurs are creating innovative ways of tackling some of our most pressing and intractable social problems: youth, crime, drugs, dependency, chronic joblessness, illiteracy, Aids and mental illness. They take under-utilised and often discarded resources – people and buildings – and re-energise them by finding new ways to use them to satisfy unmet and often unrecognised needs.' (p. 8) |
| Bornstein | 1998 | 'Ashoka's social entrepreneur is a pathbreaker with a powerful new idea, who combines visionary and real-world problem-solving creativity, who has a strong ethical fiber, and who is "totally possessed" by his or her vision for change.' (pp. 5–6) |
| Boschee | 1998 | 'Simply put, "social entrepreneurs" are nonprofit executives who pay increasing attention to market forces without losing sight of their underlying missions, to somehow balance moral imperatives and the profit motives – and that balancing act is the heart and soul of the movement.' (p. 2) |
| Dees | 1998 | 'Social entrepreneurs play the role of change agents in the social sector, by: adopting a mission to create and sustain social value (not just private value), recognizing and relentlessly pursuing new opportunities to serve that mission, engaging in a process of continuous innovation, adaptation, and learning, acting boldly without being limited by resources currently in hand, and exhibiting heightened accountability to the constituencies served and for the outcomes created.' (revised slightly in 2001: 4) |

*Table 3.2* (continued)

| Author(s) | Year | Definitions of social entrepreneur |
|---|---|---|
| Prabhu | 1999 | 'Social entrepreneurial leaders can be defined as persons who create and manage innovative entrepreneurial organizations or ventures whose primary mission is the social change and development of their client group.' (p. 140) |
| Brinckerhoff | 2000 | 'Social entrepreneurs are people who take risk [*sic*] on behalf of the people their organization serves.' (p. 1) |
| Thompson et al. | 2000 | 'Social entrepreneurs, people who realise where there is an opportunity to satisfy some unmet need that the state welfare system will not or cannot meet, and who gather together the necessary resources (generally people, often volunteers, money and premises) and use these to "make a difference".' (p. 328) |
| Brinckerhoff | 2001 | 'Social entrepreneurs have these characteristics: they are constantly looking for new ways to serve their constituencies and add value to existing services; they understand that all resource allocations are really stewardship investments; they weigh the social and financial return of each of these investments; they always keep mission first, but they know that they also need money; without it, there is no mission output; they are willing to take reasonable risk [*sic*] on behalf of the people their organization serves.' (p. 12) |
| CCSE | 2001 | 'Social entrepreneurs are leaders in the field of social change, and can be found in the private, public and not-for-profit sectors. These social innovators combine an entrepreneurial spirit with a concern for the "social" bottom line, as well as the economic one, recognizing that strong, vibrant communities are a critical factor in sustaining economic growth and development.' (p. 2) |
| Dees et al. | 2001 | 'Social entrepreneurs create social enterprises. They are the reformers and revolutionaries of our society today. They make fundamental changes in the way that things are done in the social sector. Their visions are bold. They seek out opportunities to improve society, and they take action. They attack the underlying causes of problems rather than simply treating symptoms. And, although they may act locally, their actions have the very potential to stimulate global improvements in their chosen arena, whether that is education, health care, job training and development, the environment, the arts, or any other social endeavour.' (p. 5) |

*Table 3.2*   (continued)

| Author(s) | Year | Definitions of social entrepreneur |
|---|---|---|
| Institute for Social Entrepreneurs | 2002 | 'Social entrepreneur: An individual who uses earned income strategies to pursue social objectives, simultaneously seeking both a financial and social return on investment. Said individual may or may not be in the nonprofit sector.' (p. 1) |
| Thompson | 2002 | 'Many social entrepreneurs, then, are people with the qualities and behaviours we associate with the business entrepreneur but who operate in the community and are more concerned with caring and helping than with "making money". [. . .] the main world of the social entrepreneur is the voluntary sector' (p. 413) |
| Sullivan Mort et al. | 2003 | 'Social entrepreneurs are first driven by the social mission of creating better social value than their competitors which results in them exhibiting entrepreneurially virtuous behaviour. Secondly, they exhibit a balanced judgment, a coherent unity of purpose and action in the face of complexity. Thirdly, social entrepreneurs explore and recognise opportunities to create better social value for their clients. Finally, social entrepreneurs display innovativeness, proactiveness and risk-taking propensity in their key decision making.' (p. 82) |
| Barendsen and Gardner | 2004 | 'Social entrepreneurs are individuals who approach a social problem with entrepreneurial spirit and business acumen.' (p. 43) |
| Skoll Foundation | 2004 | 'At the Skoll Foundation we call social entrepreneurs society's change agents: the pioneers of innovation for the social sector.' (in Dearlove, 2004: 35) |
| Roberts and Woods | 2005 | 'Visionary, passionately, dedicated individuals' (p. 49) |
| Schwab Foundation | 2005 | 'A social entrepreneur has created and leads an organization whether for-profit or not, that is aimed at catalyzing systemic social change through new ideas, products, services, methodologies and changes in attitude. Social entrepreneurs create hybrid organizations that employ business method – but their bottom line is social value creation. The ability to turn new ideas into concrete transformational solutions is the hallmark of an entrepreneur.' (in Fontan et al., 2007: 23) |
| Sharir and Lerner | 2005 | 'The definition we use to characterize the activities of the social entrepreneurs is acting as a change agent to create and sustain social value without being limited to resources currently in hand.' (p. 7) |

*Table 3.2*   (continued)

| Author(s) | Year | Definitions of social entrepreneur |
|---|---|---|
| Tan et al. | 2005 | 'A legal person is a social entrepreneur from $t_1$ to $t_2$ just in case that person attempts from $t_1$ to $t_2$, to make profits for society or a segment of it by innovation in the face of risk, in a way that involves that society or segment of it.' (p. 358)<br>'Social entrepreneur = Legal person engaged in the process of entrepreneurship that involves a segment of society with the altruistic objective that benefits accrue to that segment of society.' (p. 360) |
| Ashoka | 2006 | 'The job of a social entrepreneur is to recognize when a part of society is stuck and to provide new ways to get it unstuck. He or she finds what is not working and solves the problem by changing the system, speading the solution and persuading entire societies to take new steps.' (in Grenier, 2006: 120) |
| Boschee | 2006 | 'Social entrepreneurs are different because their earned income strategies are tied directly to their mission: they either start "affirmative businesses" (known as "social firms" in the UK) that employ people who are developmentally disabled, chronically mentally ill, physically challenged, poverty-stricken, or otherwise disadvantaged; or they sell products and services that have a direct impact on a specific social problem (e.g. delivering hospice care, working with potential dropouts to keep them in school, manufacturing assistive devices for people who are physically disabled, providing home care services to help elderly people stay out of nursing homes).' (p. 361)<br>'Social entrepreneurs are driven by a double bottom line, a virtual blend of financial and social returns. Profitability is still a goal, but it is not the only goal, and profits are re-invested in the mission rather than being distributed to shareholders.' (p. 361) |
| Dorado | 2006 | 'Social entrepreneurs may or may not be public sector officials; and their defining characteristic is not whether they create or change a public agency, but the blend of business and social principles they bring to it.' (p. 322) |
| Grenier | 2006 | 'Social entrepreneurs as individual change makers and innovative leaders' (p. 121) |
| Leadbeater | 2006 | 'Social entrepreneurs aim to create social value and bring about social change usually by helping people who often cannot afford market-based solutions to their needs in |

*Table 3.2*   (continued)

| Author(s) | Year | Definitions of social entrepreneur |
|---|---|---|
| | | health, education, and welfare.' (p. 234) |
| | | 'social entrepreneurs build organizations, usually not-for-profits, which create social value by applying business-like methods to meet social needs' (p. 241) |
| Baron | 2007 | 'A social entrepreneur is willing to form a CSR [corporate social responsibility] firm at a financial loss because either doing so expands the opportunity sets of citizens in consumption-social giving space or there is an entrepreneurial warm glow from forming the firm.' (p. 683) |
| Brock | 2007 | 'Social entrepreneurs share a common dream of making their ventures sustainable and contributing positively to their home communities.' (p. 1) |
| Martin and Osberg | 2007 | 'The social entrepreneur should be understood as someone who targets an unfortunate but stable equilibrium that causes the neglect, marginalization, or suffering of a segment of humanity; who brings to bear on this situation his or her aspiration, direct action, creativity, courage, and fortitude; who aims for and ultimately affects the establishment of a new stable equilibrium that secures permanent benefit for the targeted group and society at large.' (p. 39) |
| Tracey and Phillips | 2007 | 'Social entrepreneurs, individuals who develop economically sustainable solutions to social problems.' (p. 264) |
| Vasakaria | 2008 | 'The aim of the social entrepreneur is to make the society believe that his endeavor is to bring about a social change.' (p. 39) |
| Institute for Social Entrepreneurs | nd | 'Social entrepreneur: Any person, in any sector, who runs a social enterprise.' (p. 1) |
| Skoll Foundation | nd | 'Social entrepreneurs, like their business brethren, are similarly focused; they tap into vast reserves of ambition, creativity and resourcefulness in relentless pursuit of hard, measurable results. But social entrepreneurs seek to grow more than just profits. Motivated by altruism and a profound desire to promote the growth of equitable civil societies, social entrepreneurs pioneer innovative, effective, sustainable approaches to meet the needs of the marginalized, the disadvantaged and the disenfranchised. Social entrepreneurs are the wellspring of a better future.' (in Fontan et al., 2007: 23) |

Building upon these definitions for the purposes of this work, the authors define

> social entrepreneurs as any individuals who with their entrepreneurial spirit and personality will act as change agents and leaders to tackle social problems by recognizing new opportunities and finding innovative solutions, and are more concerned with creating social value than financial value.

## ANALYSIS OF EXISTING DEFINITIONS AND CHARACTERISTICS OF SOCIAL ENTREPRENEURSHIP

In this section, we analyse different definitions of social entrepreneurship cited in the literature (see Table 3.3). Austin et al. (2006) offer a Social Entrepreneurship Framework where opportunity, people and capital combine to create a social-value proposition, set against a series of contextual forces (tax, regulatory, sociocultural, macroeconomy, political and demographic). Weerawardena and Sullivan Mort (2006) have developed what they call the Bounded Multidimensional Model for Social Entrepreneurship in which risk management, proactiveness and innovativeness are the central constructs of social entrepreneurship, constrained by three factors: the external environment, the social mission of the organization, and the need for sustainability.

In the various definitions, a consensus exists on the multidimensionality of the concept and the presence of two main components: entrepreneurship and social (Mair and Martí, 2006; Nicholls, 2006; Peredo and McLean, 2006; Sullivan Mort et al., 2003). The first component is *entrepreneurship*. Entrepreneurship refers to starting (or re-starting) a business and to value creation for the entrepreneurs or society. Innovation is used to take advantage of new opportunities. Resources are mobilized to achieve the goal. The second component is the *social* dimension (Brinckerhoff, 2000; Tan et al., 2005; Ulhoi, 2005). A social mission and social value creation are characteristics that distinguish social entrepreneurship and economic entrepreneurship.

Primary characteristics of social entrepreneurship (SE_SHIP) are:

(C1)    SE_SHIP represents a variety of activities and processes
(C2)    SE_ SHIP wants to create and sustain social value
(C3)    SE_ SHIP encourages more entrepreneurial approaches for social use
(C4)    SE_ SHIP displays varying degrees of innovation and change
(C5)    SE_ SHIP is constrained by the external environment.

*Table 3.3    Definitions of social entrepreneurship*

| Author(s) | Year | Definitions of social entrepreneurship |
| --- | --- | --- |
| Fowler | 2000 | 'Social entrepreneurship is the creation of viable (socio-) economic structures, relations, institutions, organisations and practices that yield and sustain social benefits' (p. 649) |
| CCSE | 2001 | 'Defines "social entrepreneurship" broadly to encompass a variety of initiatives which fall into two broad categories. First, in the for-profit sector, social entrepreneurship encompasses activities emphasizing the importance of a socially engaged private sector, and the benefits that accrue to those who "do well by doing good". Second, it refers to activities encouraging more entrepreneurial approaches in the not-for-profit sector in order to increase organisational effectiveness and foster long-term sustainability' (p. 1) |
| Dees et al. | 2002 | 'Social entrepreneurship is not about starting a business or becoming more commercial. It is about finding new and better ways to create social value.' (p. xxx) |
| Hibbert et al. | 2002 | 'Social entrepreneurship can be loosely defined as the use of entrepreneurial behaviour for social ends rather than for profits objectives, or alternatively, that profits generated are used for the benefit of a specific disadvantaged group.' (p. 288) |
| Institute for Social Entrepreneurs | 2002 | 'Social entrepreneurship is the art of simultaneously pursuing both a financial and a social return on investment (The "double bottom line")' (p. 1) |
| Thompson | 2002 | 'Although social entrepreneurship is in evidence in many profit-seeking businesses – sometimes in their strategies and activities, sometimes through donations of money and time' (p. 413) |
| Lasprogata and Cotton | 2003 | 'Social entrepreneurship means nonprofit organizations that apply entrepreneurial strategies to sustain themselves financially while having a greater impact on their social mission (i.e. the "double bottom line").' (p. 69) |
| Mair and Noboa | 2003 | 'SE [Social entrepreneurship] as the innovative use of resource combinations to pursue opportunities aiming at the creation of organizations and/or practices that yield and sustain social benefits.' (p. 5) |
| Pomerantz | 2003 | 'Social entrepreneurship can be defined as the development of innovative, mission-supporting, earned income, job creating or licensing, ventures undertaken by individual social entrepreneurs, non- |

*Table 3.3*   (continued)

| Author(s) | Year | Definitions of social entrepreneurship |
|---|---|---|
| | | profit organizations, or nonprofits in association with for profits.' (p. 25) |
| Sullivan Mort et al. | 2003 | 'Social entrepreneurship, the entrepreneurship leading to the establishment of new social enterprise, and the continued innovation in existing ones' (p. 76) 'Conceptualises social entrepreneurship as a multidimensional construct involving the expression of entrepreneurially virtuous behaviour to achieve the social mission, a coherent unity of purpose and action in the face of moral complexity, the ability to recognise social value-creating opportunities and key decision-making characteristics of innovativeness, proactiveness and risk-taking.' (p. 76) |
| Mair and Martí | 2004 | 'The innovative use of resources to explore and exploit opportunities that meet to [*sic*] a social need in a sustainable manner.' (p. 3) |
| Tommasini | 2004 | 'Social entrepreneurship – Defined as a professional, innovative, and sustainable approach to systematic change that resolves social market failures and grasps opportunities. Social entrepreneurship engage [*sic*] with both non and for profit organisations, and the success of their activities are [*sic*] measured first and foremost by their social impact.' (p. 3) |
| Haugh | 2005 | 'Social entrepreneurship is the process of creating social enterprise' (p. 3) |
| Roberts and Woods | 2005 | 'Social entrepreneurship is the construction, evaluation and pursuit of opportunities for transformative social change carried out by visionary, passionately, dedicated individuals' (p. 49) |
| Seelos and Mair | 2005 | 'Social entrepreneurship creates new models for the provision of products and services that cater directly to basic human needs that remain unsatisfied by current economic or social institutions.' (pp. 243–4) |
| Austin et al. | 2006 | 'Innovative, social value creating activity that occurs within or across the nonprofit, business, or government sectors' (p. 2) |
| GEM | 2006 | 'Social entrepreneurship is any attempt at new social enterprise activity or new enterprise creation such as self-employment, a new enterprise, or the expansion of an existing social enterprise by an individual, teams of individuals or established social enterprise, with social or community goals as its base and where the profit |

*Table 3.3*    (continued)

| Author(s) | Year | Definitions of social entrepreneurship |
| --- | --- | --- |
| | | is invested in the activity or venture itself rather than returned to investors.' (p. 5) |
| Leadbeater | 2006 | 'One way to define social entrepreneurship would be through what motivates the actors, i.e. they want to create social value and put a higher value on their social mission than a financial one. [. . .] Another way to define social entrepreneurship would be through outcomes: anyone who creates lasting social value through entrepreneurial activities is a social entrepreneur.' (p. 241) |
| Mair and Martí | 2006 | 'First, we view social entrepreneurship as a process of creating value by combining resources in new ways. Second, these resource combinations are intended primarily to explore and exploit opportunities to create social value by stimulating social change or meeting social needs. And third, when viewed as a process, social entrepreneurship involves the offering of services and products but can also refer to the creation of new organizations.' (p. 37) |
| Nicholls | 2006 | 'Innovative and effective activities that focus strategically on resolving social market failures and creating new opportunities to add social value systematically by using a range of resources and organizational formats to maximize social impacts and bring about changes' (p. 23) |
| Peredo and McLean | 2006 | 'Social entrepreneurship is exercised where some person or group: (1) aim(s) at creating social value, either exclusively or at least in some prominent way; (2) show(s) a capacity to recognize and take advantage of opportunities to create that value ("envision"); (3) employ(s) innovation, ranging from outright invention to adapting someone else's novelty, in creating and/or distributing social value; (4) is/are willing to accept an above-average degree of risk in creating and disseminating social value; and (5) is/are unusually resourceful in being relatively undaunted by scarce assets in pursuing their social venture.' (p. 64) |
| Perrini | 2006 | 'Entailing innovation designed to explicitly improve societal wellbeing, housed within entrepreneurial organizations that initiate this level of change in society' (p. 247) |

*Table 3.3* (continued)

| Author(s) | Year | Definitions of social entrepreneurship |
|---|---|---|
| Weerawardena and Sullivan Mort | 2006 | 'Social entrepreneurship strives to achieve social value creation and this requires the display of innovativeness, proactiveness and risk management behavior. This behavior is constrained by the desire to achieve the social mission and to maintain the sustainability of existing organization. In doing so they are responsive to and constrained by environmental dynamics. They continuously interact with a turbulent and dynamic environment that forces them to pursue sustainability, often within the context of the relative resource poverty of the organization.' (p. 32) |
| Zhara et al. | 2006 | 'Social entrepreneurship concerns the processes related to the discovery of opportunities to create social wealth and the organizational processes developed and employed to achieve that end.' (p. 12) |
| Cochran | 2007 | 'Social entrepreneurship is the process of applying the principles of business and entrepreneurship to social problems' (p. 451) |
| Haugh | 2007 | 'Social entrepreneurship, the simultaneous pursuit of economic, social, and environmental goals by enterprising ventures [. . .] Social entrepreneurship is first and foremost a practical response to unmet individual and societal needs.' (p. 743) |
| Martin and Osberg | 2007 | 'We define social entrepreneurship as having the following three components: (1) identifying a stable but inherently unjust equilibrium that causes the exclusion, marginalization, or suffering of a segment of humanity that lacks the financial means or political clout to achieve any transformative benefit on its own; (2) identifying an opportunity in this unjust equilibrium, developing a social value proposition, and bringing to bear inspiration, creativity, direct action, courage, and fortitude, thereby challenging the stable state's hegemony; and (3) forging a new, stable equilibrium that releases trapped potential or alleviates the suffering of the targeted group, and through imitation and the creation of a stable ecosystem around the new equilibrium ensuring a better future for the targeted group and even society at large' (p. 35) |
| Wei-Skillern et al. | 2007 | 'We define social entrepreneurship as an innovative, social value creating activity that can occur within or across the nonprofit, business, or government sector.' (p. 4) |

*Table 3.3*    (continued)

| Author(s) | Year | Definitions of social entrepreneurship |
|---|---|---|
| Brock | 2008 | 'Innovative approaches to social change' or 'using business concepts and tools to solve social problems' (p. 3) |
| CASE | 2008 | 'Innovative and resourceful approaches to addressing social problems' (p. 1) |
| Zhara et al. | 2009 | 'Social entrepreneurship encompasses the activities and processes undertaken to discover, define and exploit opportunities in order to enhance social wealth by creating new ventures or managing existing organizations in an innovative manner.' (p. 522) |

Secondary characteristics of social entrepreneurship (SE_SHIP) are:

(C6)    SE_ SHIP may have varying degrees of positive social transformation
(C7)    SE_ SHIP may take advantage of new opportunities
(C8)    SE_ SHIP may use business concepts, principles, models and tools
(C9)    SE_ SHIP may be constrained by relative resource poverty
(C10)   SE_ SHIP may resolve social market failures
(C11)   SE_ SHIP may invest the profit in the activity of the venture itself rather than return it to investors
(C12)   SE_ SHIP may take a wide variety of legal forms
(C13)   SE_ SHIP may be achieved by creating a new business.

Building upon these definitions for the purposes of this work, the authors define

> social entrepreneurship as a concept which represents a variety of activities and processes to create and sustain social value by using more entrepreneurial and innovative approaches and constrained by the external environment.

The three definitions of the three concepts being given, it is clear that there are three separate theoretical items. But the clarification would not be complete if the practical relationships between them were not explicated.

## RELATIONSHIPS BETWEEN THE CONCEPTS

As a synthesis, the authors propose a framework depicting relationships between the three concepts. There might be other ways of depicting these

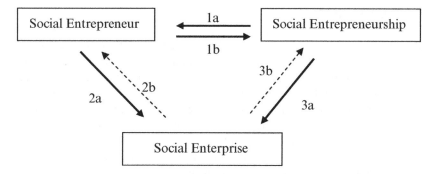

*Figure 3.2    Theoretical relationships between concepts*

relationships (for instance, inclusion relationship, as drawn in Figure 3.1), but a focus on intensity and causality of their links was chosen. This model enforces the clarification of the way the three concepts are related to each other.

If social entrepreneur and social entrepreneurship are two separate theoretical concepts, they are strongly linked in practice (the first one embodies the second one). On the other hand, we believe that a social enterprise can exist without them. A social enterprise might have been created by a social entrepreneur that is no longer a real entrepreneur but has become a manager, or might have left. So a social enterprise might not always be engaged in social entrepreneurship. This is why links 2b and 3b (see Figure 3.2) are weak links. However, in a process of social entrepreneurship, a social entrepreneur will always have to gather his or her resources in an organization (Verstraete and Fayolle, 2005), which might be a simple project, but will anyway be called a social enterprise.

The six links in Figure 3.2 are described as follows:

1a.   A social entrepreneur is necessarily engaged in social entrepreneurship (strong link).
1b.   Social entrepreneurship is necessarily embodied by (at least) one social entrepreneur (strong link).
2a.   A social entrepreneur's project has to be crystallized in an organizational form called social enterprise (strong link).
2b.   A social enterprise can be run by a social entrepreneur or not (weak link).
3a.   Social entrepreneurship leads to the creation or the development of a social enterprise (strong link).
3b.   A social enterprise is not necessarily or permanently engaged in a social entrepreneurship process (weak link).

## CONCLUSION

Based on a literature review and analysis of various definitions, the objective of this chapter is to present the main characteristics of social enterprise, social entrepreneur and social entrepreneurship concepts, to provide a definition for each concept, and to clarify their relationships. Hopefully this research will contribute to the field by establishing concrete definitions which could overcome the vagueness of many definitions. It will be useful for academics in their research and their teaching, and for practitioners and policy makers in their decisions by offering a better understanding of the different characteristics and relationships.

Even if our methodology was to perform an extensive literature review, it is not exhaustive. Our focus was only on English-language literature to avoid translation problems. Future research could look at our classification of primary and secondary characteristics of each concept and could assess our definitions. Future research could also look at the characteristics cited in the literature in addition to characteristics coming only from the definitions and to develop and revise existing typologies for each concept.

## REFERENCES

Alter, K. (2006), 'Social enterprise typology', (20 September, 2004; updated version 13 April, 2006), available at http://www.virtueventures.com/setypology.pdf.

Austin, J., H. Stevenson and J. Wei-Skillern (2006), 'Social and commercial entrepreneurship: same, different, or both?', *Entrepreneurship: Theory & Practice*, **30**(1), 1–22.

Babos, P., E. Clarence and A. Noya (2007), 'Reviewing OECD experience in the social enterprise sector', paper presented at OECD LEED Centre for Local Development international seminar held in conjunction with the Third DECIM Roundtable, 15–18 November, Trento, Italy, available at http://www.oecd.org/dataoecd/22/58/38299281.pdf).

Bacq, S. and F. Janssen (2008a), 'From social entrepreneurship as a practice to legitimate field of research: literature review and classification', working paper 06/2008, Center for Research in Entrepreneurial Change & Innovation Strategies – Louvain School of Management.

Bacq, S. and F. Janssen (2008b), 'Définition de l'entrepreneuriat social: revue de la littérature selon les critères géographique et thématique', paper presented at 9e Congrès international francophone en entrepreneuriat et PME, October, Louvain-la-Neuve, Belgium.

Barendsen, L. and H. Gardner (2004), 'Is the social entrepreneur a new type of leader?', *Leader to Leader*, No. 34, 43–50.

Baron, D. (2007), 'Corporate social responsibility and social entrepreneurship', *Journal of Economics & Management Strategy*, **16**(3), 683–717.

Bates Wells and Braithwaite and Social Enterprise London (2001), *Keeping it Legal – Legal Forms for Social Enterprises*, London: Social Enterprise London.

Bibby, A. (2002), *Climbing the Ladder – Step by Step Finance for Social Enterprise*, London: Social Enterprise London.

Bornstein, D. (1998), 'Changing the world on a shoestring', *The Atlantic Online*, January, available at http://www.theatlantic.com/issues/98jan/ashoka.htm.

Borzaga, C. and J. Defourny (eds) (2001), *The Emergence of Social Enterprise*, London: Routledge.

Boschee, J. (1998), 'Merging mission and money: a board member's guide to social entrepreneurship', available at: http://128.121.204.224/pdfs/MergingMission.pdf.

Boschee, J. (2006), 'Social entrepreneurship: the promise and the perils', in A. Nicholls (ed.), *Social Entrepreneurship: New Models of Sustainable Social Change*, Oxford: Oxford University Press, pp. 356–90.

Brinckerhoff, P. (2000), *Social Entrepreneurship: The Art of Mission-Based Venture Development*, New York: John Wiley & Sons.

Brinckerhoff, P. (2001), 'Why you need to be more entrepreneurial – and how to get started', *Nonprofit World*, **19**(6), 12–15.

Brock, D.D. (2007), 'Best practices for teaching social entrepreneurship: moving the field forward', paper presented at *USASBE+SAI Conference*, 11–14 January, Lake Buena Vista.

Brock, D.D. (2008), *Social Entrepreneurship Teaching Resources Handbook For Faculty Engaged in Teaching and Research in Social Entrepreneurship*, Ashoka's Global Academy for Social Entrepreneurship.

CASE (2008), 'Developing the field of social entrepreneurship', The Center for Advancement of Social Entrepreneurship (CASE), Duke University, Fuqua School of Business.

CCSE (2001), 'Social entrepreneurship', Discussion Paper No 1, Canadian Center for Social Entrepreneurship (CCSE).

Certo, S.T. and T. Miller (2008), 'Social entrepreneurship: key issues and concepts', *Business Horizons*, **51**(4), 267–71.

Christie, M.J. and B. Honig (2006), 'Social entrepreneurship: new research findings', *Journal of World Business*, **41**(1), 1–5.

CICA (n.d.), *Public Sector Accounting Standards*, Toronto: Canadian Institute of Chartered Accountants, looseleaf service.

CICA (1992), *Terminology for Accountants*, 4th edn, Toronto: Canadian Institute of Chartered Accountants (CICA).

Cochran, P.L. (2007), 'The evolution of corporate social responsibility', *Business Horizons*, **50**(6), 449–54.

CONSCISE (2001). 'The contribution of social capital in the social economy to local economic development in Western Europe – report of workpackage 2: baseline local socioeconomic profiles: methodology', Middlesex: Middlesex University (M. Evans).

Crossan, D., J. Bell and P. Ibbotson (2004), 'Towards a classification framework for social enterprises', University of Ulster working paper.

Dart, R. (2004), 'The legitimacy of social enterprise', *Nonprofit Management & Leadership*, **14**(4), 411–24.

Dearlove, D. (2004), 'eBay's Jeff Skoll', *New Zealand Management*, **51**(3), 34–6.

Dees, G. (1998), 'The meaning of social entrepreneurship', 31 October, available at www.gsb.stanford.edu/services/news/DeesSocentrepPaper.html.

Dees, G. (2001), 'The meaning of social entrepreneurship', 30 May, available at www.fuqua.duke.edu/centers/case/documents/dees_SE.pdf.

Dees, J.G., J. Emerson and P. Economy (2001), *Enterprising Nonprofits: A toolkit for Social Entrepreneurs*, New York: John Wiley & Sons.

Dees, J.G., J. Emerson and P. Economy (2002), *Strategic Tools for Social Entrepreneurs: Enhancing the Performance of your Enterprising Nonprofit*, New York: John Wiley & Sons.

Defourny, J. and M. Nyssens (2006), 'Defining social enterprise' in M. Nyssens (ed.), *Social Enterprise: At the Crossroads of Market, Public Policies and Civil Society*, London: Routledge, pp. 3–26.

Defourny, J. and M. Nyssens (eds) (2008a), 'Social enterprise in Europe: recent trends and developments', WP no. 08/01, Liege: EMES European Research Network.

Defourny, J. and M. Nyssens (2008b), 'Conceptions of social enterprise in Europe and the United States: convergences and divergences', paper presented at *8th ISTR International Conference 2d EMES–ISTR European Conference*, University of Barcelona, 9–12 July.

Desa, G. and S. Kotha (2006), 'Ownership, mission and environment: an exploratory analysis into the evolution of a technology social venture', in Johanna Mair, J. Robinson and K. Hockerts (eds), *Social Entrepreneurship*, New York: Palgrave-MacMillan, pp. 155–79.

Dorado, S. (2006), 'Social entrepreneurial ventures: different values so different process of creation, no?', *Journal of Developmental Entrepreneurship*, **11**(4), 319–43.

DTI (2002), *Social Enterprise: a Strategy for Success*, London: Department of Trade and Industry (DTI), Secretary of State for Trade and Industry, HM Government.

Favreau, L. (2006), 'Economie sociale et politiques publiques – l'expérience québécoise', *Horizons*, **8**(2), 7–15.

Fontan, J.-M., J. Allard, A. Bertrand-Dansereau and J. Demers (2007), *Enquête auprès d'entrepreneurs sociaux*, Réseau québécois de recherche partenariale en économie sociale (RQRP-ÉS), working paper, ARUC-ÉS, no. RQ-03-2007, March.

Fowler, A. (2000), 'NGDOs as a moment in history: beyond aid to social entrepreneurship or civic innovation?', *Third World Quarterly*, **21**(4), 637–54.

Fulton, K. and G. Dees (2006), 'The past, present, and future of social entrepreneurship. A conversation with Greg Dees', pre-reading for Gathering of Leaders, CASE, Duke University's Fuqua School of Business.

GEM (2006), *Social Entrepreneurship Monitor United Kingdom 2006*, Global Entrepreneurship Monitor (GEM), R. Harding.

Gould, S. (2006), 'Social enterprise and business structures in Canada', Fraser Valley Centre for Social Enterprise, February, available at http://www.fvcse.stirsite.com/F/SEandBusinessStructures.doc.

Gray, M., K. Healy and P. Crofts (2003), 'Social enterprise: is it the business of social work?', *Australian Social Work*, **56**(2), 141–54.

Grenier, P. (2006), 'Social entrepreneurship: agency in a globalizing world', in A. Nicholls (ed.), *Social Entrepreneurship: New Models of Sustainable Social Change*, Oxford: Oxford University Press, pp. 119–43.

Harding, R. (2004), 'Social enterprise: the new economic engine?', *Business Strategy Review*, **15**(4), 39–43.

Hare, P., D. Jones and G. Blackhedge (2007), 'Understanding social enterprise: a case study of the childcare sector in Scotland', *Social Enterprise Journal*, **3**(1), 113–25.

Haugh, H. (2005), 'A research agenda for social entrepreneurship', *Social Enterprise Journal*, **1**(1), 1–12.

Haugh, H. (2006), 'Social enterprise: beyond economic outcomes and individual returns', in Johanna Mair, J. Robinson and K. Hockerts (eds), *Social Entrepreneurship*, New York: Palgrave Macmillan, pp. 180–205.

Haugh, H. (2007), 'Community-led social venture creation', *Entrepreneurship: Theory & Practice*, **31**(2), 161–82.

Haugh, H. and P. Tracey (2004) 'Role of social enterprise in regional development', in Cambridge-MIT Institute (eds), *Social Enterprise and Regional Development Conference*, Cambridge, UK: Cambridge-MIT Institute.

Henton, D., J. Melville and K. Walesh (1997), *Grassroots Leaders for a New Economy: How Civic Entrepreneurs Are Building Prosperous Communities*, San Francisco, Jossey-Bass Publishers.

Hibbert, S., G. Hogg and T. Quinn (2002), 'Consumer response to social entrepreneurship: the case of the Big Issue in Scotland', *International Journal of Nonprofit & Voluntary Sector Marketing*, **7**(3), 288–301.

Hockerts, K. (2006), 'Entrepreneurial opportunity in social purpose business ventures', in J. Mair, J. Robinson and K. Hockerts (eds), *Social Entrepreneurship*, New York: Palgrave Macmillan, pp. 142–54.

Institute for Social Entrepreneurs (n.d.), 'Social enterprise terminology', available at http://www.socialent.org/Social_Enterprise_Terminology.htm.

Institute for Social Entrepreneurs (2002), 'A glossary of useful terms', The Institute for Social Entrepreneurs, available at http://www.socialent.org/pdfs/GLOSSARY.pdf.

Lasprogata, G. and M. Cotton (2003), 'Contemplating "enterprise": the business and legal challenges of social entrepreneurship', *American Business Law Journal*, **41**(1), 67–113.

Leadbeater, C. (1997), *The Rise of the Social Entrepreneur*, London: Demos, available at http://www.dsi.britishcouncil.org.cn/images/socialentrepreneur.pdf.

Leadbeater, C. (2006), 'The socially entrepreneurial city', in A. Nicholls (ed.), *Social Entrepreneurship: New Models of Sustainable Social Change*, Oxford: Oxford University Press, pp. 233–46.

Mair, J. and I. Martí (2004), 'Social entrepreneurship: what are we talking about? a framework for future research', IESE Business School, University of Navarra, working paper No. 546, March.

Mair, J. and I. Martí (2006), 'Social entrepreneurship research: a source of explanation, prediction, and delight', *Journal of World Business*, **41**(1), 36–44.

Mair, J. and E. Noboa (2003), 'Social entrepreneurship: how intentions to create a social enterprise get formed', IESE Business School, University of Navarra, working paper No. 521, September.

Martin, R.L. and S. Osberg (2007), 'Social entrepreneurship: the case for definition', *Stanford Social Innovation Review*, Spring, pp. 29–39.

Nicholls, A. (ed.) (2006), *Social Entrepreneurship: New Models of Sustainable Social Change*, Oxford: Oxford University Press.

OECD (1999), *Social Enterprises*, Paris: Organisation for Economic Co-operation and Development (OECD), available at http://www.oecd.org/.

OECD – LEED Programme (n.d.), *The Social Enterprise Sector: A Conceptual Framework*, Paris: Organisation for Economic Co-operation and Development (OECD)/Local Economic and Employment Development Programme (LEED), available at http://www.oecd.org/dataoecd/43/40/37753595.pdf.

Office of the Third Sector (2006), *Social Enterprise Action Plan – Scaling New Heights*, London: Office of the Third Sector, Cabinet Office, HM Government.

Office of the Third Sector (2007), *Social Enterprise Action Plan – One Year On*, Social Enterprise Day, 15 November 2007, London: Office of the Third Sector, Cabinet Office, HM Government.

Painter, A. (2006), 'The social economy in Canada: concepts, data and measurement', *Horizons*, **8**(2), 30–34.

Paton, R. (2003), *Managing and Measuring Social Enterprises*, London: Sage Publications.

Pearce, J. (2003), *Social Enterprise in Anytown*, London: Calouste Gulbenkian Foundation.

Peredo, A.M. and M. McLean (2006), 'Social entrepreneurship: a critical review of the concept', *Journal of World Business*, **41**(1), 56–65.

Perrini, F. (ed.) (2006), *The New Social Entrepreneurship. What Awaits Social Entrepreneurship Ventures?*, Cheltenham, UK and Northampton, MA, USA: Edward Elgar.

Pomerantz, M. (2003), 'The business of social entrepreneurship in a "down economy"', *In Business*, **25**(2), 25–8.

Prabhu, G.N. (1999), 'Social entrepreneurial leadership', *Career Development International*, **4**(3), 140–45.

REDF (1996), Roberts Enterprise Development Fund (previously Roberts Foundation Homeless Economic Development Fund), available at http://www.redf.org/.

Roberts, D. and C. Woods (2005), 'Changing the world on a shoestring: the concept of social entrepreneurship', *University of Aukland Business Review*, **11**(1), 45–51.

Seelos, C. and J. Mair (2005), 'Social entrepreneurship: creating new business models to serve the poor', *Business Horizons*, **48**, 241–6.

Shane, S. and S. Venkataraman (2000), 'The promise of entrepreneurship as a field of research', *Academy of Management Review*, **25**(1), 217–26.

Sharir, M. and M. Lerner (2005), 'Gauging the success of social ventures initiated by individual social entrepreneurs', *Journal of World Business*, **41**(1), 6–20.

Smallbone, D., M. Evans, I. Ekanem and S. Butters (2001), 'Researching social enterprise', final report to the Small Business Service, London: Centre for Enterprise and Economic Development Research – Middlesex University Business School.

Social Enterprise Alliance (n.d.), 'Social enterprise defined', available at http://www.se-alliance.org/resources_defined.cfm.

Social Enterprise London (n.d.), *Social Enterprise in the 3rd Sector*, London: Social Enterprise London.

Sullivan Mort, G., J. Weerawardena and K. Carnegie (2003), 'Social entrepreneurship: towards conceptualization', *International Journal of Nonprofit & Voluntary Sector Marketing*, **8**(1), 76–88.

Tan, W.-L., J. Williams and T.-M. Tan (2005), 'Defining the "social" in "social entrepreneurship": altruism and entrepreneurship', *International Entrepreneurship and Management Journal*, **1**(3), 353–65.

Thompson, J., G. Alvy and A. Lees (2000), 'Social entrepreneurship – a new look at the people and the potential', *Management Decision*, **38**(5), 328–38.

Thompson, J.L. (2002), 'The world of the social entrepreneur', *The International Journal of Public Sector Management*, **15**(5), 412–31.

Thompson, J.L. and B. Doherty (2006), 'The diverse world of social entreprise – A collection of social enterprise stories', *International Journal of Social Economics*, **33**(5/6), 361–75.

Tommasini, G. (2004), *The Meaning of Social Entrepreneurship for Congruent Regional Development*, ADEST Srl – Irecoop – Veneto.

Tracey, P. and N. Phillips (2007), 'The distinctive challenge of educating social entrepreneurs: a postscript and rejoinder to the special issue on entrepreneurship education', *Academy of Management Learning & Education*, **6**(2), 264–71.

Ulhoi, J.P. (2005), 'The social dimensions of entrepreneurship', *Technovation*, **25**(8), 939–46.

Valéau, P., P. Cimper and L.-J. Filion (2004), *Entrepreneuriat et organisations à but non lucratif (OBNL)*, Montreal, working paper 2004-10, Chair of Entrepreneurship Roger-J.A. Bombardier, HEC Montréal.

Vasakaria, V. (2008), 'A study on social entrepreneurship and the characteristics of social entrepreneurs', *The ICFAI Journal of Management Research*, **7**(4), 32–40.

Verstraete, T. and A. Fayolle (2005), 'Paradigmes et entrepreneuriat', *Revue de l'Entrepreneuriat*, **4**(1), 33–52.

Waddock, S.A. and J.E. Post (1991), 'Social entrepreneurs and catalytic change', *Public Administration Review*, **51**(1), 393–401.

Weerawardena, J. and G. Sullivan Mort (2006), 'Investigating social entrepreneurship: a multidimensional model', *Journal of World Business*, **41**(1), 21–35.

Wei-Skillern, J., J.E. Austin, H. Leonard and H. Stevenson (2007), *Entrepreneurship in the Social Sector*, Los Angeles: Sage Publications.

Zhara, S.A., E. Gedajlovic, D.O. Neubaum and J.M. Shulman (2006), 'Social entrepreneurship: domain, contributions and ethical dilemmas', paper presented at University of Minnesota Conference on Ethics and Entrepreneurship, April.

Zhara, S.A., E. Gedajlovic, D.O. Neubaum, J.M. Shulman (2009). 'A typology of entrepreneurs: motives, search processes and ethical chellenges', *Journal of Business Venturing*, **24**(5), 519–32.

# 4   Concepts and realities of social enterprise: a European perspective
*Jacques Defourny*

## INTRODUCTION

Although rarely used until the mid-1990s, the concepts of 'social enterprise', 'social entrepreneurship' and 'social entrepreneur' are now increasingly discussed in various parts of the world. The bulk of the literature is still being produced in Western Europe and the United States but those three 'SE flags' are attracting much interest in other regions, such Central and Eastern Europe, South-Eastern Asia (especially South Korea, Japan and Taiwan) and Latin America.

In Europe, the concept of social enterprise made its first appearance in 1990, at the very heart of the third sector, following an impetus which was first an Italian one and was closely linked with the cooperative movement: a journal named *Impresa Sociale* (Social Enterprise) started to study new entrepreneurial initiatives which arose primarily in response to social needs that had been inadequately met, or not met at all, by public services (Borzaga and Santuari, 2001). In 1991, the Italian parliament adopted a law creating a specific legal form for 'social cooperatives' and the latter went on to experience an extraordinary growth. Around the same period, European researchers noticed the existence of similar initiatives, though of a lesser magnitude, in various other EU countries and in 1996, they decided to form a network to study 'the emergence of social enterprise in Europe'. This network, which was named EMES and covered all of the fifteen countries that then made up the European Union, gradually developed a common approach of social enterprise.

In the United States, the concepts of social enterprise also met with a very positive response in the early 1990s. In 1993, for instance, the Harvard Business School launched the 'Social Enterprise Initiative', one of the milestones of the period. Since then, other major universities (Columbia, Berkeley, Duke, Yale, New York and so on) and various foundations have set up training and support programmes for social enterprises as well as social entrepreneurs. As to the latter, Ashoka, an organization which has identified and supported such individuals since the beginning of the 1980s, has played a pioneering role in this line.[1]

In a first period – and still today outside specialists' circles – the three SE concepts have been used more or less along the same lines: although simplifying a little, one could say that social entrepreneurship was seen as the process through which social entrepreneurs created social enterprises. Afterwards, various definitions of and approaches to each of these concepts have been proposed. However, what is striking is the fact that the debates on both sides of the Atlantic took place in parallel trajectories, with very few connections among them throughout the 1990s and even the first half of the following decade.[2] Moreover, during this time in Europe, the concept of social enterprise was the only one which really became increasingly used, although to various extents across countries. In such a context, it surely makes sense to analyse carefully how the social enterprise idea spread throughout Europe and gave birth to a quite distinct literature as well as to show how the European conceptual landscape evolved in the last years, including through a much deeper dialogue with US academic and field actors.

Before going further, it should be noted that the SE concepts can in practice be used to point out two quite different phenomena: on the one hand, they designate new organizations, created *ex nihilo*, that may often be viewed as a sub-group of the third sector; on the other hand, they can also designate a process, a new entrepreneurial spirit influencing and reshaping older third sector initiatives.

In this perspective, we therefore begin with a brief discussion of the main approaches that, for more than a quarter of a century, have been developed to apprehend the realities of the third sector (section 1). Subsequently, we will assess the extent to which one can speak of the rise of a new social entrepreneurship within this sector in Europe (section 2) and how this social entrepreneurship can be apprehended from a conceptual point of view, both through the definition proposed in 2002 by the British government when it launched an active policy for the development of social enterprises and through the approach built by the EMES European Research Network since the mid-1990s (section 3). Because of their truly European scope, particular attention will be paid to EMES empirical works in the first 15 EU member states and in the new member countries from Eastern and Central Europe (section 4). The theoretical potential of this approach will be highlighted (section 5). It will also be analysed in the light of the most recent evolutions on the North American scene (section 6).

## 1    THE (RE)DISCOVERY OF THE THIRD SECTOR

The idea of a distinct third sector, made up of enterprises and organizations which are not part of the traditional private sector nor of the public sector, began to emerge in the mid-1970s. Such organizations were already very active in many areas and were indeed already the subject of scientific works and specific public policies. But the idea of bringing these bodies together and the theoretical basis on which this might be done were not really put forward until 30 years ago.

In the United States the work of the Filer Commission and, in 1976, the launch of Yale University's 'Program on Non-profit Organisations', involving 150 researchers, marked a decisive step in the conceptualization of non-profit organizations (NPOs) and the non-profit sector. Since then, a vast scientific literature on NPOs has been developed, with contributions from disciplines as diverse as economics, sociology, political science, management, history, law and so on.[3]

In Europe, the broad diversity of socio-political, cultural and economic national circumstances has not allowed such a wide-ranging and rapid development of analytical works emphasizing the existence of a third sector. However, the economic entities that gradually came to be perceived through a third sector approach were already important in most countries. They were also rooted in solid and long-standing traditions: mutual organizations and cooperatives had existed more or less everywhere for more than a century, and association-based economic initiatives had also been multiplying for a considerable time.

In fact, without denying that the general public's view is still strongly characterized by the historical context of each country, it may be said that two conceptual approaches aiming to embrace the whole third sector gradually spread internationally, accompanied by statistical work aiming to quantify its economic importance. One is the already-mentioned 'non-profit sector' approach; the other, mainly French in origin, forged the concept of the 'social economy' to bring together co-operatives, mutual societies and associations (and, with increasing frequency, foundations).[4] Although the first approach has the great advantage of having been conveyed, from the outset, by the English language, the second approach has found an ever-greater resonance throughout Europe and in other parts of the world.[5] It has also been taken up, although not always with the same meaning, by the European Union's institutions.[6]

Other conceptualizations of the third sector have also been developed and have met with a positive response at the international level. This is particularly the case of approaches based on a 'tri-polar' representation of the economy, where the three 'poles' either represent categories of agents (private enterprises, the state and households), or correspond to logics or modes of regulation of exchanges (the market, public redistribution and reciprocity), which in turn refer to the types of resources involved (market, non-market and non-monetary resources). In such a perspective, the third sector is viewed as an intermediate space in which the different poles combine.[7] The analytical grid of the solidarity-based economy belongs to such a perspective. Although sometimes regarded as competing with the first two concepts, these last approaches rather provide analytical grids which enrich the understanding of the non-profit sector and the social economy.

The importance of this third sector is nowadays such that one can affirm that it is broadly associated with the major economic roles of public authorities: the third sector is involved in the allocation of resources, through the production of many quasi-public goods and services (in the fields of health, culture, education, social action, proximity services, sport, leisure, the environment, advocacy and so on); it has a role of redistribution of resources, via the voluntary contributions (in cash, in kind or through volunteering) which many associations can mobilize and through the provision of a wide range of free or virtually free services to deprived people; and it is also involved in the regulation of economic life when, for example, associations or social cooperatives are the privileged partners of public authorities in the task of helping low-qualified unemployed people, who are at risk of permanent exclusion from the labour market, and reintegrating them back into work.

The persistence of high structural unemployment in many countries, especially across Europe, as well as the difficulties of traditional public policies in coping with new economic and social challenges, have naturally raised the question of how far the third sector can help to meet these challenges and perhaps take over from public authorities in some areas.

Of course there is no simple answer to this question, and the debate is today wide open. Some regard associations and other third sector entities as made-to-measure partners for new transfers of responsibility and parallel reductions in public costs. The qualities usually attributed to private enterprise (flexibility, rapidity, creativity, a willingness to take on responsibility and so on) are also expected to lead to improvements in the services provided.[8] Others, on the other hand, fear that the third sector might become an instrument for privatization policies, leading to social deregulation and the gradual unravelling of acquired social rights. Others still stress the fact that our societies are moving towards a redefinition of relationships between the individual, the intermediate structures of civil society and the state.

In any case, most would share the view that Western European countries are moving from a 'welfare state' to a new 'welfare mix', where new bases are to be found for the sharing of responsibility among public authorities, private for-profit providers and third sector organizations.

## 2  A NEW SOCIAL ENTREPRENEURSHIP

Why does it make sense to talk about a new social entrepreneurship and not simply of an evolution of non-profit or social economy organizations? This question refers directly to the theories about entrepreneurship, which we do not intend to review in the present chapter. We will simply refer to the classic work of Schumpeter, for whom economic development is a 'process of carrying out new combinations' in the production process, (Schumpeter, 1934: 66) and entrepreneurs are precisely the ones whose role it is to implement these new combinations. According to this author, entrepreneurs are not necessarily the owners of a company, but they are responsible for introducing changes in at least one of the following ways: i) the introduction of a new product or a new quality of product; ii) the introduction of a new production method; iii) the opening of a new market; iv) the acquisition of a new source of raw materials; or v) the reorganization of a sector of activity.

Following the work carried out by Young (1983) and Badelt (1997), this typology can be adapted to the third sector; for each of the levels mentioned by Schumpeter, it can be asked to what extent a new entrepreneurship can be identified within the European third sector.[9]

### New Products or a New Quality of Products

Numerous analyses of the third sector have already demonstrated that the latter has often developed in response to needs to which the traditional private sector or the state were unable to provide a satisfactory answer.[10] There are countless examples of organizations that have invented new types of services to take up the challenges of their age. To this extent, many of these organizations can be said, nowadays as in the past, to be born or have been born from an entrepreneurial dynamic. But have the last two decades been different in any specific way? We believe that it is possible to speak of a new entrepreneurship, which is probably more prevalent in Europe than in the United States, because the crisis of the European welfare systems (in terms of budget, efficiency and legitimacy) has resulted in public authorities increasingly looking to private initiatives to provide solutions that they would have implemented themselves if the economic climate had been as good as in the glorious 1945–75 period. It is undoubtedly in the United Kingdom that this trend was first seen as the most striking, but it is now apparent, to varying degrees, in most member states of the European Union. The two main fields of activity covered by the works of the EMES European Research Network, namely work integration of low-qualified jobseekers and personal services, have seen multiple innovations in terms of new activities better adapted to needs, whether in regard to vocational training, childcare, services for elderly people, or aid for certain categories of disadvantaged persons (abused children, refugees, immigrants and so on).[11]

This entrepreneurship seems all the more innovative as, even within the third sector, it contrasts sharply with the highly bureaucratic and only slightly innovative behaviour of certain large traditional organizations (for example, the very large welfare organizations – *Wohlfahrtsverbände* – in Germany).

### New Methods of Organization and/or Production

It is common to see the third sector organize its activities in ways which differ from the traditional private and public sectors. But what is most striking in the current generations of social enterprises is the involvement of different partners, of several categories of actors: salaried workers, volunteers, users, support organizations and local public authorities are often partners in the same project, whereas traditional social economy organizations have generally been set up by more homogeneous social groups.[12] If this does not necessarily revolutionize the production process in the strict meaning of the term, it nevertheless often transforms the way in which the activity is organized. In some cases, one could even talk of a joint construction of supply and demand, when providers and users cooperate in the organization and management of certain proximity services. The setting-up of childcare centres run by parents in France or in Sweden is just one of many examples of such cooperation.

### New Production Factors

One of the major but long-standing specific characteristics of the third sector is its capacity to mobilize volunteer work. In itself, the use of volunteers is thus not innovating; however, it is innovating in numerous recent initiatives in so far as it makes it possible to produce goods or provide services that were not previously available.

It is also noteworthy that volunteering has profoundly changed in nature over the last few decades: it seems to be not only much less charitable than forty or fifty years ago, but also less 'militant' than in the 1960s or 1970s. Today's voluntary workers are fairly pragmatic and focus more on 'productive' objectives and activities that correspond to specific needs. It is not unusual indeed for the entrepreneurial role, in the most commonly used sense of the term (launching an activity), to be carried out by voluntary workers.

Paid work has also seen various innovations. On the one hand, many third sector organizations have been at the forefront of experiments regarding atypical forms of employment, such as the hiring of salaried workers in the framework of unemployment reduction programmes, the development of semi-voluntary formulas or of part-time work with very reduced working hours, and so on.[13] On the other hand, it can be said that the traditional status of the workers is often 'enriched' when the latter are recognized as fully-fledged members of the governing bodies of the social enterprise, with the resultant control and decision-making powers that this implies.[14]

**New Market Relations**

In a growing number of countries there is a trend of public authorities towards 'contracting out' practices and towards the development of quasi-markets for certain services which were previously provided by the state or by non-profit private bodies long favoured by the state. Indeed, with a view to reducing costs and ensuring that the services are better adapted to users' needs, public authorities are making an increasing use of calls to tender, which bring different types of providers into competition for public funding linked to the carrying out of previously defined contract specifications. The Conservative governments in the UK during the 1980s are those that have gone furthest in this direction, but this switch from 'tutelary control' to 'competitive control' through quasi-markets is becoming more and more commonplace almost everywhere.

Such profound changes in the welfare state inevitably have major consequences at different levels. It is sufficient here to emphasize the factors that tend to accentuate the entrepreneurial character of associations, in the sense that they have an increasing number of characteristics in common with traditional companies and also, in part, in terms of the 'new combinations' referred to by Schumpeter:[15]

- existing associations find themselves in competitive situations, increasingly with for-profit companies when tendering, and they are consequently obliged to install or reinforce an internal management culture very much modelled on that of the commercial sector;
- the ending of certain public monopolies (for example in Sweden) or of the monopolies enjoyed by large national federations providing social services (for example in Germany) encourage the emergence of new private initiatives (for-profit or non-profit organizations) whose structure, from the outset, is designed taking this context into account;

- last but not least, both for old and for new associations, the economic risk is greater, since their financing henceforward depends on their ability to win these quasi-markets and to satisfy users.

Finally, it goes without saying that market relations are reinforced by the increased demand, among private individuals with adequate financial resources, for certain services that become accessible because of the continued rise in the living standards of an important part of the population. Thus for example, elderly people who receive a decent pension or who have accumulated considerable savings represent new markets, but these are often very competitive. This trend is still reinforced by the fact that money is made available to fund the demand for some proximity services through public policies which cover a significant part of the production costs (for example through a 'service voucher' system for house cleaning services, as in Belgium).

### New Forms of Enterprises

The recent introduction of new legal frameworks in the national legislation of various European states tends to confirm that we are dealing with a somewhat original kind of entrepreneurship (Defourny and Nyssens, 2008). These legal frameworks are intended to be better suited to these types of initiatives than the traditional non-profit or cooperative legal forms.

We have already mentioned the new status created in 1991 for Italian social cooperatives. Laws were introduced in other EU countries as well, along the same 'cooperative' line, to create new legal forms: the 'social solidarity cooperative' in Portugal (1997); the 'social initiative cooperative' in Spain (1999); the 'limited liability social cooperative' in Greece (1999), the 'collective interest cooperative society' in France (2001), and the 'social cooperative' (2006) in Poland. Other laws have also been introduced which do not refer explicitly to the cooperative model, even though the latter sometimes inspired them. Thus, in 1995, Belgium created the 'social purpose company', and a new law creating the 'community interest company' legal form was passed in the United Kingdom in 2004. Moreover, Finland (in 2004) and Italy (in 2006) created a 'social enterprise' legal framework which goes beyond the social cooperative model.

Generally speaking, these new legal frameworks are designed to encourage entrepreneurial dynamics towards the fulfilment of a social mission, often with a dominant market orientation. They are sometimes linked to specific public programmes aiming at work integration of the hard-to-place (for instance in Poland and Finland). In various cases, they also provide a way of formalizing the multi-stakeholder nature of numerous initiatives, by involving the various stakeholders (paid workers, voluntary workers, users and so on) in the decision-making process. However, it must be emphasized that in many countries the great majority of social enterprises are still using traditional third sector legal forms.

## 3   EUROPEAN APPROACHES OF SOCIAL ENTERPRISE

Although current debates on social entrepreneurship in Europe are more influenced by US debates than before 2005, especially through business schools and a few foundations, it may be stated that two definitions of the social enterprise have been emerging consistently in Europe and now constitute conceptual reference points for a set of international works: the definition forged by the EMES European Research Network in the late 1990s, and that put forward by the British government in 2002.[16]

### The British Approach

In a paper entitled 'Social enterprise: a strategy for success', (2002), the Secretary of State for Trade and Industry, P. Hewitt, and the Social Enterprise Unit (SEU) within her department put forward a definition which served as a basis for a whole policy of the Blair government fostering social enterprises. It states that 'a social enterprise is a business with primarily social objectives whose surpluses are principally reinvested for that purpose in the business or in the community, rather than being driven by the need to maximise profit for shareholders and owners' (DTI, 2002). Based upon this definition, a series of empirical studies were carried out across the country and the Social Enterprise Unit commissioned a synthesis of these works (Ecotec, 2003). That report underlined a series of difficulties in terms of consistency and compatibility to make the definition operational. With a view to redressing these shortcomings, the report recommended breaking down the definition into a set of characteristics or indicators, which would be more useful than an 'overall statement' in creating an inventory of social enterprises in the United Kingdom. In the same perspective, the Social Enterprise Coalition, the main umbrella body which also plays a key role in fostering a national strategy, proposed to use three main criteria: in addition to a market orientation and social aims, it highlighted a third criterion of social ownership defined by governance and ownership structures based on participation and control by stakeholder groups or by trustees or directors.

In spite of such conceptual efforts, various criteria were used in subsequent surveys, notably regarding the proportion of market-based income in social enterprise's resources and the legal framework under which the enterprise is registered. A survey only covering entities registered as Companies Limited by Guarantee or Industrial and Provident Societies concluded there were around 15000 social enterprises in the UK in 2004, employing 475000 workers and a further 300000 people on a volunteer basis. It was estimated that 88 per cent of those social enterprises had generated at least 50 per cent of their income from trading (IFF Research Ltd, 2005). An even greater majority described their mission in terms of helping people, especially those with disabilities, children or young people, the elderly and people with low incomes. The main way in which people were helped was through training/education and various forms of personal support (housing, childcare), professional support (business advice, help in looking for jobs) and cultural and recreational opportunities (sports clubs, arts groups).

One year later, the Annual Survey of Small Businesses included four questions to enable the identification of social enterprises. Now covering all types of SMEs, it came out with a much larger figure: 5 per cent of all businesses, that is 55000 enterprises with employees, were said to satisfy all the following: think themselves as a social enterprise; never pay more than 50 per cent of profits to owners/shareholders; generate more than 75 per cent of income from traded goods/services (or receive less than 20 per cent of income from grants and donations); and think they are a very good fit with the government definition of a social enterprise (Institute for Employment Studies, 2006). Although that impressive figure is now often quoted, the understanding of the definition may have been somehow influenced by the fact that 'social/environmental objectives' are not defined at all and are instead indirectly presented as opposed to 'the need to maximize (not just make) profits for shareholders and owners'. Another key item of the definition states that surpluses may be simply 'reinvested in the business' (or the community), a rather natural strategy for small businesses owned by sole proprietors which represent a significant part of SMEs surveyed.

In addition to operational limits of the government's definition of social enterprise, the concept itself is still heavily debated in the UK, including as to governance issues (Spear et al., 2009). Indeed it is sometimes seen as a 're-branding' strategy to foster market orientation and business methods in existing third sector organizations as well as a major risk of weakening other specificities of the latter.[17] This probably explains why the British government appointed a Minister of the (whole) Third Sector within the Cabinet Office in 2006 and decided to locate the Social Enterprise Unit in the Office of the Third Sector (in charge of the entire 'world' of voluntary and community organizations, charities, cooperatives, mutuals, social firms, and so on). Such a move has sometimes been interpreted as weakening the very specific attention paid to social enterprises. From an academic point of view, however, there is still a growing interest in those organizations, as shown by initiatives such as an annual 'Social Enterprise Research Conference' (since 2004), the publication of a *Social Enterprise Journal* (since 2005) and the setting up of a major Third Sector Research Centre heavily financed by the Economic and Social Research Council, including various activities related to social enterprise (2008).

Moreover, it should be stressed that some university centres such as the Skoll Centre for Social Entrepreneurship at Oxford University and others have played a major role in building bridges between European and US debates on social enterprise[18] as well as between the UK and continental Europe.[19]

Finally, the most recent works in the UK are clearly less focused on the frontiers of a social enterprise sector or its overall economic weight. They rather acknowledge the very wide diversity of forms, contexts and dynamics which may be observed, as shown by Peattie and Morley (2008).

**The EMES Approach**

It is precisely the need to account for such a diversity which was the major concern of the EMES European Research Network formed in 1996 by researchers from all fifteen countries which constituted the European Union at that time. Through a major research project financed by the European Commission and covering five years, those scholars tried to analyse to what extent social enterprises were emerging throughout the EU, not only in Italy.[20] Key features of this approach include the fact that it derived from extensive dialogue among several disciplines (economics, sociology, political science and management) as well as among the various national traditions and sensitivities present in the European Union. Moreover, it was guided by a project that was both theoretical and empirical.

From the outset, the EMES approach gave priority to the choice of various indicators which would help identify social enterprises over a concise and elegant definition. It was also clear that those indicators should not be seen as conditions to be fulfilled to deserve the name of social enterprise. In order to make this key point even clearer, it was explained in a second EMES major work, that 'rather than constituting prescriptive criteria, these indicators describe an "ideal-type" (i.e. an abstract construction in Weber's terms), which constitutes a tool, somewhat analogous to a compass which can help the researchers locate the position of certain entities relative to one another (. . .) within the galaxy of social enterprises.'[21]

The EMES conceptual framework is based on two series of indicators, some being more economic and the others predominantly social.[22]

To reflect the economic and entrepreneurial dimensions of initiatives, four criteria have been put forward:

a.  **A continuous activity producing goods and/or selling services**
    Social enterprises, unlike some traditional non-profit organizations, do not normally have advocacy activities or the redistribution of financial flows (as, for example, many foundations) as their major activity, but they are directly involved in the production of goods or the provision of services to people on a continuous basis. The productive activity thus represents the reason, or one of the main reasons, for the existence of social enterprises.

b.  **A high degree of autonomy**
    Social enterprises are created by a group of people on the basis of an autonomous project and they are governed by these people. They may depend on public subsidies but they are not managed, be it directly or indirectly, by public authorities or other organizations (federations, private firms and so on). They have the right both to take up their own position ('voice') and to terminate their activity ('exit').

c.  **A significant level of economic risk**
    Those who establish a social enterprise assume totally or partly the risk inherent in the initiative. Unlike most public institutions, their financial viability depends on the efforts of their members and workers to secure adequate resources.

d.  **A minimum amount of paid work**
    As in the case of most traditional non-profit organizations, social enterprises may also combine monetary and non-monetary resources, voluntary and paid workers. However, the activity carried out in social enterprises requires a minimum level of paid workers.

To encapsulate the social dimensions of the initiative, five further criteria have been proposed:

e.  **An explicit aim to benefit the community**
    One of the principal aims of social enterprises is to serve the community or a specific group of people. In the same perspective, a feature of social enterprises is their desire to promote a sense of social responsibility at the local level.

f.  **An initiative launched by a group of citizens**
    Social enterprises are the result of collective dynamics involving people belonging to a community or to a group that shares a well-defined

need or aim; this collective dimension must be maintained over time in one way or another, even though the importance of leadership – often embodied by an individual or a small group of leaders – must not be neglected.

g.  **A decision-making power not based on capital ownership**
    This criterion generally refers to the principle of 'one member, one vote' or at least to a decision-making process in which voting power is not distributed according to capital shares on the governing body which has the ultimate decision-making rights. Although the owners of capital are important when social enterprises have equity capital, the decision-making rights are generally shared with the other stakeholders.

h.  **A participatory nature, which involves various parties affected by the activity**
    Representation and participation of users or customers, influence of various stakeholders on decision-making and a participative management are often important characteristics of social enterprises. In many cases, one of the aims of social enterprises is to further democracy at the local level through economic activity.

i.  **A limited profit distribution**
    Social enterprises not only include organizations that are characterised by a total non-distribution constraint, but also organizations which, like cooperatives in many countries, may distribute profits, but only to a limited extent, thus allowing to avoid a profit-maximizing behaviour.

As already underlined, these economic and social indicators can be used to identify totally new social enterprises, but they can also lead to designate as social enterprises older organizations which have been reshaped by new internal dynamics. In such a perspective combined with its 'ideal type' nature, the EMES approach proved to be empirically fertile. For example, when J.-F. Draperi (2003) studied 151 organizations subsidized over a twenty-year period by France's Fondation Crédit Coopératif, he found in varying degrees most of the features outlined above. Although he did not intend originally to adopt the 'social enterprise' approach, this is what he finally ended up doing; with reference to the EMES approach, he underlined the capacity for social innovation demonstrated by these organizations.

In a similar perspective, EMES researchers made an inventory of the different types of social enterprises working in the field of on-the-job training and occupational integration of low-qualified individuals. This survey, which covered 12 EU countries, combined the indicators to which we have referred above with criteria peculiar to this field and came up with the concept of the 'work-integration social enterprise' (WISE). This conceptual framework allowed the identification of 39 categories or models of WISEs in the twelve countries surveyed.[23] On that basis, another major research project funded by the European Commission was also carried out to test empirically various hypotheses which may be seen as the first building blocks of a European theory of social enterprise (Nyssens, 2006).[24]

## 4   SOME EXAMPLES FROM THE EUROPEAN UNION

### The European Union before its Enlargement in 2004 (EU-15)

In their first study (1996–99), which included the 15 countries composing the European Union at the time, the EMES Network's researchers had devoted themselves to describing and analysing social enterprises emerging in one or several of the three following fields: training and reintegration through work, personal services and local development (Borzaga and Defourny, 2001).

Some of the national realities surveyed are listed in Table 4.1, whose main objective is to provide an illustration of the conceptual developments we have described above.

More generally, social enterprises in France (as in Belgium) seem to be particularly innovating in the area of 'proximity services'. These social enterprises often mobilize additional resources beside resources from the market and the state, and they go beyond the functional logic of the latter. This also clearly shows in the thousands of Italian cooperatives providing social services (residential or not), in particular services intended for the handicapped, elderly people, drug-users and young people with family problems. In the United Kingdom as well, home-care cooperatives emerged in answer to state or market failures, in a specific context characterized by the rapid development of quasi-markets.

The border between the provision of social services and activities aiming to reintegrate people excluded from the labour market is relatively blurred. Indeed, in several countries, social work or services for handicapped people or those with other difficulties evolved towards more productive activities. The latter then served as the basis for the creation of social enterprises offering temporary (or even stable) jobs. The case of Denmark provides a good illustration of this hybrid nature; in this country, social work, community development and productive activities are intertwined in various types of initiative such as 'production communities', 'social

*Table 4.1    Examples of social enterprises in EU-15*

| Sectors | Countries | Examples |
| --- | --- | --- |
| Personal services | Austria | Children's groups: childcare services supported by a high level of parental involvement. |
| | France | *Crèches parentales* (parent-led childcare organizations): childcare services partly led and managed by parents. These organizations have formed a national network. |
| | Denmark | *Opholdssteder* (social residences): residential institutions designed as an alternative to conventional institutions for children and adolescents with difficulties. They focus on training and care services. |
| | United Kingdom | Home care co-ops: cooperatives employing their members, mainly women with dependents at home, on a part-time basis. |
| | Sweden | *LKUs*: cooperative local development agencies organized at the national level (FKU); their objective is to rehabilitate and reintegrate individuals with a mental handicap. |
| | Italy | *Cooperative sociali di tipo A* (A-type social cooperatives): cooperatives active in the fields of health, training or personal services, operating within the legal framework adopted by Italy's national parliament in 1991. |
| | Portugal | *CERCIs*: cooperatives for the training and rehabilitation of handicapped children; they merged into a national federation in 1985. |
| Training-integration through work | Belgium | *Entreprises de formation par le travail* (EFTs, on-the-job-training enterprises) and *enterprises d'insertion* (EIs, work-integration enterprises) in the southern part of the country; *invoegbedrijven* (work-integration enterprises) and *sociale werkplaatsen* (social workshops) in the northern part of the country. |
| | Italy | *Cooperative sociali di tipo B* (B-type social co-operatives): co-operatives active in the field of work-integration of individuals in precarious situations (1991 legal framework). |
| | Germany | *Soziale Betriebe* (social enterprises): these market-oriented social enterprises receive temporary public assistance. Their goal is to create jobs and promote economic development while aiming at the social and |

*Table 4.1*   (continued)

| Sectors | Countries | Examples |
|---|---|---|
| | | development while aiming at the social and occupational integration of the long-term unemployed. The jobs are created either in existing private enterprises or within the framework of the starting-up of new enterprises. |
| | Luxembourg | Associations (and sometimes cooperatives) providing their members with integration through work and economic activities in various fields, including environment, agriculture, construction, recycling of waste etc.; most are pilot projects subsidized by the state. |
| | Spain | Work-integration enterprises for the handicapped or individuals excluded from the conventional labour market. In both cases, the current trend is to provide access to transitional employment designed to ultimately integrate the target groups into the conventional labour market, rather than providing them with long-term 'sheltered' jobs. |
| Local development | Finland | Labour co-ops, organized by region into nine Cooperative Development Agencies (CDAs); they constitute an important lever for economic development at the local and regional levels. These cooperatives differ from traditional workers cooperatives in that they subcontract their members services to other enterprises. |
| | The Netherlands | *BuurtBeheer Bedrijven* (BBB, neighbourhood management enterprises): independent enterprises developing proximity services; they provide the inhabitants of disadvantaged neighbourhoods with the opportunity to perform paid work either in the maintenance/improvement of private residences and shared infrastructure or by providing social services in their neighbourhood. |
| | Greece | Agri-tourism cooperatives: cooperatives set up by women living in rural areas with tourism potential; they provide services in the areas of accommodation, catering and small crafts. |

*Table 4.1* (continued)

| Sectors | Countries | Examples |
| --- | --- | --- |
| | Ireland | Local community development enterprises with various legal forms; they provide a variety of services, including social housing, work-integration, credit (credit unions), proximity services etc. |

residences' (*opholdssteder*) or 'people's high schools' (*folkehøjskoler*) – the last two being known for their capacity to deal with young people with social problems. In Sweden, since the state initiated a reform including the phasing out, during the 1980s, of the large mental health institutions, social work cooperatives have developed for the former patients of these institutions, as well as for the handicapped. Although these cooperatives do not provide 'traditional' jobs, they demonstrate an entrepreneurial spirit which is encouraged by cooperative local development agencies. In a very different context, Portuguese CERCIs (cooperatives for the training and rehabilitation of mentally handicapped children) were originally special schools; they gradually evolved as their users grew up, acquiring an increasingly marked orientation towards production and job creation.

In many cases, the border is not clear-cut either between social enterprises aiming at the occupational integration of handicapped people and those targeting socially excluded individuals (drug-users, prisoners, young drop-outs and so on). Social enterprises of the two types (and sometimes even mixing the two target groups) can be identified in Italy, Luxembourg, Greece and Spain, in various fields of activity. In Spain, collection of waste and recycling activities are particularly important.

Many social enterprises offer stable jobs, but many others must be considered as linked to 'transitional labour markets'; in other terms, these enterprises constitute a stage on the reintegration path towards the traditional labour market. For example, various initiatives in Germany (in particular those specifically termed 'social enterprises' in three Länder) and Finnish labour cooperatives (which provide jobs to their members by 'subcontracting' their work to other employers) can be considered as transitional institutions receiving temporary support from public authorities.

Finally, we should also underline the participation of social enterprises to local development dynamics in disadvantaged areas. This is particularly true of organizations of the 'ABS' type in the new Länder of the former East Germany, of agri-tourism cooperatives (managed by women in isolated rural regions) in Greece, as well as of neighbourhood development/rehabilitation programmes in rural zones in the Netherlands. Sometimes concerns for local development are predominant, as in Ireland, where a large array of initiatives in the area of proximity services as well as community enterprises would not have emerged without the mobilization of local populations and the setting up of local partnerships.

**The Central and Eastern European Countries**

There has not yet been an in-depth study of the realities of social enterprises in most Central and Eastern European Countries (CEEC) comparable to the one conducted by EMES in the 15 countries which constituted the European Union prior to its enlargement in 2004. Nevertheless, with support of the UNDP, EMES recently carried out an overview study on the potential of social enterprises in CEE and several countries of the CIS.[25] Combined with some earlier works,[26] that study highlighted some general trends.

In contrast to the situation in Western Europe, several obstacles are hampering recognition of the real potential of social enterprises:

- the dominance of the 'transition myth' which, until now, induced policies highly reliant on the creation of a free market and failing to appreciate the value of 'alternative' organizations and enterprises as *bona fide* forces for local and national development;
- the neo-liberal paradigm (espoused by the media, the elites and the politicians), dismissive of collective and solidarity values;
- a cultural opposition to cooperatives and a belief that they are somehow politically suspect. In many countries, there is a negative perception of old cooperatives as organizations with ties to former Communist regimes – even though many of these organizations were actually created before the Communist era;
- an excessive dependence of social enterprises on donors, combined with a limited view of the role that alternative organizations can play. As regards associations, it appears that many NGOs are created, but they often suffer from two weaknesses. First, they are highly dependent on external donor agencies – especially American foundations – that tend to use them for their own purposes and significantly limit their autonomy. Second, while NGOs sometimes emerge as forces that are certainly associative, they are often less an authentic expression of civil society than the upshot of strategies linked to funding opportunities;
- a general lack of confidence in solidarity movements – the concept of solidarity being used primarily to describe an individual's

relationship with friends and family – and a view of economic activity as oriented towards the pursuit of personal gain, rather than as an activity with positive benefits for the community as a whole;

- the predominance of a 'parochial' political culture inducing, among social economy actors, a tendency to limit their horizons to the pursuit of their immediate interests; the networking capacity of third sector organizations (be it among the various 'families' of the third sector – associations, cooperatives, foundations – or within families) is low;
- the difficulty in mobilizing the necessary resources.

However, despite the cultural, political and legal difficulties they face, both traditional cooperatives and the new generations of non-profit organizations display a real potential for growth. Indeed, several factors affect the third sector in a positive way: the legacy of the strong pre-soviet tradition of charitable organizations and cooperatives constitutes an asset for the third sector; the level of education of third sector leaders is high; all countries covered by the EMES study display a capacity to create grassroots initiatives; and rural areas are characterized by strong social capital and local links.

It has also been noted that when cooperatives return to their roots, they can play an important role in regions with underdeveloped markets. The re-emergence of credit cooperatives in Lithuania bears testimony hereto. So does the example of Poland, where interesting cooperative initiatives have arisen in different areas, including credit, housing and agriculture. In Estonia, the cooperative sector, which took off in the 1990s, has now become a cornerstone of Estonia's social economy, among others through the creation of the Estonian Union of Co-operative Housing Association, which emcompasses more than 7000 organizations (Otsing, 2004).

New types of third sector organizations are also emerging in Central and Eastern Europe. Some of these can be seen as forms of social entrepreneurship, provided the latter is understood in a reasonably 'flexible' way.[27] These organizations are starting to provide services of general interest, redressing the failures of the social system. There are now associations in all CEECs, and foundations in all except Latvia and Lithuania. A few countries have also created 'open foundations', which result from the convergence of some associations and foundations.

The legal environment in CEECs indeed appears as rather favourable; some countries have even gone so far on the way to the legal recognition of social entrepreneurship as to create specific legal frameworks for social enterprises. In Hungary, for example, public interest companies (closely related in form to the UK's Community Interest Company) provide public services, while pursuing economic activities to raise funds for these services. Poland, Slovenia, the Czech Republic and Lithuania all provide examples of recently adopted specific legal frameworks for social enterprises.[28] In Poland, the Act on Social Employment (2003) and the Act on Employment Promotion and Institutions of the Labour Market (2004) already constituted a legal recognition of social entrepreneurship of low-income groups; further recognition was attained in June 2006 with the creation of a separate legal form for social cooperatives, whose aim is the social and occupational integration of jobless or handicapped people (CECOP, 2006). In Slovenia, a specific form of income-generating non-profit organization has been introduced: the private not-for-profit institute. The latter is a legal entity performing activities in the field of education, science, culture, sports, health or social affairs; private not-for-profit institutes' most important source of income is constituted by commercial activity on the market. The Czech law instituting the Public Benefit Company (which, as its name indicates, is committed to supply services of public benefit) and the Lithuanian law on social enterprises are not flawless, but they nonetheless both constitute significant steps towards the legal and institutional recognition of social entrepreneurship in the CEECs.

In sum, despite the problems associated, *inter alia*, with the process of economic transition in which CEECs are engaged, social enterprises in these countries are showing significant growth potential. Cooperatives are regaining ground in some of their traditional roles, and the new associative models that have emerged in Eastern Europe confirm the relevance of the social enterprise model.

## 5   PAVING THE WAY TO A THEORY OF SOCIAL ENTERPRISE

In the last phase of its first major research, the EMES Network took the initial steps towards the progressive development of a specific theory of social enterprise. In such a perspective, Bacchiega and Borzaga (2001) used tools from the new institutional economic theory to highlight the innovative character of social enterprises; the characteristics defining the social enterprise were interpreted as forming an original system of incentives that takes into account the potentially conflicting objectives pursued by the various categories of stakeholders. Evers (2001) developed a more socio-political analysis to demonstrate that such a 'multi-stakeholder, multiple-goal' structure was more easily understood if making use of the concept of 'social capital'. For Evers, creating social capital can also constitute an explicit objective of organizations such as social enterprises. Laville and Nyssens (2001b) came up with elements for an integrated theory of an 'ideal type' combining the economic, social and political dimensions of social enterprise. Like Evers, they emphasized the role of social capital, which is mobilized and reproduced in specific forms by social enterprises. In addition, they stressed the particularly hybrid and composite nature of social enterprises' resources (made of market, non-market and non-monetary resources such as volunteering), viewing this as a major asset of these organizations to resist the trend towards 'institutional isomorphism' that threatens all social economy organizations.

Within a second major research project, those theoretical lines were transformed into hypotheses to be tested for work integration social enterprises through a large survey conducted in twelve EU countries (Nyssens, 2006). Carried out over ten years, those two EMES projects and books may be regarded so far as the most comprehensive integrated work combining an original theoretical perspective with a large comparative empirical research across Europe.

Theoretically, the social enterprise concept could also point the way towards a more integrated approach to the entire social economy. As a matter of fact, when perceiving the social economy, two sources of tension appear as recurrent and difficult to overcome. One source of tension originates in the gap between enterprises offering their entire output for sale on the market (as do most cooperatives) and associations whose activities do not have a strong economic character (such as youth movement activities) and whose resources are totally non-market (grants, subsidies, and so on), or even non-monetary (volunteering). A second tension exists between so-called mutual interest organizations (cooperatives, mutual societies and a large part of associations) which, at least in principle, aim to serve their members, and general interest organizations, serving the broader community or specific target groups outside their membership (such as organizations fighting poverty and exclusion, or those involved in development cooperation, environmental protection and so on).[29]

These two sources of tension are partly illustrated in Figure 4.1. The first source of tension is represented by the coexistence of two distinct spheres: one sphere represents the cooperative tradition (which generated specific literature and schools of thought), while the other sphere represents the tradition of associative initiatives and movements (which has also inspired numerous sociologists and political scientists, especially in the North American literature on non-profit organizations). The second source of tension is more difficult to depict: it may be seen, although partly, within each of the two spheres, where general interest organizations are rather located in the area towards the centre, whereas the mutual

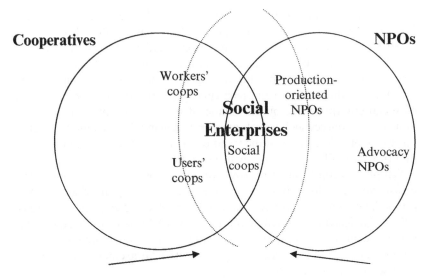

*Source:*   Adapted from Defourny (2001: 22).

*Figure 4.1   Social enterprises at the crossroads of the cooperative and
non-profit sectors*

interest organizations tend to be located either on the left or on the right of
the diagram (although some advocacy NPOs may of course be of general
interest).

The unifying role of the social enterprise concept resides primarily in the
fact that it generates mutual attraction between the two spheres. It accom-
plishes this by drawing certain organizations within each sphere towards
the central zone and by including them in a single group of organizations
because they actually are very close to each other. Whether they choose a
cooperative legal form or an associative legal form depends primarily on
the legal mechanisms provided by national legislations.

On the left hand (cooperative) side, social enterprises may be seen as
more oriented to the whole community and putting more emphasis on
the dimension of general interest than many traditional cooperatives.
This is of course the case for enterprises registered as social cooperatives
(which, like NPOs, do not generally distribute any profit) as well as,
among others, for cooperatives for the handicapped in most CEE countries. On the right hand (non-profit) side, social enterprises place a higher
value on economic risk-taking related to an ongoing productive activity
than many traditional associations, including advocacy or grant-making
organizations.

Lastly, by going beyond the two spheres, the dotted lines suggest yet another point to be considered: although most social enterprises take the form of cooperatives or associations across Europe, they can also develop, as already mentioned, within the framework of other legal forms.

## 6   TOWARDS A DIALOGUE WITH ANGLO-SAXON APPROACHES

Figure 4.1 could also be used to illustrate, although imperfectly, the two initial movements which, in Italy and the US, led to the emergence of the notion of social enterprise. Italian social cooperatives have embodied, from the early 1990s, a desire to use the cooperative model to develop the provision of social services to disadvantaged groups, often in the framework of contracts with local public authorities. By doing so, they broadened the traditional cooperative model and moved closer to areas traditionally occupied by non-profit organizations in many European countries. Conversely, the quest for market resources by US non-profit organizations led the latter to adopt commercial practices inspired by the business world. As commercial enterprises, cooperatives do belong to this business world although the proximity of social enterprises and coopera- tives appears more clearly in the British context as described earlier.

In order to adequately depict the US scene, which does not seem to give an explicit place to cooperatives, one should emphasize the whole business community and its various interactions with social entrepreneurship. One should first recall the major role played by a growing number of private foundations. Most of these are endowed by large family fortunes, often originating in business activities. They encourage initiatives with a social purpose, generally of the non-profit type, to adopt income-generating strategies inspired by the business world.[30] Another aspect of social enter- prises' interactions with the business world is constituted by the partner- ships which are established, with increasing frequency, between large private groups and non-profit organizations, be they for the commerciali- zation of products linked to societal issues (for example in the field of fair trade or ethical finance), for the joint creation of societies in new industries (for example linked to sustainable development) or for any other form of collaboration. Finally, a great variety of initiatives – from sponsoring and patronage to other, more innovative forms such as social venture capital – can occur in the framework of 'corporate social responsibility' (CSR) strategies, and many business schools will be keen to consider these as 'social entrepreneurship'.

In other words, one of the most prominent/outstanding characteristics of US social entrepreneurship is certainly its quest for commercial resources and, more generally, a kind of 'tropism' towards the market and the business world (Kerlin, 2006). Although such dynamics do also exist in Europe, social enterprises there are influenced, to a much more significant extent, by the evolution of public policies, be it in the fight against unemployment, the development of personal services or other fields deemed important by governments. This major difference is clearly reflected in scientific works. Scholars and consultants from the Anglo-sphere, for example, often consider the degree of self-funding (through sales) as the key criterion or, still better, as the main axis along which initiatives that can be considered as forms of social entrepreneurship can be classified (always keeping in mind, though, that social entrepreneurship's main goal is to serve a more or less innovating 'social mission'). Nicholls (2006), for example, puts forward a classification of social entrepreneurship along a continuum ranging from 'voluntary activism', based only on gifts and volunteering, to 'corporate social innovation', which consists in risky investment for a social purpose within the framework of a for-profit private company. Between these two extremes, he describes various types of non-profit organizations, ranging from those which are totally funded by subsidies to those which are totally self-funded. In his analysis, only the latter deserve the 'social enterprise' label; this indeed corresponds to a dominant trend in the US context as well as to the vision of the Social Enterprise Coalition in the UK when stating that a social enterprise is a business that trades for a social purpose.

In Continental Europe, the notion of social entrepreneurship is becoming more popular although still less widespread than in the US. As in the latter, it seems increasingly easy to speak of social entrepreneurship as a very broad array of initiatives, well beyond the third sector: the notion of entrepreneurship itself can be understood in many different ways and its combination with a social orientation may refer to practices including various forms of corporate social responsibility, public-private partnerships with a social aim, or even public sector adoption of business skills.[31] The EMES Network itself has never claimed to circumscribe, in its works, all the forms of social entrepreneurship; these works have mainly focused on social entrepreneurship dynamics within the third sector. But a radical divergence between the dominant US approach and this European one appears as regards the more narrow notion of social enterprise: in the European context, it is impossible to ignore the embedding of very numerous social enterprises in public policies and the existence of social enterprises that derive a great deal of their income from non-market sources (Defourny and Nyssens, 2010). For instance, the EMES study of work integration social enterprises (WISEs) throughout the EU abundantly

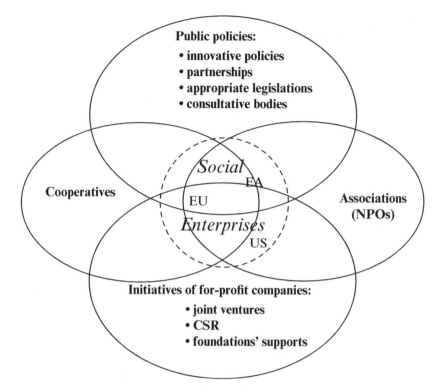

*Figure 4.2   Social enterprises at the crossroads of the third sector, public policies and the private for-profit sector*

documented the threefold orientation of these enterprises, which are situated at the crossroads of civil society, public policies and market dynamics (Nyssens, 2006).

If European and North American approaches were to be shown graphically, a possible way to do so might be the one suggested by Hulgård (2007): two spheres should be added to Figure 4.1, representing respectively the role of public authorities and the influence of the business world (Figure 4.2). Indeed, considering social enterprises as located in a central zone, more or less extended as suggested by the dotted lines, it is possible to see them as possibly resulting from a great variety of interactions. Going downwards, public policies tend to get closer to business methods and market dynamics. This can mean various public authorities' supports to social enterprises or the latter may be considered as having potentially important roles in the restructuring of public services (Spear et al., 2009). When moving upwards, the business world tends to be increasingly concerned with the public good and to get more deeply involved in the setting up of social enterprises.

Beyond comparisons between Europe and the US, such a representation even makes it possible to integrate development paths of the social enterprise landscape such as those emerging in South-Eastern Asia. In South Korea for instance, part of the associative movement which was at the forefront of the struggle for democracy in the 1990s is now advocating and setting up service-providing third sector organizations, especially for those most in need. On its side, the Korean parliament passed a law in 2006 for the promotion of social enterprises devoted to social service delivery or work integration of the hard-to-place while keeping a strong control over those initiatives (Bidet, 2008). Moreover, it is interesting to note that the official website of South Korean social enterprise[32] claims a dual influence from Europe (mentioning France, Italy and the UK) and from the United States (stressing the need to raise more funds from domestic leader companies). As to Japanese social enterprises, they seem to be heavily influenced by US models, but a good deal of them are quite close to the cooperative sector, especially some work integration social enterprises looking like workers' cooperatives and consumer cooperatives which have developed social services for the benefit of the community at large. Public policies launched in the last decade, such as a long-term care insurance system (2000), also played a critical role by increasing the scope for social enterprises' development, especially in the field of personal services to the elderly.

On the basis of a more detailed comparative analysis also covering other East Asian countries (Defourny and Kim, 2010),[33] it seems feasible to suggest the average or typical social enterprises of the three major industrialized regions can be located in Figure 4.2 as suggested by the letters EU (European Union), US (United States) and EA (East Asia), although such a synthetic representation involves of course strong limitations.

## CONCLUSIONS

Even though not all the practices that it encompasses are new, social entrepreneurship is obviously 'trendy', and it keeps diversifying, whether along organizational, industrial, geographical or other dimensions.

Since it is a very recent notion, this growing diversity and the very openness of the concept probably constitute strengths, and reasons to take it seriously. These are also the reasons for its rapid success, both among public authorities and private sector actors who, both in their own way, are discovering (or rediscovering) new possibilities to promote simultaneously entrepreneurial dynamics and social purposes.

However, beyond this 'fashionable' aspect, unstable by nature, which is supported and nourished by enthusiastic and committed promoters, it is important that rigorous analyses be developed – analyses going beyond the success stories and the 'heroes' repeatedly set under the limelight. In order to do so, thorough surveys – providing data about actual practices and about failures as well as successes – are absolutely necessary. Moreover, interdisciplinary dialogues are needed to avoid interpretations neglecting fundamental dimensions of the phenomenon. Until now, the entrepreneurial aspect and all issues related to the management of such organizations have been highlighted mostly by management sciences. This is all the more interesting that such approaches contribute to introduce into business schools forms of entrepreneurship that have hitherto hardly been considered. But as far as the social aspect is concerned, management sciences have probably much to learn from other disciplines which have been exploring the third sector for several decades, even though some trends hereof can sometimes seem to convey an 'anti-business' discourse (Dees and Anderson, 2006).

Several works carried out in the US underline the fact that social entrepreneurship tends to blur the borders between the non-profit and the for-profit sectors; these borders are then being replaced by a continuum of forms whose market orientation and for-profit character vary. However, this trend towards 'blurring boundaries', which has already been highlighted by several European specialists of the third sector[34] (also stressing interactions with the public sector), by no way reduces the increasingly recognized importance of the 'social economy' or the 'non-profit sector' in contemporary economies. Moreover, because the bulk of the third sector remains quite distinct, the fact that many or a majority of social enterprises are rooted in this specific field may well constitute the most reliable guarantee that to avoid social entrepreneurship will avoid being progressively diluted and losing most of its strength after an initial decade or two of interest due to its novelty.

## NOTES

1. First referred to as 'public entrepreneurs' by B. Drayton, who founded Ashoka, these individuals have been termed 'social entrepreneurs' from the mid-1990s onward, and increasingly presented as heroes of modern times (see for example Bornstein, 2004). Dees (1998) put forward the most often referred to definition of a social entrepreneur.
2. From a scientific point of view, the first bridges were built by Nicholls (2006), Mair et al. (2006) as well as Steyaert and Hjorth (2006).
3. See journals such as *Nonprofit and Voluntary Sector Quarterly* published by the Association for Research on Nonprofit and Voluntary Action and *Voluntas* published by the International Society for Third Sector Research.

4.  See for instance the French *Revue des Etudes Coopératives, Mutualistes et Associatives* (RECMA). The concept of social economy had already been used across various European countries in the nineteenth century to refer to the emerging cooperative societies, the friendly societies, the developing building society movement and other philanthropic and charitable organizations. See, for instance, the Scottish political essayist and historian Samuel Smiles in his work *Thrift* first published in 1875 or Gueslin (1987) for an overview of all schools of thought which contributed to the development of the social economy in France during the nineteenth century.

5.  Worldwide social economy research conferences are being organized every two years under the auspices of CIRIEC which also publishes the *Annals of Public and Cooperative Economics*, a 100-year old scientific journal rather close to social economy topics.

6.  There has existed for a long time now an inter-group 'social economy' within the European Economic and Social Committee and the European Parliament. Moreover, the action programmes as well as the decisions made by the European Council of Ministers increasingly refer to the social economy.

7.  See, among others, Evers and Laville (2004).

8.  Such an argument had become classical in the Blairist construction of the 'Third Way'.

9.  See also Defourny (2001).

10. That is indeed one of the major themes of the whole literature aiming to identify the main reasons for the existence of the third sector.

11. On the subject of work integration, see Spear et al. (2001) or Davister et al. (2004); on personal services, see Laville and Nyssens (2001a).

12. The greater homogeneity of 'traditional' social economy organizations is reflected in particular in the names of the different types of cooperatives or mutual societies, for example workers' cooperatives, agricultural cooperatives, mutual societies for civil servants, craftsmen, farmers and so on.

13. These evolutions are noted here obviously without saying that they constitute social advances.

14. Once again, care must be taken when interpreting this evolution: part of this innovative behaviour comes from the organizations themselves, but it is also a question of reactions and adaptations to the impetus or constraints inherent in public policies.

15. On this subject, see Laville and Sainsaulieu (1997).

16. Of course, the Italian law adopted in 1991 also remains a milestone and still inspires various policies in Europe and elsewhere. However, it is dedicated to two specific types of social cooperative: those delivering social, health and educational services, called 'A-type social cooperatives', and those providing work integration for disadvantaged people, referred to as 'B-type social cooperatives'.

17. In contrast to its three above-mentioned criteria, the Social Enterprise Coalition which is 'the voice of the sector' often uses an even more simple definition of social enterprise described as 'a business that trades for a social purpose'.

18. See especially Nicholls (2006) in the UK.

19. See for instance Spear et al. (2001) or Spear and Bidet (2003).

20. The letters EMES stand for 'EMergence des Enterprises Sociales en Europe', the title in French of the first research project of this network. The acronym was first used for the researchers' network for the DG Research of the European Commission, which funded the project; it was subsequently retained when the network went on to conduct other research projects on social enterprises and the social economy as a whole. Nowadays, the EMES European Research Network brings together ten university research centres specialized in these fields and several individual researchers throughout Europe. See www.emes.net.

21. Defourny and Nyssens (2006: 7). In spite of this, EMES indicators have often been seen as the EMES definition of social enterprise in a rather traditional way. In its first book, EMES had probably contributed to such a misunderstanding as those indicators were presented as a 'working definition' which proved to be fairly robust and reliable

22. although it was also stressed that social enterprises were appearing in each country as a wide spectrum of organizations for which the fulfilment of those criteria varied greatly (Defourny, 2001).
22. They are presented here as in the introduction of the first EMES book (Defourny, 2001: 16–18). This set of criteria had already been identified in the interim reports to the European Commission (EMES European Research Network 1997 and 1998) as well as in a short unpublished paper (EMES, 1999). It inspired the OECD as early as 1999.
23. The country studies were published in the EMES *Working Papers Series*. For a synthesis, see Spear and Bidet (2003) and Davister et al. (2004).
24. See section 5 below.
25. Borzaga et al. (2008). That study was carried out in collaboration with local researchers and it covered six new EU member countries (Bulgaria, Czech Republic, Estonia, Lithuania, Poland and Slovenia), two Balkan countries (Macedonia and Serbia) and four countries of the Community of Independent States (CIS) (Belarus, Kazakhstan, Russia and Ukraine). It also included a more detailed analysis for three countries selected from those sub-groups (Poland, Serbia and Ukraine).
26. In particular Borzaga and Spear (2004) and Borzaga and Galera (2004).
27. The EMES approach of social enterprise has been adapted for the purpose of the study conducted in CEE and the CIS, in order to take into account the local contexts and specificities. This 'adapted' working definition only includes three economic and three social criteria (EMES, 2006: 61; Borzaga et al., 2008: 75–6).
28. However, not all these laws explicitly use the term 'social enterprise'.
29. This second tension should not be exaggerated, though; it conveys a 'historical' difference between two models of actions rather than a clear-cut difference between the contemporary practices. For example, gradually, along their development path, many mutual societies and user cooperatives have started to offer their goods and services to non-member customers, with advantages very similar to those offered to members.
30. According to the 'Social Enterprise Alliance', created in 2002 by various foundations and support organizations, a social enterprise is *'any earned-income business or strategy undertaken by a nonprofit to generate revenue in support of its charitable mission'*. This vision is also found for example in the various programmes of the NESsT (Nonprofit Enterprise and Self-sustainability Team). In reality, as early as the 1980s, many works analysed the question of the funding of non-profit organizations, although these works did not use the term 'social enterprise' (see, for example, Skloot, 1983 or Young, 1983).
31. Leadbeater (1997) already acknowledged the presence of social entrepreneurship across all three sectors of society.
32. http://www.socialenterprise.go.kr/.
33. Since 2008, the EMES European Research Network and a group of East Asian researchers have carried out a joint research project on the emerging models of social enterprise in China, Hong Kong Japan, South Korea and Taiwan.
34. For example, among many others, Evers (1995) and Dekker (2004).

# BIBLIOGRAPHY

Bacchiega, A. and C. Borzaga (2001), 'Social enterprises as incentive structures: an economic analysis', in C. Borzaga and J. Defourny (eds), *The Emergence of Social Enterprise*, London and New York: Routledge, pp. 273–94.
Badelt, C. (1997), 'Entrepreneurship theories of the non-profit sector', *Voluntas*, **8**(2), 162–78.
Bidet, E. (2008), 'The rise of work integration and social enterprise in South Korea', paper presented at the second EMES-ISTR International Conference, Barcelona, 9–12 July.
Bornstein, D. (2004), *How to Change the World: Social Entrepreneurs and the Power of New Ideas*, New York: Oxford University Press.

Borzaga, C. and J. Defourny (eds) (2001), *The Emergence of Social Enterprise*, London and New York: Routledge (paperback edition: 2004).

Borzaga, C. and G. Galera (2004), 'Social economy in transition economies: realities and perspectives', discussion paper presented at the First Meeting of the Scientific Group on Social Economy and Social Innovation of the OECD Centre for Local Development, Trento, Italy.

Borzaga, C. and A. Santuari (2001), 'Italy: from traditional co-operatives to innovative social enterprises', in C. Borzaga and J. Defourny (eds), *The Emergence of Social Enterprise*, London and New York: Routledge, pp. 166–81.

Borzaga, C. and R. Spear (2004), *Trends and Challenges for Co-operatives and Social Enterprises in Developed and Transition Countries*, Trento: Edizioni31.

Borzaga, C., G. Galera and R. Nogales (eds) (2008), *Social Enterprise: A New Model for Poverty Reduction and Employment Generation*, EMES and UNDP Bratislava Regional Bureau.

CECOP (2006), 'Social enterprises and worker cooperatives: comparing models of corporate governance and social inclusion', CECOP European Seminar, Manchester, 9 November.

Davister, C., J. Defourny and O. Grégoire (2004), 'Work integration social enterprises in the European Union: an overview of existing models', *EMES Working Papers Series*, no. 04/04, available at: http://www.emes.net.

Dees, J.G. (1998), 'The meaning of social entrepreneurship', Stanford University, mimeo.

Dees, J.G. and B.B. Anderson (2006), 'Framing a theory of social entrepreneurship: building on two schools of practice and thought', in *Research on Social Enterpreneurship*, ARNOVA Occasional Paper Series, **1**(3), 39–66.

Defourny, J. (ed.) (1994), *Développer l'entreprise sociale*, Brussels: Fondation Roi Baudouin.

Defourny, J. (2001), 'From third sector to social enterprise', in C. Borzaga and J. Defourny (eds), *The Emergence of Social Enterprise*, London and New York: Routledge, pp. 1–28.

Defourny, J. and S. Kim (2010), 'A cross-country analysis of social enterprises in Eastern Asia', paper presented at the International Conference on Social Enterprises in Eastern Asia, Taipei, 14–15 July. Forthcoming in J. Defourny and Y.Y. Kuan (eds), 'The emergence of social enterprise in Eastern Asia', *Social Enterprise Journal* (special issue), 2011-1.

Defourny, J. and M. Nyssens (2006), 'Defining social enterprise', in M. Nyssens (ed.), *Social Enterprise – At the Crossroads of Market, Public Policies and Civil Society,* London and New York: Routledge, pp. 3–26.

Defourny, J. and M. Nyssens (2008), 'Social enterprise in Europe: recent trends and developments', *Social Enterprise Journal*, **4**(3), 202–28.

Defourny, J. and M. Nyssens (2010), 'Conceptions of social enterprise and social entrepreneurship in Europe and the United States: convergences and divergences', *Journal of Social Entrepreneurship*, **1**(1), 32–53.

Defourny, J., L. Favreau and J.-L. Laville (eds) (1998), *Insertion et nouvelle économie sociale. Un bilan international*, Paris: Desclée de Brouwer.

Dekker, P. (2004), 'The Netherlands: from private initiatives to non-profit hybrids and back?', in A. Evers and J.-L. Laville (eds), *The Third Sector in Europe*, Cheltenham, UK and Northampton, MA, USA: Edward Elgar, pp. 144–65.

Draperi, J.-F. (2003), 'L'entreprise sociale en France, entre économie sociale et action sociale' *Revue des Etudes Coopératives, Mutualistes et Associatives (RECMA)*, no. 288, 48–66.

DTI (2002), 'Social enterprise: a strategy for success', Department of Trade and Industry, London, available at: http://www.dti.gov.uk/socialenterprise/strategy.htm.

Ecotec (2003), 'Guidance on mapping social enterprise', final report to the DTI Social Enterprise Unit, London.

EMES European Network (1997, 1998), 'The emergence of social enterprises. A new answer to social exclusion in Europe', Semestrial Progress Reports to the European Commission.

EMES European Network (1999), *The Emergence of Social Enterprises in Europe. A Short Overview*, Brussels: EMES.

EMES European Research Network (2006), 'Study on promoting the role of social enterprises in CEE and the CIS', Initial Overview Study for the UNDP-BRC (Bratislava Regional Centre).

Evers, A. (1995), 'Part of the welfare mix: the third sector as an intermediate area', *Voluntas*, **6**(2), 159–82.

Evers, A. (2001), 'The significance of social capital in the multiple goal and resource structure of social enterprise', in C. Borzaga and J. Defourny (eds), *The Emergence of Social Enterprise*, London and New York: Routledge, pp. 296–311.

Evers, A. and J.-L. Laville (eds) (2004), *The Third Sector in Europe*, Cheltenham, UK and Northampton, MA, USA: Edward Elgar.

Gueslin, A. (1987), *L'invention de l'économie sociale*, Paris: Economica.

Hulgård, L. (2007), 'Differences between American and European conceptions of social entrepreneurship', paper presented at an international EMES Seminar, Roskilde University.

IFF Research Ltd (2005), *A Survey of Social Enterprises across the UK*, Report prepared for the Small Business Service, London: IFF Research Ltd.

Institute for Employment Studies (2006), *Annual Survey of Small Businesses: UK 2005*, London: Small Business Service, DTI.

Kerlin, J. (2006), 'Social enterprise in the United States and Europe: understanding and learning from the differences', *Voluntas*, **17**(3), 247–63.

Laville, J.-L. and M. Nyssens (eds) (2001a), *Les services sociaux entre associations, Etat et marché*, Paris: La Découverte et Syros.

Laville, J.-L. and M. Nyssens (2001b), 'The social enterprise: towards a theoretical socio-economic approach', in C. Borzaga and J. Defourny (eds), *The Emergence of Social Enterprise*, London and New York: Routledge, pp. 312–32.

Laville, J.-L. and R. Sainsaulieu (eds) (1997), *Sociologie de l'association*, Paris: Desclée de Brouwer.

Leadbeater, C. (1997), *The Rise of the Social Entrepreneur*, London: Demos.

Mair, J., J. Robinson & K. Hockerts (eds) (2006), *Social Entrepreneurship*, New York: Palgrave Macmillan.

Nicholls, A. (ed.) (2006), *Social Enterpreneurship, New Models of Sustainable Social Change*, Oxford: Oxford University Press.

Nyssens, M. (ed.) (2006), *Social Enterprise: At the Crossroads of Market, Public Policies and Civil Society*, London and New York: Routledge.

OCDE (1999), *Les entreprises sociales*, Programme LEED, Paris: OCDE.

Otsing, M. (2004), 'How to develop a co-operative movement. The case of co-operative housing in Estonia', in C. Borzaga and R. Spear (eds), *Trends and Challenges for Co-operatives and Social Enterprises in Developed and Transition Countries*, Trento: Edizioni31, pp. 247–52.

Peattie, K. and A. Morley (2008), 'Social enterprises: diversity and dynamics, contents and contributions', London: Social Enterprise Coalition and ESRC.

Schumpeter, J.A. (1934), *The Theory of Economic Development*, 3rd edn, 1963, New York: Oxford University Press.

Skloot, E. (1983), 'Should not-for-profits go into business?', *Harvard Business Review*, **61**(1), 20–27.

Spear, R. and E. Bidet (2003), 'The role of social enterprise in European labour markets', *Working Papers Series*, Liège: EMES European Research Network, no. 03/10.

Spear, R., C. Cornforth and M. Aiken (2009), 'The governance challenges of social enterprises: evidence from a UK empirical study', *Annals of Public and Co-operative Economics*, **80**(2), 247–73.

Spear, R., J. Defourny, L. Favreau and J.-L. Laville (eds) (2001), *Tackling Social Exclusion in Europe. The Contribution of the Social Economy*, Aldershot: Ashgate.

Steyaert, C. and D. Hjorth (eds) (2006), *Entrepreneurship as Social Change*, Cheltenham, UK and Northampton, MA, USA: Edward Elgar.

Young, D. (1983), *If Not for Profit, for What?*, Lexington, MA: Lexington Books.

# 5 Socially constructed opportunities in social entrepreneurship: a structuration model*

*Giovany Cajaiba-Santana*

## INTRODUCTION

Social entrepreneurship is still emerging as an area for academic inquiry. Its theoretical frameworks have not yet been adequately explored, and there is considerable room for contributions to theory and practice (Short et al., 2009). Research on this subject has increased over the last 10 years and there is a considerable body of literature concerned with its definitions (Dees, 1998; Weerawardena and Mort, 2006; Mair and Martí, 2006), the social value creation (Stevens et al., 2008), motivations (Mair and Noboa, 2005) and case studies. However, there is still a void concerning what is already broadly accepted as central in the study of traditional entrepreneurship: the very concept of opportunities. To date, researchers have failed to distinguish the particularities of the concept of social entrepreneurship opportunity.

Shane and Venkataraman's seminal work (Shane and Venkataraman, 2000) played a decisive role in placing the concept of opportunity as a paradigm for entrepreneurship research. They defined opportunity as 'those situations in which new goods, services, raw materials, and organizing methods can be introduced and sold at greater than their cost of production' (p. 207). This definition is not adequately applicable to the field of social entrepreneurship for two main reasons. First because it does not take into account the social value creation element of social entrepreneurship which is seen as central to the definition of the phenomenon (Mair and Martí, 2006). Second because it does not embrace the socially constructed nature of an opportunity which, as will be shown later in this chapter, is central for the study of social entrepreneurship opportunities. Shaw and Carter (2007) empirically show the socially embedded characteristic of a social entrepreneurship project during its first stages of evolution, and previous research on opportunity legitimate its study based on a socially constructed perspective (Fletcher, 2006; Sarason et al., 2006). This implies that both the opportunity and the entrepreneur are intrinsically linked to the social context where they are embedded; they co-evolve with the opportunity and should not be studied separately from each other.

Although some research has considered social value creating within social entrepreneurship (Stevens et al., 2008; Smith et al., 2008) we are yet to learn about social entrepreneurship opportunities as socially constructed phenomena, and how research should be conducted (Zahra et al., 2008). This account of opportunity based upon its evolution vis-à-vis the entrepreneur entails a more explicitly sociological commitment in social entrepreneurship research and calls for a constructivist approach able to frame all elements of this social construction process, its linkages, interactions, and changes over time. Along with other researchers (Whittington, 1992; Pozzebon and Pinsonneault, 2005; Sarason et al., 2006), it will be demonstrated here that structuration theory is a suitable theory to accomplish this task. Structuration theory stresses the importance of investigating through a processual perspective the recursive relationship between everyday practices and the social system where they are embedded; this relationship is central to the understanding of entrepreneurial and social context co-evolution. A critical review of Giddens's view of structuration theory can help us to predict, explain and model the phenomenon of opportunity construction in a social entrepreneurship context.

In an assessment of the state of social entrepreneurship research, Short et al. (2009) point out that to date there are no social entrepreneurship articles that portray opportunities based on a constructivist theory, and such an endeavour could fill conceptual and empirical gaps in social entrepreneurship research. In the same vein this chapter aims to open up a path of exploration for social entrepreneurship theory development and practice by presenting a model for the analysis of the relationship between the social entrepreneur and social entrepreneurship opportunity.

The contribution to the theory is twofold: first, present social entrepreneurship opportunities as a social constructed process. They are not objective phenomena as defined in economic literature; they are ontologically different from social needs, which represent only the structural side of an opportunity. Secondly, increase the empirical relevance of structuration theory by the proposition of a model to guide future inquiry drawn upon a critical review of Giddens's structuration theory.

The chapter is structured as follows. First, it will be shown why the nature of social entrepreneurship opportunities is better conceived as a socially constructed phenomenon. The main perspectives used to study opportunities – discovery and creation perspective – will be discussed.

After a critical review of Giddens's structuration model, this chapter will then address how structuration theory is a powerful device that can be used to study, model and guide empirical research on social entrepreneurship opportunities.

Finally, a model will be developed to enrich future theory building and to guide empirical research on the subject. The chapter concludes by discussing contributions and implications for future research.

## SOCIAL ENTREPRENEURSHIP

The dominant paradigm used in evaluating entrepreneurship has studied its impact on economic growth and its role in economic prosperity (Acs, 2008). Only recently a number of scholars have recognized the importance both of social entrepreneurship as a driver of social value creation, and of conducting research on the field (Mair and Martí, 2006; Dees and Anderson, 2002; Peredo and McLean, 2006; Gawell, 2007). The term 'social entrepreneurship' or 'social entrepreneur' has appeared in the literature in different contexts such as 'social economy' (Peredo and McLean, 2006), 'activist movements' (Gawell, 2007), 'environmental movements' (Taylor and Walley, 2003) or 'sustainable economy' (Mair and Seelos, 2005). In all those contexts, the term 'social entrepreneurship' 'has emerged as a new label for describing the work of community, voluntary and public organizations, as well as private firms working for social rather than for-profit objectives' (Shaw and Carter, 2007: 420). This does not imply that social entrepreneurship endeavours occur only in not-for-profit contexts. Not all non-profits are socially entrepreneurial, just as not all for-profit businesses are entrepreneurial. Social entrepreneurship catalyses social transformation by meeting social needs, whereas economic value creation is simply a necessary condition to guarantee financial viability (Zahra et al., 2008).

The definition proposed by Mair and Martí (2006: 37) comprehends these dimensions:

> First, we view social entrepreneurship as a process of creating value by combining resources in new ways. Second, these resource combinations are intended primarily to explore and exploit opportunities to create social value by stimulating social change or meeting social needs. And third, when viewed as a process, social entrepreneurship involves the offering of services and products but can also refer to the creation of new organizations.

They present social entrepreneurship as a process resulting from the continuous interaction between social entrepreneurs and the social context in which they are embedded. This will be central to our discussion about opportunity.

# OPPORTUNITIES

The study of opportunities has been identified as a central concept in entrepreneurship research (Buzenitz et al., 2003; Casson, 2005; Shane and Venkataraman, 2000; Singh, 2001). Its concept has been developed within a framework of economic rationality theory, the works of Schumpeter (1934) and Kirzner (1973; 1997) being seminal texts on the subject.

During the last decade a new approach to the study of opportunity arose using a more social and constructionist view (Casson, 2005; Fletcher, 2006 and Fayolle, 2005). Today, we can separate the research on entrepreneurship opportunities into two internally consistent different visions: the discovery view and the creation view (based on Alvarez and Barney, 2007; Gartner et al., 2003; Fayolle, 2007). In the discovery tradition we find those who believe that opportunities are an objective reality and exist independently of entrepreneurs – (Shane and Venkataraman, 2000; Casson, 2005; Singh, 2001). Alternatively, the creation tradition postulates that opportunities do not exist independently of the entrepreneurs but are rather created as entrepreneurs enact with the environment (Fayolle, 2007; Fletcher, 2006, Jack and Anderson, 2002, Gartner et al., 2003).

One of the main arguments of this chapter is that social entrepreneurship opportunities are by nature creation opportunities. But before embarking on this reasoning it is important to present these two views in order to accentuate their discrepancy and justify the foundation upon which the argument is based.

## Discovery Tradition

Arguably one of the most influential conceptual contributions to the study of opportunities which use the discovery vision in recent years has been Shane and Venkataraman's (2000) work. The basis of their framework is that opportunities are real and independent of the entrepreneurs who perceive them. To be consistent with this approach, the authors define entrepreneurship in terms of an individual's response to an opportunity. This response comprises three activities – discovery, evaluation and exploitation – and the success with which each of these activities is carried out determines the ultimate performance of the venture (Casson, 2005).

Shane and Venkataraman use Casson's definition of entrepreneurial opportunities as 'those situations in which new goods, services, raw materials, and organizing methods can be introduced and sold at greater than their cost of production' (Shane and Venkataraman, 2000: 207). As Singh

(2001) indicates, this requires that entrepreneurial opportunities must generate profit. This positivist view of opportunity is based on an economic disequilibrium model developed by the Austrian school of economy, notably in the work of Kirzner (1973). In this model, opportunities are formed by exogenous shocks caused by imperfections in the market; they exist objectively as 'market gaps' just waiting to be discovered and exploited independently of entrepreneurs' actions and perceptions (Alvarez and Barney, 2007). A core idea in the disequilibrium model is that in the market there are several mismatches in perceptions and opportunities. The entrepreneurial opportunities only take place when 'alert entrepreneurs' correct those mismatches by noticing them by 'surprise' (Gartner et al., 2003). According to Kirzner:

> What distinguishes discovery (. . .) from successful search (. . .) is that the former (unlike the latter) involves that surprise which accompanies the realization that one had overlooked something in fact readily available . . . The notion of discovery, midway between that of the deliberately produced information in standard search theory, and of sheer windfall gain generated by pure chance, is central to Austrian approach (Kirzner, 1997: 72).

So, in the Austrian disequilibrium approach opportunities are not noticeable to 'non-alert' individuals. Davidsson (2005) proposed a more dynamic view of opportunity in keeping with the discovery perspective. He asserts that discovery is a process and that we cannot just disregard the idea of 'opportunity formation'. He also argues that 'exploitation' and 'discovery' are overlapping processes that co-evolve as the entrepreneurial project moves forward. What still characterizes this approach as being within the discovery perspective is the absence of co-evolution of the individual and opportunity as well as the role of societal, economic or cultural structures shaping entrepreneurial practices.

**Creation Tradition**

In the creation tradition opportunities do not exist independently of the actions taken by entrepreneurs to create them (Alvarez and Barney, 2007). In other words, opportunities are enacted, to use Weick's (1979) concept of enactment. It is the enactment process between individual and the environment that will create opportunities which would not exist without the entrepreneur's actions.

Sarason et al. (2006: 290) highlight the 'idiosyncratic, path dependent nature of venture creation', arguing that enactment of individual and opportunity is a unique process. They argue that what appears to external observers as different individuals pursuing the same opportunity is not so. In fact, the construction process of an opportunity is specific to the individual as will be shown later when discussing the utilization of the structuration theory.

Gartner et al. (2003) provide interesting empirical evidence from a study using discourse analysis about the nature of opportunities. In this study Gartner shows that an opportunity enactment perspective provides a different way to look at opportunity without the use of the dominant economic stance. Analysing the discourse of nascent entrepreneurs, Gartner tried to find whether individuals use words in their vocabulary that reflect the discovery or creation perspective. He asked 443 nascent entrepreneurs to openly answer the question: 'Briefly, how did the original idea for starting a business develop?'

In only 38 statements (9 per cent) were 'discovery verbs' found (specifically 'saw', 'find' or 'found', 'looking' and 'notice'). The words 'discovery' or 'surprise' did not appear at all. The respondents were also asked to answer the question: 'Which came first to you, the business idea or your decision to start some kind of business?' The answers were analysed as follows:

- 35.0 per cent: Business idea or opportunity came first;
- 44.5 per cent: Desire to start a business came first;
- 20.1 per cent: Idea or opportunity and desire to have a business came at the same time.

The answers showed that in most cases the process of creating a new venture starts before the 'recognition' of an opportunity. Even in statements where the 'discovery' verbs were used, we notice a process of opportunity enactment; for instance:

'I was injured and had to find a new way to make a living.'
'Saw a business similar to what I would like to open.'

Gartner shows that the vocabulary of the discovery perspective is not part of the entrepreneurs' discourse, which seems to be more in line with creation perspective. He concludes that 'pursuing a belief in the opportunity discovery perspective will mean ignoring a significant portion of entrepreneurial activity' (p. 119). It means that the discovery perspective seems to explain part of the variance in the entrepreneurial opportunity phenomenon but it is not capable of explaining opportunity as the outcome of a sensemaking process between individuals and their context.

This brings forward some implications for research. Indeed, since Berger and Luckmann (1996) coined the term 'social construction of reality' to emphasize the socially dependent processes in which people engage to create meaning, there has been increased application of these ideas in business, management and entrepreneurship (Fletcher, 2006; Steyaert and Katz, 2004). Scholars have acknowledged the socially embedded and socially constructed dimensions of entrepreneurship as variables in entrepreneurship studies, and also the fact that economic deterministic models used until then do not embrace those dimensions. Some ideas have been put forward based on a social constructionist approach in order to expand research on entrepreneurship beyond the narrow confines of the economic rationality and encompass the role that societal, economic and cultural structures play in shaping entrepreneurial practice (Steyaert and Katz, 2004; Fayolle, 2005; Fletcher, 2006). Since social entrepreneurs act directly upon social systems in order to create social change, the interplay between individuals and their context is crucial to the study of this kind of social opportunity. This is empirically demonstrated by Shaw and Carter (2007) and Parkinson and Howorth (2008).

The argument here is that the study of social entrepreneurship opportunities calls for a constructionist approach as proposed by the creation tradition.

## THE NATURE OF THE SOCIAL ENTREPRENEURSHIP OPPORTUNITY

The word 'opportunity' comes from the Latin expression '*ob portus*', which means 'toward the port' (referring to the wind) (Wood, 1908). It refers to the favourable wind that leads the boat to the port. From its root we can notice the evolutionary and uncertain characteristic of the term. In order to get to the port, a sailor must sail with the wind, which may change direction or intensity. It is also implied in the root of the term that it has no meaning to talk about a favourable wind in any context other than that of sailing a boat. Coherently with this view, McKendall and Wagner (1997) give their definition by explaining that 'whereas motive refers to the arousal of behaviour, opportunity means the presence of a favourable combination of circumstances that makes a particular course of action possible' (p. 627). In these definitions, as well as in the etymological root of the term, we find the same aspects of evolution over time and implicitly the interplayed presence of the individual as the agent who 'steers the boat to the port' or to the expected future state.

This implies that the answer to the question concerning how opportunities are constructed, operationalized and studied must take into consideration not only the opportunity as an independent phenomenon but the construction process between opportunity and individual. To do that in the social entrepreneurship context we must be able to differentiate the manifestation of opportunity with other phenomena such as unmet socio-economic needs.

In previous research, some scholars have pointed out that the 'disequilibria' which exist in social structures are social opportunities themselves (Dees and Anderson, 2002; Weerawardena and Mort, 2006).

An ontological discussion is necessary because until now the concepts of 'unmet social need' and 'social entrepreneurship opportunity' have been used interchangeably, whereas there is, fundamentally, an ontological difference. Social entrepreneurship opportunities are geographically situated and materialize in social projects that emerge only when individuals mobilize themselves in the effort to give an entrepreneurial answer to a social need. Social needs are not necessarily geographically situated and do not generate social projects on their own – they are, therefore, a necessary but not sufficient condition to the emergence of social opportunities. A social entrepreneurship opportunity only emerges when individuals create entrepreneurial ventures in order to address clearly identified social needs – and these entrepreneurial ventures are generally referred to as 'social projects'.

Social entrepreneurs identify a situation as opportunity when they think they will be able to use their abilities (or resources as we will see later) to act upon the social context. Let us take the practical example of Karen Tse to clarify this important distinction. The case is presented by Ashoka Foundation,[1] an organization that finances social entrepreneurship projects. Karen Tse, a social entrepreneur, has founded International Bridges to Justice[2] to give people throughout the world the right to equal and fair legal defence. She has seen Cambodian people spend years in prison without the right to fair judgment. That situation is what is called an unmet social need; there is a suboptimal equilibrium on the distribution of legal defence among Cambodians. But the fact is that in the same place (Cambodia) and at the same time, other unmet social needs exist (such as unemployment, famine, social exclusion, lack of adequate health care and others). Why, for instance, did she not choose to act upon the health care need? The answer may be as simple as the fact that she is a lawyer specialized in international law, and not a doctor. The wind is favourable to a specific boat at a specific moment. As pointed out by Luksha (2008), opportunities may be created when entrepreneurs set to induce changes to the environment. Indeed, inductive data revealed that, for most social entrepreneurs, the recognition of a gap in the provision of services or an unmet social need had been the key driving force in the creation and development of their social entrepreneurship project (Mair and Noboa, 2005;

Shaw and Carter, 2007), but, as will be discussed later in this chapter, the social need is only the structure side of the social opportunity and cannot be analysed separately from the individual.

Opportunity in a social entrepreneurship context is a socially constructed phenomenon; entrepreneur and opportunity cannot exist independently, and therefore cannot be conceived as separated and distinct from one another. This implies that opportunities are by nature communally and relationally constituted rather than only derived from disequilibria in the socioeconomic structures. This approach is, of course, consistent with the constructionist view, but it also raises a new challenge regarding its operationalization to conduct empirical research. Structuration theory provides convincing explanatory power to take up the challenge.

## STRUCTURATION THEORY: THE CHOICE OF A THEORY

Structuration theory has been used in different fields of social sciences and has proved its capacity as a general theory for explaining social action and social evolution (Sarason et al., 2006; Wendt, 1987). Organization studies have also been the arena of rich theoretical discussion about the use of this theory to study organizational phenomena (Pozzebon and Pinsonneault, 2005; Whittington, 1992). It has also been used as a theoretical framework to guide empirical research (Barley and Tolbert, 1997; Jarzabkowski, 2008). Arguably, Giddens's most important contribution to the social sciences with structuration theory is the connection between structure and action. Fundamentally, the focus of structuration theory is the reciprocal interaction of human actors and social structure across time and space. Giddens proposes the concept of 'duality of structure'. This refers to the fact that social structures are both constituted by human agency, and yet at the same time are the medium of this constitution (Giddens, 1979: 121). So, the structure acts on the agents, constraining and enabling their practices, and through these practices social systems are recursively created. Epistemologically Giddens argues that agent and social systems are mutually constitutive in a dialectic relationship, whereas they do not share the same ontological status.

Bringing this assumption to the entrepreneurial context, the interactive coming together of entrepreneur and opportunity may be conceptualized as a dialectic relationship as well, whereby the entrepreneur and opportunity cannot exist independently, and therefore cannot be understood as separate or distinct from one another.

As Mair and Martí (2006) point out:

Giddens's theory may help us to better understand how social entrepreneurship comes into being by directing our attention to a fundamental unit of analysis: the interaction between the social entrepreneur and the context. That interaction is crucial to understanding the process of social entrepreneurship. Thus, structuration theory provides a promising lens to examine how the context enables and constrains the appearance of social entrepreneurship and how social change occurs' (p. 40).

Thus, using structuration theory, the entrepreneur and social system are not conceptualized as two separate domains, but as a duality that co-evolves to create the instantiated new venture. Those assumptions, as we discussed above, are totally in line with the creation perspective of opportunity; nevertheless we need to delve deeper into the grounding assumptions of the theory and look carefully at its limits and its capacity to explain the phenomenon we are tackling.

In the entrepreneurship research we can find some attempts to operationalize structuration theory (Sarason et al., 2006; Chiasson and Saunders, 2005; Jack and Anderson, 2002; Bouchikhi, 1993). Furthermore, this theory has the two elements that, according to Davidsson (2005: 35), are required in a theory in order to guide empirical and theoretical research:

- *A set of well-defined, abstracts concepts;*
- *A set of well-specified relationship among those concepts.*

We will see as we move forward in the chapter that those two elements are clearly presented in structuration theory. Moreover, many scholars have emphasized the fact that entrepreneurial activity is, in fact, a societal phenomenon (Steyaert and Katz, 2004; Fletcher, 2006) and therefore requires a social theory. Structuration theory is, according to Layder (1996), a social theory of human activity: 'These general theories tend to be quite abstract and deal with very general features of social life, such as the nature of the ties between power and social practices or links between social action and social structures' (Layder, 1996: 115). The theory is general because it deals with a comprehensive range of human activity and is only indirectly associated with any particular social setting (Chiasson and Saunders, 2005). Due to their broad concepts, general theories allow considerable room for researchers to shape theoretical and empirical studies based on these concepts. Nevertheless it is somehow ironic to realize that most academic research has not thoroughly investigated the adequacy of this theory regarding entrepreneurship research. As Zahra (2007) points out, many scholars have imported theories from other disciplines without considering the key and distinguishing qualities of entrepreneurial phenomena. Each theory has its limits and its assumptions;

violations of these assumptions can lead to questionable findings. In fact, it is noticeable through a literature review that many authors have made use of Giddens's structuration theory as a panacea for all situations in social research, notably in entrepreneurship. Therefore, a review of Giddens's view of the structuration theory is necessary in order to take into account the evolution of the theory and to narrow it down to study the phenomenon of opportunity construction in a social entrepreneurship context. This will be done first by analysing structuration theory as it was first presented by Giddens and second by adding the contribution of other scholars.

**Structuration Theory and Social Entrepreneurship Opportunities**

In *The Constitution of Society* Giddens defines structure as: 'a set of "rules" and "resources", recursively implicated in the reproduction of social systems.' Structure exists only as memory traces, the organic basis of human knowledgeability, and as instantiated in action (Giddens, 1984: 377). Structures, then, are virtual and are 'put into practice' in the production and reproduction of social life. The rules play the 'constraining side' of the structure and are defined as 'generalizable procedures applied in the enactment/reproduction of social life' (Giddens, 1984: 21). The resources act as agency enablers and are (obscurely) defined as 'the media whereby transformative capacity is employed as power in the routine course of social interaction' (Giddens, 1979: 92).

Another nuance that we need to understand in order to have a global vision of Giddens's approach is the concept of 'social system'. According to Giddens, a social system 'display(s) structure properties but is not a structure itself' (Giddens, 1984: 25). A social system would encompass what social scientists mean by 'societies' or 'social constructed entities'. Structures are not the patterned social practices that make up social systems, but 'the principles that pattern these practices' (Sewell, 1992: 18). This distinction between 'structure' and 'social system' is often misunderstood and its clarification is central to the model that will be presented further in the chapter.

In order to clarify Giddens's structuration model and its underlining definitions, let us take as an example the case of the language as a structure. According to Giddens, a given language may be seen as a structure comprised of rules (the grammatical rules) and resources (all the words that enables communication) recursively implicated in the reproduction of a given social system (in this case the process of communication) by an agent. Figure 5.1 summarizes Giddens's structuration framework.

As we can see in Figure 5.1, Giddens is not interested in the static

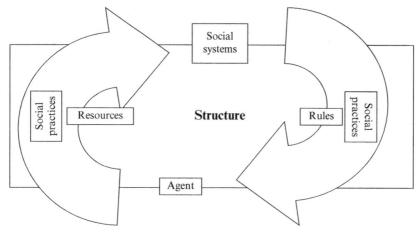

*Source:*   Nizet (2007: 16).

*Figure 5.1   Giddens's structuration framework*

entities, such as the individual or the society, but in the dynamic process represented by the arrows. The social practices must not be understood as isolated actions or behaviours, they are a flux of actions and make up the 'articulation points between agents and structures' (Giddens, 1984: 50).

The 'social context' is conceived as a movement where individual (or collective) actions 'structure' social systems and are in turn 'structured' by them. This process is recursive; there is no identifiable starting point.

Although this very model has already been applied to empirical management research (Jarzabkowski, 2008; Barley and Tolbert, 1997), further contributions to structuration theory allow us to be more coherent with the specificities of the phenomenon that we intend to study here.

In fact, structuration theory as it was first presented (Giddens, 1979) has considerably evolved through the work of other authors such as Sewell (1992) and Emirbayer and Mische (1998). Those contributions are central to the debate about the adequacy of the theory to the phenomena of social entrepreneurship opportunities. Previous theoretical contributions to the use of structuration theory for entrepreneurship research have failed to interpret and adapt the theory appropriately. Some authors have suggested that 'opportunity' as a socially constructed phenomenon may occupy the place of the 'structure' in Giddens's model (Sarason et al., 2006; Chiasson and Saunders, 2005). That is a theoretical misunderstanding. According to Giddens the concept of 'structure' is closer to the social context where actions take place. In this context, actors are enabled and constrained in their activities (by resources and rules respectively) in the construction process of social systems. Structuration is the study of the ways in which social systems are produced and reproduced in social interaction (Giddens, 1984: 25). Therefore I posit that in Giddens's model, opportunities should be represented as 'social systems' and not as 'structures'. This allows us to better conceive the dialectic relationship between opportunity and entrepreneur.

Regarding Giddens's definition of rules and resources, some remarks should be addressed based on Sewell's work. Sewell pointed out that the concept of 'rules' is not sufficiently precise. When used for instance as a routine, a rule should be viewed as a resource enabling, rather than constraining the agency. He proposed then changing the terminology to 'schemas'. According to Sewell:

> The various schemas that make up structures are generalizable procedures applied in the enactment/reproduction of social life. They are 'generalizable' in the sense that they can be applied in or extended to a variety of contexts of interaction. Such schemas or procedures [. . .] can be used not only in the situation in which they are first learned or most conventionally applied. They can be generalized – that is, transposed or extended – to new situations when the opportunities arise (Sewell, 1992: 16).

These 'schemas' might have a real or virtual nature and may enable or constrain social practices, differently from Giddens's definition of rules that are placed only on the 'constraint side' of the structure.

Concerning resources, Giddens's definition is not self-evident and does not fully suffice in an entrepreneurship context without a clear ontological definition. Looking at Giddens's definition of resources as 'the media whereby transformative capacity is employed as power in the routine course of social interaction' (Giddens, 1979: 92), we can barely establish a connection with the definition of resources in management literature (physical, human and organizational assets that can be used to implement value-creating strategies (Barney, 1991)). Sewell has contributed to the definitions of resources; he posits that resources are of two types: human (physical strength, knowledge, and emotional commitments that can be used to enhance and maintain power) and non-human (objects, animate or inanimate, naturally occurring or manufactured that can be used to maintain power). Sewell intends to conceive the agents as empowered by access to resources and also constrained by the same resources. Since resources and 'schemas' have a 'real' and 'virtual' existence, we need to change the nature of the structure. In the real world, the context in which social needs exist and social entrepreneurs act on opportunities is not virtual, although there are virtual constructs. We can infer from Sewell's assumptions that structure has a dual character since it is composed simultaneously of schemas and resources that have virtual and real existences, enabling and constraining agents' actions.

Finally there is still the concept of 'agent' that needs to be addressed. This concept is not adequately adapted to social entrepreneurship enquiry. Giddens's definition of agency is restricted to what individuals do. There is also no mention of either the temporality or how the agent makes projects of action. Those are the central dimension of the entrepreneurship process. A critical review of Giddens's theory of agency was made by Emirbayer and Mische (1998). They define human agency as: 'the temporally constructed engagement by actors of different structural environments – the temporal–relational contexts of action – which, through the interplay of habit, imagination, and judgment, both reproduces and transforms those structures in interactive response to the problems posed by changing historical situations' (p. 970). They argue that human agency must be reconceptualized as a temporally embedded process of social engagement, informed by the past, but also oriented toward the future.

Another issue that is underdeveloped in Giddens's definition concerns change. He acknowledges changes in social systems and even, to some degree, in the structure, but his theory does not encompass the evolution of the agent. Giddens argues that agents are able to change the structure but does not address the possibility of their own changing. Here we have to call upon Bourdieu's concept of 'habitus' (which is ontologically similar to the concept of 'agent'). According to Emirbayer and Mische, 'Research building upon Bourdieu's notions of habitus proves highly useful in showing how different formative experiences, such as those influenced by gender, race, ethnicity, or class backgrounds, deeply shape the web of cognitive, affective, and bodily schemas through which actors come to know how to act in particular social worlds' (p. 981). Bourdieu also argues that a formative influence of the past is determinant on the individual changing process and consequently on the individual cognitive and intentional structures of empirical action (Bourdieu, 1977). It means that the agent changes and this change will affect his/her actions.

The evolution that structuration theory has undergone over the past few years allows us now to remodel the model previously presented. The limits and the applicability of the first model perspective were reviewed and offer now a powerful tool to entrepreneurship inquiry and may be narrowed down to the specific phenomenon proposed in this chapter: the opportunity in social entrepreneurship.

Now, we can clearly perceive in Figure 5.2 how the dialectic relationship of 'social entrepreneur' and 'social opportunity' takes form, being at the same time enabled and constrained by the social context. The duality (real × virtual) of the social context is represented by the broken line and

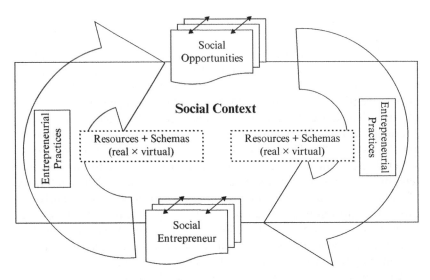

*Figure 5.2    A structuration model for social entrepreneurship research on opportunity creation*

their influence over the process is represented as schemas and resources. The evolutionary characteristic of entrepreneur and social opportunity is evidenced by the juxtaposed figures that represent the social opportunity and the social entrepreneur.

## IMPLICATION FOR RESEARCH

Giddens's theory has been criticized as being difficult to apply in empirical research (Whittington, 1992). The proposed model contributes to advancing the application of structuration theory by providing directions for framing the components that explain the recursive process of the social construction of an opportunity. It helps to delineate the fundamental interactions between entrepreneurs and the elements that will enable and constrain all the activities undertaken to create a social project. Moreover, in line with the constructionist tradition which implies that entrepreneurial processes have meaning that is specific to a particular time and place (Fletcher, 2006; Parkinson and Howorth, 2008), the structuration model emphasizes the social context of interactions across time and space.

A structuration view supports the use of both longitudinal and qualitative research methods, which allow a focus on evolutionary dynamics and process variables (Sarason et al., 2006). Barley and Tolbert (1997) suggested a way of operationalizing structuration theory by the collection of the elements highlighted in the model in different time periods in order to analyse sequential shifts amongst them. This is in line with what has already been pointed out by Fletcher (2006) and Fayolle (2003, 2007), that longitudinal study covering the whole appearance and evolution of an entrepreneurial process is needed to account for entrepreneurial situations.

In order to accomplish such a task the use of case studies may be an insightful exercise. The constructs present in the model would emerge as codes or categories of analyses using this kind of methodology. A good illustration is presented by Jarzabkowski (2008). Using structuration theory in a case methodology she shows how shifts on strategy over a seven-year period transformed and shaped the action of individuals as well as the structural context.

Pozzebon and Pinsonneault (2005) provide a repertoire of strategies for applying structuration theory in empirical IT research. Although the very context is not the same, their analysis suggests what is put forward in this chapter, that structuration theory is a powerful theory able to explain a recursive process involving different elements over time and space, which is demonstrated as being the case of the construction of social entrepreneurship opportunities.

## CONCLUSIONS

As Short et al. (2009) have pointed out, to date scholars have been focusing primarily on describing and explaining social entrepreneurship, rather than on predicting the phenomenon. Going beyond this, this chapter contributes with a framework that can be validated with rigorous research methods.

Taken together, this chapter paves the way for fine-grained studies of the dialectical relationship between social entrepreneurs and opportunity in at least two ways. First, by presenting social opportunities as socially constructed, and second, by taking up the challenge of operationalizing structuration theory. The force of a revised version of structuration theory was illustrated by showing that it allows us to problematize, refine and deepen what is at the heart of the discussion on entrepreneurial opportunities (Mitchell et al., 2008; Zahra, 2008). The theoretical approach outlined in this chapter can move us closer toward a theoretical framework of social opportunity. Empirical research is needed to verify the validity of the assumptions presented in the proposed model and prove the robustness of these concepts as well as their capacity to predict, explain and model processes on social entrepreneurship. The fact that the model emphasizes the evolutionary relationship among entrepreneurs, resources and environment leaves room for the study of discovery opportunities as well. In this case, the process of opportunity discovery and opportunity exploitation would be the independent variables.

For practitioners this model contributes first by highlighting the relationship between social context and social entrepreneur through the elements that enable and constrain entrepreneurial efforts, and second by showing that entrepreneur and opportunity are linked in a process of co-evolution while constructing a social reality.

## NOTES

*    Earlier versions of this paper were presented at the 2008 Chamonix Seminar on Entrepreneurship and at the 2008 Soci(et)al Entrepreneurship Conference. I would like to thank Heidi Dahles, Tim Folta, Frédéric Delmar, Ignasi Martí, Phillip Kim, Alain Fayolle, Grégoire Croidieu and Julienne Senyard for their insightful comments. All remaining errors are mine.
1.   http://www.ashoka.org/node/2986.
2.   http://www.ibj.org.

## REFERENCES

Acs, Z. (2008), *Entrepreneurship, Economic Growth and Public Policy: Prelude to a Knowledge Spillover Theory of Entrepreneurship*, Cheltenham, UK and Northampton, MA, USA: Edward Elgar.
Alvarez, S. and J. Barney (2007), 'Discovery and creation: alternative theories of entrepreneurial action', *Strategic Entrepreneurship Journal*, **1**(1–2), 11–26.
Austin, J.E., H. Stevenson and J. Wei-Skillern (2006), 'Social commercial entrepreneurship: same, different, or both?', *Entrepreneurship Theory and Practice*, **30**(1), 1–22.
Barley, S.R. and P.S. Tolbert (1997), 'Institutionalism and structuration: studying the links between action and institution', *Organization Studies*, **18**(1), 93–118.
Barney, J.B. (1991), 'Firm resources and sustained competitive advantage', *Journal of Management*, **17**(1), 99–120.
Berger, P. and T. Luckmann (1996), *La construction sociale de la réalité*. Paris: Meridiens-klincksieck.
Bouchikhi, H. (1993), 'A constructivist framework for understanding entrepreneurship performance', *Organization Studies*, **14**(4), 549–70.
Bourdieu, P. (1977), *Outline of Theory and Practice*, New York: Cambridge University Press.
Bryant, C.G.A. and D. Jary (1997), *Anthony Giddens Critical Assessments*, London: Routledge.
Busenitz, L.W., P. West, D. Shepherd, T. Nelson, A. Zacharakis and G. Chandler (2003), 'Entrepreneurship in emergence: past trends and future directions', *Journal of Management*, **29**(3), 285–308.
Casson, M. (2005), 'The individual-opportunity nexus: a review of Scott Shane. A general theory of entrepreneurship', *Small Business Economics*, **24**(5), 423–30.
Chiasson, M. and C. Saunders (2005), 'Reconciling diverse approaches to opportunity research using the structuration theory', *Journal of Business Venturing*, **20**(6), 747–67.

Davidsson, P. (2005), *Researching Entrepreneurship*, New York: Springer.
Dees, J.G. (1998), 'The meaning of social entrepreneurship', available at www.fuqua.duke.edu/centers/case/documents/dees_SE.pdf (accessed January, 2008).
Dees, J.G. and B.B. Anderson (2002), 'For profit social ventures', *International Journal of Entrepreneurship Education*, **2**(1), 12–38.
Emirbayer, M. and A. Mische (1998), 'What is agency?', *The American Journal of Sociology*, **103**(4), 962–1023.
Fayolle, A. (2003), 'Research and researchers at the heart of entrepreneurial situations', in C. Steyaert and D. Hjorth (eds), *New Movements in Entrepreneurship*, Cheltenham, UK and Northampton, MA, USA: Edward Elgar, pp. 35–50.
Fayolle, A. (2005), *Introduction à l'entrepreneuriat*, Paris: Dunod.
Fayolle, A. (2007), *Entrepreneurship and the New Value Creation*, Cambridge, UK: Cambridge University Press.
Fletcher, D. (2006), 'Entrepreneurial processes and the social construction of opportunity', *Entrepreneurship & Regional Development*, **18**(5), 421–40.
Gartner W.B., N.M. Carter and G.E. Hills (2003), 'The language of opportunity', in C. Steyaert and D. Hjorth (eds), *New Movements in Entrepreneurship*, Cheltenham, UK and Northampton, MA, USA: Edward Elgar, pp. 103–24.
Gawell, M. (2007), 'Activist entrepreneurship – attac'ing norms and articulating disclosive stories', PhD dissertation, Stockholm University.
Giddens, A. (1979), *Central Problems in Social Theory*, London: Macmillan.
Giddens, A. (1984), *The Constitution of Society. Outline of the Theory of Structuration*, London: Cambridge University Press.
Jack, S.L. and A.R. Anderson (2002), 'Effects of embeddedness on the entrepreneurial process', *Journal of Business Venturing*, **17**(5), 467–87.
Jarzabkowski, P. (2008), 'Shaping strategy as a structuration process', *The Academy of Management Journal*, **51**(4), 621–50.
Kirzner, I. (1973), *Competition and Entrepreneurship*, Chicago: University of Chicago Press.
Kirzner, I. (1997), 'Entrepreneurial discovery and the competitive market process: an Austrian approach', *Journal of Economic Literature*, **35**(1), 60–85.
Layder, D. (1996), *New Strategies in Social Research: An Introduction and Guide*, Cambridge: Polity Press.
Luksha, P. (2008), 'Niche construction: the process of opportunity creation in the environment', *Strategic Entrepreneurship Journal*, **2**(4), 269–83.
Mair, J. and I. Martí (2006), 'Social entrepreneurship research: a source of explanation, prediction, and delight', *Journal of World Business*, **41**(1), 36–44.
Mair, J. and E. Noboa (2005), 'How intentions to create a social venture are formed. A case study', working paper, University of Navarra, available at http://www.iese.edu/research/pdfs/DI-0593-E.pdf (accessed January, 2008).
Mair, J. and C. Seelos (2005), 'Sustainable development: how social entrepreneurs make it happen', working paper, University of Navarra, available at http://www.iese.edu/research/pdfs/DI-0611-E.pdf (accessed January, 2008).
McKendall, M.A. and J.A. Wagner (1997), 'Motive, opportunity, choice, and corporate illegality', *Organization Science*, **8**(6), 624–47.
Mitchell, R.K., J.R. Mitchell and J.B. Smith (2008), 'Inside opportunity formation: enterprise failure, cognition, and the creation of opportunities', *Strategic Entrepreneurship Journal*, **2**(3), 225–42.
Nizet, J. (2007), *La sociologie de Antony Giddens*, Paris: Editions La Découverte.
Parkinson, C. and C. Howorth (2008), 'The language of social entrepreneurs', *Entrepreneurship and Regional Development*, **20**(3), 285–309.
Peredo, A.M. and M. McLean (2006), 'Social entrepreneurship: a critical review of the concept', *Journal of World Business*, **41**(1), 56–65.
Pozzebon, M. and A. Pinsonneault (2005), 'Challenges in conducting empirical work using structuration theory: learning from IT research', *Organization Studies*, **26**(9), 1354–76.

Sarason, Y., T. Dean and J.F. Dillard (2006), 'Entrepreneurship as the nexus of individual and opportunity: a structuration view', *Journal of Business Venturing*, **21**(3), 286–305.
Schumpeter, J.A. (1934), *Theory of Economic Development: An inquiry into Profits, Capital, Credit, Interest and the Business Cycle*, Boston: Harvard University Press.
Sewell, W.H. (1992), 'A theory of structure: duality, agency, and transformation', *The American Journal of Sociology*, **98**(1), 1–29.
Shane, S. and S. Venkataraman (2000), 'The promise of entrepreneurship as a field of research', *The Academy of Management Review*, **26**(1), 217–26.
Shaw, E. and S. Carter (2007), 'Social entrepreneurship: theoretical antecedents and empirical analysis of entrepreneurial processes and outcomes', *Journal of Small Business and Enterprise Development*, **14**(3), 418–34.
Short, J.C., W.M. Tood and G.T. Lumpkin (2009), 'Research in social entrepreneurship: past contributions and future opportunities', *Strategic Entrepreneurship Journal*, **3**(2), 161–94.
Singh, R.P. (2001), 'A comment on developing the field of entrepreneurship through the study of opportunities', *The Academy of Management Review*, **26**(1), 10–12.
Smith, B.R., T.F. Barr, S.D. Barbosa and J. Kickul (2008), 'Social entrepreneurship education: a grounded learning approach to social value creation', *Journal of Enterprising Culture*, **16**(4), 339–65.
Stevens, R., N. Moray and S. Crucke (2008), 'The process of value creation in social entrepreneurial firms', paper presented at Babson Entrepreneurship Research Conference.
Steyaert, C. and J. Katz (2004), 'Reclaiming the space of entrepreneurship in society: geographical, discursive and social dimensions', *Entrepreneurship and Regional Development*, **16**(3), 179–96.
Taylor, D. and E. Walley (2003), 'The green entrepreneur: visionary, maverick or opportunist?', Manchester Metropolitan University Business School Working Paper Series, available at http://www.ribm.mmu.ac.uk/wps/papers/03-04.pdf (accessed January, 2008).
Weerawardena, J. and S.G. Mort (2006), 'Investigating social entrepreneurship: a multidimensional model', *Journal of World Business*, **41**(1), 21–35.
Weick, K.E. (1979), *The Social Psychology of Organizing*, Reading, MA: Addison-Wesley.
Wendt, A.E. (1987), 'The agent-structure problem in international relations theory', *International Organization*, **41**(3), 335–70.
Whittington, R. (1992), 'Putting Giddens into action: social systems and managerial agency', *Journal of Management Studies*, **29**(6), 693–712.
Wood, F.A. (1908), 'Greek and Latin etymologies', *Classical Philology*, **3**(1), 74–86.
Zahra, S. (2007), 'Contextualizing theory building in entrepreneurship research', *Journal of Business Venturing*, **22**(3), 443–52.
Zahra, S. (2008), 'The virtuous cycle of discovery and creation of entrepreneurial opportunities', *Strategic Entrepreneurship Journal*, **2**(3), 243–58.
Zahra, S.A., H.N. Rawhouser, N. Bhawe, D.O. Neubaum and J.C. Hayton (2008), 'Globalization of social entrepreneurship opportunities', *Strategic Entrepreneurship Journal*, **2**(2), 117–31.

# PART II

# A CONTEXTUAL PERSPECTIVE OF SOCIAL ENTREPRENEURSHIP

# 6 Social entrepreneurship in France: organizational and relational issues
## Martine Hlady Rispal and Jerome Boncler

French social entrepreneurship has developed since the 1980s in the form of work-integration social enterprise (WISE), home daycare, home helps and kitchen gardens. Its specific vocation is to build and consolidate local communities as it creates a significant number of new jobs. These enterprises belong to the social economy because they base business activity on the principle of mutual welfare in order to restructure the economic, political and social dynamics of a community (Laville, 1995). This article focuses on social enterprises that balance income generation against stated social objectives.

Economists, sociologists and political scientists have researched this topic. First, economists dissected its unique organizational features from a socio-economic perspective. They studied and pondered the economic utility of social enterprise, measured its tangible and intangible added value and examined how business operations dovetailed into one another (Vienney, 1980; Archambault, 1996). Long-term unemployment and homelessness then led sociologists and political scientists such as Laville (2000) to conclude that welfare agencies and social policy had become 'subsystems of the market economy or of public services which took no account of the emerging welfare needs of marginalized populations' (Demoustier, 2001: 114). This drew their attention to the workings of this social economy.

Then management scientists began looking at how the theories of profit-driven enterprise applied to social enterprise (Le Duff, 1992; Meunier, 1992). More recent research viewed the social economy from a purely entrepreneurial angle (Boncler and Hlady Rispal, 2003; Schieb-Bienfait and Urbain, 2004). This chapter moves on to examine the organizational and relational issues of social enterprise, especially in the planning phase and first year or so of operations prior to actual startup. It argues in terms of the groundwork, opportunities, innovation and creation of new value (Verstraete and Fayolle, 2004).

Our goal is to isolate the basic principles of social enterprise, to discover unique features and to point out any internal contradictions. We aim to show that social enterprise can sustain values other than self-interest on a marketplace that drives out uncompetitive rivals. Social enterprise must further convince public and private stakeholders of their own interest in defending its values. The tensions involved arise early in pre-startup groundwork for a social enterprise. The basic principles of social enterprise outlined herein serve as a yardstick to assess its mission and the social mutual support network it engenders. Illustrative case studies are included throughout the chapter.

## 1   CONCEPTUAL FRAMEWORK

Social entrepreneurship is an oxymoron where the loss-making 'social' goals usually relegated to government contradict the 'entrepreneurial' quest for personal profit. For better insight, we shall now review the history and key features of the social enterprise concept in France.

### 1.1   Reconciling Entrepreneurial and Social Opposites

The social enterprise concept is recent. It apparently emerged in the different contexts of the USA and Europe up to two decades ago (Alternatives économiques, 2006). Although originally designating only non-profit corporate bodies, it expanded in the USA to cover regular businesses that apply operating income to any cultural, environmental or philanthropic cause. At all events, the bottom line is to generate income that will finance any of these causes. According to Tyson (2004), a social entrepreneur is someone driven by a social mission and a desire to find innovative ways to solve social problems that have been neglected by either the market or the public sector. Gregory Dees (2001: 4) also defines a social entrepreneur as one who:

> Adopts a mission to create and sustain social values (not just private values); Recognizes and relentlessly pursues new opportunities to serve that mission; Engages in a process of continuous innovation, adaptation, and learning; Acts boldly without being limited by resources currently at hand, and exhibits heightened accountability to the constituencies served and the outcomes created.

European socio-economic studies put social enterprise at the heart of the social economy. Many highlight the institutional and historical context on one hand and the socio-political on the other. Whether economic, historical, political or sociological, the theories stress the need to consider all facets of the social economy if it is to be properly situated in the socially embedded economy (Vienney, 1994; Demoustier, 2001; Levesque et al. 2001).

Idiosyncratically, the French concepts of 'entrepreneurship' and 'social enterprise' date back to the cooperatives, mutual benefit associations and private voluntary organizations of the nineteenth-century 'social economy' as well as to the WISEs, shelters and local development associations of the 'mutual help economy' of the 1980s (Seghers and Allemand, 2007). Members of this latter group are termed 'mutual help enterprises' regardless of how they incorporate – most are registered as non-profit associations or cooperatives except for a handful operating often as mainstream limited companies. The distinction in origin serves no purpose here and this chapter refers to all of the above as social enterprise.

In 1998, France saw the release of the Lipietz White Paper which noted the 'advisability of a new type of company with a social mission'.[1] In 2001, French legislation authorized registration of a Société Coopérative d'Intérêt Collectif (SCIC), or 'public interest cooperative', although it has found few takers to date. SCIC incorporation is specifically designed to help any group of people, physical and/or moral, to respond to unmet social needs and, in doing so, to diminish burdens on local government. It also entitles employees, volunteers, users, backers, local government and other third parties to a stake in the venture.

---

### BOX 6.1   AUTOCOMM SCIC

Based in Bordeaux, AutoComm owns a fleet of vehicles it operates as a community car pool. Users book 24/7 and pay only for actual usage, which runs from several minutes to as many days. The aim is to cut city traffic congestion, given that one shared vehicle replaces eight private ones. It also changes how citizens relate to motor vehicles because they are driving less through a process of negotiating vehicle availability and transport alternatives. Finally, it reduces the mobility gap between car owners and non-owners. Overall, it combines economic development, environmental protection and social welfare, thus constituting an example of sustainable development that modifies individual behaviour beneficially.

At the outset, AutoComm was a private voluntary organization that needed substantial startup capital to purchase a fleet, hire staff and advertise. To attract that equity from Bordeaux City Government and the city's public transport contractor, it reincorporated as an SCIC.

*Source:* 'Transformer une Association en SCIC' conference held by the Union Régionales SCOP d'Aquitaine on 10 April 2008.

---

However, Seghers and Allemand (2007) observe that social enterprise only took hold in 2002 in France when ESSEC, one of the nation's top business schools, founded a chair of social entrepreneurship which it billed as 'private initiative in service of community interest'. Backers were Caisse des Dépôts investment bank, insurer MACIF, and the Fondation de France. Caisse des Dépôts then helped found AVISE (Agence de Valorisation des Initiatives Socio-Economiques), an umbrella organization for key players in the social economy.

As Clément and Gardin (1999) note, social enterprise has no legal existence under French law, contrary to Belgium, Italy and elsewhere. Nonetheless, the term is increasingly used to describe a growing number of endeavours.

### 1.2    Basic Principles of Social Enterprise

We characterized social enterprises from studies by CEGES (1995), Jeantet (1999), Lipietz (2000), Garrabé et al. (2001), Défourny (2004) and EMES (2008).[2] All of the authors just cited agree that, despite any differences of aims and activities, social enterprises have shared values and play by much the same rules. These rules include laws governing their type of incorporation (for example, cooperative, non-profit association, limited company) and collective bargaining agreements that apply to all players alike. The studies also note how social enterprises are organizing and operating in new ways, creating new relationships with the markets, taking new risks and evolving in original ways. Table 6.1 lists their key features.

Although sufficing to distinguish social enterprise from mainstream businesses, these principles do not constitute a set of prerequisites needed to qualify as a social enterprise. Rather, they merely define the centre of gravity of a mass of enterprises operating very different business models that vary with location and economic sector: EMES found 40+ different models across 12 European Union member states for ILM enterprises alone. AVISE (2003) defines the social entrepreneur as 'any person or group of persons who found an economically viable company with the core purpose of taking into account human vulnerability and/or social bonding'. Actually, there is no statutory definition of social enterprise – it is a multifaceted form of entrepreneurship that straddles private initiative and local public interest by operating a business in order to serve the interests of individuals and their community.

These principles broadly form a basis for conceptual analysis and discussion of social entrepreneurship. A finer analysis is presented in sections 2 and 3 below.

*Table 6.1   Principles of social enterprise*

| Principle | Description |
|---|---|
| 1. Profit is not the ultimate goal. | Social enterprises serve members and the local community by creating economic value to create social value. They minimize payroll costs and may or may not distribute any profits. |
| 2. Benefit to the community is a direct or indirect objective. | Social enterprises promote responsible civic engagement in the community. They may select business activities of dual social value that both serve the needs of the individual and promote responsible civic engagement in their community. |
| 3. Financial viability is essential. | Social enterprises spur the production and provision of goods and services to generate income. Managers are responsible for economic viability and ensure autonomy by securing financial resources from public bodies, private enterprise and operating revenue. |
| 4. Decisions are made jointly regardless of equity holdings and form of incorporation. | The investors are important, but the law and/or articles of incorporation require joint decision-making by all stakeholders. Cooperatives elect their chair by vote of a board of associates while non-profit associations elect her/him by vote of the board of directors; she/he and general manager run the association jointly. |
| 5. Joint involvement of all affected parties. | Joint management aims at maximizing the direct involvement of members, customers and other stakeholders. |

## 2   PRE-STARTUP ISSUES OF SOCIAL ENTERPRISE

As stated, income generation is secondary to the primary purpose of social enterprise, which is to be of (in)direct benefit to the community. How then is it to exert a positive impact in an adverse operating environment?

### 2.1   Generation of Social Value

*Principle No. 1:*   Social enterprises serve members and the community by creating economic value to create social value.

The first mission is to create social value despite a context of economic recession, high unemployment and falling household incomes. Social enterprise generates income to create social value and not the opposite. Some private corporations have long been creating social value to boost profits while its importance has only been secondary, but social enterprise puts social value first, as in the case of firms that build activity around personal vulnerability, for example by hiring the handicapped and homeless (AVISE, 2003). This applies to WISE in particular. Personal vulnerability is also factored in when the enterprise offers products or services for the elderly, illiterate, handicapped, unemployed or other marginalized individuals.

Creation of social value is not only about helping the needy but also about securing their active involvement in order to raise their social status and opportunities for gainful skilled employment; it is further about building lasting interpersonal relations and developing cost-effective services (Jeantet, 1999).

In summary, social entrepreneurs aim to meet social needs while finding new ways of securing economic viability despite a substantial share of non-paying clients (see section 3 below).

### 2.2 Creation of Societal Value

*Principle No. 2:*    Social enterprises may select business activities of dual social value that both serve the needs of the individual and promote responsible civic engagement in its community.

The management of vulnerability often involves promoting civic spirit. Social enterprise aims to act upon individuals by acting upon their context, which is inextricably linked to their immediate problems. This process also fosters interpersonal bonding, which enhances the societal impact of the enterprise.

Aside from concern for the dignity of the individual and his community, there is a vision about the role of social enterprise towards building a more humane society. Social entrepreneurs aim to benefit society as a whole and to select business activities that are in society's best long-term interests.

WISE covers a wide range of economic sectors in France. The figures below focus on the spread of economic sectors for 2005 and exclude rehabilitation workshops, neighbourhood public corporations ('régies') or other social integration enterprise. Seventy-one per cent are environment-oriented: 15 per cent heritage restoration, 5 per cent forestry and agriculture, 16 per cent public green space care and 12 per cent waste recycling, while 18 per cent provide business services, particularly cleaning of local government offices and of common areas in low-income housing, and 5 per cent supply home help to the elderly.[3] These data confirm the extent to which social enterprises have been creating social value by helping

---

## BOX 6.2   JULES GUESDES SELF-SERVICE GROCERY

The idea of an alternative grocery in Bordeaux found favour with three Christian charities as of 2006.* It opened in 2008 in a low-income district as an alternative to existing food aid and soon earned support from local government and food aid associations.

Local inhabitants played an active role in the two years of groundwork needed to start up. There were five planning groups: (1) selection of product line; (2) interior fittings and decoration; (3) liaison with local welfare services; (4) liaison with other local players; and (5) kitchen for ready-to-eat products.

Beyond bonding over convivial meals together, the kitchen group re-popularized vegetables long rejected by mainstream distributors, emphasized reliance on in-season produce, shared ethnic recipes and cooking skills, and identified ways of improving both diet and food consumption patterns.

The grocery has one employee, a workgroup manager and volunteers co-opted from the workgroups. All volunteers are community members. The grocery is open about four hours per day.

*Note:*   * Foyer Pour Tours low-income housing company, Foyer Fraternal shelter and the Reformed Church.

---

individuals and their community as well as societal value by impacting society as a whole.


# 3   SOCIAL NETWORK BUILDING

Social enterprise has its own game rules. Entrepreneurs start with an opportunity spotted inside an adverse context (see section 2). If the unmet need is easy to identify, the resources needed to meet it are more elusive. The next challenge is to build coordinated, sustainable activity from a very diverse set of in-house and outside stakeholders.

### 3.1   Pre-startup Financing

*Principle No. 3:*   Social enterprises spur the production and provision of goods and services to generate income. Managers are responsible for

---

## BOX 6.3   WISE

In 2005, X.D. and N.M. founded Greniers de l'Informatique to
recycle and market discarded computer equipment as an instrument of social rehabilitation. Their motto is 'Recycling for the
Destitute. Recovery from dustbins recovers people too'. With a
current staff of the two founders, two full-time employees and five
interns, it helps social dropouts and the unemployed to build a
future and generate income as it benefits the environment.*

*Note:*   * For details, see Hlady Rispal (2008).

---

economic viability and ensure autonomy by securing financial resources
from public bodies, private enterprise and operating revenue.

Social enterprise requires a mix of financial resources if it is to operate,
principally in the following ways: users generate operating income, government injects subsidies, volunteers invest man-hours and anyone can
contribute microsavings. The crux of this issue is to optimize the balance
of these resources.

The managerial objective is to secure respect for the independence
and autonomy of the enterprise. However, social enterprise only has full
autonomy if the bulk of its income comes from users – who are largely
cash-strapped. It is also costly to operate because it employs the handicapped, unskilled or other categories of low-productivity staff. It thus
needs additional income from a mix of sources.

Financing a social enterprise is a complex matter demanding the ability to
complete financing applications, follow up their processing and keep track
of refinancing deadlines. It also calls for the ability to interface with banks,
local government and donors, all having different expectations and oversight
demands. These relationships also assume trust, which takes time to build;
for example some banks will mediate but remain entirely risk-averse while
some associations keep a distance for fear of jeopardizing their own identity
(Guérin and Vallat, 1998). Social enterprise builds great flexibility into its
daily operations, which is anathema to the neat pigeonholes typical of government administration and to banking or to fiscal legislation that draws
a sharp line between commercial and non-commercial activity. Moreover,
donors want both oversight rights and a say in management policy. Finally
backers, both public and private, only grant term loans, with periodic rene-
gotiations of amounts and terms such that some will need to be replaced.

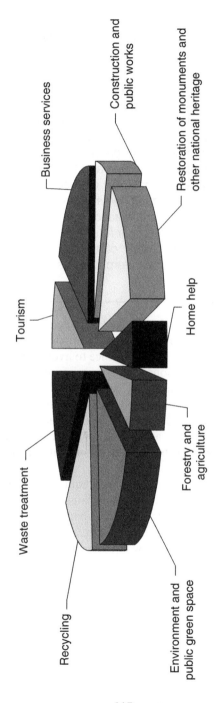

*Figure 6.1  Employment in social enterprise by economic sector*

---

## BOX 6.4    P'TITES POMMES BABYCARE CENTRE

This centre was founded in 1990 by five young mothers in a southwestern village to care for children aged 3 months to about 2 years, when they should become eligible for government daycare centres. It operates at four locations: two baby nurseries, one day nursery and a dispatch centre for mobile child minders who cover 10 municipalities. It employs 25 people and is financed by user fees, government welfare subsidies and two municipal subsidies. Finally, thrifty management has built up a cash base of €200 000 (ca. US$265 000) deposited in an interest-bearing bank account.

However, the umbrella organization for the 10 municipalities opted in 2008 to put out for tender future provision of P'tit Pomme services and has made award of the contract conditional on recovery of the €200 000 in 'overpayments'. P'tit Pomme faces a dilemma.

---

Obviously, the happy flipside of mixed funding is that it precludes takeover by any one backer and minimizes the impact of any single funding cut-off. Diluting these risks is due diligence to avoid shutdown because of overdependence on any one source or of pressure to compromise on social missions. However, social enterprise has no easy task persuading potential backers to invest in a line of business with which they may be unfamiliar, most notably when it also offers no guarantee of economic viability. As a result, social enterprises that actually happen are often those piloted by financial insiders supported by local development players and/or prominent citizens.

Financing is often compounded by legal requirements, for example non-profit associations may not raise capital because they may not pay interest and must therefore borrow at interest from banks. Inversely, cooperatives may raise capital from private sources but are ineligible for certain government subsidies because French law equates them with standard commercial enterprise. Although the law governing non-profit associations does distinguish commercial from non-commercial activity and taxes only the former, the reality is that business income pays for the social activities yet remains subject to profit tax and VAT.[4]

In short, budding social entrepreneurs should start by identifying the type of incorporation that will best enable them to efficiently mobilize the resources they need to tackle the social need they target, with due regard for the accompanying legal constraints.

## 3.2 Collegial Governance

*Principle No. 4:* Decisions are made jointly regardless of equity holdings and form of incorporation.

The social objectives assume joint decision-making and management. Before selecting her associates, the social entrepreneur should have a clear picture of the objectives. She needs to ensure everyone shares the same drive. She should finally determine how best to mobilize and stimulate the human resources involved so that they all function as an organic unit.

Joint management is a dual requirement: (1) the law stipulates that members shall enjoy equal unfettered access to all organs and executive offices based on fair, objective criteria; and (2) a social enterprise has a moral duty to empower members with enough information to participate intelligently in decision-making and oversight, which is their duty.

Management can, however, go astray in cooperatives and non-profit associations, the two top forms of incorporation. The nucleus of an association is a chair, board and general manager. In theory, the chair lays down strategy and policy, oversees compliance with the mission statement and represents the association in official capacities. The general manager supervises staff, ensures implementation of board decisions and reports back to the board on results. This goes wrong in three main ways:

1. The chair sidelines the manager and micromanages daily operations himself.
2. The manager monopolizes information and reduces the board to rubberstamping his decisions, which opens the door to fraud and embezzlement.
3. The chair and manager monopolize information and alienate staff by leaving them in the dark (Boncler, 2006).

In a SCOP cooperative, the board of 'associates' elects a general manager and co-opts new associates from the membership. Governed by the Law of 19 July 1978, as amended in 1985 and 1992, a SCOP is a limited company with a minimum of two co-founders if private, and seven if public. Uniquely, registered capital varies in function of business activity because employees supply it in exchange for 'social shares' which are an employee's option with entitlement to co-managerial, but not associate, status (Hlady Rispal et al., 2007).

According to Vienney (1994), employee status is a mix of equity and the employment contract, making each both a shareholder and wage earner. Cooperatives are employee-owned and difficult prey for hostile takeover.

---

## BOX 6.5    ATMOSPH'AIRE SCOP

This cooperative took over the recycling of computer printer cartridges by a failed association that was fighting unemployment. Beyond the will to exert positive impact on the environment, it also prioritized hiring the handicapped and those in other kinds of distress. In contrast to the 'lead entrepreneur' approach (Clarkin and Rosa, 2005), Atmosph'aire was conceived by seven jobless ex-coworkers who wanted to do 'something' together based on trust built up over the years on the job.* One dropped out in the course of brainstorming and the remaining six started networking socially. Although two crystallized the basic concept, everyone injected input and no individual stands out as the main driver, largely thanks to shared values and good interpersonal synergy. As one co-founder notes: 'When two of us were researching information and first heard about SCOPs, it clicked. We told the others and they liked it too. We then contacted the SCOP Regional Union for more details and decided it suited our need. Then we farmed out the groundwork among ourselves. Our SCOP also needed a name and we had to move fast. We appointed three or four of us to various positions. We had to move fast and everyone helped out' (Hlady Rispal et al., 2007).

---

This facilitates stable long-term planning. In addition to wages and new jobs, cooperatives may pay out dividends not to exceed average yield on corporate bonds.[5] As a rule, however, any operating surplus automatically goes into capital reserves. Managerial decisions are made by associates on the basis of 'one associate, one vote' regardless of their shareholdings.

### 3.3    From Resource Holder to Stakeholder

*Principle No. 5:* Joint management aims at maximizing the direct involvement of members, customers and other stakeholders.

Implementing this principle means facing two questions: (1) How do you make all stakeholders best fathom the way(s) in which the enterprise will create social value? And, (2) Is full disclosure of the social project to all stakeholders advisable?

The first step towards an answer requires confidence-building and a thorough understanding of each stakeholder's expectations. Joint

---

## BOX 6.6   LE LIEN

Le Lien is a WISE that was founded as a not-for-profit association in 1970 as a homeless shelter. In 1990, it started organic farming and sold the produce as prepackaged baskets to a growing membership. After a string of falling crop yields, a consultancy was hired in 2004 to reverse it. By 2007, the situation was critical: Le Lien (1) failed to secure better terms from its lead organization for the supply of staff and consumables; (2) mismanaged coordination with state welfare and other agencies, which adversely impacted its rehabilitation efforts; (3) was considering shutdown of said efforts because the evaluation criteria for renewals of government subsidies seemed to be bureaucratic and commercial rather than being based on its social efficiency, thus distracting it from its social mission; and (4) faced a shortage of quality controllers and other skilled staff, which put existing staff under enough pressure to trigger high absenteeism and ignite frustration among clients and government agencies alike.

However, relations with the municipal hospital, town hall and local rights associations remained constructive while client relations edged up despite their demanding attitude to organic produce. Le Lien also began marketing directly to consumers, restaurants and government agency cafeterias. Only with this last niche market did relations spill over into cooperation on social integration.*

*Note:*   * See Hlady Rispal (2008).

---

management goes hand in hand with careful positioning of the enterprise with respect to government backers, mainstream private enterprise, individuals, welfare agencies, like-minded associations and lead organizations. Proper positioning implies communications policy specific to each interface. Entrepreneurs should develop that policy in the early planning stages and base it on their wish list of backers who will ultimately have a stake in the venture. Positioning policy should aim for confidence-building and a full understanding of each stakeholder's needs and expectations as well as of what the enterprise will provide in return. This cuts risk and enhances teamwork for a cause that goes beyond the generation of profit without ignoring hardnosed business considerations, which is not easy.

A second issue is to earn the patronage of the client base without foisting any social aims upon it. Most corporate, government and individual clients have no grounding in social inclusion work. Thus, the relationship should be based on the business transactions, for example farming or recycling, while enabling the socially concerned among them to invest however they will. Building a community spirit assumes lasting interpersonal relationships and the satisfaction of generally accepted expectations that become the norm, for example clients expect a better product at a lower price while the enterprise expects patronage and active involvement in providing a given service, plus the word-of-mouth advertising that will increase the client base (Hlady Rispal, 2008).

As Algesheimer et al. (2005) note, the idea is to set up community activities that intensify bonding. Social ties flourish around positive consumer experiences, for example finding a healthier food product triggers individual patronage, word-of-mouth advertising snowballs into more patronage, and patrons end up making available their homes as drop-off points for distribution of the nifty new product. Meanwhile, more alert patrons will want board seats to play a more active role in social integration or environmental protection projects although this usually requires active co-opting inside local government, public hospitals and church groups: the idea is to target altruistically inclined patrons without pressuring others in the slightest.

## CONCLUSION

This study has sought to outline the aims, prerequisites and development of social enterprises in France. It covers the added economic and social value generated by its activities, products and services. It also highlights the value of the concept of local social ties omnipresent in the concept of social capital defined by Bourdieu (1986) and Putman (1995) as the aggregate of actual and potential resources available in a network. It further stresses societal value, which grows from allying sustainable development with responsible civic engagement (Evers, 1997). Generating this value in all its forms becomes feasible through innovative management and organization, a characteristic of any entrepreneurial approach. Moreover, because they target populations which cannot afford products and services at going street prices, social entrepreneurs actually create new markets. They also operate flexible, unconventional organizations, for example one WISE, intermediate labour market firm asks employees to train themselves as they work with the expectation that they will transition to a mainstream employer.

Beyond the frustrations and failures involved in reconciling end-of-year bottom lines with a social mission, the current legal framework governing social enterprise is admittedly less than ideal and there are numerous examples of moderate honesty supposedly typical of the world of mainstream business. Nonetheless, the legal safeguards are adequate for social enterprise to have become a lasting source of organizational innovation and improved interpersonal bonding, thus enabling it to further secure its niche in the French national economy.

## NOTES

1. Update report concerning the letter from the Minister of Employment and Social Solidarity, Mrs Martine Aubry, to Alain Lipietz, the Social Economy Secretary.
2. CEGES (1995) and EMES (2008) and studies found on the European Research Network (EMES) website, http://www.emes.net.
3. Data derived from statistics supplied by Centre National des Entreprises d'Insertion (http://www.cnei.org and CNEImag 2006).
4. Circular, French Finance Ministry, 15 September 1998.
5. Law of 13 July 1992.

## REFERENCES

Algesheimer, R., U. Dholakia and A. Hermann (2005), 'The social influence of brand community: evidence from European car clubs', *Journal of Marketing*, **69**(3), 19–34.
Alternatives économiques (2006), *L'économie sociale de A à Z*, Alternative économiques pratique, No. 22, January, Paris: Alternatives économiques.
Archambault, C. (1996), *Le secteur sans but lucratif: associations et fondations en France*, Paris: Economica.
AVISE (2003), 'Guide de l'entrepreneur social', September.
Boncler, J. (2006), 'De l'intérêt de la recherche en management à travailler sur la gouvernance des associations gestionnaires', paper presented at XV Conférence internationale, AIMS Congress, Annecy, France, 13–16 June.
Boncler, J. and M. Hlady Rispal (2003), 'Caractérisation de l'entrepreneuriat en économie sociale et solidaire', December, Editions d l'Adreg, available at: http://www.editions-adreg.net.
Bourdieu, P. (1986), 'The forms of capital', in J.G. Richardson (ed.), *Handbook of Theory and Research for the Sociology of Education*, New York: Greenwood Press, pp. 241–58.
Clarkin, J. and P. Rosa (2005), 'Entrepreneurial teams within franchise firms', International Small Business Journal, **23**(3), 303–4.
Clément, H. and L. Gardin (1999), *L'entreprise sociale: les notes de l'institut Karl Polanyi*, Domont, France: Thierry Quinquenton éditeur.
Dees, J.G. (2001), 'The meaning of "social entrepreneurship"', available at: http://www.fuqua.duke.edu/centers/case/documents/dees_se.pdf.
Défourny, J. (2004), 'L'émergence du concept d'entreprise sociale', *Reflets et Perspectives*, **XVIII**(3), 9–23.
Demoustier, D. (2001), *L'économie sociale et solidaire: s'associer pour entreprendre autrement*, Collection Alternatives Economiques, Paris: Syros.
Evers, A. (1997), 'Le tiers secteur au regard d'une conception pluraliste de la protection

sociale', in MIRE (ed.), *Produire les solidarités: la part des associations*, Paris: Fondation de France, pp. 51–62.

Garrabé, M., L. Bastide and C. Fas (2001), 'Identité de l'économie solidaire', *RECMA*, **280**, April, 12–35.

Guérin, I. and S. Vallat (1998), 'Les experiences du credit solidaire', *Economie et Humanisme*, No. 345, 82–7.

Hlady Rispal, M. (2008), 'Le marketing de l'économie solidaire', in M. Hlady Rispal (ed.), *Marketing Contextuels*, Paris: Dunod, pp. 163–86.

Hlady Rispal, M., J. Boncler and T. Verstraete (2007), 'Entrepreneurial teams: theoretical framework and methodology applied to an exploratory case study', paper presented at the International Council for Small Business Conference, Turku, Finland, 13–15 June.

Jeantet, T. (1999), *L'économie sociale européenne ou la tentation de la démocratie*, Paris: CIEM Edition.

Laville, J.L. (1995), 'L'économie solidaire: une nouvelle forme d'économie sociale?', *RECMA*, **255**(53), 70–80.

Laville, J.L. (2000), 'Le tiers secteur: un objet d'étude pour la sociologie économique', *Sociologie du Travail*, **42**(4), 531–50.

Le Duff, R. (1992), 'Management public ou gestion non marchande', in R. Le Duff and J. Allouche (eds), *Annales du Management*, Paris: Economica.

Levesque, B., G. Bourques and E. Gorgues (2001), *La nouvelle sociologie économique*, Paris: Desclée de Brouwer.

Lipietz, A. (2000), 'L'entreprise sociale et le tiers secteur', report to the Minister of Employment and Social Solidarity.

Meunier, M. (1992), *Le management de non marchand*, Paris: Economica.

Putman, R.D. (1995), 'Bowling alone: America's declining social capital', *Journal of Democracy*, **6**(1), 65–78.

Schieb-Bienfait, N. and C. Urbain (2004), 'L'entrepreneuriat social, un autre façon d'entreprendre', *RECMA*, **293**, July, 68–92.

Seghers, V. and S. Allemand (2007), *L'audace des entrepreneurs sociaux*, Paris: Editions Autrement.

Tyson, L. (2004), 'Good works – with a business plan', available at: http://www.business-week.com/magazine/content/04_18/b3881047_mz007.htm.

Verstraete, T. and A. Fayolle (2004), 'Paradigmes et entrepreneuriat', *Revue de l'Entrepreneuriat*, **4**(1), 33–52.

Vienney, C. (1980), *Socio-économie des organisations coopératives*, Paris: CIEM.

Vienney, C. (1994), *L'Economie sociale*, Paris: La Découverte.

# 7 Sustainable transborder business cooperation in the European regions: the importance of social entrepreneurship
## Raymond Saner and Lichia Yiu

## 1 INTRODUCTION

### 1.1 Importance of Sustainable Transborder Cooperation for European Integration

Studying regions requires an interdisciplinary approach consisting of, among other things, microeconomics (competitive firm behaviour, local labour markets), spatial economics (rural and urban planning and architecture), policy analysis (regulatory function of government), urban geography (migration patterns), institutional sociology (administrative culture), social psychology (social cohesion) and cultural anthropology (comparative religion and values).

Regional economics, the precursor of today's spatial economics or economic geography, goes back to the nineteenth century with major contributions from continental European theorists such as Thünen, Weber, Christaller and Lösch (Arnott, 1996). Some of their studies focused on the causes for variance in regional development in the newly unified Germany at the time of the creation of the German Zollverein (customs union). The main impact of the Zollverein was the creation of new market boundaries offering economies of scale, which previously did not exist in the earlier era of multiple German kingdoms and city-states. Some of the German regions thrived with the creation of a larger internal market; others stagnated or decreased in importance. The cause for growth and decline of these German regions was one of the research interests of the above-cited continental European spatial economists.

In a similar way, a growing number of today's researchers in the field of regional development focus on the impact of enlarged market boundaries, this time, however, not within a national context but rather at the level of the global economy. Liberalization of trade through continuous tariff reductions has resulted in a broadening of market scope from national to global levels. Within this enlarged context of a liberalizing and globalizing world economy, some countries have been more successful than others in making use of the new opportunities. However, successful competition in globalized markets is not evenly spread across a nation but is rather concentrated in some of its regions that have prospered more, while others stagnated or even declined. The quest for understanding why some regions succeed while others fail to meet the challenges of globalization has led to a renewed interest in regional development theory, spatial economics and economic geography, particularly in North America and Western Europe.

### 1.2 National Competitiveness Cluster

Porter (1990) has conducted an extensive comparative research of ten countries and has come up with reasons why some nations succeed in some industries but fail in others. According to Porter, the home base plays a critical role in that firms tend to build up competitive advantage in industries for which the local environment is the most dynamic and challenging. He has conceptualized his findings in his analytical 'diamond' frame, which consists of: a) factor conditions (for example, labour, capital, land); b) demand conditions; c) dynamism of related and supporting industries; and d) firm strategy, structure and rivalry. In addition to the four factors, chance (such as inventions and war) and government also play an important role in supporting a nation's aim to achieve economic success (see Figure 7.1).

Concretely, a successful region according to Porter's diamond would show the following features:

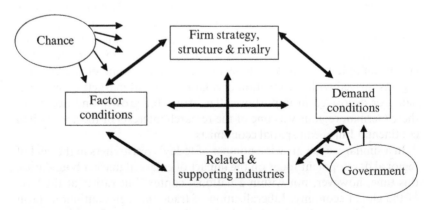

*Source:* Porter (1990).

*Figure 7.1 Successful factors of national competitiveness*

- several competing companies belonging to the same regional key industry or industries
- a large dynamic and sophisticated internal market (demand conditions)
- suppliers specialized in the activities of the regional key industry/industries
- qualified and highly qualified manpower specialized in the activities of the regional key industry/industries; educational and research institutes (factor conditions) (Borner et al., 1991, p. 62).

**Role of government**

Porter's original concept consisted only of the four diamond conditions. In later publications, Porter added more factors to his diamond model, namely: 1) chance; and 2) government. Concerning the role of government and chance in Porter's model, Oez (1999) interprets Porter's findings as follows:

> The proper role of the government should be reinforcing the underlying determinants of national advantage rather than trying to create the advantage itself. It is necessary to note that Porter anticipates a more direct but still partial role for the government in the early stage of development of a country since 'the tools at its disposal, such as capital, subsidies and temporary protection are most powerful at these stages in a nation's competitive development' (p. 4).

The role of government, and by extension the mandate and discretionary power of its civil servants, might hence vary according to the level of economic development of each country. Role adjustments are necessary to help a country move up the developmental ladder as, for instance, has been the case in Singapore since independence in 1965. This in return would imply that a country needs to know how to shift gear, so to speak, and to change policy and governmental behaviour according to levels of economic development. The question might hence be asked what is the right policy mix for what kind of stage of economic development?

Commenting on the differences between general macroeconomic principles pertaining to, for example, the competent application of inflation or monetary policy instruments, Frey (1998) points out that:

> Regional Clusters and well functioning Centers are pre-conditions to ensure the following: international competitiveness; the protection of the natural environment, transport and energy; agriculture and tourism; elimination of regional disparities between the mountainous areas and the cities and between the periphery and the center, sustainable spatial planning and utilization of land. All these issues are incompatible with economic reasoning of the type: 'wonderland of no dimension' (p. 177).

## 1.3    Social Dimension of Economic Competitiveness

There is more to regional competitiveness than the assumed rational economic behaviour of firms and the equally assumed efficient allocation of resources through assumed perfect and transparent market mechanisms as postulated by neo-classical and neo-liberal economic theory. These unsubstantiated claims have been refuted by institutional economics whose economic models offer a more interdisciplinary and holistic picture of human behaviour. Regional development consists of different, at times contradictory and conflictual factors of human behaviour which together create a mix which makes regions so uniquely different from each other.

In recent publications, Porter and Sölvell (1998) offers a more holistic explanation of regional competitiveness. Discussing innovation and sustainable competitive advantage of firms, Porter states: 'While some knowledge is embedded in materials, components, products and machinery, other knowledge is embedded in human capital, part of which is tacit' (p. 447).

Expanding on some aspects of his previous work on competitive advantage in the 1980s (Porter, 1985), Porter suggests that:

> clusters are characterised by a specific set of tangible (firms, infrastructure), intangible (knowledge, know-how) and institutional (authorities, legal framework) elements. These elements make up a complex web of *relations* that tie firms, customers, research institutions, schools and local authorities to each other. The interaction between economic, sociocultural, political and institutional actors in a given location triggers learning and enhances the ability of actors to modify their behavior and find new solutions in response to competitive changes (Porter, 1990: 443, emphasis added).

With this more complete multifactor and multidisciplinary point of view, Porter joins the existing school of institutional economists and sociologists and political scientists who have been studying the non-economic factors of regional competitiveness for quite some time and who see, for example, the emergence of new industries from the framework of a social system (Van de Ven and Garud, 1988), and from the perspective of social capital theory (Hollingsworth and Boyer, 1997; Putnam, 1993; 2000).

Van de Ven and Garud (1988, 1993) define the industrial social system as a structure that contains three key components, namely institutional, resource endowments and instrumental subsystems. These three subsystems interact in reciprocal relations, depending on an industry's conditions and development.

In particular, when looking at the non-economic contribution of a social system to competitiveness, Van de Ven and Garud (1988) suggest a framework based on the accumulation theory of change applied in the study of the social system. This framework allows the study of the process of industry emergence, as well as the role individual firms may play in this process, from a social system perspective. Putnam (1993, 2000) further elaborated on the theory of social capital by drawing a distinctive line between social and human capital. He argues that human capital relates to inherent properties of the individual, whilst social capital refers to the linkages among these individuals that create social networks. A critical distinction exists between 'bonding' social capital – connections with others 'like us' – and 'bridging' social capital connections with those 'not like us' (Gittell and Vidal, 1998). Far from mutually exclusive, bonding and bridging ties often interact to support the healthy function of a social system (Putnam, 2000).

If we link these contributions to Porter and Sölvell's (1998) more recent conceptualization, it becomes evident that developing social capital, be it at an individual, firm or industry level, is instrumental to the competitiveness and economic development of a firm, industry, region or nation.

## 1.4 Regional Competitiveness Cluster

Summarizing the results of a cross-regional survey covering 20 regions in Europe and North America, Koellreuter (1997) identified 50 factors, which have an influence on a region's economic advantage. The most decisive factors are listed in Table 7.1.

Many of the factors listed in Koellreuter's table fall into the sphere of responsibility of the respective regional government (development of highly skilled labour force, efficient tax system and issuing of permits and so on). Creating the right mix of efficient economic factor conditions, effective (consistent and predictable) regulatory framework, transparent and efficient administrative services, and high quality social and cultural institutions and services all combined obviously constitutes the right ingredients for a truly competitive region.

The table is even more significant in light of globalization. Foreign companies investing in other regions of the world make investment decisions based on most of the factors listed in Table 7.1. In other words, the ability of respective governments to design and sustain an appropriate policy environment is crucial. Equally crucial is the ability of the civil servants to apply the rules in a transparent, non-discriminatory manner to local as well as foreign investors. All this results in an increase of challenges to a region's government and civil servants, who have to honour the increasingly global requirements of good governance, meaning transparency, accessibility, non-discrimination, customer orientation and predictability. Without these requirements, foreign direct investment will go to more

*Table 7.1*   *Factors with the most decisive influence on comparative*
*advantages of a region with a future*

| Ranking | Factors |
| --- | --- |
| 1 | Availability of highly skilled labour |
| 2 | Price/performance of highly skilled labour |
| 3 | Permits (legislation, processing) |
| 4 | Corporate tax system |
| 5 | Price/performance of skilled labour |
| 6 | Availability of skilled labour |
| 7 | Work permits of transnational labour |
| 8 | Telecommunication |
| 9 | Quality of life |
| 10 | Access to EEA (EU) market |
| 10 | Working hours |
| 11 | Predictability of the politico-legal environment |
| ⋮ | ⋮ |
| 24 | Energy supply |
| 25 | Price/performance of unskilled labour |

promising pastures and local investors might 'vote with their feet' and invest elsewhere.

## 1.5   Competitive Advantage and Transborder Regional Development

From a European integration perspective, it would be useful to add to the existing literature on competitiveness of national regions a new focus on the specificities of transborder regional competitiveness. Since existing insights on competitiveness of national regions are mostly nation-specific, they are not directly transferable to the complexities of transborder cooperation and integration in the larger EU context. Hence, the discussion on competitiveness needs to be broadened in order to tackle the inter-cultural and inter-institutional aspects of transborder regional integration.

Data covering transborder regional cooperation in Europe are either scarce, incomplete or non-existent. A most useful comparative source of information on regional comparative data covering most of Europe and North America is the International Benchmark Report published annually by the BAK research group in Basle since 1998.

Collecting information concerning transborder regions (for example, the Upper Rhine Valley) has been difficult because cross-border data is not easily comparable and hence cannot easily be aggregated due to different practices of national statistical data processing. Lack of regional aggregate data, such as transborder investment flows, cross-border joint ventures and ownership patterns or comparative cross-border migration flows, makes it impossible to apply Porter's diamond concept as a means to assess competitiveness of a given European transborder region.

A second source of information which provides very illustrative insights on the importance of cross-border initiatives in the context of regional development is the Economic Reconstruction and Development in South East Europe (ERDSEE), a programme under the auspices of two joint institutions (European Commission and World Bank) and several donor institutions (European Investment Bank, European Bank for Reconstruction and Development, and so on). Among the many efforts of the ERDSEE, there are several infrastructural programmes (World Bank, 2001) and environmental projects (European Commission, 2000) destined to support economic growth and regional integration, as well as cross-border projects which focus on the promotion of networks and exchanges among the South-Eastern Europe (SEE) countries.

It is important to stress that economic development is not the only focal point of all these efforts. There is also a strong emphasis on the importance of developing social capital as a pre-condition for regional and transborder development. For example, the infrastructure programmes define from the outset that '*Building large infrastructure without* sound policies and institutions for private sector development and *social cohesion and inclusion, means wasting large amounts of resources without achieving* the objective of sustainable *economic growth and prosperity* for the region' (World Bank, 2001, emphasis added).

The current efforts demonstrate the recognition that regional development in a politically and religiously fragmented region cannot solely be achieved through economic conditioning. It needs to be streamlined with the improvement of social cohesion and social capital, if sustainable economic competitiveness at transborder and regional level is sought.

## 2 CASE STUDY OF A TRANSBORDER REGION: UPPER RHINE VALLEY

Making use of a concrete example of a transborder region, challenges will be described and analysed which local businessmen, government officials and social society representatives have to face when they attempt to create transborder competitiveness. The case in point is the Upper Rhine Valley region consisting of adjacent sub-regions from Switzerland (Province of Basle), France (Province of Alsace) and Germany (Province of Baden and Southern Palatine).

Transborder cooperation in the Upper Rhine Valley has been in existence for centuries, and movement of goods and people across the three borders was very common practice dating back to the late Middle Ages. In addition, parts of this transborder region have been politically connected in the past, and economic exchanges have only been restricted during the last two World Wars when the German and French provinces were drawn into war which opposed France and Germany and left Switzerland in an isolated position of neutrality. Today, the transborder cooperation has been formalized within the framework of a tri-national convention and organization called Conférence du Rhin Supérieur (CRS) which was established in 1975 by the respective three country governments (France, Germany and Switzerland) as depicted in Figure 7.2.

The territorial dimension of the CRS is 21 500 km$^2$ of which 38.5 per cent is French (Alsace), 44.8 per cent German (Baden and Southern Palatine),

*Source:*   EURES – Rhin Supérieur, Strasbourg (2005).

*Figure 7.2   Tri-national Upper Rhine region*

and 16.7 per cent Swiss (Basle and Northwest Switzerland). The total population in 2003 amounted to 5.813 million people who live and work in one of Europe's most densely populated territorial regions. The CRS transborder region has four main universities (Basle, Freiburg, Strasbourg and Karlsruhe), several world-known multinational companies (such as Novartis, Hofmann-LaRoche, UBS, Schlumberger SA) and houses the seat of the Council of Europe, the EU Parliament, European Court of Human Rights and Eurocorps (Strasbourg). The estimated per capita GNP for 2005 as compared to 1998 showed the following progression: namely, 25 800 (22 500) euros for Alsace province, 36 600 (30 900) euros for Basle and Northwest Switzerland province, 29 300 (26 300) euros for the province of Baden, and 23 100 (19 100) euros for the Province of Southern Palatine (see Figure 7.3).

Many inhabitants of the transborder region speak or understand Allemanisch, a German dialect spoken around the Upper Rhine Valley region. The common roots in terms of language and history made it easier for people to move across the border and 94 000 persons do cross the respective three borders both ways every day on the way to work (see Figure 7.4).

Due to a mix of economic development and historical openness to immigration, all three parts of the tri-national region show relatively high levels of foreign populations living in the three cross-border regions with Basle city showing the highest percentage of foreigners living within its territory (see Figure 7.5).

While all three subregions benefit from historical and linguistic common roots, the situation is not as simple as it might sound on first sight. Due to mandatory and exclusive use of French in the Alsatian province, French has become the preferred language of many Alsatians living in larger urban agglomerations like Strasbourg, Mulhouse or Colmar. Also, with

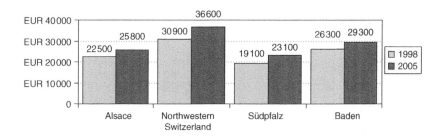

*Source:*   *Rhin Supérieur: Faits et chiffres*, No. 8, Strasbourg (2008).

*Figure 7.3   GDP per capita in 1998 and 2005*

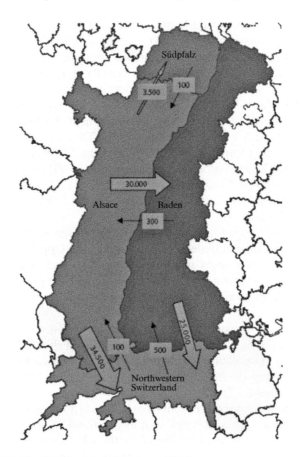

*Source:*    EURES – Rhin Supérieur, Strasbourg (2005).

*Figure 7.4    Daily cross-border movement of workforce*

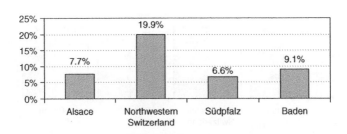

*Source:    Rhin Supérieur: Faits et chiffres*, No. 8, Strasbourg (2008).

*Figure 7.5    Foreigners living in region*

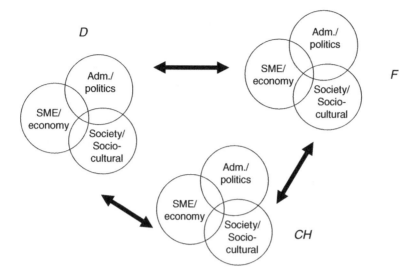

*Figure 7.6    Reality of transborder cooperation for local enterprises*

regard to the official language to be used for legal, political and contractual transactions, French and German are the two official and mandatory languages.

## 2.1   Complexity of Cross-border Cooperation

Cross-border regional cooperation between companies, governments and social society requires the management of more interfaces than is the case within national regions. To take the example of small enterprises of one country conducting business across the two borders, this would imply managing multiple interfaces: namely, dealing with three national administrations (e.g. concerning business licences), three national labour markets (e.g. recruitment of employees) and three national markets (e.g. potential buyers–sellers) (see Figure 7.6).

Taking this example further and imagining a Basle-based enterprise conducting business in Alsace/France and Baden/Germany, the complexity of interfaces would include dealing with German and French national and provincial administrations (e.g. in order to obtain business licences), German and French national and provincial labour organizations (e.g. in order to employ people), French and German local and sometimes national associations (e.g. in order to become a member of a professional organization, religious group or neighbourhood organization). This

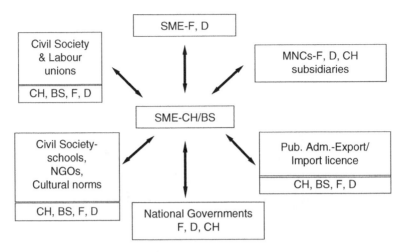

*Figure 7.7   Reality of transborder socio-economic cooperation: managing business and non-business stakeholders*

complexity of multiple interfaces would further increase with a change of personal residence or the opening of companies on the other side of the national borders. Figure 7.7 visualizes some of these interfaces mentioned above.

In addition, the hypothetical Swiss entrepreneur domiciled in Basle would also have to interface with Swiss administration officials (e.g. concerning customs declarations for goods exported or imported into Swiss territory), provincial and national authorities (e.g. federal, cantonal and municipal tax declarations and payments). The interfaces are multiple and to each cross-border interface one has to add the inevitable difficulties that would arise due to difference in national laws, administrative practices, local values and customs, including the mandatory use of the French language if business or administrative transactions involve official exchanges between Alsace and Basle.

The difficulties encountered by this hypothetical Basle entrepreneur illustrate the current limitations to the creation of competitiveness within the CRS transborder region. Transaction costs remain high, administrative obstacles substantial and the influence of the respective three national governments cannot be ignored despite all the official pronouncements of pan-European integration. All these could make it prohibitive for small to medium-sized companies to benefit from growth potential of such transborder cooperation.

## 2.2 Need for Additional Boundary Spanners

Realizing the limits of existing cooperation mechanisms, different think-tanks have come up with suggestions regarding how the CRS transborder region could deepen cooperation mechanisms by creating common physical and social infrastructures and by further increasing the existing, albeit still lightweight, cooperation in areas such as education, joint marketing, joint venturing and so on.

Taking into account the existing competitiveness in all three sub-regions with regard to financial resources, highly educated and skilled workforces, world class research institutes and large companies, successful SMEs and established cultural affinities, such efforts at transborder cooperation should succeed, provided the people involved in these cross-border development actions are cultural and professional boundary spanners who can be at home in different professional and cultural milieux, thus being instrumental in fostering bonding and bridging social capital for transborder cooperation.

The need for boundary spanners becomes clear when one considers the actions which have been proposed to create a CRS Technology Valley. Detailed proposals have been tabled to strengthen economic integration across the three national borders. However, as long as the three borders with their separate legal and administrative realities exist it will be difficult to see either full economic integration or leveraging of the potential synergy from combined resources and competitive advantages.

What follows is a selected list of the economic initiatives, which have been proposed by CRS planners. Specifically, six of the 22 proposals are identified here to illustrate the competencies needed to meet these challenges.

### Unbundling the existing proposals from a social capital perspective

The six initiatives have been grouped into three categories according to the presumed role competencies required of the experts who might be selected to implement some of them in the near future (Table 7.2). The three boundary-spanning roles are: a) Business Diplomat (Saner et al., 2000); b) Entrepreneurial Politician (Saner, 2001); and c) Cultural Ambassador (Bassand and Hainard, 1985).

The three roles suggested above should be seen as competencies which would complement or expand the expertise of traditional actors. They are entrepreneurs, government officials and politicians and representatives of civil society and cultural institutions. Together, they form the team to accumulate the social capital in support of the CRS regional development strategy.

Figure 7.8 highlights the complementary social roles as discussed above,

*Table 7.2    Transborder initiatives and role competencies requirements*

| Proposed transborder initiatives | Suggested competencies required of experts |
| --- | --- |
| A. | Business Diplomats |
| Promote regional economic market structures and networks.<br>Develop inter-municipal energy grids and telecommunication services (groupings of municipalities as 'market partners'). | Ability to develop and discuss business plans with business partners and non-business stakeholders (e.g. communes, schools, associations), understanding different national laws and practices governing employment, creation of companies and foundations, being familiar with different national management and leadership styles dominant in French, German and Swiss businesses. |
| B. | Entrepreneurial Politicians |
| Put in place legal and financial inter-municipal structures in order to better respond to entrepreneurial needs.<br>Establish the coordination mechanism and/or define specializations once the location of sites on the Upper Rhine Valley have been attributed.<br>Establish collaboration among the training and research centres and between them and the enterprises of the region. | Ability to initiate projects spanning German, Swiss and French legal and administrative laws, creating efficient cross-border administrative procedures, involving private and public sector actors to create new ventures, knowing how to mobilize financing for cross-border physical and social infrastructure projects. |
| C. | Cultural Ambassadors |
| Develop the project titled ' Cultural roadmap of the region'.<br>Create a joint offer for the regional tourism sector.<br>Develop an administration which can manage the transborder region in a competent and effective manner. | Ability to appreciate German, French and Swiss contemporary and classical art and culture, creating cultural events offering participation and benefits to existing cultural institutions of all three sub-regions, understanding processes of budgeting and approval of new initiatives in the domain of culture and tourism in all three sub-regions and respective national governments. |

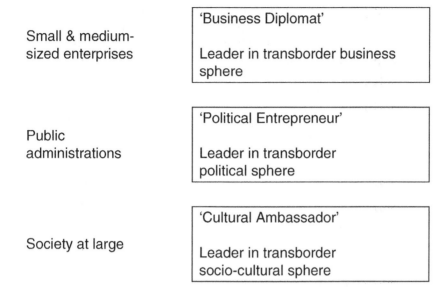

*Figure 7.8   The transborder social roles and corresponding linkages to main domain of activities and constituencies*

namely the Business Diplomat, the Entrepreneurial Politician and the Cultural Ambassador.

## 3   CONCLUSION

The goal of this chapter was to describe the importance of social entrepreneurship for sustainable cross-border business cooperation in the European region. Successful transborder cooperation requires an expanding social role repertoire of the entrepreneurs, politicians and community leaders who play a leading role in the respective transborder region.

Creating competitiveness for transborder regions requires different inputs and personal competencies than in the case for regional development at national level. This is partially due to the fact that the number of cross-border interfaces is greater and partially because specific competencies are needed to manage these inter-cultural (administrative, entrepreneurial, individual) interfaces (Gmür and Rakotobarison, 1997). Specific competencies would include for instance:

1.   foreign language proficiency (for example, French and German for the CRS region)

2. 'global-regional' mindset and a natural curiosity which enables the transborder actor to remain open for continuous learning
3. basic knowledge regarding administrative law and regulations of all three member countries
4. basic knowledge regarding policy-making procedures and framework in all three member countries
5. cross-culturally effective negotiation and communication skills
6. skills in leading and working with temporary and project task teams from one, two or all three member countries
7. networking skills suitable for different cultural contexts.

Transborder regional development requires political will, business acumen and, most importantly, the bridging roles of the Business Diplomat, Political Entrepreneur and Cultural Ambassador. These social, economic and political actors could span the social and institutional boundaries and generate social capitals to support new business development and regional dynamism.

Future research will help identify differences in achieving competitiveness in different transborder regions of Europe. It will also help deepen the understanding of the formation of bridging and bonding social capitals required for different transborder regions of Europe. It is further hypothesized that knowing more about how to create transborder competitiveness will further strengthen European competitiveness and strengthen the process of European integration. Insights gained through further research in the European region concerning the integrative dynamics and social capital formation might also be useful for sustainable transborder cooperation in other parts of the world.

## REFERENCES

Agence de Développement et d'urbanisme de l'agglomération Strasbourgeoise (ADEUS) (1999), *Lire et construire l'espace du Rhin Supérieur. Atlas transfrontalier pour aménager un territoire commun*, 99/48 PLA. Strasbourg: ADEUS.
Arnott, R. (1996), *Regional and Urban Economics*, Amsterdam: Harwood Academic Publishers.
BAK Kulturforschung (1998), *International Benchmark Report*, No. 1/1998, Basel: BAK Basel Economics.
Bassand, M. and F. Hainard (1985), *Dynamique socio-culturelle régionale*, Lausanne: Presses Polytechniques Romandes.
Borner, S., M. Porter, B. Weder and M. Enright (1991), *Internationale Wettbewerbsvorteile: ein strategisches Konzept für die Schweiz*, Frankfurt, Zurich: Campus Verlag.
Conférence du Rhin Supérieur (CRS) (2002), *Donnés statistiques 2002*, Conférence de Rhin Supérior, Strasbourg: Conférence Franco-Germano-Suisse du Rhin Supérieur.
European Commission (2000), 'Regional environmental reconstruction program. Cross

border projects: promotion of networks and exchanges in the countries of South Eastern Europe', Regional Funding Conference, 29–30 March, Brussels: European Commission.

Frey, R.L. (1998), 'Räumliche Ökonomie', in A. Brunetti, P. Kugler and S. Schaltegger (eds), *Economics Today: Konsens und Kontroverse in der modernen Ökonomie*, Zurich: Verlag Neue Zürcher Zeitung (NZZ), pp. 177–92.

Gittell, R. and A. Vidal (1998), *Community Organizing: Building Social Capital as a Development Strategy*, Thousand Oaks, CA: Sage.

Gmür, M. and A. Rakotobarison (1997), 'Organisationslehre in Deutschland und Frankreich', *Organisations Wissen*, 5, Glattbrugg: Gesellschaft für Organisation.

Grootaert, C. and T. van Bastelaer (eds) (2002a), *Understanding and Measuring Social Capital: A Multidisciplinary Tool for Practitioners*, Washington, DC: The World Bank.

Grootaert, C. and T. van Bastelaer (eds) (2002b), *The Role of Social Capital in Development: An Empirical Assessment*, Cambridge, UK: Cambridge University Press.

Hollingsworth, R. and R. Boyer (1997), *Contemporary Capitalism: The Embeddedness of Institutions*, New York: Cambridge University Press.

Koellreuter, C. (1997), 'Increasing globalisation: challenge for the European regions', *Basler Schriften zur Europäischen Integration*, no. 26, pp. 6–27, Basle: Europa Institut, Universität Basel.

Oez, O. (1999), *The Competitive Advantage of Nations: The Case of Turkey*, Aldershot: Ashgate.

Porter, M.E. (1985), *Competitive Advantage: Creating and Sustaining Superior Performance*, New York: The Free Press.

Porter, M.E. (1990), *The Competitive Advantage of Nations*, New York: The Free Press.

Porter, M.E. and O. Sölvell (1998), 'The role of geography in the process of innovation and the sustainable competitive advantage of firms', in A. Chandler, P. Hagström and O. Sölvell (eds), *The Dynamic Firm: The Role of Technology, Strategy, Organization and Regions*, Oxford: Oxford University Press, pp. 440–57.

Putnam, R.D. (1993), *Making Democracy Work. Civic Traditions in Modern Times*, Princeton: Princeton University Press.

Putnam, R.D. (2000), *Bowling Alone. The Collapse and Revival of American Community*, New York: Simon and Schuster.

Saner, R. (2001), 'Globalisation and its impact on leadership qualifications in public administration', *International Review of Administrative Sciences*, **5**(4), 650–61.

Saner, R. and L. Yiu (2000), 'The need for business diplomats, entrepreneurial politicians and cultural ambassadors', in W. Kraus and P. Trappe (eds), *Social Strategies*, Berne: Peter Lang Publishers, pp. 411–28.

Saner, R., L. Yiu and M. Sondegaard (2000), 'Business diplomacy management: a core competency for global companies', *Academy of Management Executive*, **14**(1).

Van de Ven, A. and R. Garud (1988), 'A framework for understanding the emergence of new industries', in R.S. Rosenbloom and R. Burgelman (eds), *Research on Technological Innovation, Management and Policy*, Vol. 4, Greenwich, CT: JAI Press, pp. 195–225.

Van de Ven, A. and R. Garud (1993). 'Innovation and industry development: the case of cochlear implants', in R.S. Rosenbloom and R. Burgelman (eds), *Research on Technological Innovation, Management and Policy*, Vol. 5, Greenwich, CT: JAI Press, pp. 1–46.

Weder, B. (1998), *Economics Today*, Zurich: Verlag Neue Zürcher Zeitung.

World Bank (2001), 'The road to stability and prosperity in South Eastern Europe', a Regional Strategy Paper, Washington, DC: The World Bank.

# 8 The intertwining of social, commercial and public entrepreneurship
*Elisabeth Sundin and Malin Tillmar*

## 1 INTRODUCTION

The strong connection between entrepreneurship and the private sector has resulted in entrepreneurship in other sectors being underestimated (Sundin and Tillmar, 2007). This leads to theoretical, practical and political shortcomings, as entrepreneurship and entrepreneurs are important for the development of society in other ways than through starting businesses, for example through effecting change. Thus, research on social entrepreneurship is vital in order to re-contextualize the phenomenon of entrepreneurship. However, even in this field there are taken-for-granted assumptions which may be challenged. By doing this, our ambition is to contribute methodological and theoretical input to the field of social entrepreneurship studies.

In this chapter we have drawn on Schumpeter (1934 [1994]) and argue that entrepreneurship exists in all kinds of organizations (but not in all organizations) and apply the statement to the social entrepreneurship field. Obviously, there is a 'need to move beyond not-for-profit research' (Anderson and Dees, 2006: 155). As Austin et al. (2006) noted, 'social and commercial entrepreneurship is not dichotomous, but rather more accurately conceptualized as endpoints on a continuum ranging from purely social to purely economic. Even at the extremes, however, there are still elements of both' (p. 3). To this, we would like to add that social entrepreneurship is also to be found in the public sector, in what has been termed 'public entrepreneurship'. Again, as phrased by Austin et al. (2006) 'We define social entrepreneurship as an innovative, social value creating activity that can occur within or across the nonprofit, business, or government sectors' (p. 2). We regard these standpoints as important and ones which must not be overlooked in empirical studies. Although agreeing on the broader definitions, few articles and papers on social entrepreneurship show empirical examples from all sectors (cf. Nicholls and Cho, 2006; Spear, 2006; Townsend and Hart, 2008).

**Aims**

One objective of this chapter is consequently to contribute with empirical cases of social entrepreneurship in the commercial and public sectors. We propose a typology which implies a re-contextualization of social entrepreneurship. This typology is aimed to serve as a methodological as well as theoretical guideline for future research in social entrepreneurship.

**Disposition**

In Section 2 outlines our framework which is grounded in previous studies and literature. Key concepts such as entrepreneurship and social entrepreneurship are defined. The same applies to public and private sectors, profit and non-profit and so on.

Section 3 is then devoted to describing the social entrepreneurship encountered in previous studies, and the relevant contexts.

Conclusions and implications end the chapter in section 4. This is where we outline our proposed typology.

## 2   CONCEPTS AND FRAMEWORK

**Entrepreneurship**

Entrepreneurship is nowadays on both the academic and the political agenda. The political focus is connected to the economic problems of the world economies, with unemployment and environment damage as visible signs of the shortcomings of an economic system dominated by big corporations. Entrepreneurship and small firms seem to be a way back that is also a way forwards. Back to the needs of the customer, back to the responsible individual, back to 'small is beautiful' (the title of a book published in the early 1970s by Schumacher, 1974). The 'classical characteristics' of small firms, or rather small organizations, have undergone a renaissance (Bolton, 1971; Boswell, 1973).

The entrepreneurial research field has seen a tremendous expansion (Landström, 1999) and has diversified along many lines. The trends we will acknowledge here are related to the characteristics and expressions of entrepreneurship and of the entrepreneur. Many debaters start with the writings of Schumpeter, but he is interpreted in different ways. Some, like Gartner (1989), emphasize the creation of new organizations as a sign of entrepreneurship. That justifies the mixing-up of entrepreneurship and SMEs, which is apparent both in international studies such as the Global

Entrepreneurship Monitor and on the national level as in the writings of Wiklund (2006). That the new organizations should be established in the private sector is taken for granted even when it isn't clearly articulated. That entrepreneurship is understood as the same thing as SMEs is appealing to policy-makers. They want entrepreneurship, which in hard to stimulate and measure. Therefore they choose to interpret a large number of SMEs as proof of a high level of entrepreneurship – although this is an interpretation that can be challenged for many reasons.

Another way of defining entrepreneurship, and the one we support, is to emphasize the perception or creation of opportunities, the creation of 'new combinations' and action. This, as Schumpeter says, can take place in any organizational context. Following the rise of entrepreneurship in all spheres, there is also a tendency to view entrepreneurs as the heroes of our time (Ahl, 2004; Sundin, 2002). As argued elsewhere, there is a tendency to ignore entrepreneurship at lower organizational levels (Sundin and Tillmar, 2008) and the everyday nature of entrepreneurship (Hjorth et al., 2008).

The importance of economic gains for the entrepreneur is an argument often emphasized not only in the public debate but also sometimes in research. Some like Venkataraman (1997) who states that the aim of entrepreneurship is 'to create personal wealth' have it as part of the definition. Empirical findings, however, lend weak support to that standpoint. Many studies, made both by researchers and public authorities, show that even if money is there, it is just one among many reasons for entrepreneurial actions (see Cassar, 2007; Davidsson and Honig, 2003; GEM, 2007; NUTEK, 2008). The last point of discussion leads us to the field of social entrepreneurship.

**Social Entrepreneurship**

Social entrepreneurship, just like entrepreneurship, is an expanding field in research. There have been a number of international edited volumes and special issues of journals on the subject (Nicholls, 2006a; Austin et al., 2006; International Society for Third Sector Research conferences). Both local and international agencies, such as the Swedish Knowledge Foundation which funds parts of the research reported here and at EU level, EU Training Excellence for Social Entrepreneurship Sector (www. tse.eu), are funding projects on social entrepreneurship. The background for political interest is to a great extent the same as for interest in entrepreneurship. As noted by Nicholls (2006a), the crisis of the welfare states, both in the western economies and in the former eastern bloc, gives the need for social entrepreneurship an extra dimension.

Much of the literature on social entrepreneurship is about the importance of non-profit organizations and their requirements (Waddock and Post, 1991). Often this concerns financial resources from philanthropic capitalists (Van Slyke and Newman, 2006; Osberg, 2006). Those recognizing social entrepreneurship in all sectors still tend to focus on the private sector (see for example Austin et al., 2006, and Nicholls, 2006c). An example of a subject which is often mentioned could be the choice of organizational form; that is, non-profit or for-profit organizations (Townsend and Hart, 2008; Spear, 2006). As far as we have seen, the public sector as an alternative organizational context for social entrepreneurs is not mentioned. Perhaps this can be explained by the contexts in which the studies are being undertaken. It is our contention that the international literature to date, often unconsciously or at least implicitly, is biased towards Anglo-Saxon contexts. The fact that research into social entrepreneurship is linked to research on social enterprises and stems from an Anglo-American discourse has also been noted by Palmås (2008). Research into 'social economy', however, also has continental European roots, and refers to associations, foundations and other activities in civil society. The social economy and related issues such as the informal economy (Tripp, 1997) and 'the economy of affection' (Hydén, 1983), has long been recognized within development studies. In recent edited volumes and journal articles on the concept of social entrepreneurship there are seldom insights from such contexts.

The definition of social entrepreneurship used here is that 'social entrepreneurship is an innovative, social value creating activity that can occur within or across the nonprofit, business, or government sectors' (Austin et al., 2006: 2). Apart from covering all sectors, this definition also emphasizes the activity component of entrepreneurship. The component *social value* is more problematic, since what may and may not be counted as social value is highly contested (Nicholls and Cho, 2006). The empirical examples given in the entrepreneurship literature are often the 'great men', such as the Nobel prize winner Muhammad Yunus from the micro-finance institution Grameen Bank in Bangladesh. Apart from micro-finance, Nicholls (2006b) refers to global movements within fair trade or renewable energy. As noted in a critical discourse analysis by Parkinson and Howorth (2008), there is also a need to focus on micro-level initiatives and the everyday nature of social entrepreneurship (Steyaert and Katz, 2004). Which activities create social value cannot, however, be known *ex ante*. Thus as the smallest common denominator for social entrepreneurship, we use social intention.

## Sectors: Public, Private For-profit and Private Non-profit

In the political as well as in the academic debate about entrepreneurship and social entrepreneurship, sectors play an important part. Often implicit entrepreneurship is considered to be a prerequisite for the profit part of the private sector and social entrepreneurship to be a prerequisite for the non-profit part of the private sector. The image of the public sector, from the entrepreneurship perspective, is less clear. If anything, in the common entrepreneurship debate the public sector is talked about for what it is *not* rather than for what it is – it is not entrepreneurial either in a conventional sense of the word or in its social version. Rather, the public sector is almost regarded as synonymous with bureaucracy, in the negative meaning of the word in everyday language.

In entrepreneurship studies, public entrepreneurship, however, is a specific sub-field, comprising a number of different approaches (Morris and Jones, 1999). Some of these focus on the 'reinventing government' (Osborne and Gaebler, 1992) perspective, and others focus on privatization and outsourcing, or on politicians and civil servants as entrepreneurs (Zerbinati and Souitaris, 2005).

With regard to the private and public sectors, there is an ongoing debate about whether there are differences between private and public organizations, and if so, what these are and which ones are important (cf. Brunsson and Sahlin-Andersson, 2000; Christensen et al., 2005; Morris and Jones, 1999; Rainey, 2003; Sundin, 2006). Characteristics of the public organizations are that they:

- Do not have a profit motive (but are guided by political and social objectives).
- Receive funds from taxpayers (and allocate them based on equity considerations).
- Produce services that have consequences for people other than the immediate consumers (and are held accountable for such indirect consequences).
- Are subject to public scrutiny, requirements of transparency in decision making and consensus among interest groups.

In practice the differences between the sectors is less clear than in theory (Christensen et al., 2005). The distinction can be made along several dimensions, such as ownership, finance, and service delivery. Thus there is something of a continuum between public organizations and private organizations, in between which there are a number of different hybrid organizational forms. The main reference on this point, Christensen et al.

(2005), are Norwegian researchers mainly using Scandinavia as the empirical ground for their discussion. The construction of the public sector varies from nation to nation, both in quantitative and qualitative dimensions, which are sometimes presented as different welfare regimes (Esping-Andersen, 1996). The differences have consequences for all sectors. The distribution of responsibility for children, for the elderly and other vulnerable groups differs among the welfare regimes. The Swedish daycare system for children could be used as an example. Municipalities, that is the public sector, are obliged to give all children a place at the daycare unit from an early age. In other countries, the public sector does not take that responsibility, so working parents have to find a solution themselves. As a consequence, there could be a real daycare market in these countries as well as a supply of daycare activities from the social sector. The same task – but different solutions.

The Anglo-Saxon expressions 'non-profit' and 'not-for-profit' are often used interchangeably in the social entrepreneurship field. In the USA, non-profits are social purpose organizations with special tax advantages. In the UK, not-for-profit is the common expression for voluntary organizations, cooperatives and charities (Nicholls, 2006a). In Scandinavia the concept 'the third sector' is used for organizations that are neither public nor private for-profit. In none of these contexts are the distinctions clear cut. Social motive, profit-making and distribution of profits are at times mixed as criteria. Here, we will use the term 'non-profit', and contend that there is no clear-cut distinction between non-profit and for-profit, but that it is rather a matter of a continuum.

### Summing Up: Organizational Contexts for Social Entrepreneurship

Thus, based on previous studies on SMEs, public entrepreneurship and social entrepreneurship, it has become our contention that social entrepreneurship is likely to be found in all sectors, and in a variety of organizational contexts. Focusing on only one or two sectors will lead to theoretical shortcomings and a limited understanding of the phenomena. Thus, we start by dividing social entrepreneurs into those operating in the sectors illustrated by Table 8.1.

We wish to highlight once again that the distinction between what is public and what is private is by no means clear-cut, but rather a matter of degree accounting to the welfare regime in question. The same applies to the actual interest in, and need for, profit-making. (The concept of profit is also a matter of discussion, but that would definitely lead us outside the scope of this chapter.)

*Table 8.1    Sectoral contexts for social entrepreneurs*

|            | Public       | Private       |
|------------|--------------|---------------|
| Non-profit | Situation 1  | Well-explored |
|            | Situation 4  |               |
| Profit     | Situation 2  | Situation 3   |

## 3    CASES OF SOCIAL ENTREPRENEURSHIP IN DIFFERENT SECTORS

The next section will be given to illustrating examples of social entrepreneurship in those contexts marked with a number in Table 8.1. Since social entrepreneurship in private non-profit organizations, that is associations, foundations and within families, has been so well explored in the literature, we have chosen not to present any specific example of this situation. Such examples are outside the scope of this chapter. However, that does not make the rest of the discussions in this chapter irrelevant to this context. On the contrary, similar processes seem to be taking place in all sectors.

This section will be structured in accordance with the numbers in Table 8.1, where we go through one situation at a time and give examples of social entrepreneurship in that situation.

### Social Entrepreneurship in Public Sector Non-profit Organizations (1)

Through previous studies of entrepreneurship in the public sector, we, together with our colleagues, have found many examples of social entrepreneurship in the public sector, some of which are portrayed in a Swedish book (Sundin, 2004) and in an international article (Sundin and Tillmar, 2008).

As a case in point, we will refer to a nurse who turned out to be a serial entrepreneur as she sees problems everywhere but also opportunities of how to solve them. And she does not just see – she also acts. When as a young nurse she got her first job, she was surprised by the decision-making processes in the hospital. The time schedules for the employees were decided far away from the patients' bedsides. The planning always started with the needs of the doctors – not with the needs of the patients. The nurse found that unacceptable. From friends and family, she knew that employees in many industries and service units in the private sector made their own timetables. She saw that as a solution and an opportunity to benefit both the patients and the employees at the hospital. For her, thought and action were the same. She started to work towards the implementation of this new system and was met with resistance – from doctors but also from some other groups. And still she succeeded! The system was tested and it is now spread all over the organization.

The entrepreneurial nurse is nowadays well-known in her local community, and other private companies want to recruit her. But she refuses, as she thinks it is most important to change the main provider of healthcare, as that is where most patients are. She is a social entrepreneur who wants to stay within the public sector.

One of the pioneering articles in social entrepreneurship research focused on the care for communities (Johannisson and Nilsson, 1989). Public organizations may also display such social intentions over and above their ordinary tasks. One such example is the creation of the project Close-to-Companies (CtC) (Andersson, 2008a; 2008b) in a middle-sized Swedish town. CtC is an inter-organizational cooperation between the municipality and the regional branch of the state authority, Arbetsförmedlingen. The initiative manifested joint action and the expressed aim was to give support to local industry and commerce in a proactive and innovative way. We argue that the establishment of this organization can be regarded as social entrepreneurship in itself. More about the process and its results can be read in a forthcoming dissertation.

### Social Entrepreneurship in Public Sector Profit-making Organizations (2)

In situation number 2, we will use the example of the unit 'food for the elderly and children' in a Swedish municipality (see Sundin, 2004). The municipality wanted to change along New Public Management lines, meaning that they would invite private providers to compete with their own units to make these more efficient and to cut costs. Every unit was made into a profit-unit, and therefore we can talk about for-profit units in the public sector.

The consumers in this case were children in the municipality schools and the daycare units, and the elderly who were supported by the municipality. A middle-aged woman with health problems working part-time is a typical employee. A new first line manager was recruited mainly to reduce the costs. She interpreted her new position as an opportunity to realize her ideas about the importance of 'good food for the elderly and children'. The entrepreneur argued that it means so much. It makes a change. For the elderly it could be the highlight of the day. For children, the food served could influence their whole lives in many dimensions.

To deliver this 'good food', the entrepreneur had to change both the production and the image of the unit and its employees. The manager saw qualities in the employees. They really knew how to cook. What was wrong with them, she thought, was that they had low self-confidence. The manager presented her visions to the employees. She changed the menus, the way the food was distributed, the clothing of the employees, the feedback system (which before had been non-existent) and the distribution of working hours for the employees. The numbers on sick leave were reduced and production increased. The unit was ranked top on local lists of good food! Despite this successful way of handling the unit, after some years they lost a number of public procurement negotiations. Private firms that kept their costs lower and thus charged lower prices, won the contracts.

This entrepreneur did not mind being on the market, but at times found the competition too challenging. The manager tried many different cost-cutting and price-lowering strategies to handle the situation, both for the sake of the employees and for the elderly and the children. Currently, her view is that the profit unit has reached its lower limit. It is not possible to maintain a sufficient quality at a lower price. Her social intentions and responsibility make her refuse to compromise.

### Social Entrepreneurship in Commercial Companies (3)

Private sector firms are often talked about and thought of in the ways described by Venkataraman (1997), referred to above. The fact that money and financial gains, do not play the role they are argued to play is well documented, while the social dimensions of entrepreneurship are less noticed. However, research on family firms sometimes shows social dimensions and responsibilities (Boissin et al., 2007; Salvato and Melin, 2008). In her paper from 2008, Sundin presents individuals and groups that have established enterprises to fulfil social intentions – not just commercial and individual, and not just restricted to the family – and who manage their enterprises in a social way. Sundin uses the concept 'care' for their social motives. Care for 'what' differs – from care for handicapped youngsters, to care for working class women and a local village. In the first case, a midwife was the social entrepreneur. Through her work, she knew that mentally handicapped young people needed advice and information on matters of sexuality. The need had been there all the time, but no one, before the midwife, had really tried to formulate an idea of how to deal with it. The midwife claimed that the health care units of the public sector should take responsibility for these questions and for these individuals. 'Everyone' found her ideas good and reasonable, but despite that, they were not included in the organizations. The midwife therefore started an enterprise to deliver the services she knew were needed. She did this as she cared for the youngsters and for their parents. In this case, the care dimension was a visible part of the business idea. In other enterprises, the care dimensions have to be hidden for the customers. Consequently, care could be an advantage on the market, but as a rule, it is rather a complication and a restriction.

Another more commonly described example of social entrepreneurship in the private for-profit sector is connected to care for the community (cf. Johannisson and Nilsson, 1989). Research on networks and inter-organizational relationships has explicitly or implicitly covered many such initiatives both in Sweden, in the well-known Gnosjö-region, (Wigren, 2003) and internationally, such as northern Italy, (Piore and Sabel, 1984), and in Silicon Valley (Maillat, 1995). Here we present an example studied by ourselves: the tourism association in Karlshöjden,[1] Sweden (Pettersson, 1999; Tillmar, 2002).

SMEs in the tourism industry in a small rural town in south-eastern Sweden were struggling to make ends meet. Unemployment was a problem in the region, as were conflicts and distrust between 'locals' who had lived in the town generations back, and 'newcomers' who had moved in from larger towns in Sweden. One constraint was a lack of resources for marketing the region on the national and international arena. Thus, a few key actors in the business community applied for EU grants to develop a tourism association comprising the local businesses in the industry. One of their aims was to ensure the survival of a sufficient number of tourism businesses in the community. The application was successful, a university graduate was employed as a project coordinator and the region was marketed in numerous ways. Thus, while the key actors of the association of course also benefited from the marketing, they also improved the situation for the region as such. That is, commercial and social interests went 'hand-in-hand'. As the initiator expressed it: 'I improve for everyone and then I rake in my own share later'.

### Social Entrepreneurship through Inter-organizational Cooperation across Sectoral Borders (4)

Close-to-Companies, presented above, was an inter-organizational coop-eration, and the midwife mentioned earlier moved from the public to the private sector. These examples illustrate organizational processes that also involve social entrepreneurship – not just commercial and public. As a last extreme example of social entrepreneurship processes involving differ-ent sectors, we will present Astrid Lindgrens Värld (the World of Astrid Lindgren) as the organization(s) constructed around the name and the idea include actors from the non-profit, the profit and the public sector (Johannisson and Sundin, forthcoming).

Astrid Lindgren was a Swedish author who wrote world-famous books for children. Pippi Longstocking is one of her characters. Astrid Lindgren was born in Vimmerby, a small town in southern Sweden. More than twenty years ago, just to amuse their own children, three families decided to build small houses from the Lindgren world for the children to play in. The houses were talked about and people came to have a look. The families were encouraged, built some more – and in that way the venture expanded for some years. Finally it was too much for the families. They could no longer manage and invited the municipality to join forces with them. Their success also attracted commercial actors, and over the years different constellations have been in charge – the starters, the municipality, large private for-profit companies, the local bank, third sector organizations such as the Temperance Movement, and the Lindgren family. The actors' very different aspirations could be dealt with through the construction of a new organization both dependent and independent of the key-actors' rules and restrictions. The social intentions have always been a part of the idea. For a short time one of the commercial actors tended not to work in accordance with the social norms and restrictions. After that the rules and restrictions, which had previously been informal, were put down on paper to prevent anything like that from happening again. The social intentions should be protected. The initiative to formalize these restrictions came from the Lindgren family, who in this case are the protectors of social entrepreneurship just as in some of the cases presented by Johannisson and Nilsson (1989).

## DISCUSSION AND CONCLUSION

The cases presented above illustrate not only that there are social entrepreneurs across the public/private and profit/non-profit dimensions, but they also show the blurred borders between the public and the private and how social entrepreneurship works to transcend these borders. In particular situation 4 showns that social entrepreneurship may also take place not only within, but also between, organizations. In organization theory, processes are commonly divided into those taking place within organizations (that is intra-organizational processes) and those taking place in inter-organizational relationships (IOR). The latter, in fact, constitutes a research field of its own. Also, entrepreneurship within established organizations (intrapreneurship) (Pinchot, 1985) and corporate entrepreneurship (Burgelman, 1983) have long been discussed. Studies of

*Table 8.2    Typology of social entrepreneurship: examples presented*

|  |  | Public sector | | Private sector | |
|---|---|---|---|---|---|
|  |  | Profit | Non-profit | Profit | Non-profit |
| Intra-organizational |  | Good food in the municipality | The entrepreneurial nurse | Advice for handicapped youngsters | – |
| Inter-organizational | Intra-sector | – | CtC | Tourism association | – |
|  | Inter-sector | The Astrid Lindgren World | | | |

inter-organizational entrepreneurship are, however, more rare. In situation 3, the tourism association in Karlshöjden, the inter-organizational cooperation is within the private for-profit sector. The World of Astrid Lindgren illustrates that social entrepreneurship may also be inter-sector, creating activities in cooperation between the public non-profit sector and the private for-profit sector. Thus, we wish to conclude by outlining a new typology of organizational and sector contexts for social entrepreneurship. In the Table 8.2 we have also placed each of the cases presented in its category.

Thus, we may conclude by challenging the questions posed by Austin et al. (2006), 'Social and commercial entrepreneurship: same, different or both?'. We argue that it is in fact the wrong question. Social, commercial and public entrepreneurship may not be distinguishable in that sense. The same people are often both social and commercial, both public and social, and can involve all three kinds of entrepreneurship simultaneously. Not only does entrepreneurship in general but also social entrepreneurship transcend both organizational and sectoral borders.

**Implications for Research**

The implications for future research are obvious. That is, we argue that the selection of cases and/or respondents should be a very conscious one. In particular, the social entrepreneurship that transcends organizational and sector borders is an interesting issue for further study. Perhaps social entrepreneurship studies would benefit from insights generated within the field of IOR.

The findings make us demand research with open empirical minds as well as openness towards new theoretical mixtures and constructions. Just like the entrepreneurial actors 'out there', we have to try new solutions and perspectives to elaborate knowledge and understanding and transform it adequately so the political decision-makers avoid making mistakes in their important work of making our societies welcoming and of supporting the positive (or productive in Baumol's terms) entrepreneurship. Because there is also destructive and 'necessity-driven' entrepreneurship – but that is another story.

As a final comment, we also wish to note that the insights presented here are consequences of (often longitudinal) case studies. Case study designs are likely to be especially fruitful to uncover complex patterns of entrepreneurial processes in intra- and inter-organizational contexts in intertwined sectors of the modern economy.

## ACKNOWLEDGEMENT

This research has been funded by Vinnova through the HELIX Vinn Excellence Centre at Linköping University, by the knowledge foundation through the OSIS (Organising Social Initiatives in Sweden) programme, and by the Swedish Council for Working Life and Social Research.

## NOTE

1. The name of the town is fictitious.

## REFERENCES

Ahl, H.J. (2004), *The Scientific Reproduction of Gender Inequality: A Discourse Analysis of Research Texts on Women's Entrepreneurship*, Stockholm: Liber.
Anderson, B.B. and J.G. Dees (2006), 'Rhetoric, reality, and research: building a solid foundation for the practice of social entrepreneurship', in A. Nicholls (ed.), *Social Entrepreneurship, New Models of Sustainable Social Change*, New York: Oxford University Press.
Andersson, L. (2008a), 'Interprenörskap – Ett FöretagsNära Entreprenörskap i det Offentligas Regi', in A. Lundström and E. Sundin (eds), *Perspektiv på Förnyelse och Entreprenörskap i Offentlig Verksamhet*, Örebro: FSF.
Andersson, L. (2008b), 'Hybrid aspects in a public collaboration project: a sensemaking approach to understanding hybridization', Linköping University, Sweden, paper presented at 2nd Latin American European Meeting on Organization Studies Colloquium: Rio de Janeiro, Brazil.
Austin, J., H. Stevenson and J. Wei-Skillern (2006), 'Social and commercial entrepreneurship: same, different, or both?', *Entrepreneurship: Theory & Practice*, **30**(1), 1–22.
Boissin, J.-P., J.-C. Castagnos and A. Fayolle (2007), 'Family business and social responsibility

of the managing director: a French case study', *International Journal of Entrepreneurship and Small Business*, **4**(4).

Bolton, J.E. (1971), 'Bolton Report: Report of the Committee of Enquiry on Small Firms', London: HMSO.

Boswell, J. (1973), *The Rise and Decline of Small Firms*, London: Allen & Unwin.

Brunsson, N. and K. Sahlin-Andersson (2000), 'Constructing organizations: the example of public sector reform', *Organization Studies*, **21**(4), 721–46.

Burgelman, R.A. (1983), 'Corporate entrepreneurship and strategic management: insights from a process study', *Management Science*, **29**(12), 1349–64.

Cassar, G. (2007), 'Money, money, money? A longitudinal investigation of entrepreneur career reasons, growth preferences and achieved growth', *Entrepreneurship & Regional Development*, **19**(1), 89–107.

Christensen, T., P. Lægreid, P.G. Roness and K.A. Løvik (2005), *Organisationsteori för Offentlig Sektor*, Malmo: Liber.

Davidsson, P. and B. Honig (2003), 'The role of social and human capital among nascent entrepreneurs', *Journal of Business Venturing*, **18**(3), 301–31.

Esping-Andersen, G. (1996), *Welfare States in Transition: National Adaptions in Global Economics*, London: SAGE.

Gartner, W. (1989), 'Who is an entrepreneur? is the wrong question', *Entrepreneurship: Theory & Practice*, **11**(3), 47–68.

Global Entrepreneurship Monitor (GEM) (2007), Wellesley, MA: Babson College.

Hjorth, D., C. Jones and W.B. Gartner (2008), Introduction to 'Recreating/recontextualising entrepreneurship', *Scandinavian Journal of Management*, **24**(2), 81–4.

Hydén, G. (1983), *No Shortcuts to Progress: African Development Management in Perspective*, Los Angeles: University of California Press.

Johannisson, B. and A. Nilsson (1989), 'Community entrepreneurs: networking for local development', *Entrepreneurship & Regional Development*, **1**(1), 3–19.

Johannisson, B. and E. Sundin (forthcoming), 'Astrid Lindgren's World – Enacting Multi-Sectorial Entrepreneurship'.

Landström, H. (1999), *Entreprenörskapets Rötter*, Lund: Studentlitteratur.

Maillat, D. (1995), 'Territorial dynamic, innovative milieus and regional policy', *Entrepreneurship & Regional Development*, **7**, 157–65.

Morris, H.H. and F.F. Jones (1999), 'Entrepreneurship in established organisations: the case of the public sector', *Entrepreneurship: Theory & Practice*, (Fall), 71–91.

Nicholls, A. (2006a), 'Introduction', in A. Nicholls (ed.), *Social Entrepreneurship, New Models of Sustainable Social Change*, New York: Oxford University Press.

Nicholls, A. (2006b), 'Endnote', in A. Nicholls (ed.), *Social Entrepreneurship, New Models of Sustainable Social Change*, New York: Oxford University Press.

Nicholls, A. (2006c), *Social Entrepreneurship, New Models of Sustainable Social Change*, New York: Oxford University Press.

Nicholls, A. and A.H. Cho (2006), 'Social entrepreneurship: the structuration of a field', in A. Nicholls (ed.), *Social Entrepreneurship, New Models of Sustainable Social Change*, New York: Oxford University Press.

NUTEK (2008), *Fakta och statistik. Motiv för företagsstarter* (*Facts and Statistics. Motives for Establishing an Enterprise*), Swedish Agency for Economic and Regional Growth.

Osberg, S. (2006), 'Wayfinding without a compass: philanthropy's changing landscape and its implications for social entrepreneurship', in A. Nicholls (ed.), *Social Entrepreneurship, New Models of Sustainable Social Change*, New York: Oxford University Press.

Osborne, D. and T. Gaebler (1992), *Reinventing Government: How the Entrepreneurial Spirit is Transforming the Public Sector*, New York: William Patrick.

Palmås, K. (2008), 'Social entreprenörskap: Ny sector eller rebranding av ideellt arbete?', in A. Lundström and E. Sundin (eds), *Perspektiv på förnyelse och entreprenörskap i offentlig verksamhet*, Örebro: FSF.

Parkinson, C. and C. Howorth (2008), 'The language of social entrepreneurs', *Entrepreneurship & Regional Development*, **20**(3), 285–309.

Pettersson, M. (1999), *Förtroende i Samverkan: En Studie av Småföretagare i ett Regionalt Utvecklingsprojekt*, Linköping: Linköpings Universitet.
Pinchot, G. (1985), *Intrapreneuring*, New York: Harper & Row Publishers.
Piore, M. and R. Sabel (1984), *The Second Industrial Divide: Possibilities for Prosperity*, New York: Basic Books.
Rainey, H.G. (2003), *Understanding & Managing Public Organizations*, San Fransisco, CA: Jossey-Bass.
Salvato, C. and L. Melin (2008), 'Creating value across generations in family-controlled businesses: the role of family social capital', *Family Business Review*, 21(3).
Schumacher, E.F. (1974), *Small is Beautiful: A Study of Economics as if People Mattered*, London: Sphere.
Schumpeter J.A. (1934 [1994]), 'The theory of economic development', in R. Swedberg (ed.), *Om Skapande Förstörelse och Entreprenörskap: I urval av Richard Swedberg*, City University: Press Ratioklassiker.
Spear, R. (2006), 'Social entrepreneurship: a different model?', *International Journal of Social Economics*, 33(5/6), 399–410.
Steyaert, C. and J. Katz (2004), 'Reclaiming the space of entrepreneurship in society: geographical, discursive and social dimensions', *Entrepreneurship & Regional Development*, 16(May), 179–96.
Sundin, E. (2002), 'Företagandets manliga prägling: orsaker och konsekvenser', in C. Holmquist and E. Sundin (eds), *Företagerskan: Om Kvinnor och Entreprenörskap*, Stockholm: SNS Förlag.
Sundin, E. (2004), *Den Offentliga Sektorns Entreprenörer: En Porträttbok*, Stockholm: Kommentus.
Sundin, E. (2006), Företagsekonomiska styridéer och offentlig sektor', *Nordiske Organisasjons-Studier*, 1, 57–79.
Sundin, E. and M. Tillmar (2007), 'Organizational entrepreneurs in the public sectors – social capital and gender', in I. Aaltio, P. Kyrö and E. Sundin (eds), *Women Entrepreneurship and Social Capital: A Dialogue and Construction*, Copenhagen: Copenhagen Business School Press DK.
Sundin, E. and M. Tillmar (2008), 'A nurse and a civil servant changing institutions: entrepreneurial processes in different public sector organizations', *Scandinavian Journal of Management*, 24, 113–24.
Tillmar, M. (2002), 'Swedish tribalism and tanzanian agency: preconditions for trust and cooperation in a small-business context', dissertation, Linköping: Linköping University.
Townsend, D.M. and T.A. Hart (2008), 'Perceived institutional ambiguity and the choice of organizational form and social entrepreneurial ventures', *Entrepreneurship: Theory & Practice*, (July), 685–700.
Tripp, A.-M. (1997), *Changing the Rules: The Politics of Liberalization and the Urban Informal Economy in Tanzania*, Los Angeles: University of California Press.
Van Slyke, D.M. and H.K. Newman (2006), 'Venture philanthropy and social entrepreneurship in community redevelopment', *Nonprofit Management & Leadership*, 16(3), 345–68.
Venkataraman, S. (1997), 'The distinctive domain of entrepreneurship research', in J. Katz and E. Brockhaus (eds), *Advances in Entrepreneurship, Firm Emergence, and Growth*, Greenwich, CT: JAI Press, pp. 119–38.
Waddock, S.A. and J.E. Post (1991), 'Social entrepreneurs and catalytic change', *Public Administration Review*, 51(5), 393–401.
Wigren, C. (2003), 'The spirit of Gnosjö: the grand narrative and beyond', dissertation, Jönköping: Jönköping International Business School.
Wiklund, J. (2006), 'Commentary: family firms and social responsibility: preliminary evidence from the S & P 500', *Entrepreneurship: Theory & Practice*, November, 803–8.
Zerbinati, S. and V. Souitaris (2005), 'Entrepreneurship in the public sector: a framework of analysis in European local governments', *Entrepreneurship & Regional Development*, 17, 43–64.

# 9 The promise of social franchising as a model to achieve social goals
## Thierry Volery and Valerie Hackl

Social entrepreneurship implies a blurring of sector boundaries. In addition to innovative not-for-profit ventures, social entrepreneurship can include social purpose business ventures, such as for-profit community development banks, and hybrid organizations mixing not-for-profit and for-profit elements (Dees, 1998). Despite this broad playing field, it is generally agreed that the central driver for social entrepreneurship is the social problem being addressed, and the particular organizational form a social enterprise takes should be a decision based on which format most effectively mobilizes the resources needed to address that problem (Austin et al., 2006). Social entrepreneurs, therefore, look for the most effective methods of serving their social missions.

One of the main challenges for social entrepreneurs has been to scale up their venture. Although these entrepreneurs may have a clear understanding of the needs in a given community and be able to raise the necessary capital to start a social venture, they are frequently unable to develop or scale up the service delivery, marketing and accountability challenges that all small businesses face (Zahra et al., 2008). Consequently, the impact of social entrepreneurs is usually limited to a specific region and there is a growing interest in business models which could help extending initiatives to further locations and let more people benefit from the products and services.

Franchising can represent an effective approach to mastering the complexities to replicate a proven concept. It not only promises to help address the question of how to provide innovative entrepreneurs with the structure and support necessary to convert their interest in social enterprises into sustainable businesses, but it also provides a roadmap for implementing these ventures. Social franchising is an adaptation of commercial franchising in which the developer of a successful social concept (franchisor) enables others (franchisees) to replicate the model using a proven system and a brand name to achieve a social benefit. Social franchising can be defined as a system of contractual relationships, which uses the structure of a commercial franchise to achieve social goals (Tracey and Jarvis, 2007). As such, it is a new institutional arrangement in the field of social entrepreneurship and it represents a promising leverage tool to achieve social goals.

The goal of this chapter is to outline the potential of social franchising as an organizational form to grow social ventures. Specifically, we examine the relevance of two main theories – agency theory and social capital theory – for social franchising. This leads to a description of the data collection and analysis procedure. Following an account of a multiple case study, we then consider the structure and coordination features of social franchising and distinguish them from commercial franchises.

# 1   THEORETICAL FRAMEWORK

Commercial franchising is essentially a long-term contractual relationship, where one party, the franchisor, provides a business concept to one or more other parties, the franchisees, who in return agree to pay a franchise fee. The franchisor is generally obliged to continuously refine the concept, provide training to the franchisees and arrange a consistent marketing presence. The franchisees usually are responsible for delivering performance reports and market information to the franchisor, and for handling all customer business (Skaupy, 1995).

Social franchising, however, differs greatly from traditional franchising structures in several ways. The first difference pertains to the underlying mission (social vs. profit), which in turn may lead to different types of franchise concepts (social vs. business programme) and different types of target groups (beneficiaries vs. customers). Second, the franchise units involved in social franchising vary from their commercial counterparts (for example, social enterprises vs. individual business people) (Ahlert et al., 2008). Third, the actors engaged in social franchising usually adhere to different values: social entrepreneurs are more concerned with caring and helping than with merely 'making money' (Thompson, 2002).

Three main approaches have been used to explain business format franchising: resource scarcity, social capital theory and agency theory. While the agency and social capital theories have applied widely in the field of franchising, the potential of resource scarcity remains doubtful (Combs et al., 2004). Accordingly, we focus on the agency and social capital perspectives.

## 1.1   Agency Theory

Agency theory is concerned with contractual relationships between a principal (the franchisor) and an agent (the franchisee) where the former delegates a set of tasks to the latter (Ross, 1973). Two assumptions are inherent to the theory and drive complexity in agency relationships (Spremann, 1987). First, external effects arise as the agent's behaviour affects not only its own but also the principal's success. This fact is particularly problematic when it comes to the second assumption of information asymmetries between the principal and his agent. Information asymmetries are caused by a loss of control over intentions and behaviours of the agent, because the principal cannot monitor all actions of the agent. Therefore, agency theory considers economic actors as self-interested and most likely to engage in opportunistic behaviour.

This blend of factors demands coordination mechanisms that enable the principal to exercise a certain level of control over his or her agent. While agency theory considers contracts as the main coordination mechanism to steer actions in a favourable way, it is impossible to specify all future circumstances. The inability to establish complete contracts leads to agency threats, namely adverse selection, moral hazard and hold-up (Carney and Gedajlovic, 1991). The former refers to the risk of selecting actors not well suited to achieving desired outcomes. Moral hazard relates to potential risks when contracting with individuals who withhold effort (shirking) or misappropriate firm resources (free-riding). Hold-up describes risks stemming from unequal bargaining power between cooperation partners due to specific investments.

In the context of franchising, agency theory suggests, 'there is likely to be greater goal divergence between franchisors and hired managers than between franchisors and franchisees' (Garg and Rasheed, 2003: 331). The basic premise of this argument focuses on the variability of the franchisee's compensation with unit performance. Consequently, a franchisee has a dual incentive to maximize sales revenue through effective management and promotion of the franchise concept, while minimizing variable costs. Under a franchising contract, franchisees bear the undiversifiable residual risk tied to their particular units, and therefore, 'the costs and benefits of franchisees' actions that affect the value of their individual units are capitalized onto their own shoulders'. The moral hazard of suboptimal efforts is thus less likely by franchisees than it is by hired managers (Shane, 1996).

Being residual claimants to net proceeds, franchisees have an incentive not to shirk. As a result, the need for monitoring is reduced, as a franchisee's effort is self-enforced. However, the franchisor still maintains some decision rights such as menu selection, building design, and site location. The franchisor has authority to monitor the franchisee for product quality, and franchisee shirking, if detected, could result in the termination of the contract.

## 1.2   Social Capital Theory

Social capital theory is characterized by an interdisciplinary heterogeneity and it has only recently found its way into economics (Adler and Kwon, 2002). Despite its relatively young age, it has been widely adapted in various disciplines, such as sociology, political science, and economics. As suggested by Nahapiet and Ghoshal (1998: 243), social capital is 'the sum of the actual and potential resources embedded within, available through, and derived from the network of relationships possessed by an individual or social unit'.

Social capital can be tackled either from a macro-level or from a micro-level perspective (Lin, 2001). On the macro level, social capital is recognized as a collective good or asset produced by a group of people. This view is called internal perspective, because the relations within social systems are the primary focus of analysis. Social capital can also be tackled from a micro-level perspective when the emphasis is on individuals rather than groups. This view is called external perspective as it deals with individuals as part of a web of relations.

While these two perspectives help in classifying social capital, we would like to draw attention to two dimensions clustering attributes of social capital: the structural and the relational dimension. Both of them are highly interrelated and provide a theoretical basis for the theoretical framework of social franchising.

The structural dimension refers to patterns of relations within a social system or, in other words, 'who you reach and how you reach them' (Burt, 1992). Important aspects of the structural dimension are the access to resources of other members within the social system and the structure of the social network. Some scholars, like Granovetter (1973) and Burt (1992), point to the value of structural holes in networks enabling a bridging function to access resources beyond those available in their own social surroundings. Others, such as Coleman (1990), emphasize the function of closed networks with a high number of ties between the members of a network. Here the bonding function enables the observance of norms and the power of sanction in case of violation.

The relational dimension refers to the substance and quality of social relations. The focus lies on the resources embedded in and activated through relations. These resources include trust, norms and identity. Trust is an actor's expectation of the other party's competence and goodwill and is both a requirement and a result of social relationships (Blomqvist, 1997). A norm can be defined as a rights allocation under which control over a target action is held by actors other than the one who might take the action, and Coleman (1990) stresses the importance of closed networks for the emergence of norms. One norm worthy of special attention is the concept of reciprocity, where one individual is obliged to return someone else's previous favour (Schechler, 2002). Identification can be described as the perception of oneness with or sense of belonging to some human aggregate (Ashforth and Mael, 1989) and plays an important role when it comes to collective networks.

## 1.3 Towards an Integrated Framework

An integrated theoretical framework on social franchising can be built on the agency theory as a traditional franchising approach and on social capital theory as a complementary bundle of constructs. In this section, we suggest that the sound, albeit limited contribution of agency theory be taken as a starting point, and that it be expanded gradually by adding concepts from social capital theory. This approach is based on three premises. First, the traditional view of economic actors as *homo economicus* is inadequate for social franchising. We propose the concept of *homo reciprocans* to characterize the parties involved in social franchising. Second, contractual arrangements must be completed by social concepts such as trust, commitment and identification. Third, social franchises can be described as networks where the social dimensions play a central role.

The concept of '*homo economicus*' has been traditionally employed in economics to describe economic actors characterized by self-interest, rational behaviour, and profit maximization. This view results in a short-run perspective pervasive in agency theory, which forces the rational individual to prioritize actions generating immediate, positive returns (Franz, 2004). This narrow view does not necessarily hold true, especially when dealing with socially engaged individuals where cooperative behaviour is the norm. Therefore, we suggest a departure from *homo economicus* and that the concept of reciprocity be adopted from the social capital theory. This implies that individuals do not only consider short-term objectives, but also rather adopt a longer-term view where rights, obligations and returns will balance out in a more or less distant future. By integrating the concept of reciprocity into *homo economicus*, cooperative behaviour becomes reasonable also from a rational point of view (Adler et al., 2002). This new concept is called *homo reciprocans* and represents the foundation of our framework.

When scholars write about contracts regulating agency relationships they typically refer to explicit contractual documents (Ripperger, 1998). However, legal contracts are incomplete and their value in holding off undesired behaviour is limited (Macaulay, 1963). Regardless of the duration of an exchange, it is practically impossible to specify contractually all dimensions of the exchange. Further, managers are constrained in their capacity to anticipate and contractually resolve all potential future contingencies. As a result, contracts are limited in their effectiveness in maintaining continuity in the relationship.

We therefore point to the importance of social governance systems as a complementary coordination tool. Morgan and Hunt (1994) have argued that trust, commitment and identification are central to any relationship. In the case of social franchising, these encourage franchisors and franchisees to work together to preserve relationship investments and to minimize opportunistic behaviour by resisting attractive short-term alternatives in favour of the expected long-term benefits of staying together. According to Morgan and Hunt (1994: 22), 'when both commitment and trust are present, they produce outcomes that promote efficiency, productivity and effectiveness.' In short, commitment and trust lead to cooperative behaviours that are conducive to relationship, including franchise relationship, success.

In order to generate a holistic view on social franchising it is also necessary to take a closer look at the underlying structure of the franchise. For this, we suggest using the structural perspective of social capital theory. This view considers the social franchise system as a network consisting of franchisees at the network intersections as do strategic network scholars looking at traditional franchise networks (Sydow, 1998). Most likely the system follows an egocentric structure with the franchisor positioned in the centre. Various aspects of the network dimensions can be considered to describe the franchise. This includes the density of the network as an indicator of the quality of internal relations, as well as the strategic positioning of franchise actors indicating key actors within the system. Similarly, the concept of 'structural holes' as proposed by Granovetter (1983) and Burt (1992) reflects the effect of the relationship between the franchise partners in gaining access to local networks and resources of the franchisee (that is, bridging function).

## 2 METHOD

A case study approach was adopted to collect data. A case study is considered an appropriate strategy for answering research questions that ask 'how' and 'why', and that do not require control over events (Robson, 1993) because such questions deal with operational links that need to be traced over time, rather than mere frequencies or incidence. By using a case study approach, the reasons why particular decisions were made, how they were implemented and results obtained can be identified and understood.

This research method is ideal to investigate the social franchise phenomenon. On the one hand, scant research has been conducted in this field to date. On the other hand, the specific questions about the steering mechanisms and structural features of the franchise system call for a method that provides a rich and holistic analysis, which is extremely useful in revealing complexity and dynamism. Moreover, a quantitative evaluation can hardly be imagined if we consider the small number of existing social franchises.

The exploratory case study seeks to find out what is really happening, to scale new heights, to ask new questions and to assess phenomena in a new light (Robson, 1993). Consequently, we focus on current events and concerns and seek to answer questions of how and why. Yin (2003) favours exploratory case studies only when available research or the existing knowledge base is poor, as in the field of social franchising.

This present study was designed as a multiple-case study comprising three specially selected social franchises (Dialogue in the Dark, Science-Lab and VisionSpring). The data were collected from two different sources – documents and interviews – to provide triangulation. Documents included franchise agreements, online materials, newspaper clippings and magazine articles. In addition, we conducted a series of semi-structured interviews with the franchisor and at least one franchisee in each franchise system. We also interviewed employees in key positions if this was desirable. A total of 11 interviews were conducted.

We adopted the following techniques suggested by Eisenhardt (1989) to analyse the data: (1) analysing within case data; (2) searching for cross-case patterns; (3) enfolding literature; and (4) reaching closure. The case analysis is based on classic content analysis but does not require data to be quantified. To begin with, a system of categories was developed based on a theoretical treatment of the data (theoretically deductive). In a second phase, this category system was complemented with results from the field under investigation (empirically inductive).

## 3 DESCRIPTION OF THE THREE CASES

### 3.1 Dialogue in the Dark

Dialogue in the Dark was established by Andreas Heinecke in Hamburg, Germany, in 1988. The organization aims to 'promote social creativity and new opportunities to raise social awareness about issues of old age, troubled youth, the poor, the unemployed, and the conditions of differently-abled people'. The social venture organizes exhibitions in which blind people lead sighted people through darkened rooms, thus providing them with an idea of their own dark world. Visitors, who are merely armed with sticks, are led by blind people in small groups through varying everyday situations such as a park or streets. Besides guiding groups of visitors, blind people, partially sighted people and people with other disabilities largely manage the exhibition locations themselves.

The programme thus pursues two objectives: on the one hand, it makes sighted people sensitive to and understanding of the special needs and challenges of blind people, and provides them with an educational experience that transcends typical stereotypes. On the other hand, blind people are given meaningful employment and training opportunities that will facilitate their return to a working environment in private industry.

The revenue model is based on admission fees (between €9 and €16 per visitor) and additional takings from affiliated cafés and special programmes, or from 'Dinners in the Dark'. As such, the venture is capable of funding itself almost entirely through the revenues it generates itself and is thus largely independent of donations and third-party funds. To date, more than 5 million visitors have been guided through exhibitions, and more than 4000 blind people have found meaningful jobs through Dialogue in the Dark. This growth results from expanding to several locations. Based on a tested and efficient business model, Dialogue in the Dark has succeeded in extending the social programme by means of social franchising.

A systematic expansion through social franchising requires clear-cut organizational structures, which is why Consens Ausstellungs GmbH was set up in 1996. This company is the owner of the standardized concept governing the guided tours through darkened rooms (system package) and simultaneously acts as the franchisor. Dialogue in the Dark makes a distinction between two main forms of franchising: temporary exhibitions, which typically run for six to twelve months and for which the franchisees are predominantly museums, and permanent exhibitions such as those in Holon (Israel) and Campinas (Brazil), for which the franchisees are predominantly social entrepreneurs.

Besides an initial fee for the acquisition of the concept knowledge, the ongoing franchise fees amount to between €130 and €180 per day. Since the launch of the idea in 1988, more than 140 exhibitions in over 20 countries have been staged in this manner, among them more than ten as permanent exhibitions.

### 3.2   Science-Lab: Natural Sciences for Children

Science-Lab was established in 2002 in Starnberg, Germany as an independent educational initiative for children and primary school teachers. The programme aims 'to promote inquiry-based thinking to lay a basis for the long-term development of a different understanding of the natural sciences'. The founders, Heike Schettler and Sonja Stuchtey, noticed that people generally shied away from the natural sciences and that natural science subjects produced low numbers of graduates. They developed a modern curriculum that provides children aged between four and ten with easy access to various topics in biology, chemistry, physics, astronomy and the geosciences. Course formats have been tailored to small children, who are able to get closer to these subjects by means of doing scientific experiments in a playful way.

Science-Lab funds itself both through the offer of supplementary teaching and training for independent infant and primary school teachers, and through course fees amounting to €10 per course unit and child. Since the launch of the courses, more than 10 000 children have participated in natural science courses, and there are further efforts under way to extend the system throughout Germany. This expansion into new locations takes place through social franchising.

Today, Science-Lab courses are offered in over 70 locations in Germany and abroad. Science-Lab plays the role of the franchisor and course leader. From its headquarters, the company pursues various activities, including the development of the curriculum, the training of new course leaders (franchisees), the continuous training of existing course leaders, as well as all the public relations. The course leaders, in turn, are responsible for all the activities on site.

### 3.3   VisionSpring: Glasses to Restore Eyesight

VisionSpring was established by Jordan Kassalow and Scott Berrie in New York, in 2001. Originally, it was called the Scojo Foundation. The organization describes its mission as follows: 'To reduce poverty and generate opportunity in the developing world through the sale of affordable eyeglasses.'

VisionSpring produces high-quality yet affordable reading glasses for developing countries. The organization pursues two objectives: on the one hand, it supplies glasses to people in developing countries who otherwise have no access to opticians and/or who do not have the money to afford glasses. On the other hand, VisionSpring provides people with work based on the 'Business in a Bag' philosophy, in that individual distributors actually sell those glasses. A majority of these distributors are women, who are thus able to earn a living and have the opportunity to pursue a flexible business besides family and household.

The organization's revenue model is based on proceeds from glass sales. The final prices of these glasses differ depending on markets and costs but have to satisfy the requirements of cost coverage and affordability for the population. What is important is not only that all the variable costs can be covered, but also that a profit margin is assured at every value creation level. The organization's overheads are financed by payments from the original company, Scojo Vision LLC, which is a classically profit-oriented enterprise for the production of spectacles, and donates 5 per cent of its pre-tax profits every year.

Since its launch, VisionSpring has managed to sell almost 150 000 pairs of glasses and provide 900 people with a job through the distribution of these glasses. VisionSpring, too, makes use of the social franchising approach to expand its business model. The company has expanded to nine countries to date, of which five are served through social franchising.

In its capacity as the franchisor, VisionSpring is responsible for the handover of the concept and the training of the franchisees, as well as for the production of the ophthalmic lenses. In addition, the company constantly supports its franchisees through supplementary training and consultation services, and it takes on part of the marketing activities. The franchise partners organize the entire eyeglass sales operation on site. The franchising fee to be paid to VisionSpring is a function of the number of glasses sold and mainly serves to cover production and transport costs.

## 4   GENERAL INSIGHTS INTO THE CONCEPT OF SOCIAL FRANCHISING

The three cases demonstrate a method of multiplying social value creation as opposed to the multiplication of economic value creation pursued by commercial franchises. Cooperation is based on a legal agreement between franchisor and franchisee as is customary with the traditional franchising model. In this agreement, the social enterprise appears as franchisor, while the local multipliers are autonomous units and act as franchisees. As in traditional franchises, cooperation is conceived of as a long-term relationship, with the exception of Dialogue in the Dark, whose franchisees deliberately agree on temporary cooperation (in the case of temporary exhibitions).

In all three cases, the business model on which the franchise package is based is of a social nature as opposed to the profit orientation of classic franchising. However, as in commercial franchising, all three social franchises attach a great deal of importance to a shared brand for the standardization of market presence. Science-Lab and VisionSpring insist on their franchisees using the brand. In future, Dialogue in the Dark will also enforce the use of a standard brand and corporate identity by all its franchisees.

## 4.1   Roles and Functions

The distribution of roles and functions in social franchises largely matches that of commercial franchises. Besides the initial preparation of the concept and the consistent development of the franchise package, the franchisor takes on central activities to support the entire system. Such activities include the administration and control of the franchise system with a special focus on the continuous development (franchise recruitment) and continued existence (quality assurance) of the system, ongoing training, as well as specific on-demand support for franchisees.

To a large extent, the franchisors' responsibility focuses on marketing activities, especially on branding and public relations. Owing to their interest in a standardized market presence, the franchisors support their franchisees through centrally organized public relations efforts and the provision of standardized advertising materials. In contrast to commercial franchises, however, social franchisees directly organize their specific advertising activities themselves. Only advertising measures that are of benefit to the overall system are carried out centrally. Accordingly, the three social franchises do not charge their franchisees for the current marketing and advertising expenses as is typically done by traditional franchises.

The franchisees for their part are responsible for all the activities at their individual locations. This includes the implementation of the social programme on site, which has to be done according to franchise standards. Franchisees are obliged to provide the franchisor with information about the flow of their business activities. Moreover, the payment of a financial franchise fee is contractually agreed in all the social franchises that were investigated. Contrary to the assumptions expressed in the theoretical part, the franchise fees of all three cases observed are thus monetary in nature, corresponding to the traditional franchises. Besides these running fees, whose amount is either set as a function of turnover (Science-Lab and VisionSpring) or represents a fixed sum subject to the capacity of the franchisee (Dialogue in the Dark), initial payments are also customary. Science-Lab, for instance, charges a franchisee an admission fee as compensation for initial expenses such as starter or marketing packages, whilst Dialogue in the Dark receives a consultancy fee for consultation services concerning location start-ups.

## 4.2   Degree of Standardization

With regard to standardization, a distinction can be made between two competing aspects: the necessity of a sufficiently flexible system package for adaptation to local conditions, and the significance of a standardization of products and processes. Just like commercial franchises, social franchises adapt to local conditions. The three social franchises allow all their franchisees the necessary leeway for the implementation of the concept on site. Carrie Magnuson, Franchise Partner Manager of VisionSpring, says, 'It's really important that we are able to offer all the tools, but the organization has to learn how to deploy the services within the context of their particular region.'

A high degree of flexibility dominates cooperation with the franchisees in Dialogue in the Dark. Sandra Ortiz, Assistant Manager, points to the efforts made by Dialogue in the Dark to adapt the programme to fit individual franchisees and local circumstances: 'First of all, we have to adapt to customers without losing the core . . . without losing Dialogue in the Dark.'

Science-Lab, too, leaves franchisees every possible freedom for entrepreneurial decision-making with regard to the implementation of the programme on site, provided franchisees comply with the contractually agreed quality standards. Sonja Stuchtey, co-founder of Science-Lab, puts it like this: 'As long as the franchisees remain within the limits of the quality corridor, our partners are very free.'

While social and classic franchises are largely comparable in respect of the necessity to adapt to local conditions, this does not apply to the extent of local freedoms and thus to the extent of the standardization of products and processes. The above observations alone demonstrate that all three social franchises evidence an extremely high degree of flexibility in that franchisees only have to satisfy minimum standards with regard to the fundamental social concept and qualitative aspects. Thus Andreas Heinecke, the founder of Dialogue in the Dark, only points to three minimum standards that franchisees must categorically adhere to in the preparation and implementation of a local exhibition: 'It must be dark, it must be safe, and the blind people are the kings.'

### 4.3 Structure

An overview of the basic structure of the three social franchises will serve as the starting point for this section. It is striking that the structures of the three case studies differ greatly from each other, ranging from flat structures with a high number of employees to strongly subdivided configurations with hierarchical structures.

Dialogue in the Dark is characterized by very flat structures, as shown in Figure 9.1. There is no interim hierarchical level between franchisor and franchisees; all the franchisees report directly to headquarters.

The franchisee units vary a great deal and range from private individuals who initiate the social programme at their locations, to organizations,

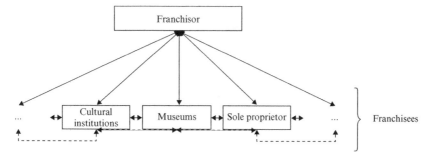

*Figure 9.1   Franchise structure of Dialogue in the Dark*

which integrate the programme into their existing operations. The latter are predominantly cultural institutions such as museums and cultural centres, which integrate the exhibition concept of Dialogue in the Dark on their own premises. This mixture of various franchisees shows a very heterogeneous group of units. Different thematic origins and diverse infrastructural circumstances result in a situation whereby the franchisor has to respond to each single franchisee in a flexible and individual manner. Whereas existing cultural institutions already have an entire infrastructure, such as box office systems, cloakroom and distribution channels, individual entrepreneurs usually have to set up the entire operation from scratch. The heterogeneity of the franchisees is intensified by the varying geographical locations.

With regard to its hierarchical structure, Science-Lab has a similarly flat structure to Dialogue in the Dark. As depicted in Figure 9.2, the course leaders largely occupy the same level and report directly to headquarters. However, Science-Lab has appointed regional heads who fulfil a supporting function.

All the individual network units are private individuals. Cooperation with organizations was once considered to scale up the business, but this strategy was rejected because of quality requirements and the risk of dilution. In spite of the standard network nodes, the individual franchisees differ greatly in terms of their personalities, which are the result of their varying backgrounds. Sonja Stuchtey (Science-Lab) says: 'They all have similar motives. [. . .] but otherwise they're completely different people.'

By contrast, the structure of VisionSpring is somewhat more complex. As depicted in Figure 9.3, VisionSpring uses two franchise channels: a direct one on the right-hand side of the figure, and an indirect one. Whereas the hierarchy is very flat in the direct channel, where there is a direct contact between headquarters and the franchisees, the so-called 'Vision Entrepreneurs' is a multilevel organization. Here, there is first a

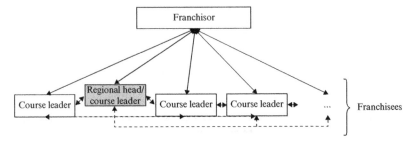

*Figure 9.2    Franchise structure of Science-Lab*

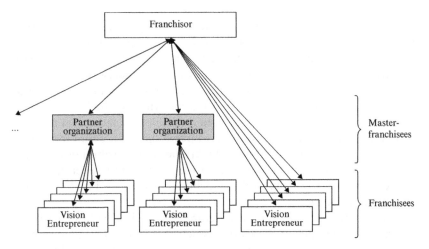

*Figure 9.3    Franchise structure of VisionSpring*

master franchisee, which in turn serves a number of Vision Entrepreneurs. Generally, there is a master franchisee in each country that is responsible for a up to 25 Vision Entrepreneurs.

Generally, it can be concluded that a specific structural pattern for social franchises does not exist. Rather every social entrepreneur has to decide individually what kind of structure works best, as can be seen with the analysed case studies.

### 4.4    Intensity of Relations

The aspect of the intensity of relations refers to the micro-level of social capital theory and addresses the nature of relations between the actors according to the distinction between 'weak ties' and 'strong ties'. Overall, the three cases show relations of greatly varying intensity. Bilateral relations between franchisor and franchisees are given and can be called strong in most cases. Whilst many are actively strong in that they are cultivated and are based on regular interaction, others must be conceived of as passively strong since, although there is no regular interaction, the relationship can quickly be activated and intensified if need be. Andreas Heinecke (Dialogue in the Dark) says, 'There's everything from zero, little, hardly any interaction to very, very lively, intensive exchange.'

Sonja Stuchtey (Science-Lab) confirms this: 'There are course leaders from whom you hear relatively little, with relatively little happening there. All those who are committed and do a lot, though, those are in a close exchange, [. . .] it's really intensive then.' Carrie Magnuson (VisionSpring) also refers to the intensive relationship with franchisees: 'It's pretty constant communication. [. . .] When they have problems or run into obstacles or successes we are on the phone and talking through all of those things.'

In contrast to the vertical relations between franchisor and franchisees, the franchisees' horizontal relations tend to be weak to non-existent. In the cases of Dialogue in the Dark and Science-Lab, there are predominantly loose relations between franchisees. These relations find place within annual general meetings (Dialogue in the Dark), further training (Science-Lab) or on the basis of individual franchisees' geographical proximity (Science-Lab). In the case of VisionSpring, however, any relations between franchisees are purely accidental.

The reason for the relatively weak ties among franchisees in all three social franchises is likely to be the wide geographical distribution of the actors (Dialogue in the Dark, VisionSpring) and the high degree of individuality and entrepreneurial freedom at the various locations.

Given these insights, one can conclude that the network metaphor derived from the social capital theory cannot be applied for social franchising. While social networks are considered as a 'structure which depicts persons as points and relations as connecting lines' (Granovetter, 1976) and imply flat, dense relational patterns, the analysed cases point to hierarchical and loose structures, contrary to network theory.

## 5  MANAGEMENT AND COORDINATION IN SOCIAL FRANCHISES

### 5.1  The Selection of Franchisees

The internal coordination of a social franchise starts with the selection of franchisees. It is particularly important to ensure that partners' selection guarantees that the franchise's overall objective can be successfully pursued at the various locations. Therefore, it is necessary to be aware of the qualifications that potential franchisees require and to be able to vet these candidates accordingly.

In all three cases, the assurance of a moral consensus was given the greatest importance in the selection of franchisees. This consensus can be described based on two factors. First, a potential franchisee must truly embrace the social cause pursued by the franchise and be enthusiastic about it. Second, franchisees generally have a similar conception of how the objectives should be attained and they can therefore actively contribute towards the development of the initiative. VisionSpring, for example, links this criterion to a similar mission and similar objectives to be pursued by a partner organization, as Carrie Magnuson remarks: 'We seek out organizations that have similar missions and goals to implement our program.'

Enthusiasm is the driving force that prompts a potential franchisee to support the initiative. This is of immanent significance as a prerequisite since a shared idealism for the social theme is often not complemented fully by classic incentive systems. Silvia Haubs, a franchisee of Science-Lab, says, 'I wrote my application on the same day because I was convinced that this was simply a fantastic concept.' Andreas Heinecke (Dialogue in the Dark) remarks for his part: 'This means that all our franchise partners approached us, they somehow got to know [. . .] that there was something there that was said to be terrific.'

The franchisee's entrepreneurial spirit constitutes a further qualification criterion. This includes a high degree of self-reliance, as well as a mastery of key organizational and management skills. In the case of VisionSpring, particular attention is given to franchisees' business acumen to reach a social objective, whereas Science-Lab and Dialogue in the Dark investigate potential franchisees' entrepreneurial suitability. Anke Burfeind-Herrmann (Dialogue in the Dark) says: 'This is why selection is very important. We have to choose the right franchisees . . . They must also be good on the business side of things, because idealism alone doesn't help.'

The selection process for franchisees is important because it stresses both signalling and screening of candidates. The principal–agent theory makes a distinction in the context of establishing contact between signalling, that is the provision of information to the better informed party, and screening, the collection of information by the less well-informed party.

The case studies show that signalling can take place in different ways either by the franchisor, the franchisee, or third parties. The franchisor provides franchisee candidates with information, particularly to ensure a moral consensus. Since franchisors create an atmosphere of transparency about the low compensation for franchisee activity right from the start, candidates' genuine motivation and expectations are subjected to a test. Sonja Stuchtey (Science-Lab) says, in respect of ensuring a moral consensus: 'It's relatively easy to make sure it's there. It's because you don't get rich with this business. That means that someone who does it for purely economic reasons may not even get as far as the personal meeting with us.' Andreas Heinecke (Dialogue in the Dark), too, says in this context that he is 'the worst salesman', since he deliberately reveals unpleasant facts even in the very first cooperation meetings.

With regard to screening, a distinction can be made between two courses of action: a rigid examination, which is driven by facts, and an intuitive examination, which is driven by emotion. A rigid, fact-driven examination is characterized by a thorough analysis of the candidate to throw light on his or her qualifications. Practices range from the classic application procedure, including an examination of the curriculum vitæ and a personal meeting (Science-Lab), a thorough due diligence examination of the applicant organization (VisionSpring) to the completion of a qualifying period (Science-Lab, VisionSpring).

Conversely, the intuitive, emotion-driven examination, which Dialogue in the Dark used in the past, encompasses elements where the assessment consisted mainly of soft factors such as credibility, cooperation skills, and the interpersonal 'fit' among the actors. This happened through long personal meetings aiming to establish a relationship between the potential partners. As Andreas Heinecke (Dialogue in the Dark) recounts:

> The understanding of where kind of person you actually are; where we actually have some common ground, and whether we are able to do something together is paramount for the selection process of franchisees. [. . .] There is no examinations as such, but you find out in discussions where you come from, what you do, what you have, and what you are.

### 5.2   Contractual Coordination

As a rule, contractual coordination constitutes the main instrument for the control of commercial franchises and is emphasized by the principal–agent theory. Generally, a legal agreement, which governs determinants of cooperation (for example remuneration, premium payments and control systems) is the main coordination mechanism.

In all three case studies, there is a legal agreement, which stipulates the parameters of the franchise relationship. It sets out the franchisors and franchisees' rights and obligations, including the monies to be paid, the type and extent of control systems, the communication requirements, as well as territorial coverage. Despite this clear weighting of contractual agreements, it is a common feature of all three social franchises that the legal agreement has only a minor significance as a steering instrument in the actual cooperation between the parties. This is, however, the case in many commercial franchises.

The contract is regarded as a necessary legal basis for the partnership, but perhaps most importantly, the coordination is constituted by the social relationships between the people involved. Carrie Magnuson (VisionSpring) explains: 'We obviously have the contract to back us up, and that's really important to have that like in any business. But at the same time it's better if we don't necessarily have to call on that contract, to enforce it.'

When asked whether the contract is really used to deal with irregularities in the franchise relationship, franchisee Anke Burfeind-Herrmann (Dialogue the Dark) says, 'No, it says right at the start in the preamble that you try to get your rights by mutual consent and do business together. This agreement is only meant to lay down some benchmark standards. We actually try to sort out problems through a dialogue between the parties involved.'

The analysis of the three social franchises reveals that franchisees always receive financial compensation for their activities and that this compensation represents the residual amount of turnover less franchise fee. Consequently, the principle of franchising, whereby franchisees act as entrepreneurs and thus bear part of the risk, holds true. In all three cases, the franchisees' business success determines the size of the actual remuneration, thus constituting a classic motivation instrument in accordance with the principal–agent theory. In the cases of Science-Lab and VisionSpring, the beneficiaries themselves pay for the social assistance (the children's parents pay for the course units provided by Science-Lab, while people with deficient eyesight pay for the glasses provided by VisionSpring). In the case of Dialogue in the Dark, franchisees are remunerated by the exhibitions' visitors. The importance of a service that results in financial compensation is emphasized by all three social franchises alike. 'A very important aspect, we don't cooperate with people who do voluntary work. We all feel responsible for what we do because we're paid for it. How much doesn't matter at all,' says Sonja Stuchtey, co-founder of Science-Lab.

Control plays an important part in the overall coordination of commercial franchise systems and is an important factor in franchisor–franchisee relations. The principal–agent theory postulates that hidden activities and information result in moral hazard such as quality uncertainties, and hold-up hazards such as the appropriation of the business concept by a franchisee.

The importance of control in cooperation with franchisees is shared by all the social franchises that were analysed. However, control systems varied greatly in the three organizations analysed. Indeed, very rigid, structured and rather less structured control procedures could be observed. The most comprehensive measures are taken by Science-Lab. The franchise contract requires that franchisees submit written feedback forms on every course unit and distribute questionnaires to the children's parents in the courses. These questionnaires must be submitted for central evaluation. Moreover, franchisees have to participate in annual training courses to extend their competencies.

VisionSpring control mechanisms are organized in a similarly formal way. This organization uses an Internet database into which franchisees regularly log their key turnover figures. This benchmark reporting has a two-tier structure in that so-called District Managers agree a loose form of turnover objectives with headquarters and coordinate their 20 to 25 Vision Entrepreneurs accordingly. In addition, VisionSpring provides training courses for Vision Entrepreneurs to improve service quality.

By contrast, Dialogue in the Dark only recently included control mechanisms in its agreements. Previously, reporting by franchisees was predominantly based on 'personal relations' and took place on a voluntary basis. The control mechanisms implemented by Dialogue in the Dark are less formal than in the two other cases. Regular personal contact and on-site inspections play a central role in Dialogue in the Dark's quality assurance. This can also be recognized from their consulting activities for each newly admitted franchisee, which are personnel intensive and are mostly conducted on site.

### 5.3   Social Coordination

As we outlined in the review of the literature, coordination in franchises takes place not only through legal contracts and control procedures but also through different social mechanisms. Among those, trust is often mentioned as the bedrock of commercial franchises. Our analysis shows that this is also an important factor for social franchises.

Trust is not only an admission criterion for the selection of new franchisees and thus a constituent feature, but it is further strengthened by cooperation during the social franchise launch and development. Since social franchises are systems that consist of people, a strong interweaving of different forms of trust can be discerned: trust in the organization and in people, with the latter form being subdivided into horizontal trust between franchisees and vertical trust between franchisor and franchisee. Although the cause-and-effect relationship between trust and social relations often remains unclear, three elements of trust are worth mentioning.

First, in all three cases trust has a particularly fertile soil in the collective, charitable objective of the social franchise in question. The shared mission and goals provide a thrust for cooperation and make transparent what the social franchise system as a whole stands for. In her answer to the question concerning the problems and conflicts in the cooperation among franchisor and franchisees, Silvia Haubs (Science-Lab) refers to the fact that cooperation has been free of trouble to date owing to the high density of connecting elements: 'The absence of problems is due to the fact that we all pull together, that is, we're all equally enthusiastic and one profits from the other.'

Second, the interviews make clear that organizational trust is of great significance. This trust is generated by professional competence on the part of the franchisor. The knowledge of the social franchise acquired at headquarters generates trust among franchisees if this knowledge is made available when the need arises. Then again, this access requires a further ingredient, namely an open, trusting climate within the franchise system. In addition, this manifests itself in fair interpersonal relations, open communication channels, and the greatest possible readiness to cooperate with each other. Bettina Deutsch-Dabernig (Dialogue in the Dark) refers to the trusting, open climate in the organization and points to: 'The people at headquarters, who really give the impression that they care about things. If you have worries during the ongoing operation, you can always go to these people.' Silvia Haubs (Science-Lab) also emphasizes the trusting climate: 'There's always a perfectly open relationship and everyone also knows that suggestions are always warmly welcomed.'

Third, when it comes to establishing organizational trust, the closely associated feeling of personal trust between the franchise partners has a role to play. Contrary to the original assumption of a high level of horizontal trust among franchisees, the cases investigated hardly provide any evidence of this. However, a strong vertical trust between headquarters and franchisees emerged as a pattern in all three cases. Trust is built on the support provided by the franchisor to their franchisees. Continuous communication and a constant readiness to provide help are typical characteristics of this relationship. 'When we get the impression that there's a quality problem, we get into contact at once. That is, we immediately offer support for qualification,' says Sonja Stuchtey (Science-Lab).

Andreas Heinecke (Dialogue in the Dark) goes even further and conceives trust in franchisees not only as the basis for cooperation but as a substitute for contractual arrangements:

> When all is said and done, the lack of legal exactitude and the possibility of financial pressure can only be balanced out if you have an open personal relationship. This is where you have to invest, you have to be open, to be able to

*Table 9.1   Overview of the coordination mechanisms in the three cases*

|  | Dialogue in the Dark | Science-Lab | VisionSpring |
|---|---|---|---|
| **Selection of franchisees** | | | |
| Requirement | *Moral consensus*, entrepreneurial spirit | | |
| Selection process | Thorough examination (curriculum vitae, due diligence, personal meeting, qualifying period) | | |
| | (in past: *intuitive examination*) | | |
| **Contractual coordination** | | | |
| Legal contract | Rights and obligations of franchise parties | | |
| Compensation | Residual of revenue and franchise fee, *high importance of non-material forms of compensation* | | |
| Control systems | High importance of contractual controls | | |
| | (in past: *low importance of contractual controls*) | | |
| **Social coordination** | | | |
| Trust | Organisational and vertical (franchisor and franchisees) trust of high importance, horizontal trust of low importance, complementary coordination function | | |
| Social standards | *Substitute for lack of process-related standards, corroboration of contractual agreement with regard to quality and behavioural aspects* | | |
| | Reciprocity standard | | |
| Identity | Varying, complementary coordination function | | |
| | | High importance of consistent brand for internal identity | |

approach people, to be able to let yourself in for a surprise, and this is precisely where you shouldn't act according to revenues and expenses.

Whereas the level of trust in social franchises is very high, in all three case studies control is exercised solely from the centre, or in isolated cases by individuals within the system, but not by the entire group as a collective as proposed by social capital theory (see Table 9.1). In the light of the above-mentioned gaps inherent in the franchise structures, this appears logical. Network-specific social standards require closed network structures, which do not exist in social franchising. The interviewees were unable to name any structure or relation patterns that underpin network dynamics and no special extent of social standards can be made out at first. However, deeper analyses reveal that social standards do exist and furthermore play a critical role throughout all three social franchises.

First, social franchises represent subsystems of the society and naturally are subject to the same rules of behaviour as the wider societal system. Therefore, reciprocity standards typical of social systems are also in place. 'Give and take' symbolizes that distinctly cooperative behaviour in social franchises and shows the great importance of reciprocity in social relations. Second, the franchisors themselves induce social standards due to their strong and powerful position within the systems as is shown by the example of Heinecke referring to quality as a 'huge topic' throughout Dialogue in the Dark, where the franchise centre acts 'very rigidly'. By stressing the importance of adhering to non-negotiable quality levels, franchisors automatically set social standards acting as a social coordination mechanism in the respective social franchise system.

## 6    CONCLUSION

The chapter provided an insight in the nature of social franchises as a business model to scale up social ventures. Our analysis focused on the structure and coordination of social franchises. The results confirm the original assumption that social franchising does indeed represent a form of franchising as seen in the commercial sector. Typical franchise elements such as an agreement on longer-term cooperation between franchisor and franchisee based on a legal contract, the payment of a franchise fee, as well as the interplay between control and entrepreneurial freedom in the actors' relationships are applied in social franchising, too. However, the transposition into social entrepreneurship results in differences from the commercial form.

The most important difference from traditional franchises concerns the ultimate goal of social franchising. Although both the traditional model and social franchising aim to distribute a business concept, the latter does not accord primary importance to a uniform market presence intended to generate a high degree of brand recognition and to build up a customer base which will buy the product again and again. In contrast to the economic objective of generating the highest possible financial profit, social franchises strive to achieve the highest possible social profit. The goal of social franchises is a far-reaching and optimal satisfaction of social needs as opposed to the high degree of brand recognition and customer loyalty pursued by traditional franchises.

A second differentiating feature can be recognized in the different incentive structures offered by social and commercial franchises. The pervasive lack of funds in the social sector prevents its actors from being paid adequate financial compensation, which is why the franchisees' motivation and commitment is largely non-material. Thus the incentive for social franchisees may reside in the fun and pleasure derived from the activities, the recognition received for their work, the creative leeway provided by entrepreneurial activities on site, or the high degree of meaningfulness generated by the social value creation.

The third difference between social and commercial franchises is to be found in the importance of quality. In analogy with the difference in objectives, the quality of service/product provision to customers serves to fulfil different purposes. Whereas for commercial franchises the importance of quality lies in maintaining customer loyalty through the provision of satisfactory or exciting products/services, the quality offered by social franchises is not primarily intended to create customer ties. Rather, its object is the best possible satisfaction of customers, which means that quality plays a part in the assurance of qualitative minimum standards and the prevention of loss in the generation of social goods.

With regard to the chosen theoretical frame of reference, results suggest that the principal–agent theory offers a valuable approach for social franchising. Although the validity of the approach was assumed to be given, albeit limited, in the theoretical part, the economic orientation of the approach allows for an excellent depiction of the professional, business side of social franchising that was so often emphasized by the interviewees. Basic agency-theoretical findings could be positioned in relation to social franchising, and concrete findings were generated: besides the validity of the principal–agent relationship between franchisor and franchisees and their typical risks, the theory provides suggestions for control mechanisms to reduce uncertainty that are either relevant (legal agreement, remuneration, control systems, standards) or less relevant (trust, identity). Once again, the 'business' character of social franchising and social entrepreneurship can thus be emphasized.

Concepts of social capital theory also provided interesting findings. The clarification of the meaning of trust, standards and identity with relation to internal coordination gives evidence of the mode of operation and the interaction of cooperation between franchise partners. However, the findings also show that this has only been an initial step and that further research is required. Thus a more detailed investigation of the social capital features, such as the multi-layered construct of trust, against the background of the special way of thinking and the attitudes of the actors involved, would be interesting. Moreover, the findings reveal the relevance of other constructs such as power and influence and the significance of social obligations in social franchise systems, whose examination would have been beyond the scope of this chapter.

## REFERENCES

Adler, P.S. and S.-W. Kwon (2002), 'Social capital: prospects for a new concept', *Academy of Management Review*, **27**(1), 17–40.
Ahlert, D., H. Fleisch, H.V.D. Dinh, T. Heussler, L. Kilee and J. Meuter (2008), *Social Franchising – A Way of Systematic Replication to Increase Social Impact*, Berlin: Bundesverband Deutscher Stiftungen.
Ashforth, B.E. and F. Mael (1989), 'Social identity theory and the organization', *The Academy of Management Review*, **14**(1), 20–39.
Austin, J. et al. (2006), 'Social and commercial entrepreneurship: same, different, or both?', *Entrepreneurship Theory & Practice*, **30**, 1–22.
Blomqvist, K. (1997), 'The many faces of trust', *Scandinavian Journal of Management*, **13**(3), 229–329.
Bradach, J.L. (1997), 'Using the plural form in the management of restaurant chains', *Administrative Science Quarterly*, **42**(2), 276–303.
Burt, R.S. (1992), *Structural Holes – The Social Structure of Competition*, Cambridge: Harvard University Press.
Carney, M. and E. Gedajlovic (1991), 'Vertical integration in franchise systems: agency theory and resource explanations', *Strategic Management Journal*, **12**, 607–29.
Coleman, J. (1990), *Foundations of Social Theory*, Cambridge: Harvard University Press.
Combs, J.G., S.C. Michael and G.J. Castrogiovanni (2004), 'Franchising: a review and avenues to greater theoretical diversity', *Journal of Management*, **30**(6), 907–31.
Dees, J.G. (1998), 'The meaning of "Social Entrepreneurship"', unpublished first draft, Stanford University, Stanford.
Eisenhardt, K.M. (1989), 'Agency theory: an assessment and review', *Academy of Management Journal*, **14**(1), 57–74.
Franz, S. (2004), 'Grundlagen des ökonomischen Ansatzes: Das Erklärungskonzept des Homo Oeconomicus', unpublished working paper, Universität Potsdam, Potsdam.
Garg, V.K. and A.A. Rasheed (2003), 'International multi-unit franchising: an agency theoretic explanation', *International Business Review*, **12**, 329–48.
Granovetter, M.S. (1973), 'The strength of weak ties', *The American Journal of Sociology*, **78**(6), 1360–80.
Granovetter, M.S. (1976), 'Network sampling: some first steps', *The American Journal of Sociology*, **81**, 1287–1303.
Granovetter, M.S. (1983), 'The strength of weak ties: a network theory revisited', *Sociological Theory*, **1**, 201–33.
Kleine, A. (1995), *Entscheidungstheoretische Aspekte der Principal–Agent-Theorie*, Heidelberg: Physica Verlag.
Lin, N. (2001), *Social Capital – A Theory of Social Structure and Action*, Cambridge: Cambridge University Press.
Macaulay, S. (1963), 'Non-contractual relations in business: a preliminary study', *American Sociological Review*, **28**(1), 55–67.
Morgan, R.M. and S.D. Hunt (1994), 'The commitment–trust theory of relationship marketing', *Journal of Marketing*, **20** (July), 20–38.
Nahapiet, J. and S. Ghoshal (1998), 'Social capital, intellectual capital, and the organizational advantage', *Academy of Management Review*, **23**(2), 242–66.
Ripperger, T. (1998), *Ökonomik des Vertrauens – Analyse eines Organisationsprinzips*, Tübingen: Mohr Siebeck Verlag.

Robson, C. (1993), *Real World Research: A Resource for Social Scientists and Practitioner-Researchers*, London: Blackwell.
Ross, S.A. (1973), 'The economic theory of agency: the principal's problem', *American Economic Review*, **63**, 134–9.
Schechler, J.M. (2002), *Sozialkapital und Netzwerkökonomik*, Frankfurt am Main: Peter Lang Verlag.
Shane, S.A. (1996), 'Hybrid organisational arrangements and their implications for firm growth and survival: a study of new franchisors', *Academy of Management Journal*, **39**(1), 216–34.
Skaupy, W. (1995), *Franchising: Handbuch für die Betriebs- und Rechtspraxis*, Münich: Franz Vahlen Verlag.
Spremann, K. (1987), 'Agent and principal', in G. Bamberg and K. Spremann (eds), *Agency Theory, Information, and Incentives*, Heidelberg: Springer Verlag, pp. 3–42.
Sydow, J. (1998), 'Franchise systems as strategic networks: studying network leadership in the service sector', *Asia Pacific Journal of Marketing and Logistics*, **10**, 108–20.
Thompson, J.L. (2002), 'The world of the social entrepreneur', *The International Journal of Public Sector Management*, **15**(5), 412–31.
Tracey, P. and O. Jarvis (2007), 'Toward a theory of social venture franchising', *Entrepreneurship Theory and Practice*, **31**(5), 667–85.
Yin, R.K. (2003), *Case Study Research: Design and Methods*, 3rd edn, Thousand Oaks, CA: Sage Publications.
Zahra, S.A., H.N. Rawhouser, N. Bhawe, D.O. Neubaum and J.C. Hayton (2008), 'Globalization of social entrepreneurship opportunities', *Strategic Entrepreneurship Journal*, **2**, 117–31.

# 10 Social entrepreneurs' actions in networks
## Chantal Hervieux and Marie-France B. Turcotte

## INTRODUCTION

Research has shown that social entrepreneurship (SE) organizations present many different variations: cooperatives, non-profits, for-profits, hybrids, partnerships, collaboration, alliances (Dees, 1998; Dees and Anderson, 2003), hence no one legal form of organizing can be said to account for all SE initiatives. The only common feature found in SE literature is the priority placed on social value creation and the socio-economic orientation of the initiative (Hervieux et al., 2010).

The challenge in defining any phenomenon is to provide for a definition that is neither too narrow nor too broad. In SE, narrow definitions are those that define SE as solely the commercial or business ways of non-profit organizations (Austin et al, 2006). Adoption of such a definition would thus exclude all for-profits that have as priority the pursuit of a social mission. We feel this is not warranted, and our position on this matter is supported by previous SE literature as most would not favour a definition based mainly on the legal status of the organization. At the other end of the spectrum, overly broad definitions of SE go as far as to include all socially entrepreneurial activity in its definition even when the organization does not have as priority the pursuit of a social mission (Peredo and McLean, 2006). In these definitions of SE, one would thus include for-profit organizations involved in innovative corporate social responsibility (ICSR). In our definition of the boundaries of SE we choose to see SE as ending where profits and commercial activities take priority over the social mission. When this happens we prefer to refer to these responsible social acts as corporate social responsibility and not SE, thus keeping the two yet connected domains separated by the priorities of the organization. The borders of SE are represented by Figure 10.1.

It has been stated that SE involves a double, or even a triple bottom line (Thompson and Doherty, 2006) and thus multiple goals. The presence of these multiple and at times opposed objectives brings many challenges for the management of SE initiatives such as goal displacement and legitimacy issues (Hervieux et al., 2010). In focusing on these initiatives, we aim to highlight the creative management solutions put in place by these social

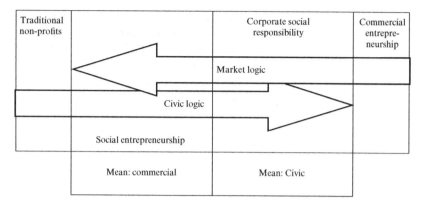

*Source:* Hervieux et al. (2008).

*Figure 10.1 Borders of the social entrepreneurship domain*

entrepreneurs that endeavour to increase the social value they create in a situation of diffused power.

We have organized our chapter as follows. First we present a brief review of SE literature, focusing on three actions to be carried out to instigate a network: proactive network construction, involvement of external actors and filling the gaps in the network. We proceed by connecting the SE literature to network literature and more specifically to Granovetter's (1973) theory of weak ties. We then present the methodology that was followed for the case study used to deepen our understanding of pluralistic SE and thus its domain specification. Following the methodology, we present the narrative of our case study, the case of Cooperative Coffees, revealing how the management of strong and weak ties brings density and solidity to the network by enabling knowledge sharing and collective solutions to problems.

## SOCIAL ENTREPRENEURSHIP AND NETWORKS

There is evidence of many collective, network forms of enterprise in SE, and SE has often been discussed as partnerships and alliances between actors of different sectors and the mobilization of these actors towards a common goal or mission (Leadbeater, 1997). For instance, case study research done by Spear (2006) highlighted how entrepreneurship within these organizations is distributed and while the leaders of the organization do have a central role in its management, these initiatives are characterized by the close involvement of external stakeholders. Mair and Schoen (2007)

highlight the proactive development of value networks by social entrepreneurs and how these networks come to be appropriated by the target
groups of the initiative. In their research, they found that in fragmented
contexts, the value networks shaped by social entrepreneurs were crucial
for the creation of social and economical value and its appropriation by
the target group. By creating a new organization, going into partnership
with another or themselves filling the missing services they identified (Mair
and Schoen, 2007), these social entrepreneurs manage to fill the gaps that
could have diminished the value returned to the population they aimed to
help.

Another important element of these value networks is how in many
cases SE initiatives involve the target group in the initiative (Shaw, 2004),
in this way empowering them to become not the recipient of charitable
contributions, but proactive actors in the solution. For some these pluralistic social organizations have great potential as

> the most enduring impacts are likely to come from organisations that tackle
> social exclusion on both fronts – embracing a trading purpose that addresses
> the perceived needs of socially excluded groups, and allowing participation
> by them in decision-making and wealth creation processes. This will promote
> solutions more closely matched to actual (rather than imagined) needs while
> encouraging sustainability (Ridley-Duff, 2007: 390).

From the literature, we identified three actions contributing to the
creation, development and reinforcement of networks: 1) involvement of
external actors and target population (Spear, 2006; Shaw, 2004); 2) proactive actions in the development of their network (Mair and Schoen, 2007);
and 3) providing missing links when needed in this network (Mair and
Schoen, 2007).

Research is needed to gain a better understanding of these organizations, for while much of the SE research has studied the leader or the
founder of the initiative (Spear, 2006; Mair and Schoen, 2007), too little is
known about how they involve their networks in finding sustainable solutions for the problems they address. The case we present in this piece of
research, Cooperative Coffees, will illustrate this. It will tell the story of a
social entrepreneur that valued highly democratic and collective decision
making and that accordingly encouraged the participation of others to
take charge of these actions. The case thus offers a valuable illustration of
what actions and roles contribute to the creation of a network and how
these roles can be shared.

# SOCIAL ENTREPRENEURS AS NETWORK ACTORS

In our framework we choose to conceptualize social entrepreneurs as playing various roles (bridges, or ties, between the various actors and groups) within networks and networks of networks. Studying the structure and functioning of networks, Granovetter (1973) developed the theory of weak ties. According to Granovetter (1983) the ties that link individuals can either be strong (ties between friends) or weak (ties between acquaintances). While strong ties are important in how they help to build trust between individuals, weak ties between an individual and his or her acquaintances are also important in that these can be used as bridges between his/her group of friends and the group of friends of each one of his/her acquaintances. Weak ties bring new information to the network, information not available in the more personal strong ties. The consequence of this is that an individual having little or no weak ties will be deprived of knowledge coming from areas more distant than that of his close friends. On a macro level, this implies that a social system composed of few weak ties will be fragmented and incoherent (Granovetter, 1983: 202). The implication for our research on social entrepreneurship is that, as previously observed by Mair and Schoen (2007), social entrepreneurs have the potential to be important actors in a fragmented system by providing the needed ties, both strong and weak, between the different actors of the social system.

Analysis of SE networks will make it possible to bind our research to network investigations in the larger entrepreneurship domain. Research on this level shows that a key benefit of networks is the access entrepreneurs gain to information and recommendations (Hoang and Antoncic, 2003). Important for the entrepreneurial initiatives at the time of their implementation, networks continue to provide access to contacts and thus to multiple needed resources (Hoang and Antoncic, 2003). The capacity to manage network ties is thus an important and essential resource for SE initiatives. In the case we present, we will see how the creation of both strong and weak ties enables the elaboration of collective, mutually beneficial solutions to the problems faced by various actors of the network.

# METHODOLOGY

As the domain of SE research is still in its infancy, there have been few theoretical developments. Our objective is hence to generate theory on SE, and in such instances qualitative, grounded theory generated from field work is indicated (Patton, 2002). Following contextual analysis of the sector, the choice of the organization to study was made by purposeful sampling (Patton, 2002) in that we aimed to identify a typical case (Yin, 1988) of an SE organization that was of pluralistic form.

**Data Collection**

Data for our analysis was collected during a 10-month period using multiple methods and data sources (interviews, participant observation, published articles on the organization, internal documents, and so on). Multiple sources of data permits triangulation and make it possible to test if results are reliable by enabling the confrontation of the different types of data (Patton, 2002).

During the phase of participant observation which lasted five months and included observation of the annual reunion in Guatemala in 2005, data was recorded using the ethnographic method. Choice of the ethnographic method was made because it systematizes note-taking, permits the organization of large amounts of data and facilitates the establishment of relations between data (Bernard, 2002). For note-taking during the field observation we used multiple journals; we present these in Figure 10.2.

The four different journals each consist of a type of note. Brief notes were collected in a small journal or notepad during the day when note-

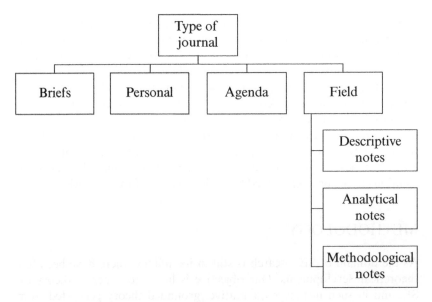

*Figure 10.2    Data collection: journals*

taking had to remain discrete. These are some quick observations that are noted in order to help in the writing of the other journals at the end of each day. The personal journal consisted of the recording of feelings or conflicts that happened during the day and that affected the observer. These notes, when combined with the other journals, help to diminish the personal biases in guiding the interpretation of the data.

The next journal is the agenda. In this journal are noted all that is planned for the next days, meetings, interviews, and so on. At the end of the day, we noted what had been accomplished and what remained; this helped in planning the next observation days. The final and most important journal is the field journal. In this journal, systematically and at the end of each day of observation, data and information were transcribed. The information collected in this journal was also classified according to the type of data: descriptive, analytical or methodological.

Data was also collected using non-directive interviews of members of Cooperative Coffee's network. Before each interview, written consent was obtained from the interviewee. Confidentiality of the interviewee was assured, and in the narrative presented in the next section, no names are used. In the case of the organization, Cooperative Coffees (CC), because the organization is well known and since it could be easily recognized, we obtained permission to use the organization name in our research publications.

Further data was also collected by participating observation of CC's management committees, by the collection of corporate documents and by collecting articles written on this organization and its members. In all, we collected 947 pages of data consisting of our field notes, 29 interviews and producer testimonies. Overall, we observed the interactions between 44 actors of CC's network; this was made possible by our presence at the annual meeting held in Guatemala in 2005. Other than this data, we also followed CC and its members as they visited five producer cooperatives in Guatemala, enabling us to observe directly the interactions between CC members and the members of the producer cooperatives.

Once the observation data was collected and the first interviews were conducted, we then proceeded by grounded theory method. We alternated phases of data collection and analysis using alternative inductive and deductive coding using Atlas ti software. The results of our analysis were presented to the members of CC in order to verify that we had not distorted the information or misinterpreted an observed situation. Thus by a prolonged engagement, persistent observation, triangulation of data and verification of our analysis by the respondents, validity, reliability and transferability of our research was assured (Lincoln and Guba, 1985).

# THE CASE: COOPERATIVE COFFEES

## Proactive Development of the Network

Founded in 1999, Cooperative Coffees (CC) is a green coffee importing cooperative, owned by the 24 roasters from the United States and Canada who are its members. The members of CC aim to source sustainably grown Fair Trade coffee from producer cooperatives they see as their partners. Being small-scale coffee roasters, the original members of CC formed the cooperative so that the combined volume of coffee they could purchase would thus make it possible to increase the variety of coffees each roaster could offer and from there increase the impact for producers. In choosing the roasters who would join the cooperative, the original members placed a priority on selecting only those that shared similar values and missions (CC's President, interviewed August 2005). CC's founder and President also chose as first members, organizations with whom he had previous business relations; thus CC was formed using the founder's network of weak ties.

## Managing the Main Organization

By adopting a cooperative form, its founder chose to put in place a demo-cratic organization, thus creating a space of shared decision making and diffused power. As the founder and President of CC explains:

> first there is the organizational structure; we are organized as a cooperative. This means one member, one vote. We have some very large members that buy a large percentage of the coffee that we buy and we have new members that are just joining. They buy a very small amount but they each get to have an equal say in who we are going to buy from, how we run the coop, and the election of the board, that ultimately elects the Chair. And the board determines who is running the coop (interview, August 2005).

Thus while there is a small staff working for CC, ultimately the organiza-tion is managed by member organizations that are situated throughout the United States and Canada. Dispersion of members over such a vast terri-tory has made it necessary for CC to hold their regular reunions through teleconferencing; critical management tasks are separated between differ-ent member-run committees (Finance, Membership, Outreach and Public Relations, Development and Green Bean). Being a member of CC hence implies not only managing one's own organization but also participating in the management of CC.

While dispersion of members at first helped in that the members were not in direct competition with each other, as CC and it member organizations grew, this could pose some problems for the organization, because 'with growth will come increased market overlap and potential territorial disputes' (interview, JHG, July 2005). Thus, growth for CC and its members is seen as an important source of challenges, because 'growth tends to have a dynamic of its own, dynamics like that have to be looked at. Competitors tend to see growth as good, but it can force choices' (interview, IDB, July 2005).

With growth of CC and the increase in membership this brings, comes the problem that it is more difficult to keep members focused on the same path, each new member having the potential to bring to CC their own values and ideas. Thus a priority for CC is:

> maintaining, keeping members interested, knowing that we have to grow, balancing our growth with wanting to maintain, to keep everyone pointing in the same direction. Wanting to maintain their ideals as some members grow very fast and other members don't grow as fast. And so that at some point they all realize that we are all in competition with each other because the market place is no longer the corner (interview, President of CC, August 2005).

It can thus be seen that dispersion of members and concerns about growth of the organization means restricting the number of issues directly addressed by CC: 'you can only keep a growing group of people that are organized cooperatively and live all over North America, you can only keep them pointed in the same direction on a certain number of issues' (interview, president of CC, August 2005).

Yet such problems are moderated by the ties that link the roasters to the cooperative and to each other. Beyond the access to more choice of coffees, it is the values of CC that serve as a bridge between its members. Accordingly with growth there is the need to keep the mission in line with members' objectives and also 'to work to spread [their] mission and shared culture among new partners' (interview, JHG, July 2005). For CC members, those values are important and they are the reasons that brought them to CC and that keep them there. These include:

- Willingness to establish close ties with the farmers:

> Because we felt that we needed to be as close as possible to the farmers and have some control over the supply chain. We were not interested in buying spot coffee (interview, ADB, August 2005).

- Social mission as priority:

> CC wanted committed people; we are part of the founding group of CC, one of seven. In CC, at the board meetings, it is obvious that all are mission driven and not money driven (interview, CTJ, July 2005).

● Strong ethics and quality standards:

> Cooperative Coffees is the only importing organization that is working to the standards of ethics and quality that fits within the mould of how we have wanted to grow our organization (interview, JHG, July 2005).

These value links between CC and its members are of fundamental importance for the cooperative as they make it possible for CC to continue to grow and change according to the needs of both its roaster members and its partner producer cooperatives. Also, while many see social entrepreneurship as for-profit social organizations, for many of CC's members, the same values that they feel are important for CC are also those they believe should be important to every business transaction: '[there is] a need to reconnect responsibility in business as it is done in human activity, the same rules that apply to everyday living and responsibility need apply to business activity [. . .] [you need to] Humanize the commodity, don't commoditize the humans' (interview, JHG, July 2005). 'Being in contact with people, you have a certain responsibility to others' (interview, AJL, September 2005).

In can thus be seen that the priorities placed on selecting members that share similar values bring coherence to the organization, limiting the negative impact that dispersion through the network could have on the initiative. Thus we propose:

*Proposition 1:* Selection of members by prioritizing shared values has a positive influence on the management of the network.

### Strong and Weak Ties between the Immediate Network of Roasters and Producers

In creating CC, the founders made the cooperative the intermediary between the roaster members and the producer cooperatives. In this way CC became the weak tie, the bridge between the roasters and the producer cooperatives, as the role of CC is

> to provide this conduit between the members of Cooperative Coffees and the producers of good coffee and, as much as we can, to not have the limelight, but instead to directly connect these guys with us as a side player. In reality, the relationship by and large is with Cooperative Coffees as opposed to with the roasters (interview with the President, August 2005).

And while CC would prefer not to be seen as the important actor, they would largely prefer to have the roasters connected more directly to the producer cooperatives so that the latter do not identify CC mainly with its employees, but rather with its members. This 'is very difficult because we are the ones paying for the coffee; we are the ones the contract is signed through. So often we are the week to week communication' (interview with the President, August 2005).

This leads us to propose:

*Proposition 2a:*   In proactively creating their networks, social entrepreneurs aim to involve actors that share similar values and goals.

*Proposition 2b:*   In the SE network, the instigating organization, or social entrepreneur, serves as the bridge (weak tie) between the different actors.

With the creation of CC, its members, the roasters, now found themselves less directly connected to the producers. To counter this, CC encourages its members to travel and visit producer cooperatives, aiming to have its members develop closer ties with a few producer communities:

> It is very difficult, but, I think that in spite of that we do a pretty good job of getting our members who otherwise might not just travel, because they are too busy, to understand that it is very important that you stop your business and go see the farmers and get down there and meet the producers. Maybe not devote a relationship with every single coop, but pick up a couple of coops that you will go back to year after year. That way you really do get to know this area, this town, these people.
>
> You are just building that relationship and that goes a long way I think in motivating, to continue to grow their business. Because they know they are growing their purchases from those farmers (interview with the President, August 2005).

Thus it can be seen that CC is the weak tie between its members, the roasters, and its partners, the producers. Yet as CC encourages its members to develop relationships with a selected group of producer cooperatives and their communities, this then means that some of its members develop stronger ties with these cooperatives than CC. In this way, CC serves as a bridge between unconnected actors and also between developing networks composed of roasters and producers, further increasing the knowledge resources that are created and shared in its network. A simplified representation of the different ties between the roasters, CC and its producer cooperatives is presented in Figure 10.3.

In the figure, broken lines represent actors involved in the smaller networks between roasters and producer cooperatives, arrows represent the network ties between the actors, thicker lines representing strong ties and thin lines representing weak ties.

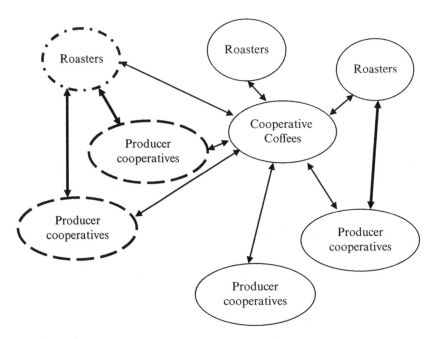

*Figure 10.3   Network ties between Cooperative Coffees, roasters and producer cooperatives*

The section above leads us to propose:

*Proposition 3a:*   The network is in itself composed of various smaller networks that are connected through the instigating social entrepreneurship initiative.

*Proposition 3b:*   Ties between the smaller networks will be stronger than those between each network and through the instigating organization.

We have now seen that the pluralistic organization, CC, was founded by the joining of actors already connected through weak ties. Furthermore, in CC's network, each of the actors involved are encouraged to develop stronger ties with some of the producer cooperatives who are the target population of the social entrepreneurship initiative. We now turn our attention to the ties created by CC and its members between external actors and the target group.

## Combined Network Development and Involvement of External Actors and Target Group

While much of the management of CC is done through its board members, employees and member committees, in order for the members to remain connected and also to address deeper and more important issues, CC organizes an annual meeting. These meetings often include the participation of members of producer cooperatives and at times take place in one of their countries. These are very important to the establishment, maintenance and strengthening of ties between the different actors of CC's network and often include external actors such as micro-financing organizations. During these meetings, important changes are discussed and adopted. It was during these annual meetings that the different management committees were formed. Following this, at each annual meeting, each committee must present the progress made during the previous year and the challenges they faced. Participation in each committee remains voluntary, but to formalize these committees, their president is elected by the members. Election of board members and president is also done each year at the annual meeting. Furthermore, at these annual meetings, new members are presented to the group and can thus start forming ties with CC's network. New members are voted in by existing members of CC, making it possible for the members to select those they feel share their common vision and values.

Furthermore, the annual meetings serve other functions as when it was decided in 2005 to hold the meeting in Guatemala in order to make it possible for many of the producer cooperatives to come and join the roasters. Holding the meetings in Guatemala was done in order to 'solicit feedback from producer partners and our roaster members on basic issues for Fair Trade, such as the market and marketing of our products, pricing, organic and Fair Trade certification costs and benefits, quality, financing and long-term planning for our future together' (Cooperative Coffees Xela Accords, 2005).

To make this exchange possible, CC brought together the majority of its members as well as members of their partner producer cooperatives from Costa Rica, Columbia, Chiapas, Peru, Nicaragua and many more. For three days they then gave the floor to the producers, inviting them to express their concerns about their organizations, their involvement in CC, the problems they faced and the reasons they perceived to be the root cause of these problems.

This willingness to exchange and involve the producers in finding together, as a group, a solution to the problems they faced is what in SE literature has been termed the involvement and empowerment of target populations. By being invited to take part in growing their relations and partnerships with CC and its members, the ties between these actors can evolve towards a more equal footing and thus become less of a paternalistic relationship where actors from the North come to tell the actors from the South how best they should manage their own lives and organizations. This leads us to propose:

*Proposition 4:* Involvement of target populations in SE networks empower them to find collective solutions to their problems.

## PROVIDING RESOURCES THROUGH NETWORKING

Hoang and Antoncic (2003) have shown the importance of networks in providing needed resources to entrepreneurs. In SE, this has also been illustrated by the case of the Grameen Bank who, with its network of millions of members and thousands of communities, has proved that the once thought unprofitable micro-loans to the poor were not only feasible but also profitable (Seelos and Mair, 2005). Networks and their management by social entrepreneurs can thus make possible what was once considered impossible by changing perceptions about what is feasible and what is not. We thus turn our attention to the ways in which CC connects the actors of its network, filling in the gaps and in this way enabling the transfer of resources through its network.

### Gaining Access to Financial Resources through Networking

Access to affordable credit and pre-financing is of critical importance to the small organizations in developing countries. As discussed by the producers during the meetings held with CC in Guatemala in 2005, affordable credit remains a problem for these producers even though Fair Trade favours a system where the buyers from the North offer pre-financing to their partners from the South. Yet, this is not always feasible for the small organizations from the North, like CC, that struggle with their own financing issues and as a result cannot afford to pre-finance the green coffee purchased from their partners. This is why CC and its members prefer to provide the needed ties between the producer cooperatives and micro-financing organizations. For the producer cooperatives, being connected to CC and having the assurance of a buyer for their production provides the guarantee that will give them access to affordable credit.

During the meetings in Guatemala, the micro-financing organization with whom CC has an alliance was also present. This bringing together of multiple actors helps everyone to gain a better understanding of the problems faced by all actors, be they the producers, roasters or even the micro-financing organization.

### Sharing and Developing Knowledge through Networking

Shared knowledge and the creation of discussion arenas are some of the more important resources that CC brings to its network. By linking the different actors, better, more adapted collective initiatives can be brought about.

One such collective solution is the Xela Accords. These Accords came about as a direct result of the meetings held in Guatemala in 2005. During these meetings, not only did the producers exchange their own experiences and problems but also those of the roasters, the other 'maillon de la chaîne'. They thus gained a more comprehensive understanding of the value chain in which they participate. From the discussions held in Guatemala in 2005, four resolutions were retained and the two sides engaged themselves in actions that would help to attain the resolutions. Two resolutions concern the commercial activities: quality of coffee sold to CC and the price paid for this coffee. While these are important in that they represent commitments above needed commercial aspects, two resolutions, presented in Table 10.1, stand out as a willingness to improve and strengthen the ties between the different actors of CC.

1.  Resolution 1: to improve the communications between the different members and partners of CC.
    In this, CC engaged itself to name a member responsible for communication in each of its different committees. The producers resolved to improve communications both internally and externally by creating new communication positions within their cooperatives and by the creation of an information exchange network between the producer cooperatives.
2.  Resolution 2: to enable the producers to have a stronger voice in CC.
    In this both sides took the resolution to work on propositions that would strengthen the ties between the important actors of CC's network. These important resolutions would lead a few years later, in 2006, to the founding of a new solidarity cooperative, CC's 'sister', Coop Sol, whose members would include roaster members of CC, producer cooperative and support organizations.[1] While this solidarity cooperative is still in its infancy, its novelty in bringing together

*Table 10.1    Xela Accords: resolutions aimed at strengthening the ties between producers and roasters*

| Resolution | Engagement resolution for CC | Engagement resolution for the producers |
| --- | --- | --- |
| Communication | Choose in each committee a member that will be responsible for communications | Choose in each producer cooperative a member that will be responsible for communications Develop an information exchange network between the producer cooperatives and partners of CC Improve communications between the members of each producer cooperative |
| Voice of the producers | Strengthen the formal ties between the producers and CC Facilitate the establishment of more direct ties between the producers | Prepare a proposition for the representation of the producers in CC |

such a diverse set of actors, from an even more dispersed geographical area and even more complex mix of objectives then CC itself, if successful, will make this organization an important source of knowledge for future SE initiatives.

This leads us to propose:

*Proposition 5a:*   The network facilitates the creation and sharing of knowledge between the different actors.

*Proposition 5b:*   The shared knowledge may contribute finding solutions to problems. These solutions may be individual or collective.

*Proposition 5c:*   Weak ties between actors enable the connection of actors in the diverse smaller networks of the initiative; thus forming new, more complex networks within the larger network.

# CONCLUSION: A FRAMEWORK FOR PLURALISTIC SE

We have illustrated, with the case study of a SE network, three types of actions that contribute to the creation or reinforcement of a network: 1) involvement of external actors and target population (Spear, 2006; Shaw, 2004); 2) proactive actions in the development of their network (Mair and Schoen, 2007); and 3) providing missing links when needed in this network (Mair and Schoen, 2007). To the first three dimensions we added a new dimension: shared knowledge. This dimension that was brought to light by our case study is also an important aspect of pluralistic organizations (Denis et al., 2007). In Figure 10.4 we now combine these dimensions with the research propositions from our case study. In Figure 10.5 the network elements, as applied by CC, are presented.

The first action concerns the *involvement of external actors*. In our case study we saw how CC engaged in discussion with the producers in order to gain a better understanding of their problems. From these discussions and the resolutions adopted during the meetings emerged the new cooperative, Coop Sol. What made this possible are the shared values and missions between the members of CC, values that include a willingness to work closely with their partners, the producer cooperatives. Hence we conclude that in pluralistic SE, shared values are important in that they help maintain cohesiveness to the initiative. Shared values and willingness to engage in collective solutions to problems thus makes it possible to strengthen the ties between the various network actors.

The second action concerns the *proactive development of the network*. Here again values are important in that they guide the selection of actors to include in the network. Also of importance for pluralistic SE is how the instigating social entrepreneur can have an important role to play in the formation of multiple smaller networks. In the case we studied, the smaller networks that formed between producer cooperatives and some members of CC made it possible for these actors to develop stronger ties than would otherwise have been possible. These strong ties helped in that they made trust possible between actors and thus the sharing of knowledge.

The third action concerns: *providing the missing links in the network*. In the case of CC, this is closely connected to the development of its network. As discussed, the founder of CC preferred that CC did not become too important for the producers, preferring to encourage the development of closer, more involved ties between its members and the producers. The reason for this is that, according to the founder of CC, it is only by developing closer relationships with the producers that the roasters can gain a better understanding of their conditions. Consequently, rather

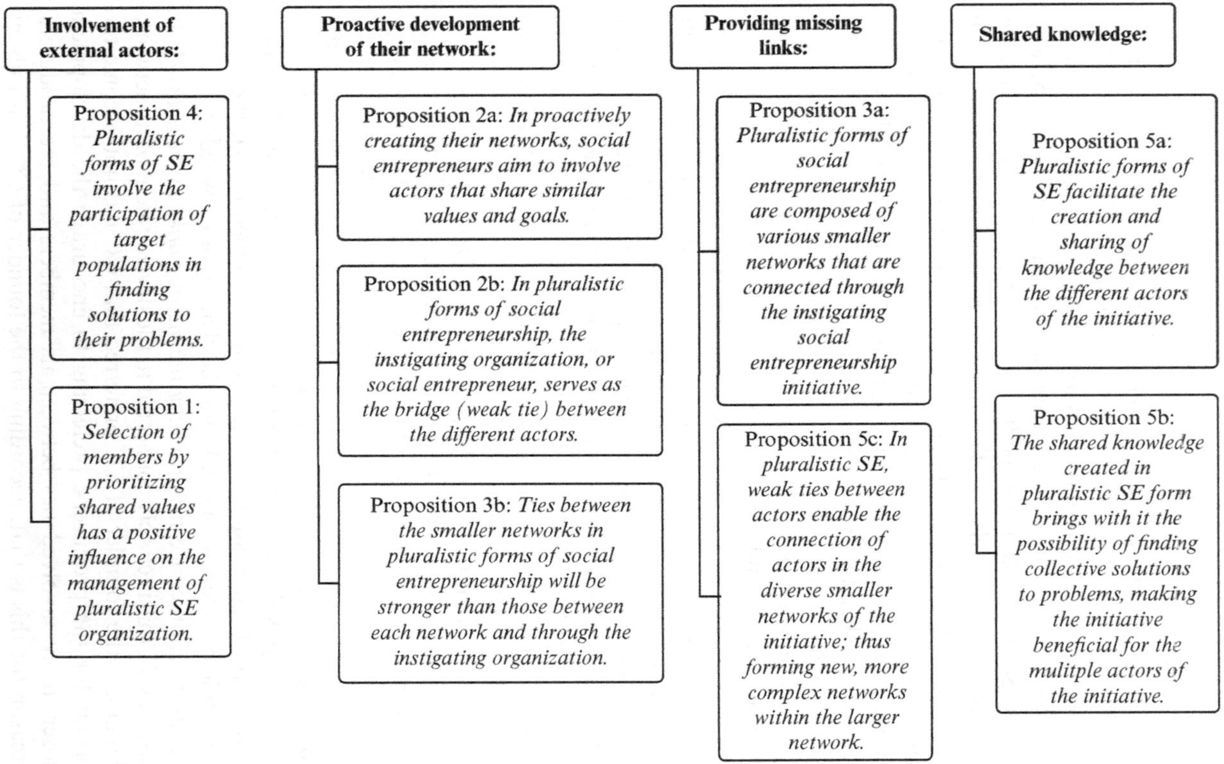

**Involvement of external actors:**

**Proposition 4:** *Pluralistic forms of SE involve the participation of target populations in finding solutions to their problems.*

**Proposition 1:** *Selection of members by prioritizing shared values has a positive influence on the management of pluralistic SE organization.*

**Proactive development of their network:**

**Proposition 2a:** *In proactively creating their networks, social entrepreneurs aim to involve actors that share similar values and goals.*

**Proposition 2b:** *In pluralistic forms of social entrepreneurship, the instigating organization, or social entrepreneur, serves as the bridge (weak tie) between the different actors.*

**Proposition 3b:** *Ties between the smaller networks in pluralistic forms of social entrepreneurship will be stronger than those between each network and through the instigating organization.*

**Providing missing links:**

**Proposition 3a:** *Pluralistic forms of social entrepreneurship are composed of various smaller networks that are connected through the instigating social entrepreneurship initiative.*

**Proposition 5c:** *In pluralistic SE, weak ties between actors enable the connection of actors in the diverse smaller networks of the initiative; thus forming new, more complex networks within the larger network.*

**Shared knowledge:**

**Proposition 5a:** *Pluralistic forms of SE facilitate the creation and sharing of knowledge between the different actors of the initiative.*

**Proposition 5b:** *The shared knowledge created in pluralistic SE form brings with it the possibility of finding collective solutions to problems, making the initiative beneficial for the multiple actors of the initiative.*

*Figure 10.4   Network elements of social entrepreneurship*

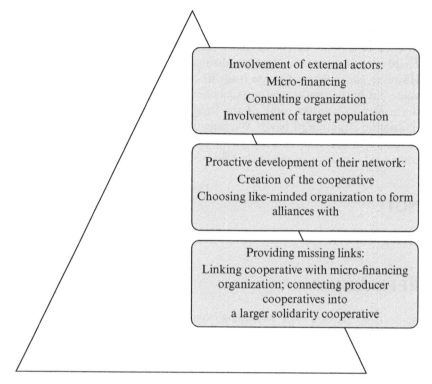

*Figure 10.5   Network elements of social entrepreneurship applied to Cooperative Coffees*

than directly providing the missing links in its network, CC encourages other actors of the network to connect in informal or formal networks; the informal networks being the smaller networks between the members and the producers and the formal networks being here represented by the new solidarity cooperative, Coop Sol. Each of these informal and formal networks increases the connections between the actors and helps fill gaps in the network.

The final observation from the case is *shared knowledge*. The sharing of knowledge resulted from the three previously discussed networking actions. Hence, by involving external actors, including the target group, developing a network where shared values guided the actions of these actors and the choice of new members and by linking them in other networks, the sharing of knowledge was possible. In turn, the sharing of knowledge increases the probability of developing beneficial solutions to problems encountered by members of the network.

We have used a well-established theory on the functioning of networks and illustrated it with the case of a SE network. The case leads us to advance a series of propositions concerning actions in SE networks. There are of course limits to generalizing propositions based on one case. However, the validity of a case study has to be judged not by its universal value but by its transferability (Lincoln and Guba, 1985). Does it allow the reader to transfer some of the insights provided by a specific case to another situation at hand? We hope it can and that the propositions advanced in this chapter may guide the actions of social entrepreneurs embedded into their specific networks.

## NOTE

1. http://coopcoffees.com/who/about-coop-sol/history, accessed 1 June 2009.

## REFERENCES

Austin, J., H. Stevenson and J. Wei-Skillern (2006), 'Social and commercial entrepreneurship: the same, different or both?', *Entrepreneurship Theory and Practice*, **30**(1), 1–22.

Bernard, H.R. (2002), 'Field notes: how to take them, code them, manage them', in *Research Methods in Anthropology: Qualitative and Quantitative Approaches*, 3rd edn, Walnut Creek, CA: Alta Mira Press, pp. 365–89.

Cooperative Coffees Xela Accords (2005), available at: http://www.alternativegrounds.com/show.php?ID=44, accessed 5 July 2010.

Dees, J.G. (1998), 'The meaning of Social Entrepreneurship', available at: http://www.fuqua.duke.edu/centers/case/documents/dees_SE.pdf, accessed December 2006.

Dees, J.G. and B.B. Anderson (2003), 'Sector-bending: blurring the lines between nonprofit and for-profit', *Society*, **40**(4), 16–27.

Denis, J.-L., A. Langley and L. Rouleau (2007), 'Strategizing in pluralistic contexts: rethinking theoretical frames', *Human Relations*, **60**(1), 179–215.

Granovetter, M. (1973), 'The strength of weak ties', *The American Journal of Sociology*, **78**(6), 1360–80.

Granovetter, M. (1983), 'The strength of weak ties: a network theory revisited', *Sociological Theory*, **1**, 201–33.

Granovetter, M. (1985), 'Economic action and social structure: the problem of embeddedness', *American Journal of Sociology*, **91**(3), 481–510.

Hervieux, C., E. Gedajlovic and M.-F.B. Turcotte (2008), 'Social entrepreneurship: management under conflicting logics', paper presented at the Soci(et)al Entrepreneurship Conference, VU University Amsterdam, 6–8 April.

Hervieux, C., E. Gedajlovic and M.-F.B. Turcotte (2010), 'The legitimization of social entrepreneurship', *Journal of Enterprizing Communities: People and Places in the Global Economy*, **4**(1), special issue: Soci(et)al Entrepreneurship, 37–67.

Hoang, H. and B. Antoncic (2003), 'Network-based research in entrepreneurship: a critical review', *Journal of Business Venturing*, **18**, 165–87.

Leadbeater, C. (1997), *The Rise of the Social Entrepreneur*, London: Demos.

Lincoln, Y.S. and E.G. Guba (1985), 'Establishing trustworthiness', *Naturalistic Inquiry*, Newbury Park, CA: Sage, pp. 289–331.

Mair, J. and I. Martí (2007), 'Entrepreneurship for social impact: encouraging market access in rural Bangladesh', *Corporate Governance*, 7(4), 493–501.

Mair, J. and O. Schoen (2007), 'Successful social entrepreneurial business models in the context of developing economies: an explorative study', *International Journal of Emerging Markets*, 2(1), 54–68.

Patton, M.Q. (2002), *Qualitative Research and Evaluation Methods*, 3rd edn, Newbury Park, CA: Sage.

Peredo, A.M. and M. McLean (2006), 'Social entrepreneurship: a critical review of the concept', *Journal of World Business*, 41, 56–65.

Ridley-Duff, R.R. (2007), 'Communitarian perspectives on social enterprise', *Corporate Governance: An International Review*, 15(2), 382–92.

Seelos, C. and J. Mair (2005), 'Creating new business models to serve the poor', *Business Horizons*, 48, 241–6.

Shaw, E. (2004), 'Marketing in the social enterprise context: is it entrepreneurial?', *Qualitative Market Research: An International Journal*, 7(3), 194–205.

Spear, R. (2006), 'Social entrepreneurship: a different model?', *International Journal of Social Economics*, 33(5/6), 399–410.

Thompson, J. and B. Doherty (2006), 'The diverse world of social enterprise', *International Journal of Social Economics*, 33(5/6), 361–75.

Yin, R.K. (1988), *Case Study Research*, Newbury Park, CA: Sage.

# PART III

# A STRATEGIC PERSPECTIVE OF SOCIAL ENTREPRENEURSHIP

# 11  Social entrepreneurs in non-profit organizations: innovation and dilemmas
*Patrick Valéau*

## INTRODUCTION

Non-profit organizations (NPOs) provide modern society with a large variety of services: they look after people's children, take care of the elderly, help the weakest, defend their rights and even entertain them. Above and beyond these activities, these organizations produce additional social benefits such as jobs and community links. Most of all, they question the market, public institutions and the whole of society with new ideas and new values and contribute to making them change. Behind each of theses organizations there is an entrepreneur, or a group of entrepreneurs, who have a vision of a better world and turn it into organized action.

Surprisingly, until quite recently, non-profit organizations have been almost ignored by researchers in the domain of entrepreneurship. One explanation could be that their entrepreneurial performances cannot be completely perceived within the classical approach. The rise of 'social entrepreneurship' as an instituted area of research may be an opportunity for the non-profit sector to get some acknowledgement and feedback on its work. Many definitions of social entrepreneurship have been proposed in the past 15 years, some including profit-orientated entrepreneurs taking social responsibilities, others requiring some more fundamentally philanthropic orientations. Beyond these differences, all these authors include more or less the same issue: an entrepreneurial process simultaneously targeting economic and social goals.

This chapter's main argument is that the introduction of non-economic goals and values within the entrepreneurial process can change its nature. It does not erase economic targets related to sustainability, growth and efficiency, but adds some other concerns. The examples analysed in this chapter fit the theory that efficiency and non-economic concerns may be temporally complementary, but also show that these different values and goals will sooner or later meet a situation that will put them in contradiction. As a result, the entrepreneur passes from a logic of optimization to a logic of arbitration between dilemmas.

Social entrepreneurs are often idealists, hoping to contribute to a better world. For them, their personal and entrepreneurial challenge consists of finding a way to make their vision, somehow, possible, which will in turn involve a certain amount of pragmatism. Based on 90 interviews with the paid and unpaid entrepreneurs of NPOs, this chapter develops a 'grounded theory' trying to capture these critical moments in the development of NPOs and, in doing this, to allow their leaders to be respected as entrepreneurs in their own right. This chapter begins with a literature review of social entrepreneurship, followed by the description and presentation of data gathered for this study and finishes with a discussion about the nature of social entrepreneurship.

# 1  THEORETICAL BACKGROUND

This chapter examines two theoretical fields still being worked on: entrepreneurship and non-profit organizations. We aim to find a definition of entrepreneurship that would allow us to maintain the core concept of entrepreneurship, but in a version open enough to respect the diversity of visions and orientations that arise at a higher level in the context of NPOs. This chapter hopes to make a contribution to the concept of social entrepreneurship.

## 1.1  Classical Entrepreneurship

A large part of the research on entrepreneurship is about what the entrepreneur actually does (Gartner, 1988). With this in mind, entrepreneurship can be defined as a core of activities related to the creation and development of a venture. The entrepreneur stands, above all, as someone innovating, (Schumpeter, 1934) taking risks (Mill, 1848: Say, 1803; Knight, 1921) and always looking for new business opportunities to seize (Cantillon, 1755; Say, 1803, Kirzner, 1993). These approaches introduced by classical authors from the past centuries still constitute the heart of entrepreneurship literature. For many authors, these activities are part of the creation process (Van de Ven et al., 1984; Bygrave and Hofer, 1991; Gartner et al., 1992; Gatner and Gatewood, 1992; Hofer and Bygrave, 1992; Davidsson et al., 2001; Fayolle, 2007). For others, the entrepreneurial phase carries on as long as the entrepreneur keeps taking risks and seizing new opportunities (Filion, 1997; Shane and Vankatamaran, 2000; Ucbasaran et al., 2001; Ireland and Webb, 2007) and keeps developing the venture (Carland et al., 1984; Shane and Vankatamaran 2000; Davidsson and Wiklund, 2001; Verstraete, 2002).

Many authors also study the characteristics of the individuals producing these activities. Summarizing past research, Brockaus and Horwitz (1985) present an individual driven by a strong achievement motive, independent and possessing an internal locus of control higher than average. This stream of research still continues today: some of the authors still emphasize the specificity of the entrepreneur's personality (Johnson, 1990), but others, more recently, admitted that entrepreneurs may not be totally different from non-entrepreneurs (Vesalainen and Pihkala, 1999). Some, like Shaver (1995), denounce the myth of the entrepreneur. Facing the empirical difficulty of identifying a common profile, many articles claim the diversity of this population. For Gartner et al. (1994) the entrepreneur is plural: there are many different types, there is no average; for them entrepreneurship is an idiosyncratic phenomenon. In fact, typologies of all kinds have been contributing to the acknowledgement of this diversity for a very long time. Since Smith's distinction (1967) between an artisan and an opportunist and the eleven styles introduced by Vesper (1980), these typologies have progressively asserted the plurality of entrepreneurs (Filion, 1997).

These typologies described different kinds of motivations and commitments (Naffziger et al., 1994). More directly, Fayolle (2007) has described the initial escalation commitment that will irreversibly engage the entrepreneur in a process that binds his or her own development to the development of his/her venture. Sharma and Irving (2005), in the context of family business, have, in a different way, connected the different types of commitment defined by Allen and Meyer (1990) to their decision to continue and to work beyond their duty. This emerging new stream of research, as part of what Ireland and Webb (2007) define as the identity construction, may help to link together the entrepreneur and the development of his/her venture (Bruyat, 1994; Verstraete, 2002; Fayolle, 2007).

As a result of the acknowledgement of the diversity of entrepreneurs and of the venture they create, it has become more and more difficult to assess entrepreneurial performance (Ucbasaran et al., 2001). Actually, the relevance of including a large variety of entrepreneurs does not gain unanimity among the entrepreneurship research community: the 'purists' consider that this conception including all kinds of small business owners, just because they have once created a new venture, without considering their actual development and performance, dilutes the concept of entrepreneurship (Carland et al., 1984; Van de Ven et al., 1984; Gartner, 1988). On the other hand, the partisans of a more open vision denounce the classical vision as being far too restrictive, centred on the venture and then ignoring the entrepreneur.

One of the key issues is the question of measurement. The authors from the 'classical' approach still want to evaluate the entrepreneurial process

*Table 11.1   Different approaches to and different dimensions of NPOs*

|  | Means – Ways | Result – Ends – Output |
|---|---|---|
| Techno-economic level | Efficiency, productivity | Goods and services responding to a demand or a need |
| Sociopolitical Level | Collective action, shared values, socialization | Impact, social change |

by growth. The 'progressive' group argues that not all entrepreneurs are always looking for profit and growth (Naffziger et al., 1994; Valéau, 2001; Ucbasaran et al., 2001), as they may have other motivations, aspirations and abilities and they may imagine and realize different visions (Filion, 1997). For Gartner et al. (1994), entrepreneurship remains a fundamentally idiosyncratic phenomenon. Authors such Carland et al. (1984) value innovation as the key criterion for assessing entrepreneurial performance. Low and MacMillan (1988), Valéau (2001) and Fayolle (2007) emphasize a broader contribution of entrepreneurs to the development of the society surrounding them, providing it with new solutions to its economic as well as its social problems. Obviously, these approaches, considering a broader entrepreneurial performance and being more open to diversity, open the doors to a more social version of the entrepreneur that fits better with the non-profit sector.

## 1.2   The Non-profit Sector

The non-profit sector can be seen as a major challenge for management sciences, as these sciences have been designed to study 'for-profit' companies. One of the main issues is the development of a concept of performance that doesn't refer to the maximization of profit. A second issue concerns considering organizations that are simultaneously driven by several goals and values.

From an economic point of view, NPOs are often referred to as the 'third sector' (see Table 11.1). They are analysed as organizations producing goods or, more often, services with the purpose of supplying demands that have been ignored or neglected by the private profit sector and by public services (Salamon and Anheier, 1997). With this in mind, one of the main issues with the economic view of NPOs concerns the added value of this production. For many authors, one of the main difficulties is the separation between those who finance and those who benefit from these activities (Valéau, 2001). Beyond the economic value of the means involved, many authors underline the social, and sometimes indirect, usefulness of these goods and services.

The sociological view of non-profit organizations analyses the NPO as a social network integrating individuals within the society (Laville and Sainsaulieu, 1997) (see Table 11.1). Through shared values and spontaneous collective action (Dawley et al., 2005; Boezeman and Ellemers, 2007), NPOs would reintroduce to modern society a primary socialization as in traditional societies. This social integration would include the creation of jobs for people who are usually excluded from the other sectors as well as the sense of belonging provided by volunteering. As a result, volunteers' and paid workers' motivations (Smith, 1981; Van Til, 1994; Bagozzi et al. 2003; Jamison, 2003) and commitment (Dailey, 1986; Pearce, 1993; Boezeman and Ellemers, 2007; Van Vuuren et al., 2008) often significantly differ from those of other organizations. According to this approach, the performance of these organizations relies, beyond activities, on the way they work.

Other sociologists emphasize the part NPOs play as agents of change within the society in which they find themselves: most of them may be more or less directly and more or less explicitly working for a 'better world' (Kanter and Summers, 1987; Cooperrider and Passmore, 1991; Valéau, 2001) (see Table 11.1). Different NPOs may target different levels of change: some are trying to change people's mentality; others want to alter their behaviour. These actions involve very open and sometimes indirect impacts, and as such remain very difficult to measure (Kanter and Summers, 1987).

Management sciences integrate the economic and sociological added values, trying to assess the level of efficiency of these organizations (Herman, 1994; Brudney, 1994) (see Table 11.1). This approach will often involve a ratio confronting the output produced with the means invested. There is still debate about how this management approach will measure the value of the services provided.

### 1.3 The Literature about Social Entrepreneurship

Authors such as Gartner (1990) have always kept the door of the field of entrepreneurship open to NPOs, but it is only during the last decade that this issue has been institutionalized as part of a new stream of research labelled: 'Social entrepreneurship'. Social entrepreneurship research plans to study a large variety of activities developed along a continuum going from the profit to the non-profit sector, even including the public sector (Dees, 1998; Johnson, 2000; Austin et al., 2006; Townsend and Hart, 2008). It can either concern businesses with a social commitment or non-profit or public organizations trying to improve their efficiency (CCSE, 2001). Johnson (2000) explains the emergence of this concept by the evolution of modern society such as the social demand for business to endorse more responsibility and, for the non-profit sector, to become more efficient due to the reduction of funds traditionally available. As noticed by Dees (1998), with all these very different contexts, it can be confusing to understand what social entrepreneurship is.

For his part, Prabhu (1999) considers that social entrepreneurship can take all kinds of legal forms, including new ones. A large number of texts even value this 'in between' as part of social entrepreneurship. For Townsend and Hart (2008), the choice of a given form of organization depends on the nature of the project: including social goals within a project essentially for profit or introducing efficiency in a venture fundamentally not for profit. For Wallace (1999), social entrepreneurs create new models of organizations that narrow the border between the profit and the non-profit sector. For Johnson (2000) this hybridization is a fundamental part of the innovations that social entrepreneurship produces to answer the complexity of the problems it addresses.

Social entrepreneurship is also often defined by referring to its goals as the use of entrepreneurial behaviours for social purposes (Hibbert et al., 2002) and an attempt to solve social problems efficiently and creatively (Wallace, 1999; Johnson, 2000; Hibbert et al., 2002). Social entrepreneurship is driven by individuals who want to improve society and who consider that the classical approach of profit and non-profit organizations cannot correctly address this issue. Social entrepreneurship reintroduces values and social considerations within the profit context and assesses performance in attracting and retaining human resources, fund-raising and finance in a non-profit sector often viewed as inefficient (Dees, 1998). Most authors agree on the difficulty, in the for-profit as well as in the non-profit sector, of measuring this entrepreneurial achievement of social value (Dees, 1998; Austin et al., 2006).

Beyond innovation, seizing opportunity and risk-taking, some of the authors address the question of the compatibility of economic efficiency and social value. Dees (1998) refers to them as the 'two bottom lines'. Townsend and Hart (2008) map the different cases through a table crossing the respective importance of economic and social goals. They evoke the possibility of maximizing the most important one with respect to the bottom line of the secondary one, but then point out the ambiguity of entrepreneurs giving high importance to both sets of goals. In most of the texts about social entrepreneurship, the term 'social value' is a synonym for 'social goals'. In the profit sector, authors admit these goals can be in contradiction to other goals related to profit. In the non-profit sector, authors connect social value to efficiency, coming back to a kind of maximization. Surie and Ashley (2008) consider the question of ethical value, which refers to a moral evaluation of the manners and the means followed to achieve the goals. For them, neither are incompatible as value creation necessitates ethical action to build legitimacy. Some authors, such as Austin et al. (2006), seem to consider the respect of ethical value as a social value in itself.

Social entrepreneurship literature has helped to import the concept of entrepreneurship within the context of NPOs. As part of this new stream of research, this chapter focuses on entrepreneurship in NPOs. Considering the fact that these organizations often give equal importance to several goals, values and considerations, we explore the 'ambiguity' (Townsend and Hart, 2008) that can occur in between the different 'bottom lines' (Dees, 1998), and we question the compatibility of entrepreneurship and ethics asserted by Surie and Ashley (2008). NPOs are often expected, and would often like, to achieve several goals according to several ethical and social values. This situation of the NPO trying to achieve different goals and values can be compared to that of mathematicians trying to optimize several functions simultaneously. Apart from random exceptions, this is not possible as in a large majority of cases, these functions take different directions, the maximum distance between them often moving according to situations and moments (Pareto, 1906 [1966]). There are ways in which one can try compromise, such as maximization of the sum of the two functions, and a middle way may be worked out, but this is not always the best solution. Furthermore, sometimes such compromise may not be possible. In other words, it can be difficult to 'run with the hare and hunt with the hounds' at the same time.

*Proposal 1:*  Social entrepreneurship often consists of dilemmas.

*Proposal 2:*  Social entrepreneurship often involves arbitrations.

## 2  METHODS

The phenomena studied in this research concern facts and situations that can be observed during the creation and development of non-profit organizations but also integrate and emphasize the subjective experiences and interpretations entrepreneurs make about them according to their goals, values and feelings. This is why the methods of data collection value particularly semi-directive interviews. The units analysed (Yin, 1984) were the activities and decision processes developed by these individuals. An important focus was the gap between the decisions they actually made

*Table 11.2    Sample*

| Sector of activity | Number of paid workers | Number of volunteers | Date of creation | Budget | Country |
|---|---|---|---|---|---|
| Education, health, social, sport, culture, leisure | Min 3 Max 1000 | Min 5 Max 300 | Min 0 Max 44 yrs | Min 0 Max £140 million | France |

and their initial and often idealistic vision. We identified and categorized different kinds of dilemmas concerning the orientation of the development of the NPO, the collective and democratic aspects of their governance and their personal commitment. These dilemmas provide a global overview of social entrepreneurship in the context of NPOs.

The 30 interviews used in this research deliberately included a large variety of NPOs (see Table 11.2). For comparison purposes, we decided to keep to smaller and, at first sight, less innovative NPOs, representing about half of our sample. These NPOs helped us to assert the limits of entrepreneurship (Gartner et al., 1994) as discussed at the end of this chapter. Another part of our sample definitely matched the archetypes of growth and efficiency suggested by social entrepreneurship literature. As a result, our sample contained a maximum of diversity (Morse, 1994) including small and big NPOs that had been operating for more or less time in different fields, developing all kinds of activities with and for all kinds of people.

One of the difficulties with NPOs is a 'bicephal' entrepreneurship shared by a chairman and an executive director (Fjellvaer et al., 2009). In half of the cases, we conducted two separate interviews or interviewed the chairman and the executive director together. In the other half, we had just one of them. From now on we will refer to both of them as entrepreneurs. We met these entrepreneurs, *in situ*, in their organizations. Most of the time, interviews were preceded by a visit to the structure. This observation would become a shared experience that has proven to be very useful in conducting and interpreting the interviews.

Interviews always started with an introduction about the entrepreneur and their NPO. Beyond the information collected, this objective topic helped to initiate the relationship. Our question was formulated as follows: 'Can you give me an overview of your NPO, trying to identify the important decisions that have shaped its development?'. Then we would listen to what the entrepreneurs had to say, simply asking for more details when necessary or asking them to elaborate or express their feelings. Progressively, their description of the facts would include more subjective aspects: opinion, goals, values and feelings. The most delicate parts of interviews were those concerning the dilemmas. As addressed in the conclusion, entrepreneurs often feel uncomfortable about what they perceive as a kind of failure. 'Congruence' and 'unconditional acceptance' (Rogers, 1961) promoted in the interviews helped the entrepreneur to overcome these feelings of failure and express themselves honestly. Exceptionally, only when not spontaneously discussed, we would ask: 'have you ever had to choose between the survival or development of your NPO and your values?'

Our interpretation of the words of the social entrepreneurs we have met do not pretend be 'true' but to be credible (Guba and Lincoln, 1994; Adler and Adler, 1994). These interpretations are developed following three steps:

- A first level of interpretation aims to understand the sense meant by the entrepreneur, being as empathic as possible.
- The second look is more critical, looking at words of the entrepreneur as a set of cognitive activities developed to make sense of actual experience.
- The third and ultimate interpretation of the interviews consists of a systematic comparative analysis between the experiences of the different entrepreneurs met that has led to the different proposals introduced in this chapter.

The quotations displayed in Tables 11.3, 11.4 and 11.5 are the final result of this empirical-formative process. They are examples of the different cases we have met. They illustrate the different categories of goals, values, considerations and preoccupations to which the entrepreneurs we have met refer. The overall idea of 'dilemma–innovation–arbitration' itself 'emerged' from the study of the interviews:

- First, identifying recurrent hesitations the social entrepreneurs had in their management and decision-making, observing their obsession to innovate, to 'find the solution'.
- Second, with Pareto's theory in mind (1906 [1966]), analysing that in most cases a large part of the difficulties faced were related to the incompatibility of their different sets of values and goals.
- Third, comparing different decisions finally made by entrepreneurs asserting the fundamentally subjective nature underlying them.

This model of 'dilemma–innovation–arbitration' presented and discussed in this chapter provides a 'representation', a map, emphasizing what has emerged from our set of interviews, as a crucial activity of social entrepreneurs in the non-profit context.

Qualitative research is a piece of craftwork that has its limits as well as its strengths, and our categories and models may not be absolutely universal. Other research with other samples may discover new elements that could necessitate revisions (Yin, 1984). Statistics would be useful to measure the frequency and probability of the cases identified. Nevertheless, the propositions formulated in the next section give an account of all the 30 cases that composed our sample (Guba and Licoln, 1994): this 'grounded theory' (Glaser and Strauss, 1967) has 'saturated' our data (Morse, 1994; Adler and Adler, 1994). Beyond internal coherence (Guba and Licoln, 1994; Adler and Adler, 1994), the trustworthiness of our results and models has been confirmed by the entrepreneurs themselves (Glaser and Strass, 1967; Morse, 1994; Wacheux, 1996). As a result, this grounded middle range theory allows us to start a conversation (Huff, 1999) with more universal theories (Popper, 1934, [1968]) about entrepreneurship, social entrepreneurship and NPOs.

## 3   RESULTS

This section presents the results. Each part deals with a specific set of dilemmas. We begin with a confrontation of the most frequent theoretical points of view and our data to introduce the proposal we develop. Data is presented in the form of a table including a series of summaries and quotations that are discussed later.

### 3.1   Dilemmas between Efficiency and Ethical Values

The literature about social entrepreneurs often emphasizes their ability to raise the funds they need to create and then efficiently develop the organizations they are running. The French sociological literature about non-profit organizations pays more attention to the fundamental part played by values in these organizations. Our data shows these two logics of action are sometimes difficult to handle simultaneously.

*Proposal 1 bis:*   Social entrepreneurs sometimes have to arbitrate between economic efficiency and the respect for their values.

As illustrated by the first two quotations (1.1 and 1.2) of Table 11.3, NPOs can't escape economic and financial issues as they determine their sustainability. Obviously, just like any other businesses, NPOs can reach a situation

*Table 11.3   Quotations about the dilemmas between efficiency and values*[1]

| No. | Summary | Content |
| --- | --- | --- |
| 1.1 | The need for money | 'The problem concerns the financial aspect. I can't do anything right now. I have used all the money from all our accounts. [. . .] Hopefully, I'll have a new subsidy coming next month!' |
| 1.2 | The need for competence in finance | 'People can't manage thousands and thousands of Euros, if they don't have a background in finance. [. . .] That's what causes problems in the non-profit sector.' |
| 1.3 | The worries about the renewal subvention | '. . .we always struggle. At the end of the year, we have to prepare our next task, then we have to wait until December to know how much we are going to get [. . .] are we going to get enough to develop all our projects? [. . .] Will we be able to survive all year? [. . .] all this is a permanent worry for us.' |
| 1.4 | The worries about the renewal of donations | 'As far as we are concerned, we don't get any subsidy from the public sector, we don't demand any and we're proud of it. We are self financing!' <br> 'The donors express their will through the renewal of their donation.' (site MSF) |
| 1.5 | Efficiency and controversy | 'As far as I am concerned, I want to be as useful as possible. I want to be efficient and offer as many services as possible. This is my style, even if everybody does not appreciate it.' |
| 1.6 | Making or not someone redundant | 'Of course, we would have liked to keep him but we could not afford it any longer.' |
| 1.7 | The price issue | 'At the moment, there is a lot of talk about price issues: some of us would like to raise the prices to get more money, others would like to give our services for free. At the moment, we just give free services to people who don't pay tax which serves as evidence of their low income.' |

*Note:*   1. Translated from French.

where they are not able to pay their debts (1.2) and may go bankrupt. As shown by quotation 1.3, in France, far more than in Anglo-Saxon countries, one of the most common means of financing NPOs is through government grants. The literature about social entrepreneurship unanimously rejects this option as it may compromise the NPOs' independence. However, it is also possible that the support and legitimacy gained from the beneficiaries and the general community can become a counter-power allowing a more balanced collaboration. Entrepreneurial and innovative projects can be developed in the framework of what can be a respectful partnership.

The literature about social entrepreneurship values fundraising from individuals and private companies, but as shown by quotation 1.4, these donations introduce another kind of dependency: advertising used to obtain funds needs to 'touch' the public. For instance, humanitarian NPOs often show their most spectacular achievements. Dramatization may help in raising more money but may also give a condescending image of the beneficiaries that could be seen as demagogy.

As illustrated by quotations 1.5, 1.6. and 1.7, the development of technical and financial efficiency in NPOs is not always as obvious as the recommendations made by the social entrepreneurship literature suggest. In France, the managers recruited in the 1980s who had been trained in business schools often had to face questions about the legitimacy of their management style. There may be some prejudice against innovation coming from the business sector but there may also be some actual contradictions between these solutions and the traditional values of the non-profit sector.

The two issues illustrated by quotations 1.6. and 1.7, having to make someone redundant and raising the prices of services, are the most commonly shared examples of these contradictions. Making someone redundant may be the only solution to overcome a reduction in financial means, but most NPOs find this hard or even impossible, referring to the fraternity and altruism that inspires their mission. These values can apply to paid workers who are often considered as part of the collective and communitarian action. Raising the prices of the services provided is obviously a pragmatic solution to secure the sustainability of an NPO that fits the recommendations of the models promoted by the social entrepreneurship literature, but on the other hand, this limits access to the goods and services provided for poorer people, just like any business would do.

### 3.2 Dilemmas between Leadership and Democracy

Research about the non-profit sector as well as literature in social entrepreneurship, often describes these organizations as collective and democratic. Our data shows that, in practice, they fit this description to a certain extent, but sometimes, in order to be more efficient, the entrepreneurs leading them introduce some form of hierarchy, exerting some form of power.

*Proposition 2 bis:*　Social entrepreneurs in the context of non-profit organizations sometimes have to arbitrate between participative democracy and more traditional, organized and professional forms of leadership.

As shown by the figure displayed at the top of Table 11.4 and as illustrated by quotation 2.1, NPOs are often democratic, and significantly more so than other organizations. In fact, democracy is one of the main criteria for identifying the organizations that should be counted as part of the sector (for example European Chart of Social Economy). Most of the entrepreneurs we have met introduce this principle within their speeches and work to gain this kind of legitimacy. But, as shown by all the other quotations from Table 11.4, the actual reality of these collective actions is more complex. This complexity, sometimes ambivalence, can be identified in the relationship with all the stakeholders involved in the organization: among members of the board and the directors, with human resources, with the customers and with the financers.

As shown by quotation 2.2, one of the obstacles to making NPOs more collective is the lack of candidates. This ability to commit people to an organization and its project may be at the heart of social entrepreneurship. As shown by quotations 2.3 and 2.4, conscious of this need for legitimacy, some entrepreneurs gather a lot people around them, but still, by vocation or necessity, do most of the work and decision making. This decision making can be seen as a responsibility, but also a power. As a matter of fact, NPOs are not always exempt from power games and sometimes look like Mintzberg's (1983) political arena. In France, one of the most well-known examples of this aspect of NPOs' lives is the tension that occurred within Médecin Sans Frontières, which led to the departure of Bernard Kouchner who then created Médecins du Monde. According to some entrepreneurs, the dilemma exists between a democracy that may bring opposition and a control of membership entering the board that will give them some means of carrying on their actions with more ease and efficiency.

As shown in quotations 2.5 and 2.6, another specificity of entrepreneurship in the non-profit sector is the dual leadership combination of Chairman–Paid Director. Beyond their complementary skills, the possible tension between them reflects the heterogeneity of these organizations (Reid and Karambayya, 2009): often but not always, the chairman communicates the vision, while the paid director works to make it possible. Legally, the paid director is under the chairman in hierarchy, but in practice, the asymmetry in the technical and financial skills currently required in the development of NPOs partially or substantially reverses the direction of the relationship.

More generally, collectivization of entrepreneurship in the non-profit sector also concerns the volunteers and paid human resources working for the organization. At least two visions can be found in the literature about this issue: the first one, brought about by French sociologists such as Laville and Sainsaulieu (1997), emphasizes progressive management

*Table 11.4   Data and quotations about the dilemmas between democratic management and classical leadership*[1]

| No. | Summary | Data |
|-----|---------|------|
|  | Evaluation of the collective nature of NPOs Quantitative Data / the collective dimension of a Non-Profit Venture | |

15%

18%

67%

☐ Collective Action
■ Mix of Collective and Individual
☐ Individual Action

| No. | Summary | Data |
|-----|---------|------|
| 2.1 | Reliability of the team | 'We have a team of very reliable people. It is a lot better than it used to be. . . .' |
| 2.2 | Volunteers' commitment | 'Today, we realize that it has become more and more difficult to find committed volunteers.' |
| 2.3 | Someone has to lead | 'Without being pretentious, I set up 70% of our projects. I like organising, I am good at it. We need a good group but also someone leading.' |
| 2.4 | Giving more | 'I give what I can, sometimes maybe I give too much. The problem is when you give more, the others give less.' |
| 2.5 | Chairman and paid director | 'The president visits us every week. I give him all the information and we make the decisions together.' |
| 2.6 | Professionalization | 'I don't believe in volunteering any more. We must professionalize [. . .] Responsibilities should not be given to the volunteer. We need professionals that have been trained for that. [. . .] volunteers are welcome but it is not they who make our organization go ahead.' |

*Table 11.4* (continued)

| No. | Summary | Data |
|-----|---------|------|
| | Definition of the relationship between entrepreneurs and their human resources Quantitative Data / collective dimension of Non Profit Venture | |
| 2.7 | Coordination | 'I am someone who coordinates, who asks questions, who coaches but I don't give any orders.' |
| 2.8 | Hierarchy and authority | 'No, I don't want to. [silence] no, [silence] maybe yes. I suppose I can force them to do what I want. I have the authority to do that.' |
| 2.9 | Members' commitment | 'Members behave more and more like customers [. . .] parents leave their children and we don't see them, the parents, any more. . .' |

*Note:* 1. Translated from French.

practices based on autonomy as part of the social innovation introduced by this organization. On the other hand, Anglo-Saxon literature about NPOs recommends more formalized and professional management forms with job description, training and evaluation. As shown by the second figure displayed in Table 11.4, an important part of the non-profit entrepreneurs we have met exercise an authority (38 per cent) but, within the French context, because of the social norms of the sector, as illustrated by quotation 2.7, most non-profit entrepreneurs often emphasize the responsibilities and the autonomy given to their human resources, introducing themselves as relatively or even absolutely equal coordinators (62 per cent). Digging a bit deeper, talking about extreme cases such as a worker disrespecting a beneficiary, these entrepreneurs admit they can exert directivity and authority. Valéau (2009) connected this to power and dependency. The entrepreneurs of NPOs can 'play' on members' wishes to remain members of the organization in order to get their way. Part of the dilemma is solved within an autonomy a priori given and emphasized but remaining implicitly conditional and if necessary, reduced.

The social entrepreneurs in NPOs may try to commit the other stakeholders in their democracy. One main step in the evolution of NPOs is the opening of their governance to their beneficiaries. We interpret this invitation as a move from an altruistic approach based on the idea of a giving organization to a more communitarian movement, where beneficiaries become part of the actual entrepreneurship, NPOs becoming an action for, by and with the beneficiaries. But, as shown by quotation 2.9, this ideal is difficult to achieve, because of the lack of motivation or competencies among beneficiaries. As far as finances are concerned, donations often give access to membership, but subvention forbids it: in France a law called the 'Loi Sapin' prevents representatives from the public sector from joining NPOs.

For some of the non-profit social entrepreneurs in our sample, despite their inherent difficulties, democracy and collectivization remain challenges that represent an added value and an end in themselves. These entrepreneurs see themselves as helping the rise of this dynamic without trying to control its output. For others, this collectivization is seen more as a limitation of their power which they accept as a part of a normal system of governance. Beyond its difficulties and constraints, part of the dilemma of collectivization can be reduced, as democracy may help social entrepreneurs to gain some kind of legitimacy that can become a valuable resource for action.

### 3.3    Dilemmas between Giving and Giving Up

Theory often describes the entrepreneur as someone who is never self-indulgent and never doubts. These individuals remain very focused on their activity and they adapt but persist in the same direction. They have a very strong achievement motive, a great need for control of events, they do not care about risk, and even like it. These assumptions are part of what Shaver (1995) refers to as the entrepreneurial myth. The literature about non-profit organizations and the research on social entrepreneurs also describes individuals full of passion with a high sense of their mission. As shown in the graph in Table 11.5, our data supports the importance of altruism and achievement motives. Creating an activity useful for others

*Table 11.5   Data and quotations about the motivations and doubts of entrepreneurs*[1]

| No. | Summary | Content |
|-----|---------|---------|
| | Motivations of social entrepreneurs in NPOs<br>Quantitative data | 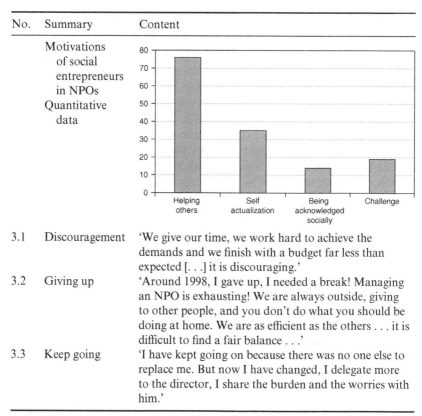 |
| 3.1 | Discouragement | 'We give our time, we work hard to achieve the demands and we finish with a budget far less than expected [. . .] it is discouraging.' |
| 3.2 | Giving up | 'Around 1998, I gave up, I needed a break! Managing an NPO is exhausting! We are always outside, giving to other people, and you don't do what you should be doing at home. We are as efficient as the others . . . it is difficult to find a fair balance . . .' |
| 3.3 | Keep going | 'I have kept going on because there was no one else to replace me. But now I have changed, I delegate more to the director, I share the burden and the worries with him.' |

*Note:*   1. Translated from French.

may often give entrepreneurs a sense of achievement, but as illustrated by the next quotations, sometimes they can feel like 'giving up'.

*Proposition 3*   Social entrepreneurs in the context of NPOs often go through moments of self-doubt during which they feel like giving up.

As illustrated by the data introducing Table 11.5, social entrepreneurs become committed to new or existing NPOs, driven by different motivations. This set of motivations fits quite well with the ones found in the literature on volunteering in terms of motivation and commitment: a general background of altruism taking the form of affective and normative commitment combined with personal and social achievement. The connection between altruism and personal motives often lies in the feeling of an efficient usefulness.

As illustrated by quotation 3.2 and 3.3, the motivations of these entrepreneurs cannot be taken for granted. Despite their sense of responsibility and commitment, they sometimes feel at these moments like giving up. Talking to them, it appears that the discouragement and weariness they then feel comes partly from the time taken by their activity but also from the responsibilities and the worries that come with it. Sometimes, as shown by quotation 2.4, they regret the absence of feedback or reward or the reciprocal commitment they expected from others. Chairmen often spend time wondering if they are going to quit. They often feel stuck because of their responsibilities and the expectations of the other members.

Some chairmen may quit with bitterness, but a lot of them overcome their discouragement and disappointment and carry on. This time of doubt often appears to be very useful in finding a second wind based on a renewed commitment more adjusted to their actual experience. One common pattern is a second wind inspired by a more distant commitment, less affective, more balanced, and eventually leading to more efficiency.

It is important to mention that the data presented in Table 11.5 and the following comments only refers to the unpaid chairman. The situation of the paid director is to a certain extent similar as they often choose the non-profit sector by vocation. But, as measured by Van Vuuren et al. (2008), immediate material investment connected with remuneration as well as long-term investment in terms of career can lead to different types of commitment. Their doubts may be about quitting a specific organization or even quitting the non-profit sector to join the public or for-profit sector.

## 4  DISCUSSION

The objective of this chapter was to contribute to the development of the concept of entrepreneurship within the non-profit sector. It explored the conditions under which innovation in terms of efficiency as recommended by the social entrepreneurship literature could be achieved with respect to the ethical values of independence, equality and solidarity to which NPOs often refer. In doing so, this chapter provides an in-depth exploration of what happens in between the 'bottom lines' to which social entrepreneurship literature sometimes adheres (Dees, 1998; Townsend and Hart, 2008). The different proposals grounded in the empirical data gathered for this research show an entrepreneurship experience made up of contradictions and dilemmas. Cases of complementarities between goals often happen

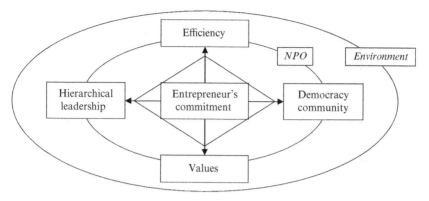

*Figure 11.1   Social entrepreneurship in NPOs*

(Surie and Ashley, 2008) but sooner or later, contradictions will occur. As a consequence, the main challenge of the social entrepreneur will be to make legitimate arbitration to create a course of organized action not too far from his or her initial vision (Figure 11.1).

The first dilemmas observed occur due to conflict between the respect for ethical values such as independence, equality or solidarity, and that of efficiency. Arbitration at this level actually determines the direction followed by the NPO. We agree with the idea from social entrepreneurship literature that in trying to improve some crucial aspect of the life of a given population, the volume of the contribution provided does matter. We think there is always a way to measure performance, even if it requires complementary qualitative investigations. It may be done by measuring the number of beneficiaries, the number of hours of cumulated service provided, the number of jobs created or even the number of actions made to broadcast the vision in the media. It is also possible to measure the evolution of these indicators through time to assess different aspects of growth. The social entrepreneurship literature often promotes innovation in accessing more resources and in organizing them in a more efficient manner. Indicators of the volume of activity can also be compared to the volume of resources actually used to achieve them to assess elements of productivity. However, our results also show that with these developments in efficiency, there is still a risk of not meeting the social values (Dees, 1998; Townsend and Hart, 2008). Furthermore, different cases indicate that the bottom lines (Dees, 1998; Townsend and Hart, 2008) of the different goals often come very close to each other, that is, where there is no space or margin to find a compromise. The idea of the social entrepreneur always doing well may be, using Shaver's word, a myth. As illustrated with the issue of making someone redundant, the entrepreneur has to arbitrate between efficiency and ethical value. There is no good solution, but the entrepreneur will choose what he or she considers the least damaging one.

The second dilemma was about the kind of leadership and the decision-making process developed. Social entrepreneurs have to choose between collectiveness and democracy versus a more hierarchical leadership. Arbitration at this level stands as a means to an end in terms of legitimacy and efficiency. We agree with Austin et al. (2006) and Townsend and Hart (2008) that this collectiveness, in other words this alignment with the stakeholders, represents a main characteristic of social entrepreneurship, especially in the NPOs. This legitimacy can not only be seen as a constraint, but also as a resource (Zimmerman and Zeitz, 2002). Beyond financing, legitimacy constitutes strength of negotiation. When dealing with public institutions, this legitimacy can become a counter power that can warrant independence. On the other hand, this research requires a need for coordination to direct all energies in the same direction. Mintzberg (1983) asserted the risk of the NPO becoming an 'political arena'. Leadership may be part of entrepreneurship (Becherer et al., 2008). The idea of the charismatic social entrepreneur leading his or her people toward a common goal may be another myth. In practice, part of the job of the social entrepreneur is to arbitrate, in particular when there is tension between the stakeholders involved in the governance.

The third dilemma was about the intensity and nature of the commitment of the social entrepreneur. Arbitration at this level obviously determines the development of the structure and the way the two other dilemmas will be treated. This third dilemma can be studied as part of the construction of identity as defined by Ireland and Webb (2007). This part of our study contributes to the introduction of commitment in the context of entrepreneurship by Sharma and Irving (2005) and Fayolle (2007) through an exploration of the process after the launching of an organization, focusing on momentary fall in commitment and then changes that may have an impact on the social entrepreneur'ss intention to proceed or the way he or she will do it. The idea of the missionary social entrepreneur who will always sacrifice everything he or she has to succeed in helping others is another myth of social entrepreneurship. Social entrepreneurs very often hesitate to carry on. Human failure is one of the major risks for NPOs' survival.

Considering these three sets of dilemmas, non-profit organizations present a very challenging research problem for entrepreneurship theory: a problem of measurement. Dees (1998) and Austin et al. (2006) have already asserted the difficulty of quantifying the social impact of the NPOs on their environment. Taking into account the dilemmas we observed introduces further complication. For instance, in the context of the NPO, entrepreneurs sometimes refuse an opportunity to grow because they do not want any funds from the government. This decision can be interpreted as an entrepreneurial act, and because of it, social entrepreneurs assert their vision and orientate the development of their venture according to it.

Facing the same dilemma with a similar set of goals and values, two social entrepreneurs can make very different decisions and take their venture along very different paths. There are different ways to develop NPOs entrepreneurially (Valéau, 2003). We believe that, in this context more than anywhere else, considering these dilemmas, entrepreneurship stands as an idiosyncratic phenomenon (Gartner et al., 1994). With this in mind, entrepreneurial performance can no longer be assessed only through comparative quantitative methodologies; it also requires qualitative interpretations. Following other authors from the social entrepreneurship literature, we will revisit some of the core ideas of entrepreneurship: risk-taking, innovation and seizing opportunity.

Risk-taking has often been introduced as a constitutive aspect of entrepreneurship (Mill, 1848; Say, 1803; Knight, 1921; Low and MacMillan, 1988; Davidsson et al. 2001; Ireland and Webb, 2007). This research reminds us that the risk of financial failure and bankruptcy is as high in the NPOs as in the profit context. Financial survival risks are related to other risks. This risk of failure threatens, and at the same time allows the personal achievement process: success cannot exist without this risk (MacClelland, 1961; Argyris, 1965). A financial failure also introduces a social risk as these entrepreneurs invest their reputation in a project. Standing out in their community and taking charge of some of its needs, their ability to act depends on the legitimacy and trust they get from all the stakeholders who give their money and time, or simply their approbation. This social judgement about success or failure also takes into account the other 'bottom line': as shown by our data, people can be against efficient social entrepreneurs because they think the way they work does not properly respect certain social values. Social aspects of failure may, in a way, be more stigmatizing than financial ones and can constitute a bigger handicap for further ventures.

Innovation has been identified as another fundamental aspect of entrepreneurship (Schumpeter, 1934; Carland et al., 1984; Low and MacMillan, 1988; Ucbasaran et al., 2001; Davidsson et al. 2001; Verstraete, 2002; Ireland and Webb, 2007; Fayolle, 2007). In the context of 'non-profit' as in 'for-profit' organizations, innovation covers all kinds of areas: it can concern the needs and demands taken in charge, the access to larger funds through new forms of marketing, the development of new forms of

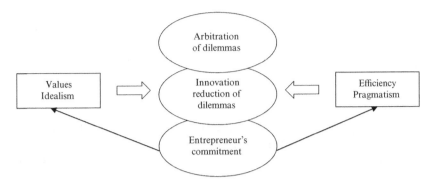

*Figure 11.2   Innovation as a way to make NPOs' projects possible*

organization as traditionally promoted by social entrepreneurship literature, but also new ways of managing and governing human resources and
stakeholders. A large part of this creativity is devoted, at least partially, to
solving the dilemmas and overcoming the contradictions encountered.

Innovation can be connected to seizing opportunity (Cantillon, 1755;
Say, 1803; Low and MacMillan, 1988; Kirzner, 1993; Ucbasaran et al.,
2001; Ireland and Webb, 2007). Shane and Vankataraman (2000) asserted
that this activity is at the heart of entrepreneurship. For us, as for many
authors (Fayolle, 2007), opportunity is not always pre-existing. In the
non-profit sector even more than anywhere else, seizing opportunity consists of creating the conditions to make the project possible (see Figure
11.2). Changing their environment can be seen as a positive effect of entrepreneurial activity (Schumpeter, 1934; Fayolle, 2007). For the NPO, this
is part of their mission. Social entrepreneurs judge the actual society and,
identifying its shortcomings and needs, try to make it a better place. To
this extent, seizing opportunity is about realizing a vision, and somehow
making it possible. This involves an overall arbitration between pragmatism and idealism.

### 4.1   Final Proposals

- Social entrepreneurship often consists of dilemmas.
- Dilemmas can sometimes be partially solved through innovation.
- Social entrepreneurship often involves arbitration (arbitration
  begins where innovation ends).
- The challenge of the social entrepreneur consists in making ambi-
  tious and inspired visions, economically, socially and personally
  possible.

# CONCLUSION

Social entrepreneurship can be seen as an approach combining pragmatism with idealism or idealism with pragmatism. The dilemmas identified in this chapter occur with situations where two sets of goals cannot be simultaneously achieved, obliging the social entrepreneur to choose what he or she will judge is the 'least bad' alternative. These dilemmas are relatively frequent and constitute, in our opinion, the turning points of social entrepreneurship: that is, crucial moments during which entrepreneurs push their venture in the direction they have decided. During this very challenging moment, they confront their ideal vision with reality and show their ability to make it technically and economically possible without deviating from its core values.

As a result, NPOs remain very open spaces that are defined only according to what they cannot be. Their actual activities, their goals and the way they operate are more than ever inspired from the vision of the entrepreneur. But these lines of action are also defined through this confrontation of the vision with reality, day after day, dilemma after dilemma. Acknowledging the absence of the ideal decision and the necessary subjectivity of the arbitration required to solve these dilemmas, the question of the measurement of entrepreneurial performance becomes more uncertain than ever (Carland et al., 1984; Van de Ven et al., 1984; Low and MacMillan, 1988; Gartner, 1988; Davidsson et al. 2001; Ireland and Webb, 2007; Fayolle, 2007). Should we try to quantify the fit between the way the venture is actually developed and the initial vision? Should we take into account the level of ambition of the social entrepreneur? In other words, to what extent should we take the growth of the NPO into account? One of the limitations of this chapter is that it does not bring any answer to these crucial questions, but, on the other hand, it does offer a very idiosyncratic idea of entrepreneurship.

These questions of measurement are connected to questions of definition and have a direct impact on the development of future research (Whetten, 1989; Sutton and Staw, 1995; Davidsson et al. 2001; Ireland and Webb, 2007). As in any other domain of research, social entrepreneurship should develop quantitative approaches to try to identify antecedents and consequences of the phenomena studied. One possibility could be to carry on with the tradition of typologies (Smith, 1967; Vesper, 1980; Filion, 1997) and to work on mean comparison to try to identify the types of personality and motivations (Brockaus and Horwitz, 1985; Naffziger et al., 1994; Vesalainen and Pihkala, 1999) that lead to a certain type of arbitration, or the specific risks that accompany the different ways of being a social entrepreneur.

These questions of definition and measurement of the social entrepreneurial phenomena also have an impact on practical issues as these methods of evaluation and their resulting recommendations will influence the individuals running NPOs, either directly or through the people, books and classes that help them to learn their job (Fayolle, 2007). One important issue brought out by this chapter is that the difficulty of continuously and simultaneously achieving different goals does not always come from a lack of skill, but depends, at least partially, on the characteristics of the situation: some situations allow complementarity, others don't. Bearing this in mind, we invite social entrepreneurs not to give up their core values too easily for the profit of an efficiency that would not be legitimate (Zimmerman and Zeitz, 2002). Facing these dilemmas, we recommend creativity and innovation to help build new opportunities, explore new ways of doing things and push back the constraints of the situation faced. When all the possibilities have been analysed and contradictions are still there, social entrepreneurs should look to arbitrate between goals as part of the job.

# BIBLIOGRAPHY

Adler, P.A. and P. Adler (1994), 'Observational techniques', in N.K. Denzin and S.Y. Lincoln, *Handbook of Qualitative Research*, Thousand Oaks, CA: Sage.

Allen, N.J. and J.P. Meyer (1990), 'The measurement and antecedents of affective, continuance and normative commitment to the organization', *Journal of Occupational Psychology*, **63**, 1–18.

Argyris, C. (1965), *Integrating the Individual and the Organization*, New York: Wiley.

Austin, J., H. Stevenson and J. Wei-Skillern (2006), 'Social and commercial entrepreneurship: same, different, or both?', *Entrepreneurship Theory and Practice*, **30**(1), 1–22.

Bagozzi, R.P., M. Bergami and L. Leone (2003), 'Hierarchical representation of motives in goal setting', *Journal of Applied Psychology*, **88**(5), 915–43.

Becherer, R.C., M.E. Mendenhall and K. Ford Eickhoff (2008), 'Separated at birth: a conceptual inquiry of the independence of the entrepreneurship and the leadership constructs', *New England Journal of Entrepreneurship*, **11**(2), 13–25.

Boezeman, E.J., and N. Ellemers (2007), 'Volunteering for charity: pride, respect, and the commitment of volunteers', *Journal of Applied Psychology*, **92**(3), 771–85.

Brockhaus, R.H. and P.S. Horwitz (1985), 'The psychology of the entrepreneur', in D.L. Sexton and R.W. Smilor, *The Art and Science of Entrepreneurship*, Cambridge, MA: Ballinger.

Brudney, J.L. (1994), 'Designing and managing volunteer programs', in R. Herman, *The Jossey-Bass Handbook of Nonprofit Leadership and Management*, San Francisco: Jossey-Bass, Chapter 13.

Bruyat, C. (1994), 'Contributions épistémologiques au domaine de l'entrepreneuriat', *Revue Française de Gestion*, **101**, 87–99.

Bygrave, W.D. and C.W. Hofer (1991), 'Theorizing about entrepreneurship', *Entrepreneurship Theory and Practice*, Winter, **16**(2), 13.

Canadian Center for Social Entrepreneurship (CCSE), 'Social entrepreneurship', Discussion Paper No. 1.

Cantillon, R. (1755), *Essai sur la Nature du Commerce en Général*, London: Fetcher Gyler.

Carland, J.W., F. Hoy, W.R. Boulton and J.A.C. Carland (1984), 'Differentiating entrepreneurs from small business owners: a conceptualization', *The Academy of Management Review*, April **9**(2), 354.

Clary, E.G. and M. Snyder (1998), 'The motivations to volunteer: theoretical and practical considerations', *Current Directions in Psychological Science*, **8**(5), 156–9.

Cooperrider, D.L., and W.A. Passmore (1991), 'The organization dimension of global change', *Human Relations*, **44**(8), 763–87.

Dailey, R.C. (1986), 'Understanding organizational commitment for volunteers: empirical and managerial implications', *Journal of Voluntary Action Research*, **15**, 19–31.

Davidsson, P. and J. Wiklund (2001), 'Level of analysis in entrepreneurship research: current research practice and suggestions for the future', *Entrepreneurship Theory and Practice*, **25**(4), 81–100.

Davidsson, P., M.B. Low and M. Wright (2001), 'Editors' introduction: Low and MacMillan ten years on – achievements and future directions for entrepreneurship research', *Entrepreneurship Theory and Practice*, **25**(4), 5–16.

Dawley, D.D., R.D. Stephens and D.B. Stephens (2005), 'Dimensionality of organizational commitment in volunteer workers: Chamber of commerce board members and role fulfillment', *Journal of Vocational Behavior*, **67**, 511–25.

Dees, J.J. (1998), 'The meaning of social entrepreneurship', Kauffman Foundation, available at: http://www.fntc.info/files/documents.

Fayolle, A. (2007), *Entrepreneurship and New Value Creation*, New York: Cambridge University Press.

Filion, L.J. (1997), 'Le champ de l'entrepreneuriat: historique, évolution, tendances', *Revue Internationale PME*, **10**(2): 130–77.

Fjellvaer, H., W. Reid and A. Langley (2009), 'Le leadership bicephal: sa logique et ses defies', paper presented at Conférence HEC Montréal, 14 January.

Gartner, W.B. (1988), 'Who is an entrepreneur is the wrong question', *American Small Business Journal*, **12**(4), Spring, 11–32.

Gartner, W.B. (1990), 'What are we talking about when we talk about entrepreneurship?', *Journal of Business Venturing*, **5**, 15–28.

Gartner, W.B., B.J. Bird and J.A. Starr (1992), 'Acting as if: Differentiating entrepreneurial from organizational behavior', *Entrepreneurship Theory and Practice*, **16**(3), 13–21.

Gartner, W.B. and E. Gatewood (1992), 'Thus the theory of description matters most', *Entrepreneurship Theory and Practice*, **17**(1), 5–10.

Gartner, W.B., K.G. Shaver, E. Gatewood and J.A. Katz (1994), 'Finding the entrepreneur in entrepreneurship', *Entrepreneurship Theory and Practice*, **18**(3), 5–10.

Glaser, B. and A. Strauss (1967), *The Discovery of Grounded Theory, Strategies of Qualitative Research*, Chicago: Aldine Publishing Company.

Guba, E.G. and Y.S. Lincoln, Y.S. (1994), 'Competing paradigms in qualitative research', in N.K. Denzin and S.Y. Lincoln, *Handbook of Qualitative Research*, Thousand Oaks, CA: Sage, pp. 105–17.

Herman, R.D. (1994), *The Jossey-Bass Handbook of Nonprofit Leadership and Management*, San Francisco: Jossey-Bass.

Hibbert, S.A., G. Hogg and T. Quinn (2002), 'Consumer response to social entrepreneurship: the case of the big issue in Scotland', *International Journal of Nonprofit and Voluntary Sector Marketing*, **7**(3), 288–301.

Hofer, C.W. and W.D. Bygrave (1992), 'Researching entrepreneurship', *Entrepreneurship Theory and Practice*, **16**(3), 91–5.

Huff, A.S. (1999), *Writing for Scholarly Publication*, Thousand Oaks, CA: Sage.

Ireland, R.D. and J.W. Webb (2007), 'A cross-disciplinary exploration of entrepreneurship research', *Journal of Management*, **33**(6), 891–927.

Jamison, I.B. (2003), 'Turnover and retention among volunteers in human service agencies', *Review of Public Personnel Administration*, **23**(2), 114–32.

Johnson, B.R. (1990), 'Toward a multidimensional model of entrepreneurship: the case of achievement motivation and the entrepreneur', *Entrepreneurship Theory and Practice*, **14**(3), 39–54.

Johnson, S. (2000), 'Literature review on social entrepreneurship', discussion paper, Canadian Centre for Social Entrepreneurship, University of Alberta.

Kanter, R.M. and D.V. Summers (1987), 'Doing well while doing good: dilemmas of performance measurement in nonprofit organizations and the need for a multiple-constituency approach', in W.W. Powell, *The Nonprofit Sector. A Research Handbook*, New Haven and London: Yale University Press, pp. 154–66.

Kirzner, I.M. (1993), 'The morality of pure profit', *Journal des Economistes and des Etudes Humaines*, **4**, 315–28.

Knight, F.H. (1921), *Risk, Uncertainty and Profit*, New York: Houghton Mifflin.

Laville, J.-L. and R. Sainsaulieu (1997), *Sociologie de l'Association: des Organizations à l'Épreuve du Changement Social*, Paris: Desclée de Brouwer.

Low, M.B. and I.C. MacMillan (1988), 'Entrepreneurship: past research and future challenges', *Journal of Management*, **14**, 139–61.

MacClelland, D.C. (1961), *The Achieving Society*, Princeton, NJ: Van Nostrand.

Mill, J.S (1848), *Principles of Political Economy with Some of their Applications to Social Philosophy*, 9th edn London: Longmans, Green & Co., 2 volumes.

Mintzberg, H. (1983), *Power In and Around Organizations*, Englewood Cliffs, NJ: Prentice Hall.

Morse, J.M. (1994), 'Designing funded qualitative research', in N.K. Denzin and S.Y. Linclon, *Handbook of Qualitative Research*, Thousand Oaks, CA: Sage, pp. 220–33.

Naffziger, D.W., J.S. Hornsby and D.F. Kurato (1994), 'A proposed research model of entrepreneurial motivation', *Entrepreneurship Theory and Practice*, **18**(3), 29–42.

Pareto, V. (1906 [1966]), *Manuel d'économie politique*, 4th edn, Geneva: Droz.

Paulhus, D. (1984), 'Two-component models of socially desirable responding', *Journal of Personality and Social Psychology*, **46**, 598–609.

Pearce, J.L. (1993), *Volunteers: the Organizational Behavior of Unpaid Workers*, London and New York: Routledge.

Popper, K. (1934 [1968]), *The Logic of Scientific Discovery*, 3rd edn, London: Hutchinson.

Popper, K. (1968), *The Logic of Scientific Discovery*, first published 1934, London: Hutchinson.

Prabhu, G.N. (1999), Social Entrepreneurial Leadership, *Career Development International*, **4**(3), 140–47.

Reid, W. and Karambayya (2009), 'Impact of dual executive leadership dynamics in creative organizations', *Human Relations*, **62**(7), 1073–112.

Rogers, C.R. (1961), *On Becoming a Person*, Boston: Houghton Mifflin Company.

Salamon, L.M. and H.K. Anheier (1997), *Defining the Nonprofit Sector: a Cross-National Analysis*, Manchester: Manchester University Press.

Say, J.B. (1803), *Traité d'Économie Politique: ou Simple Exposition de la Manière dont se Forment, se Distribuent and se Consomment les Richesses*; English edn (1964), *Treatise on Political Economy: on the Production, Distribution and Consumption of Wealth*, New York: Kelley (1st edn, 1827).

Schumpeter, J.A. (1934), *The Theory of Economic Development*, published in German (1912), 1st English edn, Cambridge, MA: Harvard University Press.

Shane, S. and S. Venkataraman (2000), 'The promise of entrepreneurship as a field of research', *Academy of Management Review*, **25**(1), 217–26.

Sharma P., and G. Irving (2005), 'Four bases of family business successor commitment: antecedents and consequences', *Entrepreneurship Theory and Practice*, **29**(1), 13–33.

Shaver, K.G. (1995), 'The entrepreneurial personality myth', *Business & Economic Review*, **41**(3), 20–23.

Smith, D.H. (1981), 'Altruism, volunteers and volunteerism', *Journal of Voluntary Action Research*, **10**(1), 21–36.

Smith, N.R. (1967), *The Entrepreneur and his Firm: the Relationship between Type of Man and Type of Company*, Bureau of Business Research, East Lansing, Michigan State University Press.

Surie, G. and A. Ashley (2008), 'Integrating pragmatism and ethics in entrepreneurial leadership for sustainable value creation', *Journal of Business Ethics*, **81**(1), 235–46.

Sutton, R.I. and B.M. Staw (1995), 'What theory is not', *Administrative Science Quarterly*, **40**, 371–84.

Townsend, D.M. and T.A. Hart (2008), 'Perceived institutional ambiguity and the choice of organizational form in social entrepreneurial ventures', *Entrepreneurship Theory and Practice*, **32**(4), 685–700.

Ucbasaran, D., P. Westhead and M. Wright (2001), 'The focus of entrepreneurial research: contextual and process issues', *Entrepreneurship Theory and Practice*, **25**(4), 57.

Valéau, P. (2001), 'Pour une version non seulement lucrative de l'entrepreneuriat', *Management International*, **6**(1), 33–41.

Valéau, P. (2003), 'Différentes manières de gérer les associations', *Revue Française de Gestion*, **146**, 2–12.

Valéau, P. (2009), 'International volunteering and alter-globalization', in J.M. Aurifeille, C. Medhin and C. Tisdel (eds), *Trust, Globalization and Market Expansion*, New York: Nova Science Publishers Inc., pp. 149–66.

Van de Ven, A.H., R. Hudson and D.M. Schroeder (1984), 'Designing new business startups: entrepreneurial, organizational, and ecological considerations', *Journal of Management*, **10**(1), 87–98.

Van Til, J. (1994), 'Nonprofit organizations and social institution', in R. Herman, *The Jossey-Bass Handbook of Nonprofit Leadership and Management*, San Francisco: Jossey-Bass, pp. 44–64.

Van Vuuren, M., M.D.T. De Jong and E.R. Seydel (2008), 'Commitment with or without a stick of paid work: comparison of paid and unpaid workers in a non-profit organization', *European Journal of Work and Organizational Psychology*, **17**, 315–26.

Verstraete, T. (2002), *Essai sur la singularité de l'entrepreneuriat comme domaine de recherche*, Les Editions de l'ADREG, January.

Vesalainen, J. and T. Pihkala, T. (1999), 'Entrepreneurial identity, intentions and the effect of the push-factor', *Academy of Entrepreneurship Journal*, **5**(2), 1–25.

Vesper, K.H. (1980), *New Venture Strategies*, Englewood Cliffs: Prentice Hall.

Wacheux, F. (1996), *Méthodes Qualitatives and Recherche en Gestion*, Paris : Economica.

Wallace, S.L. (1999), 'Social entrepreneurship: the role of social purpose enterprises in facilitating community economic development', *Journal of Developmental Entrepreneurship*, **4**(2), 153–75.

Whetten, D.A. (1989), 'What constitutes a theoretical contribution?', *Academy of Management Review*, **14**(4), 486–9.

Yin, R.K. (1984), *Case Study Research: Design and Methods*, Beverly Hills, CA: Sage.

Zimmerman, M.A., and G.J. Zeitz (2002), 'Beyond survival: achieving new venture growth by building legitimacy', *Academy of Management Review*, **27**(3), 414–31.

# 12 Innovating for social impact: is bricolage the catalyst for change?
## *Jill Kickul, Mark D. Griffiths and Lisa Gundry*

As an alternative to the focus on financial value creation, social entrepreneurship is primarily concerned with the creation of social value for disenfranchised members of society. To date, relatively little attention has focused on understanding the process by which social entrepreneurs mobilize resources to initiate, develop and grow their enterprises. While authors such as Bornstein (2003) have provided anecdotal cases and examples to imply that social entrepreneurs make do with the resources they currently possess, very little focus has been on the types of behaviour and development that enable them to continually sustain and have an impact on assisting marginalized individuals, groups and communities. As Desa (2007) recently highlighted, social entrepreneurship is abundant and flourishes in resource-constrained environments (for example, as witnessed in the inner-city neighbourhoods in the US (Porter, 1995) and small villages in Brazil and India (Bornstein, 2003)).

We extend this literature with the first empirical study (to our knowledge) of the effect of bricolage behaviour on the growth of social impact, albeit in a relatively small but focused sample of social entrepreneurs. While economic theory predicts the rent-seeking behaviour of prospective commercial entrepreneurs, we focus instead on the prosocial behaviour of entrepreneurs whose environments are typically resource constrained and essentially present new challenges, whether opportunities or problems, without providing new resources (Baker and Nelson, 2005). Specifically, we examine the bricolage behaviour of social entrepreneurs – a set of actions driven by the pursuit of existing and often scarce resources that can be recombined to create novel and interesting solutions of value that affect their respective markets. Bricolage behaviour may predict entrepreneurs' attempts to bring social innovations to the marketplace to solve meaningful problems and challenges. Researchers such as Harding (2004) have noted that there is a need for a more expansive definition of business value creation, and the role of social enterprise in creating economic and social value deserves greater investigation. Moreover, Cornwall and Naughton (2003) questioned the assumption of entrepreneurial success, suggesting that researchers may not be accurately measuring what success means to some entrepreneurs, and that it might be broadened to include issues of principle and of a personal, moral nature. As scholars attempt to assess the motivations and desired outcomes of social entrepreneurs, it is helpful to build on and extend the existing framework of new venture creation and growth in the social arena. Research in the social entrepreneurship space can advance more quickly by utilizing the universe of knowledge gained in the study of commercial entrepreneurship. 'We should build our theory of social entrepreneurship on the strong tradition of entrepreneurship theory and research. Social entrepreneurs are one species of the genus entrepreneur' (Dees et al., 2001: 2). The logic of this approach is that both social and commercial entrepreneurship address similar conceptual questions about the processes of discovery, evaluation and exploitation of opportunities and the set of individuals who engage in these actions (Shane and Venkataraman, 2000). The increased recognition that social and commercial entrepreneurship exist on a continuum rather than as a dichotomy, and the continued blurring of boundaries between social and economic value creation suggests there may be numerous examples of cross-fertilization of knowledge between commercial and social entrepreneurship (Mair and Martí, 2006).

In comparing social and commercial entrepreneurship, Austin et al. (2006) identified four key differentiating elements: the social nature of the opportunity, motivation due to fundamentally distinct missions, human and resource mobilization, and performance measurement. Each of these represents an important potential contribution between the two domains of entrepreneurship. For example, in their theoretical work on social entrepreneurship, Zahra et al. (2006) introduced the construct of social wealth as a measure of the social value created after accounting for the associated financial and social costs. While the creation of financial value is often the dependent variable of choice when measuring the contribution of entrepreneurship, the performance measurements of social wealth and impact may complement these efforts and be more consistent with the *raison d'être* of entrepreneurship.

Underlying social entrepreneurship are the multiple tangible and intangible benefits and rewards that are exhibited by a heightened sense of accountability to the constituencies served, as well as to the impact and outcomes that are created. Social entrepreneurs seek to provide social improvements and enhancements to their communities, including an attractive return on investments (both social and financial) to their key stakeholders. Social entrepreneurs assess their impact and influence in terms of their social impact, innovations and outcomes, not simply in terms of size, growth, or processes. Realizing greater social impact through innovation may depend on the extent to which entrepreneurs can apply and combine the resources they have to new problems and opportunities – a behaviour known as 'bricolage' (Baker and Nelson, 2005).

The purpose of this chapter is to examine the relationship between entrepreneurial bricolage and firm innovation, and growth in social impact (see Figure 12.1). This study extends earlier work on bricolage behaviour in established, for-profit organizations to the social entrepreneurship arena. This research further explores the usefulness of bricolage as a key concept in the social entrepreneurship process, as recent scholarship has begun to establish (Mair and Martí, 2009). By acknowledging the resources at hand, entrepreneurs can engage in bricolage as a means to discovering problems and opportunities, enabling the development of robust innovations within constrained environments (Desa, 2008). Moreover, it investigates the influence of innovation on the growth of social impact, including the development of products and services targeted to unserved markets, and on the reduction and resolution of social problems and challenges.

## SOCIAL ENTREPRENEURSHIP AND BRICOLAGE: USING WHAT'S AT HAND TO DO GOOD

Bricolage was developed by Lévi-Strauss (1967) to suggest the creation of something new through involved actors in the process of recombination and transformation of existing resources (Venkataraman, 1997; Garud et al., 1998; Baker and Nelson, 2005). Bricolage constructs were further refined in Baker and Nelson (2005), where they defined it as a focus on using resources at hand, using existing resources for new purposes, recombining existing resources and making do to provide breakthrough solutions in firm creation. Bricolage normally is directed towards resource processes, relationships, and the interconnections among them. Existing resources are based in specific contexts and knowledge and application of local and regional resources provides resource advantages. This suggests that bricolage may be integral in the development of novel innovations, and through this, further social change and success occurs.

Bricolage recognizes the interrelationship of environment and the individual/firm, building new/novel solutions and viewing and targeting different markets (assuming path creation). It also has ties with notions of knowledge spillovers, economic regeneration, and proximity designs, that is, regeneration through firm development using local depleted or minimal resources available 'freely at little or low cost'. As posited by Desa (2007):

> Since social ventures often operate in resource constrained environments yet are required to develop and deploy complete modular packages to scale their

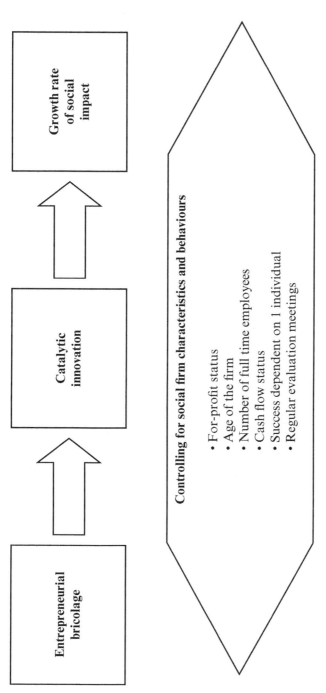

*Figure 12.1  Proposed research model: the mediating role of catalytic innovation on the relationship between entrepreneurial bricolage and growth rate of social impact*

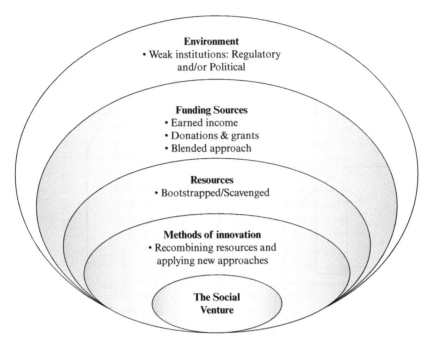

*Source:*   Adapted from Desa (2007).

*Figure 12.2   Bricolage within resource-poor environments*

social impact, it appears that bricolage can be very applicable to understanding social venture development. The reasons for using bricolage are particularly relevant to social entrepreneurship: to create within penurious environments, to create despite limited knowledge, or to build upon their existing acts of creation (Baker and Nelson, 2005; Baker et al., 2003; see adapted Figure 12.2 from Desa, 2007).

Moreover, the majority of literature on bricolage attempts to make systematic sense of what entrepreneurs do when they continue to pursue their goals despite substantial resource constraints; these may be external constraints (depleted resources/inability to access) or internal constraints (lack of knowledge, capabilities). In the literature, these resources have generally been studied in terms of finance (for example, bootstrapping), and dealt with to a limited extent in the venture creation processes (nonlinear process designs; see Bhave, 1994; Sarasvathy, 2001). More recently, scholars have addressed the question of whether the outcomes of bricolage can be extrapolated to firms in which profit maximization is not the primary priority. For example, Mair and Martí (2009) investigated bricoleurs operating under severe resource constraints who are attempting to help marginalized individuals and groups to participate in market activities in a developing country. Among the findings is the conclusion that bricolage can be a process to invoke change.

Bricolage is inherently tied to notions of creativity, and improvization. This differs from traditional linear social planning and focuses instead on social design processes, the more focused role of compressed timeframes of decision making and the frequency of connections with the environment and the resources contained within it (externally) and within the firm (internally). Because social entrepreneurs often operate within resource-scarce environments, they may be compelled to use creative approaches to attract non-traditional resources, and to apply those resources in novel ways to the social challenges of their mission. Social entrepreneurs tend to approach social problems unnoticed or unaddressed by existing organizations or institutions, and thus bricolage occurs when institutional support, such as external financing sources (Desa, 2008), is unavailable. Further, since many of the challenges pursued by social entrepreneurs have persisted for some time, and perhaps even resisted traditional methods of resolution, social entrepreneurs may be especially inclined to engage in bricolage behaviour. Simply put, the conventional approaches do not work, so they must seek creative alternatives. This makes social entrepreneurship a particularly interesting, appropriate and useful arena in which to examine bricolage behaviour.

The degree to which social entrepreneurs engage in bricolage behaviours may determine their success in developing catalytic innovations for the marketplace. Bricolage notions of making do and using whatever is at hand links with a fundamental social shift of developing smart, sustainable, projects that are integral to social change. This represents a shift from a consumption-based to a conservation-based way of doing things better through an improved understanding of existing resources, their form, function, and fungibility, thereby developing a more clever, creative means of developing products and services aligned with market needs. Bricolage may enable these entrepreneurs to use creative approaches to attract and distribute resources, identify overserved or unserved market segments, and offer products and services that are simpler, less costly, and 'good enough' – all characteristics of catalytic innovators (Christensen et al., 2006).

## CATALYTIC INNOVATION FOR SOCIAL IMPACT

Effective social change and its long-term impact rely on new approaches and methods to solve some of the most pressing and persisting problems faced by communities around the world. Christensen et al. (2006) asserted that social-sector organizations must develop fundamentally new approaches that are scalable and sustainable, with the ability to influence system-changing solutions. This 'catalytic innovation' is derived from Christensen's model of disruptive innovation, with an emphasis on creating social change.

Innovations can be separated into two distinct categories: sustaining and disruptive. Sustaining innovations include nearly all product and service innovations, whether incremental or breakthrough, that provide, for example: increased quality, better or more features and functions, and other changes targeted to existing customers of the organizations (Christensen and Bower, 1995). Disruptive innovations do not fulfil existing customers' needs as effectively as sustaining innovations. They tend to be less complex, more accessible and convenient, and less costly, therefore attracting new or different customer groups (Christensen and Bower, 1995). Disruptive innovations are likely to be attractive to markets that are not adequately served by existing product and service solutions.

Catalytic innovations, as a subset of disruptive innovations, provide 'good enough' solutions to social challenges that are not effectively addressed by existing organizations using traditional approaches (Christensen et al., 2006). Catalytic innovators, descriptive of entrepreneurs and organizations whose primary focus is on social change, share the following five characteristics (Christensen et al., 2006):

1. Creating systemic social change through scaling and replication: these innovators are often new entrants that continually improve their offerings to expand their market reach. High transferability from one location to another enables the innovation to be scaled and to be sustained across marketplaces.
2. Meeting a need that is either overserved or not served at all: new entrants to the market provide less expensive, less functional alternatives to a segment of the market that is overserved by the dominant provider, or not served at all.
3. Offering products and services that are simpler and less costly than existing alternatives, and are considered 'good enough'. These innovations bring new benefits to people in ways existing firms are not willing to provide. Maintaining the status quo prevents traditional, dominant players from trying new approaches that might cannibalize their current offerings. Catalytic innovators are thus able to attract new markets with alternatives and solutions that are affordable and effective enough to reduce the problems.
4. Generating resources, such as donations, grants, volunteers, or

intellectual capital in ways that are unattractive to incumbent competitors. Catalytic innovators tend to be creative in their approaches to identifying needed resources, and these may come from non-traditional sources, such as micro-lending programmes.

5. Often being ignored, disparaged, or even encouraged by existing players for whom the business model is unprofitable or unattractive, and who therefore withdraw from the market segment. The dominant provider places distance between it and the new entrant, and moves toward a more lucrative market segment. This enables the catalytic innovator to capture the opportunity in serving its intended market (Christensen et al., 2006).

By incorporating the specific role that catalytic innovation has in the relationship between entrepreneurial bricolage and growth in social impact, we are better able to understand the process by which social entrepreneurs adopt and utilize existing resources for future development, growth, and sustainability of their own ventures. As such, our proposed research model (as mentioned earlier and depicted in Figure 12.1) was developed, in which catalytic innovation mediates the relationship between entrepreneurial bricolage and the growth rate of social impact. The degree to which social entrepreneurs engage in bricolage behaviour, applying existing resources to problems and opportunities in new ways, can lead to catalytic innovation that ultimately strengthens their firms' social impact on the people and communities they serve.

## METHODOLOGY

### Data Collection

Participants were 41 social entrepreneurs of organizations whose business activities are directly involved with and primarily working in the social enterprise sector (for example, for-profit social ventures or not-for-profit organizations).[1] The entrepreneurs and their respective firms were sampled through an existing social entrepreneurship university database. The social entrepreneurs served a number of sectors, including education, environment, mental health, hunger, arts and culture, and social capital investing.

All information was gathered from the social entrepreneurs over a two-week period, utilizing an on-line survey. Emails were sent to the social entrepreneur of the social enterprise sampled, asking for their participation in the study. Within the text of the email was a hyperlink that would direct them to the online questionnaire. The social entrepreneurs were informed that their candid opinions would help us to clarify the different approaches that social entrepreneurs take in finding and implementing new ideas and opportunities within their respective markets. In addition to answering a series of questions on personal characteristics, the entrepreneurs were asked to provide information regarding the types of business practices and innovations implemented in their social firms. Upon completion of the survey, their responses were submitted to a secure Internet database.

## Measurement

### Entrepreneurial bricolage

To assess the entrepreneurial bricolage behaviour of the social entrepreneurial firm, we used a nine-item scale developed by Steffens et al. (2009) who used the standard protocols for scale development. In deriving their scale, they created items that were consistent with Baker and Nelson's (2005: 333) definition of bricolage as 'making do by applying combinations of the resources at hand to new problems and opportunities'. Sample items included: 'We are confident of our ability to find workable solutions to new challenges by using our existing resources'; 'We use any existing resource that seems useful to responding to a new problem or opportunity'; 'We deal with new challenges by applying a combination of our existing resources and other resources inexpensively available to us'; 'When dealing with new problems or opportunities we take action by assuming that we will find a workable solution'; and 'We combine resources to accomplish new challenges that the resources weren't originally intended to accomplish'. Social entrepreneurs indicated how much they agree or disagree with the statements on a seven-point Likert scale (1 = 'strongly disagree'; 7 = 'strongly agree'). Cronbach's alpha of this scale was .90.

### Catalytic innovations

We measured catalytic innovation, solutions to social challenges that are not effectively addressed by existing organizations using traditional approaches, by developing a 25-item scale designed to capture each of the five characteristics advanced by Christensen et al. (2006). For each of the characteristics, we created 4–6 items within each characteristic. Sample items to measure 'Creating systemic social change through scaling and replication' included: 'Our approach allows us to serve potentially large groups of people'; 'The individuals or groups we serve have traditionally been underserved by alternative services or organizations'; 'We are able to serve people whose access is otherwise limited'; and 'We are able to improve our offerings by expanding market reach (e.g. offering services to more people, adding locations, etc.)'.

For the 'Meeting a need that is either overserved or not served at all' characteristic, sample items included: 'Our services or solutions meet our clients' needs in ways more traditional providers did not'; 'Our offerings are simpler and therefore more effective as solutions than others that were traditionally available'; and 'Our clients were not served at all by traditional offerings'.

Sample items for the characteristic of 'Offering products and services that are simpler and less costly than existing alternatives, and are considered "good enough"' included: 'Our products and services are less complex than existing alternatives'; 'Our products and services are less costly than existing alternatives'; 'Our products and services are perceived as more convenient to new clients'; and 'Our products and services are perceived by new clients as less costly than alternatives'.

The 'Generating resources, such as donations, grants, volunteers, or intellectual capital in ways that are unattractive to incumbent competitors' included such items as: 'We are able to attract donors and funding based on our business model'; 'We would decline funding that requires us to alter our business model'; 'We are able to attract grants for our business model'; 'We are able to attract volunteers to our organization'; and 'Organizations with more traditional offerings would not be likely to obtain the knowledge or information (intellectual capital) that we have obtained'.

Finally, sample items for the 'Often being ignored, disparaged, or even encouraged by existing players from whom the business model is unprofitable or unattractive, and who therefore retreat from the market segment' characteristic included: 'Businesses that offer more traditional services tend to ignore our business, or its services'; 'Existing players have encouraged us to provide offerings for our market segment'; 'Existing players find our market segment unattractive and either avoid it or retreat from serving it'; and 'Existing players disparage the work we do because they believe it is unprofitable'. Social entrepreneurs indicated how much they agree or disagree with the statements on a seven-point Likert scale (1 = 'strongly disagree'; 7 = 'strongly agree'). An overall composite score of all of the characteristics to comprise catalytic innovation was then developed and used in subsequent analyses. The Cronbach's alpha of this scale was .88.

**Control Variables**

We chose six control variables that can have an influence on a social entrepreneurial firm's growth rate of social impact, including:

1. *For-profit status*: whether the social enterprise was of for-profit or not-for-profit status.

2. *Age of the firm*: age since inception, range from less from one year to over 20 years.
3. *Number of full-time employees*: full-time employees, range from one employee to more than 50 employees.
4. *Cash flow status*: whether the social enterprise had negative cash flow, break-even, or positive cash flow.
5. *Success dependent on one individual*: whether the social enterprise's success is perceived to be dependent on one individual leader/ entrepreneur.
6. *Regular evaluation meetings*: the frequency of meetings ranging from 'as needed' to 'weekly'.

Additional information and descriptives of each of the six control variables are provided in Figure 12.3.

### Data Analysis: Statistical Mediational Model

Zero-order correlations as well as the mediated regression approach recommended by Baron and Kenny (1986) were used to test our proposed model. In the mediational approach, three separate regression equations are estimated. First, the mediator (catalytic innovation) is regressed on the independent variable (entrepreneurial bricolage). Second, the dependent variable (growth rate of social impact) is regressed on the independent variable. In the last equation, the dependent variable is regressed simultaneously on both the independent and mediational variable. Mediation is indicated when the following conditions are met: the independent variable must affect the mediator in the first equation; the independent variable must affect the dependent variable in the second equation; the mediator must affect the dependent variable in the third equation; and lastly, assuming that all of these conditions are in the proper direction, the effect of the independent variable on the dependent variable must be less in the third equation than in the second equation. Full or perfect mediation is supported when the independent variable has no significant effect when the mediator is controlled, while partial mediation is indicated if the effect of the independent variable is reduced in magnitude but still significant when the mediator is controlled (Baron and Kenny, 1986).

### Results

The means, standard deviations, and zero-order correlations and reliabilities are reported in Table 12.1. The reliabilities of our continuous measures used were all over the .70 minimum established by Nunnally (1978).

As shown in Table 12.1, we found a number of zero-order correlations to be significant, including those among and between our control variables as well as our dependent variable. For example, younger firms tended to have negative cash flows ($r = -.53$) and were smaller in terms of full-time employees ($r = .63, p<.05$). Additionally, the size of the organization (full-time employees) was also related to whether they had positive cash flow ($r = .31, p<.05$), had regular evaluation performance meetings ($r = .32, p<.05$), and were less dependent on one individual to lead the efforts of the social enterprise ($r = -.39, p<.05$). Finally, in examining the control variables relationships with the growth rate of the firm's social impact, having positive cash flow and regular evaluation performance meetings were all significantly associated to this rate and type of firm growth.

In analysing the relationships, we also found initial support for the first part of our mediational model. That is, the relationship between entrepreneurial bricolage and our mediator of catalytic innovation was significant ($r = .69, p<.05$). While this was supported at a one-to-one relationship (zero-order correlations), we wanted to utilize the mediation approach to better understand and evaluate our proposed research model within the context of our social enterprises. Table 12.2 displays the approach and results to test this more stringent growth model by including our control variables, entrepreneurial bricolage, and mediator of catalytic innovation.[2] With a three-equation approach suggested by Baron and Kenny (1986), we found that the growth rate of social impact is fully mediated by catalytic innovation. That is, the relationship between entrepreneurial bricolage and growth was no longer significant when accounting for catalytic innovation. Therefore, catalytic innovation serves as an important link between a firm's bricolage behaviour and its growth rate in terms of social impact.

## DISCUSSION

The purpose of our chapter was to investigate the relationship between entrepreneurial bricolage, firm innovation, and growth in social impact. Our work and findings augment and extend previous research on bricolage behaviour in the social entrepreneurship arena. This arena presents an especially relevant experimental setting in which to examine the role of bricolage, since social entrepreneurs are compelled to use existing resources at hand, applying them in creative and useful ways to problems and new opportunities. In incorporating such behaviour, an often observed and cited trait that social entrepreneurs persist and develop, we are also able to investigate its influence on innovation and on the growth rate of social

For-profit organization

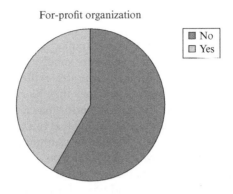

Histogram

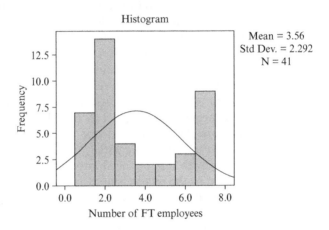

Success dependent on one individual

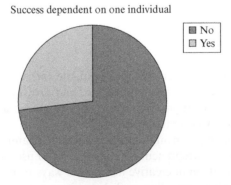

*Figure 12.3   Social firm characteristics and behaviours*

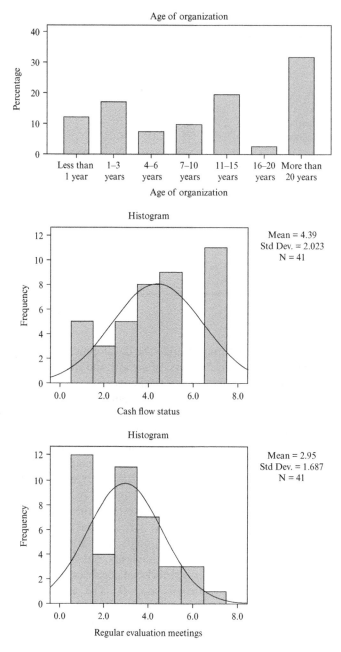

*Figure 12.3*   (continued)

*Table 12.1   Means, standard deviations and zero-order correlations*

| | Variable | Mean | Std Dev | 1 | 2 | 3 | 4 | 5 | 6 | 7 | 8 |
|---|---|---|---|---|---|---|---|---|---|---|---|
| 1 | For-profit organization | 0.42 | 0.49 | 1.0 | | | | | | | |
| 2 | Age of firm | 4.42 | 2.22 | −.18 | 1.0 | | | | | | |
| 3 | Cash flow status | 4.39 | 2.02 | −.21 | −.53* | 1.0 | | | | | |
| 4 | Regular evaluation mtgs | 2.95 | 1.68 | −.21 | .11 | −.09 | 1.0 | | | | |
| 5 | Success dependent on 1 individual | 0.27 | 0.45 | .05 | −.29 | −.09 | −.15 | 1.0 | | | |
| 6 | Number of full-time employees | 3.56 | 2.29 | −.30 | .63* | .31* | .32* | −.39* | 1.0 | | |
| 7 | Entrepreneurial bricolage | 5.30 | 1.01 | −.16 | .20 | .24 | −.14 | .11 | .08 | 1.0 | |
| 8 | Catalytic innovation | 22.39 | 4.39 | −.22 | −.05 | .13 | .20 | .20 | .12 | .69* | 1.0 |
| 9 | Social impact growth rate | 4.68 | 1.39 | −.02 | −.22 | .32* | .32* | .04 | −.19 | .33* | .46* |

*Note:*   * Significant at the 5% level.

impact. This social impact may include the development of products and services targeted to unserved markets, often with the goal of the reduction and resolution of social problems and challenges.

Our findings indicate that while entrepreneurial bricolage is associated with growth in social impact, they are mediated by the role and rate of catalytic innovation that is present within the social enterprise firm. Bricolage may assist social entrepreneurs using novel approaches to attract and distribute resources, identify overserved or unserved market segments, and offer products and services that are simpler, less costly, and 'good enough'. These types of catalytic innovations, as proposed by Christensen et al. (2006), may also help social enterprises determine their future growth in terms of their own social contribution to both internal and external stakeholders. Within their penurious environments and with limited resources, bricolage may explain one of the key behaviours that social entrepreneurs must adopt when they encounter institutional constraints and are without regulatory or political structure or support. The ability to mobilize resources known and available to social entrepreneurs may allow them to generate the types of needed solutions and innovations and drive awareness of the immediate and pressing problems of the community.

While bricolage behaviours are traditionally instigated from an ad hoc intuitive process and through research, they may also be developed into a

*Table 12.2    Mediated regression on social impact growth rate*

| Control variables | β |
|---|---|
| For-profit organization | 0.04 |
| Age of firm | −0.16 |
| Cash flow | −0.14 |
| Regular evaluation meetings | 0.40 |
| Success dependent on 1 individual | −0.09 |
| Number of full-time employees | −0.17 |
| *Mediational approach[†]* | |
| (1) Entrepreneurial Bricolage → Catalytic Innovation | 0.38* |
| (2) & (3) Entrepreneurial Bricolage → Growth Rate of Social Impact | −0.03 |
| Catalytic Innovation → Growth Rate of Social Impact | 0.54* |
| $R^2$ | 0.40 |
| Adjusted $R^2$ | 0.21 |
| F | 2.08* |

*Notes:*
\* Significant at the 5% level.
† The Beta weights represent the values in the final and last step of the mediational analyses. Entrepreneurial bricolage was found to be significantly related to the growth rate of social impact; however, when catalytic innovation is entered into the last equation, this relationship is no longer significant ($β = −.03$, $p > .05$).

more strategic tool. For social entrepreneurs, such a tool can be used to evaluate resource requirements, changes of the nature and the amount of resources needed, and its influence on the development of the firm and, more specifically, products and services that create additional benefit for society. Additionally, through attempts of bricolage, social entrepreneurs may learn through doing (for example, entrepreneurial skills) and instigate entrepreneurial behaviours linked with self-efficacy (see Hmieleski and Corbett, 2006) and building social firm capabilities in the venture creation and growth process to bring about effective social change.

## STUDY LIMITATIONS AND FUTURE RESEARCH DIRECTIONS

Although this research makes several important contributions, these contributions must be considered within the context of the limitations of this study. Limitations include the relatively small sample size and that the association between our predictor (entrepreneurial bricolage), the intervening variables (catalytic capabilities), and outcomes (growth rate of social impact) included common method variance. That is, the measures used to tap each of these constructs were taken from one source (the social entrepreneur) and these associations could, therefore, be attributed to a bias on the part of the respondent.

We could overcome this bias by bringing in alternative perspectives from multiple stakeholders (senior-level managers, employees, partnering organizations, and so on) in the social enterprise. A 'deep dive' into their viewpoints of how the social firm continually builds, adapts and reconfigures their internal and external resources to achieve congruence with the changing social, economic, and institutional environments would give us further insight into the innovation and social impact modelling and approach. More of a systematic approach at multiple levels of the firm may tell us that social entrepreneurs do not compete on introducing radically new solutions or services, but rather on a deeper factor – the capacity to develop solutions that have been traditionally overlooked by alternative services or organizations, or to serve individuals and communities whose access is otherwise limited.

An additional limitation was that our study was cross-sectional, yet the hypothesized model and relationships suggests causal direction. Causal inferences created from cross-sectional designs are only inferences (Spector, 1984). Future research should examine many of the same relationships in our study with longitudinal data to assess causality. This type of data collection along with a case study approach may provide an additional perspective of how bricolage and innovation occur throughout the life cycle and strategy of the social enterprise. As an on-going research initiative, we are in the process of capturing and completing our database which tracks not only our social entrepreneurs at one point in time but also enables us to examine longitudinally how bricolage and its associated behaviours relate to multiple and diverse social impact measures. This type of research allows us to investigate the relationship between bricolage and the stage of development of the social enterprise firm. Similar to how traditional entrepreneurial organizations often bootstrap in their early initial stages of growth, it would be interesting to examine how nascent social firms create and find the financial, social and intellectual resources needed to demonstrate the scale, sustainability and impact that attract a social capital market audience.

The social capital market is expanding to include not only traditional non-profit firms but also for-profit and hybrid entities that have strong social values and missions. The blurring of boundaries among the different types of entities creates opportunities in which non-profits are adopting and engaging in profit-seeking behaviours, for-profits aggressively seeking social value through both operating and charitable activities, and public agencies looking to develop partnerships with all in their attempts to reduce social problems and advance positive public outcomes and benefits (Austin et al., 2007; Wei-Skillern et al., 2007).

At the NYU-Stern School of Business Fifth Annual Conference of Social Entrepreneurs on 'Measuring social impact', Mission Measurement founder and president Jason Saul provided pragmatic advice by articulating a different vision of where the social benefit sector is headed and what it means for social entrepreneurs and the way they assess their impact. He emphasized that this sector is increasingly becoming a social capital market in which organizations need to be focused on the outcomes they produce and measurement that allows them to improve their impact. Social entrepreneurs have allegiance to the outcomes and innovations they are trying to create, but should be agnostic to the means. His perspective is that there are three major shifts happening in this context, including:

(1) fundraising is done – you should be selling a product called impact and find ways to measure it since the currency of the social capital market is the impact you have; (2) from activities to outcomes – we do not define ourselves by what we do, we define ourselves by what value and innovations we create, and (3) a shift from 'evaluation' to 'measurement' – it is not about 'proving', it is about 'improving.'

Saul further introduced several key principles to survive in a social capital market, all from a resource and impact perspective including engaging stakeholders, aligning resources and strategies, translating both into meaningful outcomes, and connecting back to the market and stakeholders. His perspective and suggestions may prove valuable for social entrepreneurs within resource-constrained environments who often engage in bricolage behaviour. These entrepreneurs may be looking to the social capital market to provide the funding and to ensure resources to scale and to replicate their business model for the next underserved or unmet market outside their existing community.

## CONCLUSION

As discussed by Mair and Martí (2006), the field of social entrepreneurship creates a unique opportunity to continually integrate, challenge and debate many traditional entrepreneurship assumptions in our efforts to develop a cogent and unifying paradigm. With this first empirical study to our knowledge to examine the effect of bricolage behaviour on the growth of social impact, we further develop the field of social entrepreneurship by utilizing the maxims and concepts developed in commercial entrepreneurship.

Incorporation of the concept of entrepreneurial bricolage to the field provides us with a unique perspective on how social entrepreneurs mobilize and utilize existing resources to 'catalyse' innovations that address some of society's most pressing problems. As such, they are not only directly finding creative solutions, but also engaging their own pre-existing knowledge and relationships to encourage stakeholders to take notice of these innovations and the impact they can have in driving long-term systematic change for broader social, political and economic well-being.

## NOTES

1. Social enterprise describes any non-profit, for-profit or hybrid corporate form that utilizes market-based strategies to advance a social mission (consistent with many organizational and alliance definitions, see http://se-alliance.org/).
2. The table includes standardarized Beta weight ($\beta$), $R^2$ and F value results for the last equation in the test for mediation.

## REFERENCES

Austin, J., H. Stevenson and J. Wei-Skillern (2006), 'Social and commercial entrepreneurship: same, different or both?', *Entrepreneurship Theory and Practice*, **30**, 1–22.
Austin, J.E., R. Gutiérrez, E. Ogliastri and E. Reficco (2007), 'Capitalizing on convergence', *Stanford Social Innovation Review*, Winter, pp. 21–34.
Baker, T. and R.E. Nelson (2005), 'Creating something from nothing: Resource construction through entrepreneurial bricolage', *Administrative Science Quarterly*, **50**, 329–66.
Baker, T., A.S. Miner and D.T. Eesley (2003), 'Improvising firms: bricolage, account giving and improvisational competencies in the founding process', *Research Policy*, **32**, 255–76.
Baron, R.M. and D.A. Kenny (1986), 'The moderator–mediator variable distinction in social psychological research: Conceptual, strategic, and statistical considerations', *Journal of Personality and Social Psychology*, **51**, 1173–82.
Bhave, Mahesh P. (1994), 'A process model of entrepreneurial venture creation', *Journal of Business Venturing*, **9**(3), 223–42.
Bornstein, D. (2003), *How to Change the World: Social Entrepreneurs and the Power of New Ideas*, Oxford; New York: Oxford University Press.
Christensen, C.M. and J.L. Bower (1995), 'Disruptive technologies: catching the wave', *Harvard Business Review*, January–February.
Christensen, C.M., H. Baumann, R. Ruggles and T.M. Sadtler (2006), 'Disruptive innovation for social change', *Harvard Business Review*, December.
Cornwall, J.R. and M.J. Naughton (2003), 'Who is the good entrepreneur? An exploration within the Catholic social tradition', *Journal of Business Ethics* **44**(1), 61–75.
Dees, G., J. Emerson and P. Economy (2001), *Enterprising NonProfits: A Toolkit for the Social Entrepreneur*, New York: J. Wiley & Sons.

Desa, G. (2007), 'Social entrepreneurship: snapshots of a research field in emergence', paper presented at the 2007 International Social Entrepreneurship Research Conference (ISERC), Copenhagen, 18–19 June.

Desa, G. (2008), 'Mobilizing resources in constrained environments: a study of technology social ventures', unpublished doctoral dissertation, University of Washington.

Garud, R., A. Kumaraswamy and P. Nayyar (1998), 'Real options or fool's gold: perspective makes the difference', *Academy of Management Review*, **3**(2), 212–14.

Harding, R. (2004), 'Social enterprise: the new economic engine', *Business Strategy Review*, **15**(4), 39–43.

Hmieleski, K.M. and A.C. Corbett (2006), 'Proclivity for improvisation as a predictor of entrepreneurial intentions', *Journal of Small Business Management*, **44**(1), 45–63.

Lévi-Strauss, C. (1967), *The Savage Mind*, Chicago: The University of Chicago Press.

Mair, J. and I. Martí (2006), 'Social entrepreneurship research: a source of explanation, prediction, and delight', *Journal of World Business*, **41**(1), 36.

Mair, J. and I. Martí (2009), 'Entrepreneurship in and around institutional voids: a case study from Bangladesh', *Journal of Business Venturing*, **24**(5), 419–35.

Nunnally, J. (1978), *Psychometric Theory*, New York: McGraw-Hill.

Porter, M.E. (1995), 'The competitive advantage of the inner city', *Long Range Planning*, **28**, 132.

Sarasvathy, S.D. (2001), 'Causation and effectuation: toward a theoretical shift from economic inevitability to entrepreneurial contingency', *Academy of Management Review*, **26**(2), 243–88.

Shane, S. and S. Venkataraman (2000), 'The promise of entrepreneurship as a field of research', *Academy of Management Review*, **25**, 217–26.

Spector, P.E. (1984), 'Using self-report questionnaires in OB research: a comment on the use of a controversial method', *Journal of Organizational Behavior*, **15**(5), 385–92.

Steffens, P., J. Senyard and T. Baker (2009), 'Linking resource acquisition and development processes to resource-based advantage: bricolage and the resource-based view', paper presented at the AGSE Entrepreneurship Research Exchange, Adelaide, AU, 3–6 February.

Venkataraman, S. (1997), 'The distinctive domain of entrepreneurship research: an editor's perspective', in J. Katz and R. Brockhaus (eds), *Advances in Entrepreneurship, Firm Emergence and Growth*, Vol.3, Greenwich, CT: JAI Press, pp. 119–38.

Wei-Skillern, J.C., J.E. Austin, H.B. Leonard and H.H. Stevenson (2007), *Entrepreneurship in the Social Sector*, Thousand Oaks, CA: Sage Publications.

Zahra, S., E. Gedajlovic, D. Neubaum and J. Shulman (2006), 'Social entrepreneurship: domain, contributions and ethical dilemma', paper presented at University of Minnesota Conference on Ethics and Entrepreneurship, June.

# 13 A community-wide framework for encouraging social entrepreneurship using the pipeline of entrepreneurs and enterprises model

*Thomas S. Lyons and Gregg A. Lichtenstein*

> One of the most important things that can be done to improve the state of the world is to build a framework of social and economic supports to multiply the number and the effectiveness of the world's social entrepreneurs.
>
> (David Bornstein, *How to Change the World*, 2007)

The purpose of this chapter is to present a new conceptual lens through which to view social entrepreneurship, its players, processes and objectives. In so doing, we hope to provide a framework for guiding thought and action in this rapidly emerging field. As researchers *and* practitioners, our focus is on linking both worlds. The current literature on social entrepreneurship is very broad, which is to be expected of a young field, and it is not necessarily a negative, as it lends an early inclusivity to a multi-disciplinary field (Martí, 2006). However, it lacks a structure for pulling its significant knowledge together in a way that can be acted upon.

Herein, we re-introduce a model of our creation, which we call the Pipeline of Entrepreneurs and Enterprises (hereafter referred to as 'the pipeline' or 'the pipeline model'). We created this model to facilitate thinking about commercial, or business, entrepreneurship and its relationship to community economic development. We would argue, however, that it has value in framing social entrepreneurship more broadly as well. In this chapter, we briefly explore the current literature on social entrepreneurship and where it leaves practitioners, both social entrepreneurs and those who would assist them, in their ability to take effective action. We explain the pipeline and its relationship and utility to social entrepreneurship, and we demonstrate how the pipeline can be used to manage the social assets of a community effectively. We close by noting other potential related uses for the pipeline model in social entrepreneurship research.

## BACKGROUND/BRIEF LITERATURE REVIEW

Social entrepreneurship is best described as an *emerging* field, as yet without a clear theoretical base or even a commonly agreed-upon definition. It spans disciplines, economic sectors, legal structures and communal boundaries. It is a huge field – at once exciting and overwhelming. In an effort to provide a baseline for discussion, however, we favour the definition of social entrepreneurship developed by Wei-Skillern et al. (2007: 4). It characterizes this field as 'an innovative, social value-creating activity that can occur within or across the nonprofit, business, or government sector'. We admire this definition for its recognition of social entrepreneurship's innovative core and its boundary-spanning nature. Having said that, we would also emphasize that social entrepreneurship is about the application of business discipline to the pursuit of a social or environmental mission. It is this disciplined, systematic and strategic thinking that characterizes the approach to social entrepreneurship we espouse within these pages.

To date, the literature of social entrepreneurship has been broad and relatively unfocused. It touches upon a host of topics including the characteristics and behaviours of social entrepreneurs, their similarities to and differences from commercial entrepreneurs, the nature of social enterprises, and how social entrepreneurs marshal resources in pursuit of mission, among others (Perrini and Vurro, 2006; Guclu et al., 2002; Dees, 1998).

This literature tells us that social entrepreneurs share many characteristics with commercial entrepreneurs, among them innovativeness, willingness to proceed without currently owning the resources required for success, determination, constructive impatience, and a focus on performance. They also share certain characteristics among themselves – a willingness not to be constrained by ideology, a strong belief in their and other people's innate capacity to 'do good', a comfort level with speaking for others, a focus on social value creation and mission, and so on (Bornstein, 2007).

We also know from this literature that social entrepreneurs are more likely to be women and members of ethnic minorities than are business entrepreneurs, and are also likely to be better educated. Social entrepreneurs are commonly more oriented than business entrepreneurs to think in terms of accomplishing things through cooperation and collaboration. We know that while both types of entrepreneur seek to create value, commercial entrepreneurs strive for value that generates profits; social entrepreneurs pursue social value. Unlike commercial entrepreneurs, social entrepreneurs may never achieve financial sustainability for their enterprises and may need to rely on volunteers for much of their staffing needs (Bygrave et al., 1996).

The literature also tells us much about the nature of social enterprises. These entities are diverse in their legal structure and in the way they are financed (European Commission, 2008; Cornforth, 2003; Brinckerhoff, 2000). They may be non-profit entities, for-profit businesses, or a hybrid of the two. They may rely for financing on government grants, traditional philanthropy (for example, individual donors, foundations and business giving), non-traditional philanthropy (for example, social venture philanthropy, commercial financial markets, E-philanthropy), and/or earned income (Wei-Skillern et al., 2007; Dees, 2001).

While all of this information is useful to understanding who social entrepreneurs are and how they build and sustain social enterprises, its focus is at the level of the individual entrepreneur and/or his or her individual enterprise. Some authors (Wei-Skillern et al., 2007; Robinson, 2006; Dees et al., 2001) have acknowledged that social entrepreneurship does not take place in a vacuum and, in fact, is undertaken within a context that brings political, socio-cultural, demographic and other forces to bear on the pursuit of social mission. However, little is known about the interaction between social entrepreneurs and the broader communities of which they are a part. More specifically, little is known about how the actions of communities enhance or impede social entrepreneurship or how communities can organize themselves to foster entrepreneurship as a community-wide strategy.

This chapter attempts to address this shortcoming of the literature by introducing a conceptual framework for organizing our thinking about social entrepreneurship activities in our communities. This framework is designed to allow us to map these activities, then use that map to prepare strategies for efficiently and effectively encouraging them. We call this framework the 'pipeline of entrepreneurs and enterprises'.

## THE PIPELINE OF ENTREPRENEURS AND ENTERPRISES

We first articulated the pipeline model elsewhere (Lichtenstein and Lyons, 2006) as a framework for thinking about the under-appreciated role of business entrepreneurship in community, or regional, economic development. We argued that entrepreneurship creates wealth, both for individual entrepreneurs and for the community. In order to maximize wealth creation as an economic development strategy, a community must think about its entrepreneurs and enterprises as business assets. It is the economic developer's job to effectively manage those assets as a portfolio, similar to a stock and bond portfolio.

One way to think about this portfolio of entrepreneurs and their enterprises is as a pipeline of variegated stocks and flows, as opposed to an undifferentiated pool. As with any pipeline, the goal is to maximize volume and maintain or increase flow. If this is done well, then wealth will be generated at a sufficient scale to transform the economy of the community in question.

In order to make this work, the community must segment its market; its client base. This requires being able to differentiate among entrepreneurs, among enterprises, and between the two. Our pipeline model does this by using two variables: (1) the skill level of the entrepreneur or team leading the enterprise; and (2) the stage in the business life cycle that the given enterprise has attained. At the heart of this approach is the observation that the entrepreneur and the enterprise are not one and the same. An entrepreneur must have the necessary skills to move his or her business from one stage in the business life cycle to the next. Our work in the field has demonstrated that a very different set of skills is required at each life cycle stage (Lichtenstein and Lyons, 2008). Examining each of these two variables in turn helps to clarify these distinctions.

Relative to entrepreneurship skills, we argue that these are essential to success, can be developed, and that entrepreneurs can be differentiated by their degree of skill. Skills can be measured on four major dimensions (Gerber, 1995; Lichtenstein and Lyons, 2001):

1.  Technical – those required to carry out the essential functions of the business;
2.  Managerial – those necessary for efficient and effective management of the functions of the business;
3.  Entrepreneurial – those required for recognizing opportunities and devising ways to capture them;
4.  Personal maturity – those involving personal accountability, self awareness, emotional intelligence and creativity.

When these skills are measured and assessed, entrepreneurs can be differentiated and placed at distinct skill levels, where their skills can be developed through coaching, training and resource allocation that is appropriate to the given level. The idea is to advance the entrepreneur's skills to the next level, where a new and different round of developmental activities takes place. This kind of laddered approach to skill development can be found in several areas of human activity, most notably sports. In sports as diverse as auto racing, baseball and soccer, a hierarchal league system is used to develop athletes' skills as they advance to the highest tier of their sport. The original pipeline uses American professional baseball's

*Table 13.1   The ladder of entrepreneurship skill development*

| Skills/ Maturity Level | Technical | Managerial | Entrepreneurial | Personal |
| --- | --- | --- | --- | --- |
| 5 | Outstanding | Outstanding | Outstanding | Outstanding |
| 4 | High | High | High | High |
| 3 | High | Medium | Medium | Medium |
| 2 | High/medium | Low | Low | Low |
| 1 | Low/no | Low/no | Low/no | Low/no |

*Source:*   Adapted from Lichtenstein and Lyons (2001).

'farm system' as its metaphor (Lichtenstein and Lyons, 2006); however, this can be generalized for a wider audience by using a simple numbering system, where '1' represents the lowest skill level and '5' the highest. Table 13.1 depicts this ladder of skill development.

Advancing upward from one skill level to the next involves a transformation – a long-term and fundamental change in the entrepreneur's thinking, capability and identity (Lichtenstein and Lyons, 2006). Different technical and financial assistance must be used in working with entrepreneurs at Level 2 than at Level 1, and so forth. Therefore, entrepreneurs must be properly prepared to use the resources available at each level. As an example, a social entrepreneur with a Level 2 skill set may be quite capable of handling traditional philanthropic funding sources (for example, individual donations, government grants) but may be deemed 'not ready' for social venture capital of the type garnered by Ashoka or Echoing Green fellows.

The other variable in the pipeline model is stage in the business life cycle. This variable permits the tracking and measurement of the development of an enterprise, as opposed to the development of the entrepreneur. These are distinct activities, though closely related. There are many different models of the life cycle. The one utilized in the pipeline framework is unique in that it is designed to be effectual (Sarasvathy, 2008) and not predictive (Lichtenstein and Lyons, 2008). That is, it can be used to help entrepreneurs, and those who would assist them, to make decisions about taking appropriate action. The five life cycle stages in the pipeline are described below (Lichtenstein and Lyons, 2006: 379–80):

*Stage 0 – Pre-Venture:* This phase begins with either an interest or desire on the part of an entrepreneur to start a business, or an idea for a business, and ends with the emergence or birth of an organization with an economic offering (i.e., a product or a service) ready to be sold to a potential client and to generate revenue.

*Stage 1 – Existence or Infancy:* This phase begins when the business is launched (with a product or service ready for sale) and ends when the business has reached breakeven from sales. The business has passed the first preliminary test of survival – its offering has demonstrated some interest by a small set of customers, although acceptance by the 'market' has not yet been demonstrated. Profitability has not yet been achieved, and the venture's continued viability (i.e., its ability to maintain a separate existence) is not assured. However, the business exhibits potential.

*Stage 2 – Early Growth:* This phase begins with breakeven from sales and if successful, ends with the establishment of a sustainable business – with either healthy or marginal profits. The latter pays a living wage (i.e., a 'mom-and-pop' operation), whereas the former would be positioned to grow further. This level of economic viability or measure of stability has been achieved by securing and satisfying a critical mass of customers and producing sufficient cash flow to at least repair and replace the capital assets necessary to continue the business as those assets wear out. This assures the survival of the business as long as market conditions remain the same.

*Stage 3 – Expansion or Sustained Growth:* This stage begins when a business with healthy profits and a clear indication of growth potential marshals its resources for growth by risking the established borrowing or equity power of the business to finance growth (even if profitable, cash flow is typically insufficient to supply the needed growth capital for the next phase). This stage ends when the company has emerged as a growth business, demonstrated the capability to serve many customers, deliver a variety of products and services, grow quickly, operate profitably, capture market share, defend against competitors, expand operations, and sustain increases in growth and profitability over time. If successful, the business will reach a size that is sufficiently large, given its industry and market niche, to earn a significant economic return on its assets and labor.

*Stage 4 – Maturity:* This phase begins when the company has 'arrived' – it has successfully achieved the advantages of size and stability, a strong market position (e.g., share of the market), a strong level of profitability, positive cash flow, and a strong management team with an effective system of controls in place. Growth (including the growth rate), however, has slowed, and market saturation as well as competitive pressures are on the horizon. The challenge of this phase is to avoid ossification and decline by resisting complacency and preserving or reestablishing its entrepreneurial spirit. If it has not already done so, it is important that the company make the transition from a single-product-line company to a multiproduct company, as well as from a single business to a more diversified but complementary multi-business unit operation. To continue to thrive, the company must maintain a dynamic balance between conserving existing assets and pursuing new market opportunities. This phase begins to end (not all at once) when the balance favors the status quo, even in the face of an increasingly competitive environment.

*Stage 5 – Decline:* This phase begins when, due to complacency and a desire to avoid risk, market share begins to decline, cash flow and profitability begin to decline from competitive pressures, and the company begins to feed off its accumulated assets. This phase ends when the company is either sold or closed or manages to reinvent itself, usually through the replacement of the management team.

As was the case with skill levels, movement from one stage in the life cycle to the next involves a transformation – a change in the structure of the business. This should be clearly distinguished from growth, which is merely more of the same thing. Enterprises that grow without changing their structure tend to collapse under their own weight (Lichtenstein and Lyons, 2006).

The pipeline, itself, represents the skill level and life cycle stage variables combined in a 5 × 5 matrix (see Table 13.2). Each segment, or cell, of the pipeline represents a particular convergence of skill and life cycle stage. Flow in the pipeline is upward and to the right, as skill levels increase and enterprises move through the stages in their life cycle efficiently and effectively. Volume is expressed by the number of entrepreneurs and their enterprises found in each cell.

The pipeline can be used to 'map' the entrepreneurs and enterprises operating in the given community (see Table 13.3). Empty or lightly populated cells indicate weaknesses in volume and flow that need to be addressed. Heavy concentrations in some cells reflect places where the pipeline may be over-served and could become bogged down. For example, in communities where there is a heavy concentration of entrepreneurs and enterprises in the cells in the lower left-hand corner of the pipeline, while there are only a few in the upper right-hand corner, this may suggest that there are many 'mom and pop' type enterprises but no mechanism for scaling them up. Communities with the opposite situation may be 'creaming' serial entrepreneurs and later-stage enterprises in order to pump them up with venture capital in hopes of creating 'gazelle' companies that generate hundreds of jobs and millions of dollars in revenue. While such communities may appear to be 'winning' in the short term, they are actually failing to 'make more cream', an unhealthy situation that jeopardizes the flow of the pipeline in the long run. Still other communities show a pattern of concentrations in both ends of the pipeline, with little or nothing in between. This is a broken pipeline, where the community is working at cross-purposes to itself.

## DIRECT APPLICATION OF THE PIPELINE TO SOCIAL ENTREPRENEURSHIP

The pipeline model can also be applied directly to the management of a community's portfolio of social entrepreneurs and enterprises, with some

*Table 13.2   The pipeline of entrepreneurs and enterprises*

| Life Cycle / Skill Level | Stage 0 Pre-venture | Stage 1 Existence | Stage 2 Early growth | Stage 3 Expansion | Stage 4 Maturity | Stage 5 Decline |
|---|---|---|---|---|---|---|
| D |  |  |  |  |  |  |
| C |  |  |  |  |  |  |
| B |  |  |  |  |  |  |
| A |  |  |  |  |  |  |

*Source:*   Adapted from Lichtenstein and Lyons (2006).

*Table 13.3   Mapping social entrepreneurs and enterprises in community X*

| Life Cycle / Skill Level | Stage 0 Pre-venture | Stage 1 Existence | Stage 2 Early growth | Stage 3 Expansion | Stage 4 Maturity | Stage 5 Decline |
|---|---|---|---|---|---|---|
| D | 4 | 4 | 0 | 1 | 2 | 0 |
| C | 7 | 9 | 0 | 2 | 2 | 3 |
| B | 12 | 15 | 3 | 4 | 5 | 8 |
| A | 25 | 10 | 5 | 8 | 6 | 6 |

*Source:*   Adapted from Lichtenstein and Lyons (2006).

minor modification (see Table 13.2). First, in the interest of moving away from the sports analogy to a more universally understood nomenclature, we use the simple designations of A, B, C and D for the levels of skill, with A representing the lowest skill level. Second, we revisit the dimensions of skill upon which the assessment of skill level is based to make them more relevant to social entrepreneurship:

- **Technical skills** – These are skills that are specific to carrying out the social entrepreneur's mission. If her mission is to provide affordable housing to low-income households, then she and her team must have skills in real estate development, housing construction, real property law, and so on.
- **Managerial skills** – This body of skills involves the management and administration of the social enterprise. For the most part, these skills will be the same as those required to operate a commercial enterprise, with exceptions such as grant-writing skills, non-profit accounting skills, and so forth, when the social enterprise is a non-profit.
- **Entrepreneurial skills** – These are the skills necessary to generate ideas for creating positive societal change; to assess those ideas to determine their social value, market and sustainability potential as true social entrepreneurship opportunities (Dees, 2001); and to capture those opportunities in a mission for a viable social enterprise.
- **Personal maturity skills** – These are essential 'soft' skills to successful entrepreneurship, which Goleman (1995) has called 'emotional intelligence'. Chief among these for social entrepreneurs is accountability – engendering public trust by being answerable to one's stakeholders, providing them with information regarding the achievement of mission and listening to and utilizing their feedback (Emerson, 2001).

As in the case of the application of the pipeline to commercial entrepreneurship, the ladder of skill development (rungs A, B, C and D) represents varying levels of mastery of this skill set.

The names and order of the business life cycle stages of the pipeline model remain the same as they are applied to the growth *and* development of social enterprises; however, the specifications and parameters must be modified:

- **Stage 0, Pre-venture:** This stage begins with an idea that is developed into a true opportunity to add social value. It ends when there is a clear social mission to be pursued.

- **Stage 1, Existence:** This stage begins with a mission and ends with an organization in place to take up that mission. This entity will have an identified group of primary customers (Dees et al., 2001) or target beneficiaries; however, it will not yet have a market and will not be sustainable. It will also have initial stakeholder support (for example, a grant for testing proof of concept).
- **Stage 2, Early Growth:** This stage begins with a non-sustainable social enterprise with a small group of customers and ends with a sustainable social enterprise that is both small-scale and highly local or one that is positioned to 'scale up' in revenue and reach. This sustainable social venture has a market (a critical mass of customers) and adequate long-term funding/financing. Small-scale social enterprises will not achieve expansion or complete maturity but may experience decline due to complacency on the part of management or because their mission has been achieved or falls out of favour. An example of such a small-scale social enterprise might be an organization that provides after-school computer classes for disadvantaged young people in a single urban neighbourhood.
- **Stage 3, Expansion:** This stage begins with a sustainable social enterprise with growth potential that leverages that growth through investment in its own resources, collaboration with supportive partners, and mission expansion. It ends when the social enterprise demonstrates its capacity to serve many primary customers, maintain numerous beneficial partnerships, and achieve maximum SROI (social return on investment). Examples of social enterprises in the Expansion stage are Ashoka, KaBOOM!, and the National Foundation for Teaching Entrepreneurship (NFTE).
- **Stage 4, Maturity:** This stage begins with a social enterprise that enjoys the advantages of size and stability, many partners, consistent long-term financial support, and substantial demonstrated SROI. Growth, however, has slowed. It ends, gradually, as pursuing the status quo becomes more important than innovation. A loss of momentum is most usually due to management complacency, risk aversion, or a mission that has lost its social relevance. Examples of mature social ventures include the United Way and the Girl Scouts of America, both of which are still thriving.
- **Stage 5, Decline:** This stage begins when the social enterprise loses its momentum and begins to live off of its existing assets without generating new ones. It ends when the social enterprise ceases operations or reinvents itself with a new mission.

### Using the pipeline to map social entrepreneurship activity

Now that we have modified the pipeline model to fit social entrepreneurship, we can turn our attention to employing it to help us better understand a community's social enterprise assets. Table 13.3 demonstrates how the pipeline can be used to map the social entrepreneurs and enterprises of a hypothetical Community X.

While the data in Table 13.3 has been artificially created for illustrative purposes, it is worth briefly discussing sources of the data needed to fill the pipeline. Each number in each cell represents the number of social enterprises in the community at a given stage in their life cycle whose lead entrepreneur, or combined entrepreneurial team, possesses a given level of skill. So, for example, Community X has been found to have 25 social enterprises at the Pre-venture stage whose entrepreneurs are at the 'A' skill level. But from where can this data be derived?

### Data Gathering for the Pipeline

It is most likely that there will be no one source that lists all the social enterprises in a given community. It can be useful to approach government agencies, community foundations and other philanthropic organizations that serve the community to get a list of those social enterprises they support. This can open the way to utilizing a 'snow-balling' technique to identifying still other social ventures operating locally. It can also be useful to conduct interviews with knowledgeable individuals in the community and/or to conduct focus groups with local leaders.

Once all of the community's social enterprises have been identified, each needs to be assessed relative to the skills of its entrepreneur(s) and its present stage in the business life cycle. The authors have developed a clinimetric tool for assessing entrepreneurship skills. While this tool has proven effective, it can be time-consuming and expensive to administer. We are currently in the process of developing an online version of this assessment tool that will be easier, quicker and less expensive to use. Typically, a brief conversation with a social enterprise's lead entrepreneur will reveal at which stage in the business life cycle the enterprise finds itself. Feedback from knowledgeable parties in the community can be used as a check on the accuracy of this latter assessment.

While collecting all of this information may appear burdensome, it is usually not as onerous as it seems. Because of the relative dearth of secondary data on entrepreneurial ventures and the inability of such data to shed light at an appropriate micro-level, this type of primary data collection is essential. The ability to map a community's pipeline of social entrepreneurs and their enterprises can be valuable, even if the skill and life cycle stage 'measurements' are only approximations. It is the organizing capacity – the ability to frame – that adds value.

**Looking for Patterns**

Once the social entrepreneurship landscape is mapped, it is possible to begin using the map as a strategy tool. This involves the art of pattern recognition; a form of assessment that would not be possible without the pipeline map. In carefully examining Table 13.3, one observes several relevant patterns that suggest a need for strategic intervention in order to ensure the volume and flow of Community X's pipeline:

1.  There is a heavy concentration of enterprises in Community X that are in the Pre-venture and Existence stages with entrepreneurs whose skills are at the lower levels – A and B. This is not necessarily a cause for alarm. The history of the social entrepreneurship movement in Community X must be taken into account. If social entrepreneurship was, until recently, under-represented in the local economy, this pattern would be both expected and welcomed as the early-stage development of what could be anticipated to be a complete pipeline. However, if social entrepreneurship is well-established in Community X, this pattern should elicit concern. It suggests that the community's social enterprises are stuck in these segments of the pipeline. Most likely, these social entrepreneurs are not getting the developmental assistance they need in order to enhance their skills and move their enterprises forward to ensuing life cycle stages. As a result, they are either not getting their enterprises off the ground or they are not able to get them past start-up. This situation commonly arises when there is little or no assistance available to nascent social entrepreneurs and they are left to their own struggles, or when the assistance providers, themselves, lack the capability to develop these entrepreneurs beyond a certain point.

2.  It can also be observed that Community X has a disproportionally low number of social enterprises in the middle of its pipeline. That is, there are many more enterprises in the lower left and upper right portions of the pipeline than in the middle. This suggests that community resources are being focused on either encouraging the start-up of new social enterprises or on sustaining large, already successful social ventures. Nothing is inherently wrong with either activity. A community should strive to foster new social innovations brought to market by young enterprises. A community should also seek to support strong,

stable social ventures with a track record of mission achievement. However, all communities operate in an environment of limited resources, forcing tradeoffs. If a community is spending all of its social sector resources at both ends of the pipeline and not the middle, there is no place for early stage enterprises to go, and no replenishing of enterprises at the highest levels of development. If this condition persists for too long, the flow of the pipeline will be disrupted and, ultimately, destroyed.

3.  There are clearly segments of Community X's pipeline that are completely neglected; most notably at the Early Growth stage with C- and D-level entrepreneurs. These are crucial segments of the community's pipeline because highly-skilled entrepreneurs are most likely to opt to move their enterprises to the Expansion stage, if for no other reason than they have the capability to do so. The fact that these segments are empty has important negative implications for the flow of Community X's social pipeline.

4.  One other pattern worthy of note in Table 13.3 is that Community X has an inordinate number of social enterprises that are advanced in their development (Expansion and Maturity stages) but whose entrepreneurs have low levels of skill. There will always be a few of these, but too many suggests a potentially dangerous situation. These are most likely social enterprises whose missions are so compelling that they have attracted partners and resources that have rushed them through the business life cycle, in spite of the weak skills of their entrepreneurial team. This is not sustainable. Notice that, in Table 13.3, a not insubstantial number of such enterprises have moved into the Decline stage. It is unlikely, given their entrepreneurs' lack of skill, that they will be able to reinvent themselves in time to avoid death. This situation is not healthy for the social pipeline.

The ability to map a community's portfolio of entrepreneurs and enterprises and to observe patterns of flow and volume is powerful in and of itself. However, the ultimate value of the pipeline model is that it allows the community to make strategic interventions in the social entrepreneurship landscape to correct negative and perpetuate positive patterns.

# MAKING STRATEGIC INTERVENTIONS BASED ON THE PIPELINE ANALYSIS

In our seminal article on the pipeline of entrepreneurs and enterprises (Lichtenstein and Lyons, 2006), we identify three major types of intervention that communities can use to manage their pipelines:

- Incubation: the nurturing of entrepreneurs and enterprises through the provision of technical and financial assistance, designed appropriately, to move entrepreneurs up the skill ladder and enterprises through the life cycle stages. These are strategies mostly targeted at the lower left-hand corner of the pipeline; however, they can be used in any segment.
- Performance Enhancement: this involves efforts to enhance the performance of an enterprise within a single segment of the pipeline, with no intention of advancing skills or life cycle stages. Some technology commercialization programmes use this strategy when they pour large amounts of venture capital into enterprises at the Expansion stage with highly skilled serial entrepreneurs tapped to run them.
- Strategic Recruitment: this strategy is a variation on the overused economic development strategy of attempting to lure large companies away from other communities in order to capitalize on their job creation capacity. In strategic recruitment, however, the focus is on filling empty or under-occupied segments of the pipeline by attracting from elsewhere entrepreneurs and their enterprises that have the same skills–life cycle coordinates as the segment to be filled.

To these three original intervention strategies we would add a fourth, uniquely applicable to social entrepreneurship:

- Coopetition (Brandenburger and Nalebuff, 1996): While commercial enterprises are limited by anti-trust and other collusion mitigating regulations, social ventures have no such limitations (Dees et al., 2001). Furthermore, competition in social entrepreneurship is generally not for customers but for resources. Therefore, it makes considerable sense for social enterprises to collaborate. Typically this is collaboration based on compatibility of missions, shared expertise, and/or complementary resource needs. The pipeline model permits strategic intervention to encourage another type of collaboration: that which fills mutual skill gaps and life cycle lags.

Using these broad intervention strategies, we can begin to address the challenges to pipeline management in Community X suggested by the data in Table 13.3. First, Community X's abundance of early stage social enterprises with low-skilled entrepreneurs suggests a need for ample Incubation support. These entrepreneurs need help in developing their skills so that they can effectively move their social enterprises through the business life cycle stages, rising to levels that maximize mission achievement. There are numerous tools available for this purpose, a few of which we will note here.

Some communities have created *business incubators for social ventures*, particularly non-profit enterprises. These facilities not only lower costs for social entrepreneurs by providing low-cost space and shared resources, their staff provide useful training and counselling as well. A unique example of this is The Foundation Incubator, located in Palo Alto, California. The Foundation Incubator breeds new philanthropic organizations by providing their social entrepreneurs with affordable space and access to expert advice from experienced foundation officials and through collaboration with each other (Cohen, 2002).

*Entrepreneur networks* have proven themselves to be valuable vehicles for information exchange and knowledge building among commercial entrepreneurs (Pages, 2001). This model of peer support could be employed to assist social entrepreneurs, also.

Social entrepreneurship *coaching* can also be an effective incubation technique. For example, Hustedde (2007) developed a programme in northeastern Kentucky for training local leaders to coach entrepreneurs in their communities. The Entrepreneurial Development System (EDS), a system created by the authors of this chapter (Lichtenstein and Lyons, 2001), utilizes a unique blend of coaching to develop entrepreneurs' skills. The EDS employs personal coaching (one-on-one support); peer group coaching (8–12 entrepreneurs at the same skill level who meet regularly with a coach, who acts as a facilitator, to share information and to challenge and support one another); and community coaching (entrepreneurs at different skill levels who meet periodically to share successes and lessons learned, engage in mentoring of lower-skilled entrepreneurs by higher skilled entrepreneurs, and form joint ventures where appropriate). While these example tactics were created for commercial entrepreneurs, they could easily be adapted for social entrepreneurs as well.

*Microenterprise development programmes*, the brainchild of Nobel laureate Mohammad Yunis, provide valuable technical and financial support to very small enterprises operated by nascent entrepreneurs and could be readily adapted to the incubation of new social ventures. Ernesto Sirolli's (1999) concept of 'enterprise facilitation', which involves a knowledgeable individual who organizes local support for entrepreneurs and guides entrepreneurs in the use of that support, is another promising social entrepreneurship incubation model.

When assembled in a synergistic way, these tactics, and others, can be effectively applied as an overall social entrepreneurship incubation strategy for Community X. Such a strategy should allow the community to move its low-skill, early-stage social entrepreneurs and enterprises upward and to the right in the pipeline, eliminating the log-jam at that place in the pipeline and facilitating flow.

Second, the 'missing middle' of Community X's pipeline can be addressed using tactics from three of the four major intervention strategies. Segments of the middle of the pipeline where no social enterprises are currently found can be filled using the Strategic Recruitment and Coopetition strategies. In this case, strategic recruitment could involve identifying social entrepreneurs, from places outside the community, at the appropriate skill level, whose enterprises are in the life cycle stage characterized by the empty cell in question. Luring these entrepreneurs to Community X will require offering resources that they cannot get, or cannot get easily, in their current location. Under ideal circumstances, the community within which they currently operate has also done a pipeline analysis and has an excess of entrepreneurs and enterprises in that same segment. Thus, the recruitment will not amount to 'poaching' by Community X at the expense of the other community.

Coopetition can be employed to fill the empty pipeline segment by strategically finding entrepreneurs whose combined skill levels and organizations would place them in that segment. They can then be encouraged to partner, either temporarily around a social project that has mutual relevance to their missions or permanently by merging missions.

Where segments in the middle of Community X's pipeline are not empty but have very few enterprises, approaches that employ an Incubation strategy, described above, can be used to move entrepreneurs and enterprises from segments to the left and below the lightly filled segment up and to the right. That is, their skills and business structures can be transformed to advance them to the point where they are needed.

Addressing Community X's dearth of C- and D-level entrepreneurs whose businesses are at the Early Growth stage could involve the strategies of Incubation, Strategic Recruitment, and Coopetition in much the same way they were used to deal with the problem of the missing pipeline middle. These strategies could clearly add to the number of social ventures found in these segments. However, the problem may not be one of numbers but one of relative strength. Early Growth could be a good time to employ a Performance Enhancement approach. An infusion of social venture philanthropy, or social venture capital, while it will not change the structure of these ventures or the skills of their entrepreneurs, may increase their capacity to achieve social mission, making their combined social impact substantially greater than that of the same number of enterprises without the equity injection.

Finally, the relatively large number of under-skilled social entrepreneurs with ventures in the Expansion and Maturity stage in Community X can be addressed by employing an intensive Incubation strategy. Coaching and networking with social entrepreneurs at higher skill levels would be the tactics of choice in this strategy because they provide the best opportunity for quick results. However, the quickest 'fix' for this problem may be Coopetition, which could involve partnering a more highly skilled entrepreneur with their lower-skilled counterpart to provide the level of capability necessary to sustain the social enterprise in question.

Thus, a strategic combination of interventions can be employed by Community X to manage its pipeline to encourage optimum flow and volume. This raises an important question, however: who is responsible for managing Community X's social entrepreneurs and their enterprises? In commercial entrepreneurship, it could be argued that this role could be played by the organization responsible for local economic development, representing the interests of the community. In social entrepreneurship, however, there is no comparable organization. This represents a major shortcoming of social entrepreneurship; it is highly fragmented and not systemic. As a result, it lacks the efficiency and the synergistic power it could have to transform an entire community.

The question of who should bear responsibility for managing social entrepreneurial activity in any given community is a difficult one that deserves careful consideration. The best answer could vary from community to community. In some communities, it could be a charter organization assembled for that purpose. This organization could be made up of representatives from government, business, the non-profit sector, and philanthropy. In other communities, it may be the elected legislative body. In still others, where there is a strong community foundation, that institution's deep knowledge of the non-profit landscape of its community could make it ideally suited to this function. Whatever entity plays this role, it must do so fairly, honestly, inclusively, and with the community's best interests at heart.

## CONCLUSION

The field of social entrepreneurship is ripe for research that permits it to go beyond description toward the establishment of its own theory, testing of that theory, and the creation of models for its successful effectuation.

This chapter falls into this latter category by modifying the Pipeline of Entrepreneurs and Enterprises model to make it a relevant tool for thinking about, and effectively managing, a community's social entrepreneurship assets. Our approach is intended to elevate social entrepreneurship from a set of disconnected or weakly connected social value-adding activities to a holistic, synergistic infrastructure for benefiting communities.

In doing so, we see other potential uses for the pipeline model. Among these is the fact that as this tool is used to map social entrepreneurship pipelines in a variety of communities, this permits cross-community pattern recognition relative to both the development of social entrepreneurs' skills and of the life cycle stage of their social enterprises. This knowledge could help to define the role of context in shaping such development. It could also be used to differentiate, in a more useful way, among social entrepreneurs. Finally, the pipeline model could be used as a way of organizing the body of social entrepreneurship research, itself. By being able to place each study in an appropriate cell of the pipeline, we can better understand that piece of research's relevance to the whole of our understanding and to other research, and we can see where we still have gaps in our knowledge, which can be filled through additional meaningful research.

# REFERENCES

Bornstein, D. (2007), *How to Change the World: Social Entrepreneurs and the Power of New Ideas*, Oxford: Oxford University Press.

Brandenburger, A., and B. Nalebuff (1996), *Co-Opetition: A Revolution Mindset that Combines Competition and Cooperation*, New York: Broadway Business.

Brinckerhoff, P.C. (2000), *Social Entrepreneurship: The Art of Mission-based Venture Development*, New York: Wiley.

Bygrave, W., D. D'Heilly, M. McMullen and N. Taylor (1996), 'Toward a not-for-profit analytical framework', *Frontiers of Entrepreneurship Research*, 1996 edn, Wellesley, MA: Babson College.

Cohen, T. (2002), 'Breeding philanthropies: new incubator will hatch foundations', *The Nonprofit Times*, 1 February.

Cornforth, C. (ed.), (2003), *The Governance of Public and Non-profit Organizations: What do Boards do?*, London: Routledge.

Dees, J.G. (1998), 'The meaning of social entrepreneurship', unpublished paper, Kansas City, MO: Ewing Marion Kauffman Foundation.

Dees, J.G. (2001), 'Mobilizing resources', in J.G. Dees, J. Emerson and P. Economy, (eds), *Enterprising Nonprofits: A Toolkit for Social Entrepreneurs*, New York: Wiley, pp. 63–102.

Dees, J.G., J. Emerson and P. Economy (eds) (2001), *Enterprising Nonprofits: A Toolkit for Social Entrepreneurs*, New York: Wiley.

Emerson, J. (2001), 'The accountable social entrepreneur', in J.G. Dees, J. Emerson and P. Economy (eds), *Enterprising Nonprofits: A Toolkit for Social Entrepreneurs*, New York: Wiley, pp. 103–25.

European Commission (2008), http://ec.europa.eu/enterprise/entrepreneurship/coop/social-cmaf_agenda/social-enterprises.htm, accessed October 2008.

Gerber, M.E. (1995), *The E-myth Revisited: Why Most Businesses Fail and what to do about it*, New York: HarperCollins.

Goleman, D. (1995), *Emotional Intelligence: Why it can Matter more than IQ*, New York: Bantam.

Guclu, A., J.G. Dees and B. Battle Anderson (2002), 'The process of social entrepreneurship: creating opportunities worthy of serious pursuit', Durham, NC: Center for the Advancement of Social Entrepreneurship, Fuqua School of Business, Duke University.

Hustedde, R. (2007), 'What's culture got to do with it? Strategies for strengthening an entrepreneurial culture', in N. Walzer (ed.), *Entrepreneurship and Local Economic Development*, Lanham, MD: Lexington Books, pp. 39–58.

Lichtenstein, G.A. and T.S. Lyons (2001), 'The entrepreneurial development system: transforming business talent and community economies', *Economic Development Quarterly*, **15**(1), 3–20.

Lichtenstein, G.A. and T.S. Lyons (2006), 'Managing the community's pipeline of entrepreneurs and enterprises: a new way of thinking about business assets', *Economic Development Quarterly*, **20**(4), 377–86.

Lichtenstein, G.A. and T.S. Lyons (2008), 'Revisiting the business life-cycle: proposing an actionable model for assessing and fostering entrepreneurship', *International Journal of Entrepreneurship and Innovation*, **9**(4), 241–50.

Martí, I. (2006), 'Introduction to part I – Setting a research agenda for an emerging field', in J. Mair, J. Robinson and K. Hockerts (eds), *Social Entrepreneurship*, New York: Palgrave Macmillan, pp. 17–21.

Pages, E.R. (2001), 'Building entrepreneurial networks', available at SSRN: http://ssrn.com/abstract=1244508.

Perrini, F. and C. Vurro (2006), 'Social entrepreneurship: innovation and social change across theory and practice', in J. Mair, J. Robinson and K. Hockerts (eds), *Social Entrepreneurship*, New York: Palgrave Macmillan, pp. 57–86.

Robinson, J. (2006), 'Navigating social and institutional barriers to markets: how social entrepreneurs identify and evaluate opportunities', in J. Mair, J. Robinson and K. Hockerts (eds), *Social Entrepreneurship*, New York: Palgrave Macmillan, pp. 95–120.

Sarasvathy, S.D. (2008), *Effectuation: elements of entrepreneurial expertise*, Cheltenham, UK and Northampton, MA, USA: Edward Elgar.

Sirolli, E. (1999), *Ripples from the Zambezi: Passion, Entrepreneurship and the Rebirth of Local Economies*, Gabriola Island, BC, Canada: New Society Publishers.

Wei-Skillern, J., J.E. Austin, H. Leonard and H. Stevenson (2007), *Entrepreneurship in the Social Sector*, Los Angeles, CA: Sage.

# 14 Considering social capital in the context of social entrepreneurship
## Paul Myers and Teresa Nelson

A growing academic and practitioner community is now engaged in lively and, hopefully, fruitful debate on whether and how social entrepreneurship should be distinguished from entrepreneurship generally, and why this may matter. Austin et al. (2006: 2) define social entrepreneurship as 'innovative, social value creating activity that can occur within or across the non-profit, business, or government sectors'. They make the case for building specific theory about social enterprises based on their inquiry into differences in mission, resource mobilization, performance measurement and the orientation to market failure between models of social and commercial entrepreneurship. Noting that these two models exist on a spectrum rather than as dichotomous positions (that is, social and commercial purpose is mixed for most ventures to some degree), the authors still posit that fundamental distinctions between the two supra-categories recommend that traditional entrepreneurship approaches be carefully considered before they are applied wholesale in the social venture realm.

We agree for three reasons. First, social entrepreneurship has been one of the most powerful innovations in economic practice in the last few decades; the breadth and variety of organizations (profit, non-profit, government) that are exploring this territory and its potential implications is sizable and therefore careful analysis is called for (for example, Bornstein, 2004). Second, on a national and global basis, nations and powerful global organizations and systems (for example, financial systems, UN, WTO, World Bank) define the legal territory of commercial and social entrepreneurship in quite different ways, and in newly emerging ways, and this needs to be carefully taken into account as we look at where, when and how social entrepreneurship creates value. Third, we believe that advances in knowledge on social entrepreneurship will inform us and assist us in identifying how innovative ideas and opportunities are put to work in commercial entrepreneurship. In this chapter we consider how the sources and uses of social capital by the social entrepreneur inform such understanding.

From the perspective of both theory and practice, the challenge of mobilizing appropriate and adequate resources through exchange is a most fruitful area for examining the differences between forms of entrepreneurship. By the nature of their *raison d'être*, social entrepreneurs are motivated to form partnerships with others – businesses, governments, individuals, groups, and other non-governmental agencies – to move their agendas forward. In these efforts the interests and goals of the partners may align around the social venture's mission in some respects, and diverge in others. In contrast, the parties to the commercial venture are more likely to coalesce around a common objective: the success of the new venture. The difference here pushes the social entrepreneur to reach across sectors to create complex alliances with individual and organizational members who participate for varied and even changing reasons. The challenge for the social entrepreneur is then not only to collaborate effectively with these disparate allies, but to connect with them in the first place.

While the first element of this challenge reflects an entrepreneur's human capital, the latter is what Burt (2005: 4) refers to as its 'contextual complement' – *social* capital. The degree and kind of social capital available to an actor will vary, and certain positions in the social structure enable relationships that provide access to richer information, broader opportunities, and more valuable exchanges than do others. Social capital comprises the trust, norms and mutual obligations that develop in these relationships. It is a valuable asset that can produce advantage for individuals and firms as a function of their location within a network of relationships. In this way, social capital shapes a social entrepreneur's ability to facilitate the coordination needed between and among the partners to his or her venture.

An increasingly sophisticated scholarship on social capital in the social sciences offers a structural perspective on the firm, its players, their communities and their interactions. Yet, with few exceptions (notably Stam and Elfring, 2008), Burt's (2000) observation that the field of entrepreneurship 'remains virtually un-touched by theory and empirical research on the network forms of social capital' (Burt, 2000: 372) remains accurate. We believe that theoretical extensions on the process and content of social capital creation are suggested in regard to the practice of social entrepreneurship given its core objective – radical innovation for social welfare enhancement. We also see the complex use of social capital by social entrepreneurs as an informative model generally for entrepreneurs and entrepreneurship researchers as value creation is considered.

In this chapter we use the experience of information technology (IT) executive and social entrepreneur Radha Basu to examine these conceptual areas with the purpose of understanding how social enterprise goals narrow, broaden, challenge and/or otherwise change current understandings of social capital deployment. We begin by defining the concept of social capital and how it relates to social entrepreneurship. We then present the story of Basu's social venture, the Anudip Foundation for Social Welfare, to demonstrate the role social capital can play in the formation and growth of ventures that embrace both social and commercial purposes. We conclude with a discussion of the theoretical and research implications suggested by this exploratory analysis.

## SOCIAL CAPITAL

The concept of social capital has attracted the attention of a diverse set of economists, sociologists, political scientists and management theorists in recent decades (for reviews, see Portes, 1998; Burt, 2000; Woolcock and Narayan, 2000; Mouw, 2006). Just as other forms of capital – financial, physical, human – enable action, so too does social capital (Coleman, 1988). The key difference between social capital and other forms of capital is that social capital is embedded in relationships between individuals. Unlike financial and physical capital, it is not tangible, and unlike human capital, it is not an individual trait or capability. Social capital is inherently social; that is, it 'inheres in the structure of relations between actors and among actors' (Coleman, 1988).

While no single definition unites the disparate social capital literature, a common thread is the recognition that social capital comprises both the social structure of relationships as well as the resources obtained through it and that these factors influence one's ability to act. Bourdieu defines social capital as 'the aggregate of the actual or potential resources which are linked to possession of a durable network of more or less institutionalized relationships of mutual acquaintance or recognition' (1985: 248). Such resources can include access to information and opportunities, economic benefits, and social support. Social capital provides benefits, but can also require commitments. Coleman regards social capital as the accumulation of obligations subject to norms of reciprocity (1988).

Adler and Kwon (2002) analyse and synthesize the range of definitions of social capital found in a broad selection of social science literature and propose their own: 'Social capital is the goodwill available to individuals or groups. Its source lies in the structure and content of the actor's social relations. Its effects flow from the information, influence, and solidarity it makes available to the actor' (Adler and Kwon, 2002: 23). Nahapiet and Ghoshal (1998) identify three content dimensions of social capital: structural, relational and cognitive. The structural aspect comprises the pattern of relationships, or connections between actors in terms of density, hierarchy and intensity. The relational facet refers to the affective attachments that produce psychological benefits of sociability, approbation, and prestige and the quality of those ties through which flow trust, expectations and norms, and obligations. Finally, the cognitive dimension encompasses the shared systems of meaning, language and ways of interpreting between actors, yielding durable connections.

Portes (1998) draws the distinction between the consequences of social capital (that is the content dimension) and the processes by which they are derived. Arregle et al. (2007) summarize work on social capital *process* identifying critical structural and relational factors that support the creation and maintenance of social capital. These include the interdependence of network members, the degree to which the network is interconnected, relationship stability and development over time, and the form and quality of interactions. Burt, most prominently among social network researchers (1992, 2005), describes and explains how the proximity and degree of cohesion among actors in the network matters. With the concept of closure, that is, how gaps between clusters of people or firms are bridged, Burt identifies how 'structural holes', create advantage for those who broker connections across them.

Closure and brokerage reflect two distinct functions of social capital: it bonds individuals in close-knit and intensive relationships within a community or organization, but it also bridges more diffuse and extensive inter- and extra-organizational networks (Woolcock and Narayan, 2000). Thus advantage can come from belonging to a tight network of relationships as well as from being part of a more diffuse one – provided in the latter case a person is in a position to make and maintain connections where none yet exist. Furthermore, these effects are not mutually exclusive; the actor may both bridge and bond successfully (Batjargal, 2007).

Another process issue is the actual deployment, or use, of social capital. Bourdieu theorizes that social capital is a fungible currency exchanged between actors: 'a credential which entitles them to credit' (Bourdieu, 1985: 249). In this view, each party in a relationship can take out capital of different forms. Coleman (1988) regards social capital as less fungible than does Bourdieu. His model of collective action describes actors that have interests in certain resources and events, only some of which they control (1990). For Coleman, social exchange is the process of trading resources in which one has less interest for those of greater interest. But he acknowledges that social capital that is valuable for one purpose may not be so for another.

Portes (1998) differentiates between the motivations of those who obtain resources through social capital from those who 'donate' or contribute those resources when the benefit to them may not be immediate, well defined, or even certain. He argues that the motivations of donors can be complex and plural and offers a framework that distinguishes 'consummatory' and 'instrumental' motivations. Consummatory motivations are those that represent the drive to fulfil one's normative duties and reflect a sense of bounded social solidarity. Instrumental motivations are also based on norms, but the donor seeks not personal satisfaction but rather social status, approval, or recognition. Later in the chapter we provide an example that describes how a social entrepreneur taps into both forms of motivation to gain needed support for his or her venture.

## SOCIAL ENTREPRENEURS AND SOCIAL CAPITAL

The key factor that distinguishes the social entrepreneur from the mainstream (commercial) entrepreneur is the purpose: the primary objective of the venture is to use business and/or organizational skills to create *social* value through innovation. *Economic* value creation serves as the means to that end rather than the primary end in itself. As Emerson (2003) notes, all organizations produce a mix of economic and social benefits, or what he a calls 'blended value'. The relevant question becomes the extent to which the parties of the venture, including the founder, the team, the customers, the vendors and the investors, seek each type of return, and in what combination. In this view, the legal form of incorporation – for-profit, not-for-profit, for example – becomes a strategic choice for the founder rather than simply an institutional imperative. The legal form can be an instrument for reaching the purpose; the organization design becomes a tool in pursuing the mission.

While social entrepreneurs share a common motivator, their profiles are varied (for example, Leadbeater, 1997; Bornstein, 2004; Light, 2005). Some are young Millennials who seek to improve the world with a pragmatic drive not yet diminished by disappointments. Others are non-profit managers who have identified revitalized paths to social change unencumbered by the limitations of bureaucracy and institutional inertia. Still others are professionals who desire to channel their business skills to start a second career that reflects their personal values and passions.

Whatever impulse compels them to create their social venture, each social entrepreneur must mobilize resources to achieve their objectives. This often requires bridging gaps across countries, organizations, industries and societal sectors. Social capital enables the social entrepreneur to facilitate this brokerage by tapping the resources of their social network. While their stocks of financial and human capital may be largely fixed when they launch their venture, we posit that their social capital is malleable on application and regenerative through use. The way social capital is deployed and the value it can create, then, become key factors in navigating the rough waters of social entrepreneurship.

For some aspiring social entrepreneurs, typically those launching second careers, the social credits built over years among industry peers, acquaintances and key influencers become a superlative asset, perhaps more valuable than other forms of capital. Not only is the network itself extended, but it is based in business and therefore can access a rich set of economic resources, mobilizing them in new and creative ways. While these social entrepreneurs face the particular challenge of putting their social capital to use in an entirely new context, they also have extraordinary potential to create the value they seek in the world. That their number and importance is increasing is being recognized in the mainstream. Harvard University, for example, has organized five of its graduate schools to launch the Harvard Advanced Leadership Initiative, a fellowship programme aimed at helping Baby Boomers make just such a transition from successful business and administrative careers into social entrepreneurship.

Maurer and Ebers (2006) note that an entrepreneur's social capital is an asset that provides information and learning, increases legitimacy, and coordinates benefits. The application of social capital by the entrepreneur influences innovation capacities, particularly as it relates to boundary-spanning activities (Subramaniam and Youndt, 2005), and especially as regards radical innovation (Dewar and Dutton, 1986). Social capital, then, is a resource that can be mobilized to achieve ends that would otherwise be difficult or even impossible to reach.

As resource needs get larger with new venture growth, when the needs are disparate, or when the path ahead is not well established, entrepreneurs can look to *bridging* social capital to generate the resources needed to grow and survive. Under such conditions, more diffuse and diverse networks rich in structural holes provide critical advantage. Networks of this type create opportunities for mediating the flow of information between disconnected groups (Burt, 1992). For instance, Batjargal (2007) found that more successful entrepreneurs used social networking strategies and tactics that emphasized forming ties to individuals outside of their existing cliques in order to create brokerage opportunities.

The bridging social capital deployment of social entrepreneurs brings an informative perspective not only to entrepreneurship but to social network research more generally. Social capital research to date has focused most particularly on how bridging is accomplished within industries and sectors, attending much less to deployment across industries and sectors. We propose that the ways and means that social entrepreneurs use to form bridges between apparently disconnected people and organizations moves this field of investigation beyond our current focus. The social entrepreneur's social capital is deployed and maintained in ways particular to the entrepreneur's experience, the mission of his/her social enterprise, and via conditions shared by social entrepreneurship as a field of endeavour. We turn now to an exploration of just such an entrepreneur and the role social capital plays in her venture's growth and quick success.

## SOCIAL CAPITAL IN USE: RADHA BASU AND THE ANUDIP FOUNDATION

In this section we present the example of social entrepreneur Radha Basu and her Anudip Foundation for Social Welfare (Anudip). Our data come from interviews with Basu, transcripts of her speeches, documents provided by Basu, and publicly available sources. We offer her story as a way to consider the deployment of social capital in the context of social entrepreneurship, and thus our efforts are exploratory for the purpose of theory-building.

### Background

Radha Basu is at the forefront of a global movement that is re-defining the purpose of enterprise and its role in addressing social needs. Her vision is to spread prosperity to the rural poor of India by linking the country's massive metropolitan-based information technology sector to semi-urban and rural areas through job training and entrepreneurial venturing. Leading the Anudip Foundation for Social Welfare, Ms Basu is a social entrepreneur committed to building a scalable, sustainable venture that provides livelihoods through technical training, language instruction, employment services, and new venture start-up instruction.

In creating Anudip, Basu is aligned with other social entrepreneurs who apply business skills and strategies with the goal of solving pernicious social problems. She modelled her efforts in part on those of Nobel prizewinner Mohammed Yunnis's Grameen Bank, which for the past 15 years has provided micro-credit financing for venture creation to the poor, first in Bangladesh and now in more than 60 countries around the world, including largely prosperous countries such as the United States. Projects such as Grameen Bank and Anudip address real human and social problems through grassroots economic approaches that search for non-charity sources of funding. In fact, Basu believes that the rigours of competition and meeting the demands of a business model are what provide the potential for her enterprise to develop commercial alliances with successful global businesses – a partnership, Basu asserts, providing the best formula for achieving Anudip's purpose.

Before Anudip, Radha Basu spent more than 20 years building her career as a leader in the global technology industry and a pioneer in the Indian software business (see http://www.anudip.org). College-trained in India during the 1960s, when being a female engineer was highly unusual, Basu pushed even further, arriving in Los Angeles with $8 in her pocket to pursue a graduate degree at UCLA. Basu excelled in her studies, and upon graduation, joined Hewlett-Packard (HP). She eventually reached positions with global management responsibilities, including building one of the first software outsourcing businesses in India (originally from her kitchen table in Bangalore). In her last position with HP, Basu led a $1.5 billion international software business comprising eight offshore software centres across the globe.

From Hewlett-Packard, Basu moved on to serve as CEO and later Chairman of SupportSoft, a technology start-up that moved through and beyond an initial public offering on the US stock market under her leadership. These experiences directly informed her approach to social entrepreneurship. As she told us, 'You can't change your stripes. At heart I'm very much a business person – the Foundation is something we very much run like a business. I fundamentally believe that you have to look at how to make the business sustainable. If it sustains itself, it doesn't need any external financing.' Beyond this professional orientation, Basu notes that a business-based approach is called for since her venture competes with services companies in India that are run purely for profit; she must be market-oriented when it comes to wage rates and prices, or risk failure in the marketplace.

**The Anudip Foundation**

Anudip is based in the Sundarbans region of West Bengal. Lack of development initiative and industrial growth in the region has limited the livelihood opportunities of people in its primarily agrarian communities. Yet even those with education who migrate to urban centres in search of employment find themselves ill-equipped for a job market in which even entry-level jobs require basic IT skills. With demand for skilled labour outstripping its supply, the resulting high wages at IT hubs like Bangalore, Gurgaon and Hyderabad have pushed Indian and multinational corporate giants to move operations to lower-cost locations in East Europe, China and Vietnam. Furthermore, this 'IT gap' is not only felt by the IT companies – stock and trade firms in the country must similarly cope with the scarcity of basic IT-skilled staff for back office operations such as accounting and database management.

Basu saw the opportunity to create a solution that would address the economic needs of the poor rural population by creating a nationally internal market labour pool to serve the IT industy's demand for lower cost, but skilled workers. Through its network of LINKAGE (Livelihood Initiative through Knowledge) centres, Anudip provides comprehensive computer and entrepreneurship training, hands-on practice, mentoring, and progress tracking. These *non-profit* training and job centres are operated through key partnerships with reputable rural non-governmental organizations that reach out to communities, recruit qualified trainees, and manage the centres. Operations of this segment of the business are funded by grants and donations, including money directed from the for-profit outsourcing centres described below. By the end of its second year of operations, Anudip had trained over 1000 people through the LINKAGE network, and its plan is to train 100000 within five years.

In direct association with the LINKAGE centres, Anudip also runs *for-profit* outsourcing centres that provide data entry services to large Indian firms. When individuals complete their training through the LINKAGE centre, they have the option of accepting employment through the outsourcing centre, or creating a new venture using the skills they have acquired. Of note, 75 per cent of the trainees who choose the entrepreneurial route are women. For example, Anudip heralds the case of five rural women they trained who successfully and cooperatively created the new venture DIGITAL GRAPHICS to supply invitations, letterhead and business cards from a small storefront outside the gates of IIM-Calcutta, one of India's leading business schools.

**The Role of Social Capital**

Social capital played a key role in Basu's earlier professional achievements as an IT executive in India. In the mid-1980s when she first arrived in the country to represent HP, very few people had thought about software development as a potential industry for India, let alone come to fully consider its economic potential. In fact, Basu credits the novelty of her assignment in India to HP founder Dave Packard's innovative management style; in sending her to India he told her to 'Find out what's going on over there and how HP can be involved'.

Basu's initial approaches to various government ministries were met with resistance. As word spread, however, that HP – one of the world's most highly regarded companies at the time – had appointed an Indian woman to lead its first foray into India, 'the ministers became curious about [me]', Basu relates. Her 'celebrity' status opened doors, in part because those with whom she met sought to sate their curiosity about her and to have a story to share with their friends. Basu used these opportunities to build a network that used closure and bridging elements in relation to her personal and professional social life, including her network in India, the US, and elsewhere around the globe.

Basu has now transformed the social capital accumulated in her first career to service Anudip. She has created relationships, resource flows and partnerships across economic sectors, bridging her entrepreneurial venture with a network that connects India's leading technology companies, nonprofits and NGOs, and government ministries. In addition, she has drawn in her personal and family network in a closure fashion. Her network functions and delivers in ways unattainable by traditional charitable ventures. These bridging efforts arise and are renewed because she has a level of access to decision-makers in the company partners she targets that gives her a clear advantage over other marketplace competitors. Further, the reputation she developed through her work at HP and elsewhere assuages the uncertainty her partners might have about the level of risk, quality and stability of operations they can expect when signing on a new venture as a vendor partner. Finally, her success in delivering products refreshes the network, creating new access and new business.

Part of her success is her ability to align her multiple partners' divergent goals (for example, livelihood creation, social stability, profit generation, national competitiveness, risk management, alleviation of human suffering) into one plan of action. Central to these efforts is her appeal to both the consummatory and instrumental motivations of her prospective partners. She sells her passion for the mission of her venture as she connects with allies – actual and potential – on a practical and emotional level. As a business person, she sells results. As an Indian national, humanitarian and role model, she can also convincingly make the case to fellow executives that, as members of the middle and upper class, supporting Anudip is the 'right thing' to do. Note that her client partners are not working with Anudip for philanthropic reasons alone; if the business proposition in terms of quality and price were unacceptable, there would be no deal. Ultimately, Basu, as a bridge between otherwise unconnected individuals and organizations, is able to identify even further opportunities, therefore addressing the potential diminution of her first business network as time passes.

On the legal front, the organizing structure of the Anudip 'effort' uses existing structures to build the greatest value possible. The relationship of the two entities – a non-profit foundation and a for-profit organization – takes advantage of the institutional legal arrangements of the US and India; donations to Anudip in the US are tax deductible, for instance. Having a foot in both sectors serves another purpose for Basu. As the organization's chief evangelist, she is able to put on her social enterprise 'hat' when it suits her to emphasize the organization's mission, thereby persuading donors, customers, regulators and others to ally. On the other hand, she can wear her CEO business 'hat' to communicate in terms of cost savings and business benefits, as appropriate.

Basu's experience suggests that social entrepreneurs can take what are typically and predominantly market relationships comprised of providers and customers mediating through explicit and specific economic exchanges (that is, money), and imbue them with social relationships in which the terms of the exchange are diffuse and the commitments to reciprocal benefits are tacit (see Adler and Kwon, 2002). Because social entrepreneurs, particularly that sub-group who embrace for-profit, mission-driven models of organization, see profit (money) as a critical means to an end, though not an end in itself, the social capital expenditure of the entrepreneur encounters a fuller range of motives and manifestations. It offers unique value to those who seek the advantages (for example, status, prestige, influence) that come from associating with the social entrepreneur and her mission.

This case also suggests that the role of the founder may be more critical and take on different aspects in social ventures as compared with commercial ventures. The social entrepreneur must possess the orientation to innovation, bias for action, and resourcefulness of a regular entrepreneur, but she also has the additional challenge/opportunity of spanning different networks and adjusting to their varied milieux and priorities, assuming she has the social structure in place. Moreover, the implications for succession of the social entrepreneur loom large. Social capital belongs jointly to the parties in a particular relationship and thus is not readily appropriable by a third party (Burt, 2002; Coleman, 1988). The ability of a successor to broker relations or reap the benefits of network closure established by the founder can be questioned, and that raises concerns about the venture's sustainability: the survival of social ventures may be more dependent on their founders than other ventures.

Similarly, the network structure of this type of social entrepreneur/ founder may provide a unique and valuable resource set for the organization. The existing entrepreneurship literature depicts most founders as having relatively simple inter-organizational networks typically within a single sector that they draw on in combination with their personal social network (for example, people at church, family members). The social network structure that would provide advantage to the social entrepreneur, however, is more complex, rich with structural holes, yet also containing strong ties that offer the benefits that closure provides.

Lastly, the social capital deployed by social entrepreneurs is embedded in a network structure that comprises not only different organizational fields but societal sectors as well. While social capital may be fungible to some degree, its role and effectiveness in one area may not translate across sectors. Actors may have expectations with different time horizons about how things should be done, and about the appropriate boundaries between persons and roles. This presents implications for the development and implementation of strategy, organizational design and operational capabilities. Given the social entrepreneur's goal of radical change, addressing these matters is not a small undertaking.

## IMPLICATIONS FOR THEORY AND RESEARCH

We identify three major areas for further research investigation through this work. Each concerns either implicitly or explicitly the ways that social and commercial entrepreneurship may differ, and why this may matter.

First, in terms of the construction of a value chain for the social venture's operations (that is, relations between the organization and customers on one side and vendors on the other), we posit from our analysis that the act of spanning the social welfare and commercial worlds creates new and different types of value chain relationships. More than profit may be involved in both input and output sides of the exchange, and the terms may change on a case-by-case basis depending on the individuals involved. For social entrepreneurs straddling commercial and social purpose, the relationships on the value chain might more resemble a joint venture linking organizations that share mission, rather than one would expect in a traditional supply chain relationship. The customers or vendors can join the social organization in its purposeful intent (for example, alleviating poverty) which augments a utilitarian benefit (selling product or buying inputs). As organizations, profit and non-profit alike, are joined in the social mission which may supplement or augment the commercial intent, we need to probe how business decisions are made and how organizational performance is evaluated. This brings us more clearly to the 'social environment' of business, directly challenging the conception of the business as a simple profit-making machine.

We also see significant potential in further investigation of the role of the social entrepreneur as social enterprise founder. From a social capital perspective, the relationships and network brought to work by the founder are not apparently transferable. Therefore, we wonder whether the organization can develop a stock of social capital separate from that of the founder but which offers the functional equivalent of the founder's original and refreshing social network. Further, by what processes can ventures aggregate or otherwise draw from the social capital that belongs to the founder, or any other venture member, to create a network that links structural positions independent of their incumbents, yet produces the value of the relational aspect of social capital? Without identifying some way to supplant the social capital of the founder upon her exit, perhaps social ventures are doomed either to dissolution or to transition into traditional for-profit (that is, reliant on competitive positioning) or non-profit entities (that is, reliant on charity). At the core, we are asking about the degree to which social structure makes the specific founder on whose network the venture is built essential to the social enterprise's survival.

In addition, we see another implication for the role of social entrepreneurs in terms of their key activities, both symbolic and operational. If social capital is transmutable and/or transferable, or is concomitantly created by individual and organization, we wonder to what extent founders must prioritize the task of boundary span across organizations and bonding in their own organization, to create new ways of thinking about how to create social value. This line of reasoning relates to both the content and process of social capital, including cognitive and relational aspects.

Finally, and most broadly, social entrepreneurship is a newly identified institutional approach to creating social value. While it shares many of the process and content characteristics of traditional entrepreneurship, it also requires us to think in new ways about existing practices assigned to the for-profit, non-profit and government realms. Perhaps the social capital that tends to be regarded as a personal asset drawn on to create organizational benefits will come to be considered an organizational resource that can be deployed to create value of various kinds, regardless of organizational type. If the basis of goodwill integral to social capital is subject to isomorphic pressure, we may then see a drift toward for-profit clients and non-profit providers sharing values over time. This move would be enabled by the model of organizational structures and super-structures, like Anudip, that are adapting current norms and structures in innovative ways to serve social needs.

# REFERENCES

Adler, P.S. and S.W. Kwon (2002), 'Social capital: prospects for a new concept', *Academy of Management Review*, **27**, 17–40.

Arregle, J-L., M.A. Hitt, D.G. Sirmon and P. Very (2007), 'The development of organizational capital: attributes of family firms', *Journal of Management Studies*, **44**(1), 73–95.

Austin, J., H. Stevenson and J. Wei-Skillern (2006), 'Social and commercial entrepreneurship: same, different, or both', *Entrepreneurship Theory and Practice* **30**(1), January, 1–22.

Batjargal, B. (2007), 'Internet entrepreneurship: social capital, human capital, and perform-ance of internet ventures in China', *Research Policy*, **36**, 605–18.

Bornstein, D. (2004), *How to Change the World: Social Entrepreneurs and the Power of New Ideas*, New York: Oxford University Press.

Bourdieu, P. (1985), 'The forms of capital', in J. Richardson (ed.), *Handbook of Theory and Research for the Sociology of Education*, New York: Greenwood, pp. 241–58.

Burt, R.S. (1992), *Structural Holes: The Social Structure of Competition*, Cambridge, MA: Harvard University Press.

Burt, R.S. (1997), 'The contingent value of social capital', *Administrative Science Quarterly*, **42**, 339–65.

Burt, R.S. (2000), 'The network structure of social capital', in R. Sutton and B.Y. Staw (eds), *Research in Organizational Behavior*, Vol. 22, Greenwich, CT: JAI Press, pp. 345–423.

Burt, R.S. (2002), 'The social capital of structural holes', in M.F. Guillén (ed.), *The New Economic Sociology: Developments in an Emerging Field*, New York: Russell Sage Foundation, pp. 148–90.

Burt, R.S. (2005), *Brokerage & Closure: An Introduction to Social Capital*. New York: Oxford University Press.

Coleman, J.S. (1988), 'Social capital in the creation of human capital', *American Journal of Sociology*, **93**, 291–321.

Coleman, J.S. (1990), *Foundations of Social Theory*, Cambridge, MA: Harvard University Press.

Davidsson, P. and B. Honig (2003), 'The role of social capital among nascent entrepreneurs', *Journal of Business Venturing*, **18**(3), 301–32.

Dewar, R. and J. Dutton (1986), 'The adoption of radical and incremental innovations: an empirical analysis', *Management Science*, **32**(11), 1422–33.

Emerson, J. (2003), 'The blended value proposition: integrating social and financial returns', *California Management Review*, **45**(4), 35–51.

Hansen, M.T., J.M. Podolny and J. Pfeffer (2001), 'So many ties, so little time: a task contin-gency perspective on corporate social capital', *Research in the Sociology of Organizations*, **18**, 21–57.

Leadbeater, C. (1997), *The Rise of the Social Entrepreneur*, London: Demos.

Light, P.C. (2005), 'Searching for social entrepreneurs: who they might be, where they might be found', paper presented at annual meeting of Association for Research on Nonprofit and Voluntary Associations.

Lin, N. (2001), *Social Capital: A Theory of Social Structure and Action*, Cambridge: Cambridge University Press.

Mair, J. and I. Martí (2006), 'Social entrepreneurship research: a source of explanation, pre-diction, and delight', *Journal of World Business*, **41**, 36–44.

Maurer, I. and M. Ebers (2006), 'Dynamics of social capital and their performance impli-cations: lessons from biotechnology start-ups', *Administrative Science Quarterly*, **51**(2), 262–92.

Mouw, T. (2006), 'Measuring the causal effect of social capital: a review of recent research', *Annual Review of Sociology*, **32**, 79–102.

Nahapiet, J. and S. Ghoshal (1998), 'Social capital, intellectual capital, and the organiza-tional advantage', *Academy of Management Review*, **23**(2), 242–66.

Oh, H., M. Chung and G. Labianca (2004), 'Group social capital and group effectiveness: the role of informal socializing ties', *Academy of Management Journal*, **47**(6), 860–75.

Oh, H., G. Labianca and M. Chung (2006), 'A multilevel model of group social capital', *Academy of Management Review*, **31**(3), 569–82.

Peredo, A.M. and M. McLean (2006), 'Social entrepreneurship: a critical review of the concept', *Journal of World Business*, **41**(1), 56–65.

Portes, A. (1998), 'Social capital: its origins and applications in modern sociology', *Annual Review of Sociology*, **24**, 1–24.

Reed, K., M. Lubatkin and N. Srinivasan (2006), 'Proposing and testing an intellectual capital-based view of the firm', *Journal of Management Studies*, **43**(4), 867–93.

Stam, W. and T. Elfring (2008), 'Entrepreneurial orientation and new venture performance: the moderating role of intra- and extraindustry social capital', *Academy of Management Journal*, **51**(1), 97–111.

Subramaniam, M. and M. Youndt (2005), 'The influence of intellectual capital on the types of innovative capabilities', *Academy of Management Journal*, **48**(3), 450–63.

Weerawardena, K. and G.S. Mort (2006), 'Investigating social entrepreneurship: a multidimensional model', *Journal of World Business*, **41**, 21–35.

Woolcock, M. and D. Narayan (2000), 'Social capital: implications for development theory, research, and policy', *The World Bank Research Observer*, **15**(2), 225–49.

Yli-Renko, H., E. Autio and H. Sapienza (2001), 'Social capital, knowledge acquisition, and knowledge exploitation in young technologically based firms', *Strategic Management Journal*, **22**, 587–613.

# 15 Social entrepreneurs and earned income opportunities: the dilemma of earned income pursuit

*Brett R. Smith, Christopher E. Stevens and Terri F. Barr*

## INTRODUCTION

While the increased attention on social entrepreneurship in recent years has done much to illuminate social entrepreneurs and their ventures, less is known about how social entrepreneurs make decisions and the tensions involved in making these decisions. The decision-making process is tension-laden partly because of the potentially conflicting types of value creation and the relative emphasis on each type of value. While commercial entrepreneurs focus primarily on the creation of economic value, the primary focus of social entrepreneurs is the creation of social value.[1] However, for many social entrepreneurs, the creation of social value is often facilitated through the creation of economic value, thereby bringing both types of value – social and economic – into close proximity to one another and raising questions about the tensions involved in a dual-value creation process.

For one group of social entrepreneurs – those that pursue their entrepreneurship in the form of a non-profit organization – entrepreneurship is often embodied in the pursuit of earned income opportunities (EIOs). While the practice of non-profit organizations engaging in commercial activities is not new, the scope and magnitude of these activities is growing at an increasing rate spurred in part by an increasingly competitive landscape for economic resources (Skloot, 1988). As a result, 'nonprofit organizations are becoming more dependent on commercial activities, in one form or another' (Weisbrod, 1998: 16). This increased reliance on EIOs highlights the importance of understanding the tensions involved in the identification and evaluation of EIOs by non-profit organizations.

EIOs present social entrepreneurs with the possibility of increased revenue, increased market exposure, and increased financial and intellectual independence. As such, the prospect of identifying and pursuing an EIO offers intriguing possibilities for non-profit organizations. Yet, with these benefits, EIOs carry potentially substantial burdens. As social entrepreneurs become engaged in commercial activities, a number of challenges may be encountered – financial, organization, communal, and even moral – when trying to generate both economic and social value. A better understanding of the internal debates at play when non-profit organizations consider the pursuit of new opportunities holds the potential to increase our understanding of the unique pressures faced by social entrepreneurs and the ventures they lead.

To that end, we examine the issues related to the development of earned income in 27 non-profit organizations in the United States. In a series of semi-structured interviews with the executive directors of each firm, we explore a number of the tensions related to the pursuit of EIOs. Through exploratory qualitative evidence, we identify three primary themes or 'tensions' experienced by non-profit organizations when considering EIOs. These tensions include organizational identity tensions, institutional tensions and risk-related tensions. Collectively, these tensions provide a more nuanced understanding of the dilemma faced by social entrepreneurs in the evaluation and exploitation of EIOs. Individually, each of these tensions offers a rich theoretical lens through which continued development of the emerging domain of social entrepreneurship can be developed for future empirical and theoretical research.

## SOCIAL ENTREPRENEURSHIP, NON-PROFIT ORGANIZATIONS, AND EARNED INCOME OPPORTUNITIES

### Definition of Social Entrepreneurship

In a recent review of the growing body of literature on the phenomenon of social entrepreneurship, Austin et al., (2006) define social entrepreneurship as 'innovative, social value creating activity that can occur within or across the nonprofit, business, or governmental sectors' (2006: 2). Although many definitions exist for social entrepreneurship/social enterprise, they all tend to share common elements.

First and foremost, social entrepreneurs are characterized by a focus on social outcomes – the 'social' half of the term. Dees notes that for social entrepreneurs, social mission is 'explicit and central' (1998: 3). This parallels the traditional (economic) view of entrepreneurship, which focuses on creating shareholder wealth, but identifies a non-ownership body (society) as the shareholder, and focuses on increasing social wealth (Austin et al., 2006). Second, a focus on the application of novel means provides us with the link to the 'entrepreneurship' label. Entrepreneurial activity is characterized by the application of approaches that are novel or unique, approaches that aim to solve an identified problem in an inherently different way (Gartner, 1988; Schumpeter, 1934; 1942; Vesper, 1980) and this is no different for social entrepreneurship (Austin et al., 2006). Finally, the literature suggests that we need not think of social entrepreneurship as charity – organizations may balance their dominant focus on social outcomes with a pragmatic view of economic realities. As Alter (2004) indicates, we should focus our attention on 'hybrid' organizational forms, where social motives are balanced with the economic activities needed to sustain and grow these organizations. Taken together, the innovation involved in social value creation often leads to the ongoing balancing act that occurs within these hybrid organizations. For our purposes, we focus on the tensions experienced in this balancing act that make up what we term the 'dilemma' of earned income.

### Non-profit Organizations and the Earned Income Opportunity

An important component of the domain of social entrepreneurship is the pursuit of entrepreneurial activity by non-profits (Mort et al., 2003; Thompson, 2002). Non-profit organizations are self-directed, innovative and engage in risk-bearing behaviour, albeit in pursuit of the welfare of others (Bilodeau and Slivinsky, 1996; Handy et al., 2002; Kassam et al., 2000; Pilz, 1995; Young, 1984). Non-profit organizations are also just as dependent on the consistency of mission, value and strategy (Bryson, 1988; Vernis et al., 2004) as their for-profit brethren (Johnson and Scholes, 2001). In these ways, the pursuit of EIOs by non-profit organizations represents an important and growing dimension of social entrepreneurship.

Non-profit organizations, by their nature, have a limited capacity with which to raise or use equity capital (Crimmins and Keli, 1983; Young, 1987), and their reliance on donated and granted funds for resources often makes the service of debt-based financing impractical or undesirable. For most of this century, the vast majority of non-profit organizations relied exclusively on two sources of funding – donations and grants (Zietlow, 2001). However, recent changes to economic policy (Skloot, 1988) and the offsetting growth of private foundations (Emerson, 2004) and new non-profits seeking funding (Tierney, 2006) have resulted in an economic environment that is difficult for many non-profit organizations to survive in when they rely on traditional sources alone. Therefore, there is an increasing need to consider alternative sources of funding such as earned income opportunities.

What exactly is an earned income opportunity? Two prominent views exist among practitioners and researchers. The first, championed by Dees and his colleagues (2001), suggests that earned income can include any and all revenue-generating opportunities in the non-profit sector. In this context, the focus of earned income is on the *income* portion of the term – any activity that generates income for the organization is earned income. A more limited definition, suggested by Zietlow (2001) and others argues that the *earned* portion of the term is the vital distinction – that only revenue-generating activities that would not occur but for ongoing, non-programme-dependent action on the part of the organization are earned income – in other words, activities that require additional independent effort are earned income. While legitimate arguments exist for both perspectives, the ambiguity surrounding EIO pursuit in the field suggests the broader definition is more applicable in a study of current non-profit practice.

Another key distinction evident from the literature is that an earned income opportunity need not be tied to the organization's mission. While cost recovery activities have a direct link to mission and organizing principles, earned income opportunities may focus on any area, provided they operate within certain legal frameworks (Young, 1998; Alter, 2004). Finally, earned income opportunities are characterized by their independent and self-sufficient nature. As EIOs are not tied directly to programme function, and may rely on their own customer bases for support, the goal of any earned income opportunity is generally focused on providing funding for the non-profit. Emerson and Twersky (1996) suggest that non-profits managing social ventures – even those they plan on being temporary – are inevitably drawn towards permanent ventures, as the earned income opportunity often requires the establishment of services, staffing and management that present a significant start-up cost to be recovered by the non-profit organization. Thus, we emerge with a definition of earned income opportunities that focuses on revenue generation, sustainability, and some link (be it direct or indirect) with the non-profit organization's primary mission.

**The Potential Pros and Cons of EIO Pursuit**

While the potential exists for EIOs to bring additional financial resources to organizations, there is less agreement on the related positives and negatives of EIO pursuit. Viewed positively, pursuit of EIOs may diversify the organization's funding stream (Skloot, 1988), increase its overall revenue-generating abilities (Tuckman and Chang, 1991; Tuckman, 1998), increase the organization's reputation for innovativeness and proactivity among potential donors and stakeholders (Guo, 2006), provide an improved competitive position relative to more traditionally-funded organizations (Alter, 2004), and improve its fiscal discipline (Skloot, 1988).

Against these potential benefits, potentially significant organizational burdens emerge. Perhaps most significantly, non-profit organizations that pursue independent funding streams risk impacting their 501(c) 3 status, which relies on a careful balance between revenue generation and mission fulfilment (Hopkins and Beckwith, 1988). EIOs also, by their nature, require some level of initial investment, staffing, and business acumen that may either be in short supply or absent altogether in the non-profit (Thompson, 2002; Boschee, 1998). This prospect of adopting a business perspective may seem particularly daunting to many non-profits (Young, 1999; Zietlow, 2001; Thompson, 2002), regardless of their actual business knowledge. Additionally, concerns regarding the dilution of process and product quality (Adams and Perlmutter, 1991; Boschee, 1998; Weisbrod, 2004), the ability to measure success in a socially-motivated economic pursuit (Thompson, 2002), the management of growth, success and expansion (Boschee, 1998; Thompson, 2002), pressure to enter EIOs from boards or constituents (Skloot, 1988), cause apprehension. Finally, issues related to mission creep or departure based on profit pursuits (Salamon, 1995; Thompson, 2002), the fear of increased publicity or public scrutiny (Skloot, 1988), and the fear of the impact of failure (Boschee, 1998; Skloot, 1988; Thompson, 2002) make EIOs a challenging prospect for many non-profit organizations. As a result, a major dilemma exists for non-profits as they pursue earned income opportunities, as they must balance 'the need to ensure their survival as entities without forgetting their raison d'être' with the need to ensure 'consistency between strategy, mission, and available resources' (Arenas et al., 2006). While this final point of tension may, in some respects, rest on the type of earned income pursuit undertaken and its level of departure from the organizational focus, even the pursuit of highly interrelated revenue recovery-type activities may require some level of independent organization and management, factors which have the potential to pull resources from the core activities of the organization.

While some emerging empirical research has examined the prevalence and relative financial success of EIOs by non-profits (for example, Alter, 2004; Salamon, 1999), much less work has sought to understand the tensions involved in the evaluation and exploitation of EIOs by these non-profit social entrepreneurs. Therefore, our goal in this study is to identify organizational tensions which offer some promising theoretical lenses through which the decision-making process of EIOs may be better understood. In this way, we believe one of the important contributions of this study is to provide some exploratory evidence about why certain theoretical frameworks may be useful for future inquiry in the emerging research domain of social entrepreneurship.

## METHODOLOGY

### Sample

The sample used in this research included 27 executive directors of non-profit organizations located in the United States that were considering, developing, or had developed an EIO. While quantitative research often relies on the use of statistical sampling to obtain evidence on the distribution of variables within a population, qualitative research typically uses a different form of sampling referred to as theoretical sampling (Eisenhardt, 1989). In theoretical sampling, the respondents for analysis are chosen for theoretical rather than statistical reasons (Glaser and Strauss, 1967). Such is the case with this particular sample.

The sample of organizations was identified through two different sources: first, by connecting with an organization which works with non-profits as they consider social enterprises and second, by the snow-ball method of asking people involved in the study to identify other potential participants (Miles and Huberman, 1994). Given the focus of understanding the tensions involved in evaluating and pursuing EIOs, we included organizations who were at several different stages of evaluating earned-income opportunities: (1) those who had never launched an EIO; (2) those who were in the process of launching an EIO; (3) those who had several years of experience with their EIO; and (4) those who had discontinued at least one EIO. Nearly a quarter of the organizations had no prior or current experience with EIOs; nearly a quarter had discontinued an EIO. The age of the non-profit organizations ranged from 3 years to more than 100 years, with an average of 18 years. The age of the EIOs ranged from less than 1 year to more than 20 years, with an average age of 6 years.

### Data Collection

The research design of this study included two types of data collection: archival data and interview data. The use of multiple methods is ideal to allow for convergence and triangulation of findings (Jick, 1979). First, archival data was collected from the non-profit organizations, including annual reports. A second type of data collection was done through personal semi-structured interviews with the executive directors of the non-profit organizations. Questions included topics such as career background, history of the organization, factors affecting identification of EIOs, funding of EIOs, processes of EIOs evaluation and board perspective of EIOs. The interviews lasted approximately 60 minutes on average.

A semi-structured interview included both pre-determined protocol questions and ad hoc questions that arose during the course of the interview. One of the unique benefits of qualitative data collection is the flexibility of the design that allows the researcher to adapt to the dynamic demands of the immediate research setting (Lee, 1999). As such, a semi-structured interview provides the researcher the flexibility to explore interesting themes and questions as they emerge during the interview and allows the respondents a greater opportunity to speak in *their own voice* (Kreiner et al., 2006). Ten of the interviews were conducted in person; 17 were conducted over the telephone. All telephone interviews were tape-recorded on digital audio files and then transcribed verbatim by a professional transcriber. Interview transcripts averaged over 19 pages of single-spaced text and totalled 323 pages of text.

**Data Analysis**

The data analysis began during the first interview. During each interview, several notes were taken on interesting themes or ideas that emerged during the interview. In some cases, these themes served as prompts for follow-up questions within or after the interview. In many cases, specific quotes were recorded. In every case, these notes served as the basis for beginning to understand the issues associated with EIOs. Following each interview, we wrote down all of the interesting themes that emerged and how these themes were consistent with or departed from previous interviews. This initiated the ongoing toggling back and forth between the data and the theoretical frameworks being created by the process of interviewing; as we conducted more interviews and more common themes emerged, discernible themes of pressure and conflict began to emerge – themes we were able to focus on in more detail in subsequent interviews.

The ongoing analysis of the data continued with the receipt of the telephone interview transcripts. We adhered to grounded theory techniques (Strauss and Corbin, 1998) by following a manual coding process to derive codes inductively from the transcripts. The first step of the coding process involved researchers coding a transcript and developing codes based on the content of the data. Codes are labels of condensed meaning that can be placed on any passage of text (a word, a phrase, a sentence, a paragraph, or even multiple pages). Any passage of text could have multiple codes if warranted. The creation of codes also included a toggling back and forth between the passages of text in the transcript and the previously analysed data.

The second step of the coding process occurred when two researchers sat down together to jointly code the same interview. Through comparison and discussion, the two researchers reached agreement about how to code a particular passage of the transcript. As codes were agreed upon by both researchers, a dictionary identifying and explaining each of the codes was developed. During coding sessions, the dictionary was updated as new codes emerged from the data and were jointly agreed to by the researchers. Due to the emergent nature of the coding process, traditional inter-rater reliability calculations were impractical, as codes are added, deleted, and changed throughout the analysis.

# FINDINGS

The findings of our research examining the evaluation and exploitation of EIOs centred around three major tensions that were experienced by non-profit organizations and their constituents. These tensions represented important ways in which the organizations were 'stretched' or pulled in different directions based on resource needs or the views of multiple stakeholders within their environments. The tensions included organizational identity tensions, institutional tensions and risk-related tensions. In the following paragraphs, we will provide a brief overview of the literature relevant to each of these tensions, and illustrative quotes and examples of the ways in which these tensions manifested themselves, resulting in the dilemma of EIOs for non-profit organizations.

**Organizational Identity Tensions**

An organization's identity has been defined as those features of an organization that are considered to be central, distinctive and enduring (Albert and Whetten, 1985). In this sense, organizational identity focuses on expressing 'who the organization is' and on defining the essence of the organization (Corley et al., 2006). The literature on organizational identity has also highlighted that organizations often have multiple or hybrid identities – identities that coexist but at the same time appear conflicting or unlikely (Albert and Whetten, 1985). One of the common issues associated with hybrid identity organizations is that the multiple identities are often in conflict with one another (for example, Glynn, 2000) and may have negative ramifications for the organization and its members. As non-profit organizations engage in EIOs, one of the potential tensions is the development and management of the hybrid identities of both the social service side of the organization and the business-oriented side of the organization (Tracey and Phillips, 2007).

In our study, we found several examples of the challenges of managing hybrid identities within organizations. First, several leaders of non-profit organizations experienced substantial opposition to the very thought of an EIO, based partly on the premise that an EIO undermined the character of the organization itself. For example, one executive director suggested: 'I remember one meeting where our Program Managers reacted so strongly to EIOs. They asked "What kind of organization are we becoming? Oh my God, poison just walked through the door. Put up the garlic."'

Such a reaction speaks to one of the inherent tensions of developing and managing an EIO. That is, the initiation of an EIO to a non-profit organization has the potential of introducing a competing and conflicting identity. Such concerns were not limited to the overall concern about changing the character of the organization but also to the very language of business-related practices. For example, an executive director claimed:

> The word 'marketing' in this organization is a dirty word because in the non-profit paradigm, you do outreach – you don't market. To market is to convince someone that they need something, whether they need it or not. In outreach, you let people know you've got something that can help them. We no longer think this way, but that was how we were thinking while we were walking into this world.

The concerns over language-related issues were not limited to internal stakeholders but also to external stakeholders, such as donors. One executive director commented:

> We do a fundraiser every fall, and the people are there because they love us, they love what we do and especially they love our founders. They do not want to hear about food costs and sales. They want to hear that so-and-so got a job. If I talk that other language, they'll think I'm too 'business-y', and that I'm not associated with the mission. And, that will put them off.

One of the most salient identity challenges occurred when the mission of the social side of the organization and the operation of the business side of the organization came into conflict. In our study, this challenge seemed to be particularly problematic for non-profit organizations that were focused on job training. For these organizations, the EIOs represented both a means to earn income and a means to provide their clients with real-world skills. For these organizations, there was a very delicate balancing act between these two sides of the organization.

I think what nonprofits sometimes do is that they start to run these businesses, and they are serving two gods, if you will. They are serving the clients who come to the business and they are serving the employees who are getting the job skills or training. When you do that you create a dual and sometimes opposite set of needs and requirements.

While these issues create challenges for the ongoing operation of the enterprise, such issues also pose very difficult questions about the very identity of the organization.

The other big tension I've had – the big tension – is deciding whether I am a permanent employment operation or a training operation. . .This is the issue I asked the board when they hired me. Which are we? Is the expectation that people will have a great place to work forever or is the expectation that people will graduate from us, in which case we are a training operation? If people stay forever . . . my operation will run much, much smoother. But, I chose to try the opposite. We had people who had been here for three or four years and then we graduated them . . . but, it definitely hurt the business.

In some cases, the identity challenges were not limited to the people that were being served, but were more closely related to the location that was being changed – a geographic-based identity. That is, the initiation of the EIO involved the relocation of the physical presence of the organization and its people to another geographic location. This relocation raised important concerns for the identity of the organization.

There was a big consideration about changing the neighbourhood (where we operate). We have been a West End organization and have been tied to the West End. I've been looking very carefully at how do we keep our West End contacts and how do we keep our 'West Endedness', now that we've moved to [another neighbourhood]. We still have an office in the West End, but we are rarely there. In terms of the services we offer and the people we are serving, we've lost our contact with the West End, which is traditionally where we were and who we were.

While the hybrid identities of the organization often created challenges for non-profit organizations, the initiation of EIOs was not universally viewed to be problematic. By contrast, several organizations found EIOs to be wholly consistent with not only their identity as an organization, but also with the social change the organization was trying to implement. One executive director described it to us this way:

Everybody always says to poor people, 'You've got to get off the government dole. You've got to stop waiting for people to give you stuff. You've got to earn stuff.' Well, we, the service providers can be in the same position of saying, 'You've got to get off the government dole. You've got to earn. You've got to mirror what you're asking of your clients.' So, there's a parallelism there that I find very inviting.

In this way, the multiple identities of the organization reinforced rather than pulled apart the identity of the organization. In the same way, some non-profit organizations thought the initiation of EIOs actually increased their support from donors partly because the donors recognized the organization for trying to become more self-sufficient.

> We actually have a lot of really great support (from donors) and I think it's because they recognize we're very much committed to doing things on our own but need a little more help. There's a feeling that they want to support people who, for the most part, are making it happen themselves instead of relying completely on hand-outs. They're really driving and doing their own thing. I think that actually bodes well for us. It's just a little bit more help from people. People feel better about something that's innovative and working to help themselves.

Given the issues related to hybrid identities of the initiation of EIOs by non-profit organizations, a number of important questions could be explored by future research. These questions include:

- How do non-profit organizations introduce an EIO to the organization?
- How do non-profit organizations manage the hybrid identities inherent in the evaluation and exploitation of EIOs?
- How do individuals associated with non-profits that engage in EIOs respond to the possible changing nature of the EIOs?
- Should non-profit organizations seek to integrate or segment the multiple identities of the organization?
- How do non-profit organizations manage the impression of the organization to stakeholders both internally and externally?

Each of these questions opens up important lines of inquiry that can inform not only the practice of EIOs by non-profit organizations but also the broader management literature on the topics related to the initiation and management of hybrid identities by organizations and their members.

### Institutional Form Tensions

A second theoretical framework that may be useful to understand the tensions experienced by non-profit organizations in the evaluation and exploitation of EIOs is institutional theory. Emerging out of organization theory and sociology, institutional theory attempts to explain why organizations take the form they do (Meyer and Rowan, 1977). In short, institutional theory suggests that organizations conform to the rules and belief systems of their environment and develop organizational structures that conform to these rules and belief systems (Meyer and Scott, 1983). While institutional theory was developed partly to explain non-profit organizations, it may also be applied to the tensions experienced by these same types of organizations as they consider the prospects of EIOs, and the changes in organizational form that necessarily must come about as a function of pursuing an EIO.

In the consideration of an EIO, a non-profit organization may experience pressures from several different 'actors' within their environment. In this way, the non-profit organization and its leaders are likely to experience institutional tensions when different groups of actors are pulling the organization in different directions. To understand the institutional pressures, it is important to understand the historical context in which non-profit organizations have traditionally been funded. In summarizing this perspective, one executive director commented:

> It's almost like you've learned through osmosis that you're just supposed to get grants. That's what you do. You're not supposed to think about making money or be creative about ways to support yourself. And so, it's almost like an institutionalized way of thinking . . . It's like we're supposed to be poor. We're supposed to struggle. . .we're not supposed to make money.

As such, many non-profit organizations had used traditional funding mechanisms such as foundation and government grants to support their work. However, the traditional funders were beginning to develop a growing interest in the prospects of non-profit organizations engaging in EIOs. Many of the executive directors we spoke to indicated that funders were beginning to adopt favourable attitudes toward EIOs. For example, one respondent suggested: 'Donors are getting more savvy [about EIOs], and certainly, foundations like the fact that we have earned income and we generate income to help support our mission. That's changing.'

Consistent with institutional theory, the changing attitudes by funders (whether individual donors or foundations) were resulting in a growing number of non-profit organizations beginning to explore EIOs. According to institutional theory, the processes of isomorphism – whereby organizations become similar to each other over time (DiMaggio and Powell, 1983) – suggests that organizations may follow the lead of others to maintain legitimacy with key stakeholders. In addition, institutional form pressures may extend beyond the non-profits to the funding organizations themselves. One veteran of the social enterprise movement observed:

> I have seen that (donors) have identified a lot with (social enterprise). So they really have gotten passionate about it. What's interesting to me is that a lot of foundations are reacting the same way right now. It seems like social enterprise has reached an acceptance level where everybody is trying to get on the bandwagon to a certain degree. I know ten years ago, or eight years ago, it was very hard to make the case to fund us through grants. Lately, we've been doing real well. It seems like almost every grant we do we've been funded on. It just – it's been interesting to me, the change.

Taken together, the preceding examples begin to highlight the institutional form tensions felt by non-profit organizations. On the one hand, these organizations rely primarily on historical practices such as grant making which have served as a mainstay of non-profit financing for many years. On the other hand, many different actors within the organizational field of these organizations are beginning to chart a new course.

From an institutional form perspective these institutional pressures offer many important questions for future research on EIOs which include:

- How do non-profit organizations gain and maintain legitimacy in a time of transition for funding organizations?
- How does the relative performance of EIOs by non-profit organizations affect the institutional pressures of various stakeholders?
- How do non-profit organizations determine the appropriate referent organizations to monitor changes within their organizational field(s)?
- How do non-profit organizations decide how and when to become institutional entrepreneurs (Mair and Martí, 2006) within their organizational field(s)?

**Risk-related Tensions**

A third type of tension related to the pursuit of EIOs by non-profit organizations is risk-related tension. Since the advent of research on commercial entrepreneurship, the concept of risk has generally played in important role (cf. Shane, 2003). As such, it should be no surprise that the concept of risk would be salient to non-profit organizations as they evaluate and exploit EIOs. One of the important constructs related to risk in the entrepreneurial literature is the construct of risk perception. The concept of risk perception has generally been defined as a decision maker's assessment of the risk inherent in a situation (Mullins and Forlani, 2005). In general, entrepreneurial research has found a negative relationship between risk perception and the decision to start a new business (for example, Keh et al., 2002; Simon et al., 2000).

Echoing the importance of risk perception in the entrepreneurship literature, we also found the role of risk perceptions to be an important indicator of whether or not non-profit organizations engaged in the evaluation and exploitation of EIOs. In summarizing this view, one executive director suggested that non-profits considering EIOs should answer the following questions:

> How risk-taking does your organization tend to be? I think that all needs to be in alignment because there's a lot of risk involved in establishing something like that. So I would think whoever is considering (social enterprise) needs to make sure there's support at the Board level for assuming the risk involved. Are there adequate resources to take on that risk?

These comments indicate that risk perceptions are important across a broad range of stakeholders. In addition, many non-profit organizations were also concerned with the opportunity costs of utilizing any resources or assets in the pursuit of EIOs. For example, one executive director suggested:

> I think it is risky if it takes any resources of the not-for-profit at all that should be going towards mission or supporting mission by fund-raising. I think it is risky and I think I'm saying it mostly because look at the number of fits and starts [of EIOs] we had.

Consistent with this perception, several executive directors liked the idea of earning additional unrestricted revenue from an EIO but did not want to invest any resources of the non-profit organization into the EIO.

> You need the investment to underlay it so it's not coming out of your budget – look at it as looking for investors, just as you would if you were working for – or going to issue stock. To look for something that doesn't take any of your staff time, that it's completely self-sustaining. . .separate entity.

One tactic used by non-profit organizations to reduce their risk perceptions and therefore participate in EIOs was to segment the EIO into its own entity. Consistent with this view, one respondent commented:

> I think an important criterion is: how do you keep separate assets of the parent organization from the social enterprise? If you have to put at risk the assets of the parent organization in order to fund the social enterprise, then I would have been much less enthusiastic about going after the enterprise. When we bought our enterprise, we made an arrangement with the bank that we would put none of the parent organization's assets up against the loan. That was critical, really critical.

Another approach to assessing risk perceptions related to the manner in which the success of an EIO was measured. While some organizations focused on the financial performance of the EIO, many other organizations included or even exclusively focused on social value creation of their EIO. For example, one executive director described it this way:

> So, the profit is not what you have at the end of the day in terms of your bank account. The profit is that you have a healthier family you served. The outcome is the improved life, in our case, of the child whose family came through the door. . .That's our profit margin. That's how we measure our success – not, did our bank account grow.

The integration of different forms of value creation in the measurement of success is likely to affect the risk perceptions of the organization about the EIO. In addition, the calculus of risk perception seemed to differ for the social and the business outcomes of these organizations. For example, one executive director explained the risk perceptions of investing in EIO this way:

> You're investing in inventory. What if it just sits on the shelf and no one buys it? Have we not been good stewards of the organization and misused the resources of the organization? Are people going to look at us and say, 'How could you let this happen to our [non-profit]?'

This approach was common in many of the EIOs, suggesting that the literature on mental accounting (Thaler, 1980) may be useful to understand the risk-related calculations of non-profit organizations. The concept of mental accounting explains how people code, categorize and evaluate outcomes. While commonly referred to as economic outcomes, the concept of mental accounting could be usefully applied in the evaluation of EIO performance.

While many organizations focused on the potential risks of initiating an EIO, some organizations focused on the risk of not doing so. The risk literature refers to this as the risk of missing the boat (Dickson and Giglierano, 1986). As a result, many non-profit organizations launched a business that they knew relatively little about because the opportunity presented itself.

Taken together, the concept of risk and the various risk-related tensions may lead to fruitful examination of many different questions of future research:

- How do non-profit organizations identify the various risks of starting an EIO?
- How do non-profit organizations calculate the potential and actual return on their investments in terms of both social and economic performance?

- How do non-profits mentally account for both social and economic performance?
- How do the stakeholders of non-profit organizations balance the risk of sinking the boat and the risk of missing the boat?

## CONCLUSION

The pursuit of earned income opportunities by non-profit organizations is growing, as the need to find alternative forms of funding increases. The interviews conducted in this study with the executive directors of 27 non-profit organizations which are considering or have pursued EIOs, provide evidence that these opportunities have the potential to significantly affect issues of organizational identity, institutional form and perceptions of risk. These three theoretical frameworks provide new lenses through which to consider some of the tensions that exist when non-profits consider pursuing an EIO – which we have labelled the dilemma of earned income.

Evidence from our interviews suggests that non-profit organizations struggle with the tensions often created between the social mission of the non-profit and the profit mission of the EIO. Further, this tension also has the potential to create distrust, misunderstandings and confusion in the minds of potential donors, clients and staff members, making the pursuit of EIOs for non-profits challenging. As a result, managing non-profits with hybrid identities creates an enormous burden on the organization regarding carefully and consistently communicating with all of its stakeholders. Future research focusing on how non-profits can successfully introduce and integrate EIOs into their organizations would be extremely valuable,

Our research findings also suggest that institutional form is altered as non-profits pursue EIOs, putting pressure on both the organization and the people working both in and with that organization. The tension created as a function of changes to the traditional, and recognizable organizational form as non-profits take on EIOs requires changing both attitudes and adequacies of all involved. Future research opportunities related to issues of organizational form abound, and have the potential to answer questions regarding issues of institutional legitimacy, performance and change.

Additionally, our findings suggest that the pursuit of EIOs by non-profits must be measured in terms of the risk inherent in such a decision. The lens of perceived risk provides an opportunity to examine how non-profit leaders look at EIOs as a viable method of funding. Specifically, the executive directors of the non-profits with whom we spoke identified risk-related concerns as one of the predominant factors in whether or not an organization and its multiple stakeholders would be comfortable with the uncertainties associated with any new business venture, including issues of opportunity costs, and how to evaluate both economic and social outcomes. Future research that examines perceptions of risk associated with non-profit organizations' ventures into EIOs is needed to fully understand the potential benefits and costs of such undertakings.

The increasingly competitive environment along with the faltering economic environment that non-profits are currently facing calls for some new and innovative ways for non-profits to sustain themselves, and protect the people whom they serve through their social missions. To that end, this study identifies three themes that emerge from the qualitative data that appear to cause tensions for non-profits engaged in some way with EIOs. Using the theoretical frameworks of organizational identity, organizational theory, and perception of risk, we are able to examine these tensions and make sense of them. This research, which expands our knowledge of issues associated with earned income opportunities, offers new insights to non-profits by both informing and supporting their future consideration of earned income opportunities.

## NOTE

1. For a full discussion of the different forms of value creation and the relative emphases by commercial and social entrepreneurs, please see Smith and Barr (2007).

## REFERENCES

Adams, C. and F. Perlmutter (1991), 'Commercial venturing and the transformation of America's voluntary social welfare agencies', *Nonprofit and Voluntary Sector Quarterly*, **20**(1), 25–38.
Albert, S. and D. Whetten (1985), 'Organizational Identity', in B.M. Staw and L.L. Cummings (eds), *Research in Organizational Behavior*, Vol. 7 Greenwich, CT: JAI Press, pp. 236–95.
Alter, K. (2004), 'Social enterprise typology', Virtue Ventures, LLC, online report, available at: http://www.virtueventures.com/setypology, accessed 1 May, 2007.
Arenas, D., J. Bruni, P. Marquez and A. Vernis (2006), 'Strategy in social enterprise: a comparison of business and civil society organizations in Iberoamerica', in J.E. Austin, R. Gutierrez, E. Ogliastri and E. Reficco (eds), *Effective Management of Social Enterprises: Lessons from Businesses and Civil Society Organizations in Iberoamerica*, Cambridge, MA: Harvard University Press, pp. 47–74.
Austin, J., J. Wei-Skillern and H. Stevenson (2006), 'Social and commercial entrepreneurship: same, different, or both?' *Entrepreneurship Theory and Practice*, **30**(1), 1–22.
Bilodeau, M. and A. Slivinsky (1996), 'Volunteering nonprofit entrepreneurial services', *Journal of Economic Behavior & Organization*, **31**(1), 117–27.

Boschee, J. (1998), 'Merging mission and money: a board member's guide to social entrepreneurship', available at: http://www.socialent.org/pdfs/MergingMission.pdf, accessed September 2006.

Bryson, J.M. (1988), *Strategic Planning for Public and Nonprofit Organizations: A Guide to Strengthening and Sustaining Organizational Achievement*, San Francisco: Jossey-Bass.

Corley, K., C. Harquail, M. Glynn, C. Fiol and M. Hatch (2006), 'Guiding organizational identity through aged adolescence', *Journal of Management Inquiry*, **15**, 85–99.

Crimmins, J.C. and M. Keli (1983), *Enterprise in the Non-Profit Sector*, New York: Rockefeller Brothers Fund.

Dees, J.G. (1998), 'The meaning of social entrepreneurship', unpublished paper, Kansas City, MO: Ewing Marion Kauffman Foundation.

Dees, J.G., J. Emerson and P. Economy (2001), *Enterprising Nonprofits: A Toolkit for Social Entrepreneurs*, Toronto, ON: John Wiley & Sons.

Dickson, P.R. and J.J. Giglierano (1986), 'Missing the boat and sinking the boat: a conceptual model of entrepreneurial risk', *Journal of Marketing*, **50**(3), 58–70.

DiMaggio, P.J. and W.W. Powell (1983), 'The iron cage revisited: institutional isomorphism and collective rationality in organizational field', *American Sociological Review*, **48**, 147–60.

Eisenhardt, K. (1989), 'Building theories through case study research', *Academy of Management Review*, **14**, 532–50.

Emerson, J.E. (2004), '*The 21st century foundation: building upon the past, creating for the future*', working paper, available at: http://www.blendedvalue.org/media/pdf-21st-century-foundation.pdf, accessed 20 April.

Emerson, J.E. and F. Twersky (eds) (1996), *New Social Entrepreneurs: The Success, Challenge, and Lessons of Non-Profit Enterprise Creation*, San Francisco: The Roberts Foundation.

Gartner, W. (1988), 'Who is the entrepreneur? Is the wrong question', *American Journal of Small Business*, **12**(4), 11–32.

Glaser, B.G. and A.L. Strauss (1967), *The Discovery of Grounded Theory*, Chicago, IL: Aldine.

Glynn, M.A. (2000), 'When cymbals become symbols: conflict over organizational identity within a symphony orchestra', *Organization Science*, **11**(3), 285–98.

Guo, B. (2006), 'Charity for profit? Exploring factors associated with the commercialization of human service nonprofits', *Nonprofit and Voluntary Sector Quarterly*, **35**(1), 123–38.

Handy, F., M. Kassam and S. Renade (2002), 'Factors influencing women entrepreneurs of NGOs in India', *Nonprofit Management and Leadership*, **13**(2), 139–54.

Hopkins, B. and E. Beckwith (1988), 'The revenue act of 1987 and nonprofit organizations', *Journal of National Association of Hospitality Development*, 23–6.

Jick, T. (1979), 'Mixing qualitative and quantitative methods: Triangulation in action', *Administrative Science Quarterly*, **24**, 602–11.

Johnson, G. and K. Scholes (2001), *Strategic Directions*, 5th edn, Madrid: Prentice Hall.

Kassam, M., F. Handy and S. Ranade (2000), 'Forms of leadership and organisational structure of non-profits: a study of women's NGOs in India', *Chinmaya Management Journal*, **4**(1), 30–40.

Keh, H.T., M.D. Foo and B.C. Lim (2002), 'Opportunity evaluation under risky conditions: the cognitive processes of entrepreneurs', *Entrepreneurship Theory and Practice*, **27**(2), 125–48.

Kreiner, G.E., E.C. Hollensbe and M.L. Sheep (2006), 'Where is the "me" among the "we"? Identity work and the search for optimal balance', *Academy of Management Journal*, **49**(5), 1031–57.

Lee, T. (1999), *Using Qualitative Methods in Organizational Research*, Thousand Oaks, CA: Sage.

Mair, J. and I. Martí (2006), 'Social entrepreneurship research: a source of explanation, prediction, and delight', *Journal of World Business*, **41**, 36–44.

Meyer, J.W. and B. Rowan (1977), 'Institutionalized organizations: formal structure as myth and ceremony', *American Journal of Sociology*, **83**, 440–63.
Meyer, J.W. and W. Scott (1983), *Organizational Environments*, New York: Russell Sage.
Miles, M. and A. Huberman (1994), *Qualitative Data Analysis: An Expanded Sourcebook*, 2nd edn, Thousand Oaks, CA: Sage.
Mort, G., J. Weerawardena and K. Carnegie (2003), 'Social entrepreneurship: towards conceptualization', *International Journal of Nonprofit and Voluntary Sector Quarterly*, **8**, 76–88.
Mullins, J.W. and D. Forlani (2005), 'Missing the boat or sinking the boat: a study of new venture decision making', *Journal of Business Venturing*, **20**, 47–69.
Nicholls, A. (2006), *Social Entrepreneurship: New Models of Sustainable Social Change*, Oxford: Oxford University Press.
Pilz, D.M. (1995), 'A study of characteristics and start-up activities of entrepreneurs in the nonprofit (non-governmental) organizations', unpublished DBA dissertation, Nova South Eastern University.
Salamon, L.M. (1995), *Partners in Public Service: Government–Nonprofit Relations in the Modern Welfare State*, Baltimore, MD: Johns Hopkins University Press.
Salamon, L.M. (1999), *America's Nonprofit Sector*, New York: Foundation Center.
Schumpeter, J. (1934), *Capitalism, Socialism and Democracy*, 1st edn, New York: Harper and Row.
Schumpeter, J. (1942), *Capitalism, Socialism and Democracy*, 2nd edn, New York: Harper and Brothers.
Shane, S. (2003), *A General Theory of Entrepreneurship: The Individual–Opportunity Nexus*, Cheltenham, UK and Northampton, MA, USA: Edward Elgar.
Simon, M., S.M. Houghton and K. Aquino (2000), 'Cognitive biases, risk perception, and venture formation: how individuals decide to start companies', *Journal of Business Venturing*, **15**(2), 113–34.
Skloot, E. (1988), *The Nonprofit Entrepreneur*, New York: Foundation Center.
Smith, B. and T. Barr (2007), 'Reducing poverty through social entrepreneurship: the case of Edun', in J. Stoner and C. Wankel (eds), *Innovative Approaches to Reducing Global Poverty*, Charlotte, NC: Information Age Publishing, pp. 27–42.
Strauss, A. and J. Corbin (1998), *Basics of Qualitative Research: Grounded Theory Procedures and Techniques*, 2nd edn, Thousand Oaks, CA: Sage.
Thaler, R. (1980), 'Towards a positive theory of consumer choice', *Journal of Economic Behavior and Organization*, **1**, 39–60.
Thompson, J.L. (2002), 'The world of the social entrepreneur', *The International Journal of Public Sector Management*, **15**(4), 412–31.
Tierney, T.J. (2006), *The Nonprofit Sector's Leadership Deficit*, Boston, MA: The Bridgespan Group.
Tracey, P. and N. Phillips (2007), 'The distinctive challenge of education social entrepreneurs: a postscript and rejoinder to the special issue on entrepreneurship education', *Academy of Management Learning and Education*, **6**, 264–71.
Tuckman, H.P. (1998), 'Competition, commercialization, and the evolution of nonprofit organizational structures', *Journal of Policy Analysis and Management*, **17**(2), 175–94.
Tuckman, H.P. and C.F. Chang (1991), 'A methodology for measuring the financial vulnerability of charitable nonprofit organizations', *Nonprofit and Voluntary Sector Quarterly*, **20**, 445–60.
Vernis, A., M. Iglesias, B. Sanz and S. Angel (2004), *Los Retos en la Gestion de las Organizaciones No Lucrativas*, Barcelona: Grancia.
Vesper, K.H. (1980), *New Venture Strategies*, Englewood Cliffs, NJ: Prentice-Hall.
Weisbrod, B.A. (1998), 'The nonprofit mission and its financing: growing links between nonprofits and the rest of the economy', in B.A. Weisbrod (ed.), *To Profit or Not to Profit: The Commercial Transformation of the Nonprofit Sector*, Cambridge: Cambridge University Press, pp. 1–22.

Weisbrod, B.A. (2004), 'The pitfalls of profits', *Stanford Social Innovation Review*, **2**(3), 40–47.

Young, D.R. (1984), *Caseboook of Management for Nonprofit Organizations*, New York: Haworth.

Young, D.R. (1987), 'Executive leadership in nonprofit organizations', in W.W. Powell (ed.), *The Nonprofit Sector: A Research Handbook*, New Haven: Yale University Press, pp. 167–79.

Young, D.R. (1998), 'Commercialism in nonprofit social service organizations', in B.A. Weisbrod (ed.), *To Profit or Not to Profit: The Commercial Transformation of the Nonprofit Sector*, Cambridge: Cambridge University Press, pp. 195–216.

Young, D.R. (1999), 'Economic decision-making by nonprofit organizations in a market economy: tensions between mission and market', The National Center on Nonprofit Enterprise, available at: http://www.nationalcne.org.

Zietlow, J.T. (2001), 'Social entrepreneurship: managerial, finance and marketing aspects', *Journal of Nonprofit & Public Sector Marketing*, **9**, 19–27.

# 16 Ending essay: sociality and economy in social entrepreneurship
## Daniel Hjorth

There was a time when economy was defined with reference to frugality, to saving, to the careful handling (hand, as in *manus* – Latin for hand – and later management) of resources with attention to the well-being of families, communities. Today, as we still hear the echoes of the cries of those affected by the so-called financial or credit crisis, economy is understood by reference to spending, excess, aggressive investment, competitiveness, and alluring lending–borrowing circles. For sure, economy has always been inherently tied to management, and management of one's owns affairs: the Oxford English Dictionary rightfully explains the origin of the word to be found in the Greek *oikonomia*, meaning 'household management'. We may read this as another inherent relationship between economy and the private, albeit not individual sphere. The household, the well-being of which is the purpose of economic handling in this sense, is not an autonomous, individual actor as in the much celebrated *homo oeconomicus*, always lionized by economists seeking to achieve by this offer of marriage a tie that binds (if not anchors) their models to a touchstone of the real. Economy has become a managerial economy, and in the process lost most of its attention to (or care for) community. Management is today understood as an act of an individual – the manager – for an individual: no one works merely for salary any more. You want me to lift my finger – present me to your bonus-programme. The individualistic approach, promoted by economic theory, has enjoyed tremendous success when it comes to invading other fields of social sciences and has pushed out more collectivist approaches to analysing human behaviour (Kirchgässner, 2008).

The sociological programme for analysing human behaviour (which in its modern form is shaped by Comte, Durkheim, Tönnies and Weber), with its focus on the *socius*[1] (Latin for 'companion') has gradually been pushed back by an economic programme for analysis of individual action. Rational choice theorists, game theorists, social economists have expanded the domain of economic theory much as the capitalist system continuously expands into 'virgin land' to maintain its functions. The social economy of Becker (for example Becker and Murphy, 2003) results in 'extended utility functions' – economist language for having taken the social into

306

consideration – which is how changes in the social environment are taken into consideration when analysing choice. Michel Foucault has targeted Gary Becker in particular – Becker being an economist of the Chicago school who has been particularly industrious in his pursuit of expanding the domain of economic analysis *qua* individualistic behaviour of the rational-calculative kind – as he identified the productivity of certain economics discourses affecting a gradual redescription of the social as a form of the economic (as Colin Gordon, 1991, puts it). However, Becker leading scholar in promoting this change (he also received a Nobel Prize in economics in 1992), was and is not alone in this approach, proposing 'a global redescription of the social as a form of the economic' (Gordon, 1991: 43) Economics as knowledge and economists as expertise – as we all know from daily news media – have risen to an unchallenged status as truth speakers. The financial crisis has also illustrated how these experts can work on both sides of the break-down: advising decisions leading to it and later explaining how it could happen.

Now, why is this part of an introduction to an ending essay in a social entrepreneurship book? There are two answers to this. The answers are both about recent intensifications of the relationship between the economic and the social. One is the famous (notorious) so-called financial or credit crisis that I have already started to engage with, and the way this event bears witness to tendencies of the capitalist system, tendencies that threaten to become institutionalized in people's debt-generating behaviour. The other is how the success of the 'social entrepreneurship' discourse has changed the relationship between the social and the economic. This chapter is a modest attempt to investigate this relationship between economy and sociality, and to do so from the perspective of the successful 'social entreprenuership' discourse and from the perspective of the case of the credit crunch. As such it is aimed as a minor contribution to a more nuanced inquiry into how economy and sociality are related, one of the more important questions that social entrepreneurship asks.

A conversation – over email – with Zygmunt Bauman is important for the further contextualization of this chapter, and for the choice of the two answers provided above. After having invited[2] Professor Bauman and his wife Janina to a symposium at Växjö University in 2006 (on the theme of Utopia), we were later connected via Zygmunt's latest book – *The Art of Life* (Bauman, 2008). In the afterword of the book, he generously refers to our (Monika Kostera's and my) book on the Experience Economy (Hjorth and Kostera, 2007) and notes that we pointed out that the move from an old organizational paradigm, centred on management, over to a new, centred on entrepreneurship, also meant that the most vital characteristics of experience are 'immediacy, playfulness, subjectivity and performativity' (Hjorth and Kostera, 2007). Bauman noted that this change towards entrepreneurial organizations also means that what used to be located in the natural habitats of homes, friendship relationships and neighbourhoods – that is, playfulness and even love – have now moved into work/organization. This breaks the rule, characteristic of modernity according to Weber, that suggested that we separate work from the personal, and make professionalism centred on conducting oneself as a modular human (Kallinikos, 2003), understanding that organizations (bureaucracies) called upon a particular professional role to be included in work, not humans in their full behavioural complexity. Bauman further indicates that there is a continuous expansion here, by work-organizations, which he describes by reference to aging fairy tale witches' need for ever larger supplies of virgin blood, and which takes on bulimic features (Bauman, 2008: 129). Later, as part of the process of honouring Professor Bauman with a doctorate at Copenhagen Business School, he sent me his speech, to be given in a seminar at this occasion. The speech focused on this reflection on the expansive tendencies of Capital, as he discussed the present-day credit crunch, and its never-ending craving for virgin lands in order to maintain its machinery. My chapter here makes use of Bauman's speech, as he so kindly invited me to do, as I use the credit crunch as a case that also suggests we need to inquire into how sociality and economy are created and related, and what role social entrepreneurship has in this.

## THE CASE OF THE CREDIT CRUNCH

At the opening of Bauman's speech, he writes the following, citing Rosa Luxemburg at the end (the text, not specified in the speech, must be her *The Accumulation of Capital* from 1951):

> To develop, the capitalist system needs non- or pre-capitalist social organizations to gain its surpluses, but if it is successful, it deprives of their pre-capitalist virginity the self-same organizations whose uninterrupted and abundant supply is the very condition of its continuous existence . . . Capital, she wrote, 'feeds on the ruins of such organizations, and although this non-capitalist milieu is indispensable for accumulation, the latter proceeds at the cost of this medium nevertheless, by eating it up'.

It is not difficult to imagine the parallel to social entrepreneurship, in its Anglo-American form, as an expansion of the capitalist system, feeding on what it chooses to represent as the ruins of the social system whose organization – so it suggests, cheered on by the mainstream management writers of enterprise discourse, who, so I suggest, have much to gain from such an image acquiring truth-status – has failed to solve the problems. Re-presenting the problems as *economic* problems, rather than social (not that any problem is either purely economic or social), paves the way for management as expertise, and for suggesting – as a true statement, uncontested expertise – that we fix what's wrong by using economic analysis. This is of course why management writers readily support the kind of thinking that Gary Becker represents; it expands the market for management books and consulting services almost infinitely. Economy, according to the meaning it has now acquired, is about proper/efficient *management* of resources. Now, this used to imply scarce resources and managing them in an economic way was associated – as I suggested above – with frugality and care. Management has radically changed the meaning of 'economic'. The managerial economy is characterized by ICT (information and communication technology)-enhanced systems of control, recording of performances to establish normalizing targets and correspondingly 'normal' subject-positions or roles, and assessment to appraise achievement; by excessive (some say perverse) bonus systems, and tireless chasing of 'virgin lands' into which to expand. Note that I am not criticizing management or capitalism as such (this would indeed require a much larger effort), but merely pointing out reasons to understand its role in shaping the economy and its consequences for the economy–sociality relationship.

Bauman, leaning on Rosa Luxemburg, recognizes this (the tendency to bite its own tail) in his speech as immanent to capital, but does not recall his reflection from the book, *The Art of Life*, where he associated the experience economy with a move towards the entrepreneurial. But the connection is provided by the colonizing tendency, the snake that bites its tail. The move towards the entrepreneurial organization is, in *The Art of Life*, a case of capitalist organization expanding beyond its habitat into all spheres of life. Playfulness, friendship, and even love are now to be expected from work. Management of the competitive workplace in an innovation-intense post-industrial economy thus seems to be characterized by calling upon the whole human as opposed to the modular human of modern-industrial organization (according to Weber, as pointed out in Kallinikos, see above). In the speech, the credit crunch is instead analysed with the help of Luxemburg's leading thought-figure about capital eating on its own tail, without reference to changes in organizational forms (from managerial to entrepreneurial). The credit crunch is discussed as an exemplification of how capital feeds on young people (in particular) by luring them into developing debt-generating habits as if this was the most natural way of satisfying their 'need' to consume. Bauman writes:

> All or almost all potential borrowers have been already seduced into borrow-
> ing to the limit (and often beyond the limit) of their 'debt servicing' capacity;
> acquisition of additional debtors has become therefore exorbitantly costly.
> Goaded by their own momentum, lenders carried nonetheless their already
> tested skills of 'debt production' to the territories too hopelessly barren to
> promise any return on investment (recall for instance the collapse of the 'sub-
> prime mortgages' stratagem). And so yet another strategy in the long line of
> capitalist accumulation methods exhausted its potential: once more capitalism
> 'ate up', in the course of its expansion, the milieu indispensable for its survival
> . . . (Bauman, 2009: 2).

Bauman's analysis is broader, though, than his initial focus on capital. In
this sense he is typically more sociological in his approach. He identifies
the habit of borrowing to consume as one established by the support from
the State as well. It is at the time between childhood and adulthood that
people are most vulnerable to efforts to make them develop habits and
opinions. This is a time, Bauman suggests, when young people want to
start to 'manage their affairs' (that is, becoming economic in the original
sense of the word). Not only banks and credit-card providers, but also the
state-supported university loans are part of creating the vicious circle of
debts:

> The loans unavoidable when studying for a degree have been with the help
> of governments made seductively easy to obtain and to appear seductively
> (though misleadingly) easy to repay. In the result, an average student finishes
> her or his study with a debt most graduates will find too huge to be ever repaid
> in full . . . (Bauman, 2009: 4).

So, to 'become someone', the young person joins the 'normal' habit of
creating a debt, a pattern that is then easily repeated in order to finance the
life one believes rightfully is what 'I should demand for myself'. One can
detect here a critique (which makes Bauman join Deleuze in this respect)
of Kant's transcendental-legislative subject 'as a historical construct
derived from the institution of the State' (Goodchild, 1996: 17). People,
especially young people trying to 'become someone', readily institution-
alize conventions, values, opinions, and habits that are abstracted from
State-institutional settings. Critique, change and innovation are thereby
prevented.

At this point it is necessary to distinguish two movements that I have
merely indicated above without further due explanation. First, the credit
crunch makes overt a central tendency in capital – to seek out virgin
grounds in order to generate surplus, a method that is forcing it to 'move
on' as it eats up the milieu indispensable for its survival. This is illustrated
in abundance in the credit crisis, where the snake finally reached its head

and so could not chew any further. Secondly, the inability to identify this tendency, let alone its consequences for oneself as a person, is partly explained by the entrepreneurialization that is central in late- or post-capitalism's managerialization of personal identity (Gordon, 1991). This means that management's promotion of enterprise behaviour during the 1990s (cf. du Gay, 1997), what I once called the development of mano-preneurship (Hjorth, 2003) as an idealized employee subject-position, represents a skilful extension of the domain of the market into all spheres of life – including friendship, love and playfulness (Åkerström Andersen, 2008). This expansion was made under the flag: securing the innovation-based competitiveness of globalized businesses by the means of the enter-prising (manopreneurial) employee. This would suggest that employees in general and young people in particular represent two targets of capital: two more or less virgin grounds needed to generate profit. In the case of the employee, the virgin ground represents this calling on the full human into work.

Now, what is really the role of entrepreneurship in this? I suggest that depending on how we understand social entrepreneurship, we are likely either to extend this tendency of capital and serve up ever new domains to be properly included in the economic solutions to social problems, or, alternatively, to resist this tendency by emphasizing entrepreneurship as creating *sociality* rather than economy. It falls back on how we understand entrepreneurship: as part of or distinct from management; as one total-izing concept or multiple, contextual and differing; as best theorized from the perspective of a rational choice agent, modelled on extended utility functions (à la Becker's social economics), or from accepting the behav-ioural complexity of creators of new sociality, new practices of living. Let us look closer into this idea.

## SOCIAL ENTREPRENEURSHIP: ECONOMY AND SOCIALITY

In the opening chapter to our book *Entrepreneurship as Social Change* (Steyaert and Hjorth, 2006), we asked 'What is social in social entrepre-neurship?' We did so in perspective of the hype around social entrepre-neurship, which we also suggested represented a new entrepreneuriality of society (Ibid: 1). The book affirmed a claim made in earlier publica-tions (Hjorth, 2003; Steyaert and Hjorth, 2003; Steyaert and Katz, 2004) that entrepreneurship is a social force creating society, and not only (or even primarily) an economic force creating companies and products. In a later chapter we critiqued what we understood as the Anglo-American discourse on social entrepreneurship, prioritizing an extension of the market into new areas of society in order to represent social problems as economic and make them targets for new public management. We wrote, after analysing the dominant 'social entrepreneurship' discourse, suggesting the need to move into a discussion of the public and the role of the citizen therein, rather than to stay with the social (re-described in terms of the economic) and its central figure – the consumer:

> We could then ask how the social is created today in everyday processes. A partial conclusion tells us that the social is predominantly produced as a form of the economic, with the effect that existing political tension is transformed into a discussion of active citizens as responsible consumers. However, this study has told about public entrepreneurs that don't opt for public action for economic reasons as do Hirschman's consumers, but for the kind of opportunities that are created in participating in the public space guided by *abundantia* and *aequitas* [surplus should be shared in fair and open manner]. Whereas 'social entrepreneurship' produces the 'social' as something needing to be fixed (re-described as forms of the economic and subject to management knowledge), 'public entrepreneurship' creates sociality as something missing and socialises risk in local communities as part of public space (Hjorth and Bjerke, 2006: 117).

This was an attempt to shift focus in the 'social entrepreneurship' debate: away from the entrepreneur as an instrument for solving societal problems with business skills, and towards the social role of entrepreneurship as a sociality-creating force. *Sociality* was here understood (leaning on Deleuze and Guattari's work, 1994) as collective investments in a desired image, investments that produce heterogeneous groupings (projects, communities, collective), united by co-functioning and sympathy. The purpose was to point out that entrepreneurship generates new possibilities for living, which in turn opens society up to 'missing people' (a concept we borrow from Deleuze, for example 1998). This suggestion is not based upon a change of what entrepreneurship is. Rather, it is a suggestion to see the complex and diverse force that entrepreneurship has always been. It is a disclosure – brought about by a nuanced language of social and cultural theory – of sides of entrepreneurship silenced by mainstream determination of it. This is resonant with Steyaert and Katz's (2004) plea for a more socially and culturally sensitive analysis of entrepreneurship as a societal force.

I am not suggesting that social entrepreneurship is not about economy. In the perspective of the engagement with Bauman's sociological analysis of the credit crash, I have instead found additional reasons to emphasize the social: 'We believe creativity is a genuinely social force. Our focus should be on the in-betweens, the relationships, and not on individuals.'

(Hjorth and Bjerke, 2006: 119), and to stress the pre-managerial under-standing of economy, that is, less instrumental, individualistic, and one-dimensional. Bauman uses, in his book *The Art of Life*, the helpers of Jews in Poland during the holocaust (helpers were punished by death for helping, hiding or failing to report such activities) as evidence against the dominant individualistic, rational choice approach to explaining human behaviour. One cannot explain such behaviour – choosing to help others and thereby risking one's life – by the help of individualistic approaches, but one has to look beyond this, into the sympathy holding collectives together, into a care for the other (that is, economy in the original sense): 'when it comes to moral selves and ethical judgement, inventories of deter-minants and statistics of their distribution are of little use' (Bauman, 2008: 97).

When we pretend that to study social entrepreneurship it is enough to focus on the economic and to base our analysis on the rational choices of the individual agent, I would say I sense a lie, although all the facts may be argued as true. By this I mean to emphasize that conventional wisdom (if you want to call it that) suggests to us today that such an approach would be correct in order to investigate social entrepreneurship. Facts and truths are always products of discourses and institutions operating in society within a certain period of time (Foucault, 1988). The convention has to be broken – an entrepreneurial effort per se – in order for social entrepreneur-ship as a field of study to become social in a meaningful way. This may require a more reflexive study of social entrepreneurship, one that not only includes the author's role in the field and in the creation of the text, but one that in addition observes how disciplinary, historical and institutional forces set the table for certain kinds of descriptions, analyses and conclu-sions. This is indeed also a matter of economy in its present sense. For the 'rational' researchers – according to dominant perspectives – would not engage in too much of such contextualization and reflexivity due to the simple fact that it pays very little in review processes. It also prevents, or at least makes more difficult, the delivery of neat bullet-point lists aimed at servicing the consulting efforts provided for practitioners (often man-agers of various kinds). Letting social, historical and cultural perspective into studies of social entrepreneurship (as suggested by Steyaert and Katz, 2004) – what I would describe as being more sensitive to what we study – would then not correspond to good management of resources, as this has become determined in the managerial economy. However, again, from a more original (although originality is by no means a guarantee for being right or true) meaning of economy, the household would be the manager's focus and a prudent, frugal care to be characterizing one's attention. It seems important to disassociate entrepreneurship from a managerial economy and to intensify its social, cultural and ethical sides. I cannot think of any particular study of forms of entrepreneurship where this is more important than in the case of social entrepreneurship.

What sociality, then, is social entrepreneurship creating? We have previously described sociality (again leaning on Deleuze and Guattari's philosophy, 1994) as a field of emergence from which distinctions between individual and collective, as well as the forms for their interaction, are formed (cf. Massumi, 2002). By this I mean to suggest that a processual approach provides a rich possibility for relational studies of social entrepreneurship. As Massumi (2002: 9) says, when we do not assume that societal or disciplinary conventions are correct (for example dominant ways of studying social entrepreneurship), we include finding concepts for 'interaction-in-the-making' as an important part of our study. Massumi suggests further that relation is the term for 'interaction-in-the-making'. This means, for social entrepreneurship studies, that we would include questions of *how* individuals and collectives are made distinct, how individuality is theorized, culturally supported, organizationally rewarded . . . and how forms of interaction – relations – are regulated. I believe such questions – and there is certainly a whole plethora of such that go well beyond my imagination at the present – are crucial for describing, studying, analysing and creating knowledge of social entrepreneurship. This is not the least since social entrepreneurship is a dominant discourse presently ordering and regulating the way people think and practise regarding how the distinction between the individual and the collective should look, and how the interaction between them should be formed.

## CONCLUDING

For this reason – that this distinction is made at present, and this interaction is formed at present, not the least by influences from social entrepreneurship studies, exemplified by this volume – it is important to investigate how such studies are conducted and develop. The purpose of such an investigation cannot of course be to limit or control it, or to suggest forms for conducting this research. Rather, on the contrary, it should be in our interest to open up what is about to close itself in – centripetally – around a unifying paradigm of totalizing definition. In the perspective developed here, engaging with the present via the case of the credit crunch, it is also important to emphasize (with Massumi, and process studies more generally) that societies, subjectivities, interactions are made and not given or settled. Indeed, when social entrepreneurship is understood as a force creating sociality, it is suggested that it is the becoming of the social that is affected. It is the ways we distinguish individuals from collectives, and it is the forms for interaction – relations – that we suggest for them, that are made possible by creations of sociality. This means, as most of you have observed by now, that such a conceptualization of social entrepreneurship refuses to limit the concept to the economic, managerial, strategic, or decisional nature of the practices. It stresses the need to include the political and ethical sides of the matter too.

## NOTES

1. Gilles Deleuze will later pick up the concept of socius and use it as a virtuality of 'being-with others' (Goodchild, 1996), that is, as a driving force in actualizing the social. But he also stressed the repressive nature of such concepts, and opposed Kant for this (political) reason. Totalizing concepts of the *socius* – such as the State or Capital – leads to subjects interiorizing Kant's court of Pure Reason, conventions, values (Goodchild, 1996: 17) which limits the imagination of what society could become.
2. Monika Kostera provided the direct contact with the Baumans.

## REFERENCES

Åkerstrøm Andersen, N. (2008), *Legende magt (Playing Power)*, Copenhagen: Hans Reitzels Forlag.

Bauman, Z. (2008), *The Art of Life*, Cambridge: Polity Press.

Bauman, Z. (2009), 'Life on credit: or: what lies at the bottom of the "credit crunch"', speech for the Honorary Doctorate Ceremony, at Copenhagen Business School, personal correspondence.

Becker, G.S. and K.M. Murphy (2000), *Social Economics: Market Behaviour in a Social Environment*, Cambridge: Harvard University Press.

Becker, G.S. and K.M. Murphy (2003), *Social Economics: Market Behaviour in a Social Environment*, Cambridge: Harvard University Press.

Deleuze, G. (1998), *Essays Critical and Clinical*, transl. by Daniel W. Smith and Michael A. Greco, London: Verso.

Deleuze, G. and F. Guattari (1994), *What is Philosophy?*, transl. by Graham Burchell and Hugh Tomlinson, London: Verso.

du Gay, P. (ed.) (1997), *Production of Culture, Cultures of Production*, London: Sage.

Foucault, M. (1988), 'Truth, power, self: an interview with Michel Foucault', in L.H. Martin, H. Gutman and P.H. Hulton (eds), *Technologies of the Self – A Seminar with Michel Foucault*, Amherst: The University of Massachusetts Press, pp. 9–15.

Goodchild, P. (1996), *Deleuze & Guattari – An Introduction to the Politics of Desire*, London: Sage.

Gordon, C. (1991), 'Governmental rationality: an introduction', in G. Burchell, C. Gordon and P. Miller (eds), *The Foucault Effect – Studies in Governmentality*, Chicago: The University of Chicago Press, pp. 1–50.

Hjorth, D. (2003), *Rewriting Entrepreneurship – For a New Perspective on Organisational Creativity*, Malmö/Copenhagen/Oslo: Liber/CBS Press/Abstrakt.

Hjorth, D. and B. Bjerke (2006), 'Public entrepreneurship: moving from social/consumer to public/citizen', in C. Steyaert and D. Hjorth (eds), *Entrepreneurship as Social Change*, Cheltenham, UK and Northampton, MA, USA: Edward Elgar, pp. 97–120.

Hjorth, D. and M. Kostera (2007), *Entrepreneurship and the Experience Economy*, Copenhagen: CBS Press.

Kallinikos, J. (2003), 'Work, human agency and organizational forms: an anatomy of fragmentation, Jannis Kallinikos', *Organization Studies*, **24**(4), 595–618.

Kirchgässner, G. (2008), *Homo Oeconomicus – The Economic Model of Behaviour and its Applications in Economics and Other Social Sciences*, New York: Springer.

Luxemburg, R. (1951), *The Accumulation of Capital*, London: Routledge and Kegan Paul.

Massumi, B. (2002), *Parables for the Virtual – Movement, Affect, Sensation*, Durham & London: Duke University Press.

Steyaert, C. and D. Hjorth (eds) (2003), *New Movements in Entrepreneurship*, Cheltenham, UK and Northampton, MA, USA: Edward Elgar.

Steyaert, C. and D. Hjorth (2006), *Entrepreneurship as Social Change*, Cheltenham, UK and Northampton, MA, USA: Edward Elgar.

Steyaert, C. and J. Katz (2004), 'Reclaiming the space of entrepreneurship in society: geographical, discursive and social dimensions', *Entrepreneurship and Regional Development*, **16**(3), 179–96.

# 17 Conclusions, recommendations and an agenda for future research in social entrepreneurship

*Harry Matlay and Alain Fayolle*

## INTRODUCTION

The collection of chapters published in this volume offer ample evidence of the wide variety of concepts and contexts that can be legitimately considered or examined under the scope and remit of 'Social Entrepreneurship'. This volume incorporates the latest thinking on, and 'cutting edge' research in, this fast-growing and rapidly expanding area of entrepreneurship. The handbook provides an international perspective on social entrepreneurship theory and practice, not only by virtue of its multinational authorship, but also by its cross-border focus on social entrepreneurs, their actions and their enterprises.

The rapid development of a research topic invariably results in a growing volume of mixed quality publications, which can range from empirically rigorous, peer-refereed output to dogmatic and often superficial renditions of 'how to do' books. Social entrepreneurship, as an emergent area of academic endeavour, is no exception to the rule and an extensive literature search undertaken by us has highlighted that the expansion of specialist knowledge in this area follows closely the mixed quality developmental path exhibited by related topics, such as Entrepreneurship, Entrepreneurship Education and Social Capital (Ostrom and Ahn, 2003; Matlay, 2005; 2006). Differentiating between research output that is empirically rigorous as well as useful in practice and the haphazard, but seductive superficiality and ease of read of lesser publications is a considerable challenge faced by researchers engaged in Social Entrepreneurship theory-building. Furthermore, the delivery of timely research output that is easily accessible to a wide range of stakeholders and of practical relevance to social entrepreneurs requires careful planning, in-depth knowledge and a commitment to empirical rigorousness in all its complexity and resource implications. We genuinely believe that the *Handbook of Research in Social Entrepreneurship* fulfils the quality criteria that define empirical rigour and that, as a comprehensive and cutting edge research monograph, it will withstand the test of time in this exciting and fast-growing area of scholarly endeavour.

## CONCEPTUAL DILEMMAS IN SOCIAL ENTREPRENEURSHIP

The emergence of contemporary Social Entrepreneurship has often been attributed to and explained in terms of individual, community and societal responses to profound crises and changes taking place in developed as well as developing countries (Borzaga and Defourny, 2001). An in-depth analysis of the growing socio-economic, humanitarian and environmental crisis or the declining volume of resources made available for social consumption is beyond the scope of this chapter. These, and other pertinent aspects, are competently outlined, evidenced and analysed elsewhere (see, for example, Brinckerhoff, 2000; Bornstein, 2004; Nicholls, 2006a). In a recent critical overview of the emergence and fast growth of this phenomenon, Defourny (2001: 1) argued that social enterprises 'represent the new or renewed expression of civil society against a background of economic crisis, the weakening of social bonds and difficulties of the welfare state'. It is further posited that the unprecedented expansion of the social entrepreneurship sector cannot be meaningfully considered in isolation from a long heritage of philanthropic and charitable activities that can be traced to the nineteenth century (Boettke and Rathbone, 2002; Evers and Laville, 2004; Gaudiani, 2004; Lohmann, 2007). Additionally, in recent years, both advanced and transition economies have experienced a revival of, and a renewed interest in, cooperative forms of organization and their transformation into new social enterprises (Borzaga and Spear, 2004; Perrini, 2006). As social problems and related needs have increased on a global scale, government interest in general and community involvement in particular have expanded to encompass a wide range of national and international perspectives, initiatives and solutions (Barendsen and Gardner, 2004; Christie and Honig, 2006; Fulton and Dees, 2006).

Interestingly, however, and despite the rapid growth of this variant of entrepreneurial activity, there exists a notable paucity of empirically rigorous research on the dimensions and complexities inherent in social entrepreneurship. In this context, Mair and Martí (2006: 36) point out that 'while entrepreneurial phenomena aimed at economic development have received a great amount of scholarly attention, entrepreneurship as a process to foster social progress has only recently attracted the interest of researchers'. Much of the recent writing on this topic falls into three broad areas of research interest: (i) social entrepreneurship definitions and boundaries; (ii) theory development and validation; and (iii) illustrative case studies. Developmental research, which focused specifically on social enterprises as a unit of analysis, has contributed considerably to the tentative emergence of social entrepreneurship as a new field of academic endeavour (see Nicholls, 2006b). There can be little doubt, however, that social entrepreneurship is in its theoretical infancy and that a great deal remains to be achieved and consolidated before it can empirically establish itself within the wider entrepreneurship research portfolio. Specifically, and in order to mitigate the current 'fuzziness' in its theoretical foundations, further empirically rigorous research must be undertaken on definitions, boundaries and interpretation of social entrepreneurship as well as its positioning within the wider entrepreneurial theory and practice (Brouard and Larivet, 2009).

Early descriptors of social entrepreneurship were dominated by theories of state and market failure (demand side) and related changes in patterns of entrepreneurial activities (supply side). Socially oriented theories of entrepreneurial supply and demand were usually contextualized within the dynamics and complexities of organizational choice, size, location and economic orientation (Pestoff, 1998; Spear, 2002). Some researchers argued that social entrepreneurs as well as their enterprises should be adopted as the main unit of analysis in this growing field of research (Thompson et al., 2000; Bornstein, 2004). According to Dees (2001: 5), however, 'society has a need for different leadership types and styles . . . social entrepreneurs are one special breed of leader, and they should be recognized as such'. Other researchers perceive social entrepreneurship as a process of exploring and exploiting opportunities in order to create social value (Alvord et al., 2004). It should be noted, however, that regardless of which unit of analysis is chosen, the organizational context within which social entrepreneurship takes place sets it apart from a wide range of social initiatives aimed at facilitating socially oriented change and betterment (Austin et al., 2006; Mair and Martí, 2006).

## STAKEHOLDER INVOLVEMENT IN SOCIAL ENTREPRENEURSHIP

One of the most important aspects of the recent expansion in social entrepreneurship is the potential relevance and/or usefulness of specialist research to a range of stakeholders who are involved in this growing sector of the economy. Research relevance in this area is particularly important in terms of the sector's practical potential, actual impact and growth tendencies – as evidenced over the last two decades, during a period that is often described in terms of relative economic stagnation and long periods of negative growth (see Matlay, 2008). In this context, Alter (2006) highlights an apparent paradox between social entrepreneurship as an area of practitioner growth and its relatively underdeveloped body of specialist knowledge. We posit that a useful and cost effective way of improving the quality, quantity and relevance of specialist knowledge in this topic would be to focus future research upon the specific needs of various groups of stakeholders. Support for this approach can be found in both stakeholder theory and the specialist knowledge which relates to entrepreneurship in general and social entrepreneurship in particular (Matlay, 2009). The notion of stakeholder involvement and influence in the management of change can be traced to the early 1980s and the rise of strategic management theory. Freeman's (1984: 46) definition of a stakeholder covers 'any group or individuals who can affect or are affected by the achievement of the organisation's objectives'. The stakeholder approach is particularly relevant to social entrepreneurship and the multitude of individuals who are involved in, or benefit from, related entrepreneurial activities.

Spear (2006) argues that successful social enterprises tend to rely on a range of internal and external stakeholders, whose involvement is crucial to socially oriented entrepreneurial activities. In this context, Dees (1998) found that most social enterprises represented a hybrid interaction of key stakeholder relationships that offered a compromise between non-profit and for-profit entrepreneurial perspectives and activities. His 'hybrid model' of social entrepreneurship identified four groups of stakeholders (that is, beneficiaries, capital, workforce and suppliers) on a spectrum which ranged from 'purely philanthropic' to 'purely commercial'. Typically, the motives, methods and goals of these stakeholders varied in accordance with the social enterprise's position on the spectrum. Therefore, it is not just entrepreneurs who influence or contribute towards the success of their social enterprises, but also the involvement and activities of a wide range of internal and external stakeholders. Social entrepreneurship is sometimes labelled 'caring capitalism' in view of the fact that success in achieving organizational goals is largely dependent upon competitiveness in a chosen niche market (Hibbert et al., 2005). In this context, Sharir and Lerner (2006: 7) assert that 'essential to the founding and establishing of any social venture are the individuals and groups with the vision, drive, and perseverance to provide answers to social problems and needs, whether educational, welfare, environmental or health related'.

The conceptualization of social entrepreneurship within the stakeholder perspective is, however, complicated by the recent rise to economic and political topicality of the view that all enterprises should address social issues, regardless of their size, economic activity, mission or orientation (Margolis and Walsh, 2003). As a result, various aspects of social responsiveness and corporate social responsibility are now considered important priorities in policy making, at national and international levels. Consequently, many features of corporate social responsibility, corporate social responsiveness, social issues management, corporate social performance and stakeholder management are becoming mainstream business strategies and practices (see Jenkins, 2006; Porter and Kramer, 2006). As most empirical research focusing on social entrepreneurship is qualitative or illustrative in nature, a stakeholder approach presents ample scope for larger, quantitative studies to incorporate most, if not all, the aspects relating to corporate social behaviour present in small, medium and large organizations. Furthermore, the limited stakeholder perspective proposed by Dees (1998) should be widened to embrace the interests and involvement of government and policy makers as well as those of researchers who focus specifically on this new and exciting area of academic endeavour.

# CONCLUSIONS, RECOMMENDATIONS AND AN AGENDA FOR FUTURE RESEARCH

Following on from the research disseminated in this volume, we conclude that the diversity of approaches and perspectives reflect, to a large degree, the wide range of entrepreneurial activities, goals and missions that can be legitimately considered as representative of social entrepreneurship. We identify a number of important strands that stand out as mainstream approaches to social entrepreneurship research. One of the earliest empirical approaches to gain legitimacy focused upon social entrepreneurs and highlighted several personal leadership characteristics, such as credibility, motivation, commitment and a strong belief in social values. The ability of social entrepreneurs to lead by example, to motivate followers and to secure the commitment of internal as well as external stakeholders often ensures the success of their chosen social mission. Related approaches, while recognizing the leadership value of the individual entrepreneur, expand the research focus to cover other key players as well as the social enterprise as a whole. Similarly, a plethora of new dimensions have been added to social entrepreneurship research by focusing not only on the implicit or explicit mission of social enterprises, but also on the competitive environment within which these operate and the characteristics that differentiate them from their commercial counterparts. Social entrepreneurship can also be researched as a process involving the identification, exploration and conversion of entrepreneurial opportunities with the purpose of creating social value and/or benefits. These, and other innovative research approaches, have all contributed to the development of an embryonic theory of social entrepreneurship.

An in-depth investigation of the emergent theory of social entrepreneurship uncovered a growing fragmentation and divergence of research in this area of entrepreneurial activity. Definitional difficulties and a blurring of traditional constructs, which now can include for-profit variants and commercial hybrids, have resulted in a conceptual blurring that undermines researchers' efforts to build a unified, convergent and meaningful social entrepreneurship theory. A lack of definitional cohesion and a multitude of overlapping 'umbrella' concepts in current usage tend to render national and international comparisons of social entrepreneurship research problematic or unreliable at the best of times. We conclude that research fuzziness and a lack of critical mass negatively affects the relevance and usefulness of a considerable proportion of emergent research and renders it either unusable for, or largely irrelevant to, the needs of an influential segment of practice-oriented stakeholders, including social entrepreneurs, policy makers and legislators.

We acknowledge, however, that there is some conceptual consensus on important aspects of social entrepreneurship and recommend that these should be used as the basis for building a convergent theory that focuses, in the first instance, upon the specific needs of main groups of stakeholders. Based upon our knowledge and understanding of social entrepreneurship, we tentatively group stakeholders into three main categories: primary, secondary and tertiary. Social entrepreneurs, their employees and direct beneficiaries are grouped together in the primary stakeholder category. The secondary stakeholder group would include fundraisers, donors, suppliers, customers, voluntary workers and those individuals that are engaged in socially oriented activities within commercial organizations. We envisage that the tertiary stakeholder category would incorporate representatives of government, public, community and commerce. This tentative typology is not meant to be exhaustive or exclusive and is offered here as indicative of a flexible grouping of individual, organizational, official and community interests, all of which are committed to a social agenda and/or mission. Having suggested a stakeholder focused conceptual approach to convergent theory-building, we further recommend a grounded contextual basis for the future expansion of the social entrepreneurship knowledge base.

The context of social entrepreneurship research is complex and can vary considerably in accordance with multiple stakeholder missions and objectives. The lack of a unifying social entrepreneurship paradigm has resulted in a proliferation of small-scale, qualitative research studies. To some extent, this can be justified by the heterogeneous nature of the sector and the contextual diversity (individual, local, national and international) that social entrepreneurship tends to embrace. The need for a balanced approach to theory-building, which includes qualitative, quantitative and mixed method research, has been commented upon by some of the contributors to this volume. We suggest that more quantitative and mixed method research is undertaken in order to redress the balance and ensure a wider comparability of results as well as a marked improvement in the generalization of relevant findings. In this context we also recommend that, when planning and designing their empirical studies, researchers clearly differentiate between enterprises engaged in social value creation and those that pursue economic, for-profit objectives. Hybrids, double value creation enterprises are rendered problematic in terms of stakeholder perspectives, involvement and expectations and, therefore, should be researched separately, in a category of their own.

In most emergent fields of research, a vast proportion of early studies are exploratory in nature and aim to lay the conceptual foundations upon which explanatory and prescriptive theories are later built and validated. Although social entrepreneurship initially emerged as a practice-led subtopic of entrepreneurship, much of the emergent conceptual fieldwork relied on academic and professional research and related dissemination. If we set out, as we should, to build a rigorous and legitimate field of research, then the foundations of social entrepreneurship must be convergent, empirically rigorous and replicable across a multitude of contextual perspectives. It must also embrace geographical, cultural, religious and political variety – in all its diversity and richness. An ideal 'wish list' of stakeholder-oriented research agenda would include traditional themes as well as emergent and controversial subjects. We feel that it is important to explore the meaning of social entrepreneurship, its scope and its mission in order to ensure the robustness and applicability of related research. The social entrepreneurship process is yet another important aspect of this emergent topic of research, as it involves the active participation of a number of primary stakeholders and therefore must not be neglected by the academic community.

Although many social enterprises operate locally, some can have a community or society-wide impact. Cumulatively, social entrepreneurship output can contribute to societal welfare at both micro and macro levels. Very little is known about intangible returns on social investments or social impacts attributable directly to this type of entrepreneurial activity. We would welcome research that sets out to quantify the impact that social entrepreneurship can have on employment, income generation, service provision and other micro-level indicators. Similarly, contributions to welfare reform, resource redistribution, social innovation and other aspects of macro-level social entrepreneurship activity need to be empirically investigated. Furthermore, there is a marked paucity of empirically rigorous research on social entrepreneurship failures and related negative outcomes. Practice-oriented stakeholders could benefit considerably from reliable data on the causes and consequences of social enterprise failure. Conversely, success could be disseminated in the form of best practice for the benefit of local, regional, national and international practitioners. We are confident that our recommendations to target research efforts and scarce resources upon the specific needs of stakeholders will contribute to a convergent and unified body of empirically rigorous knowledge. The emergent theoretical foundations will benefit not only entrepreneurs, researchers and policy makers involved in social entrepreneurship but also countless individuals and communities who are the recipients of social value created in these enterprises.

# REFERENCES

Alter, K. (2006), *Social Enterprise Typology*, Washington, DC: Virtue Ventures.

Alvord, S., L. Brown and C. Letts (2004), 'Social entrepreneurship and societal transformation', *Journal of Applied Behavioural Science*, **40**(3), 260–82.

Austin, J., H. Stevenson and J. Wei-Skillern (2006), 'Social and commercial entrepreneurship: same, different, or both?', *Entrepreneurship Theory and Practice*, **30**(1), 1–22.

Barendsen, L. and H. Gardner (2004), 'Is the social entrepreneur a new type of leader?', *Leader to Leader*, **34**(1), 43–50.

Boettke, P. and A. Rathbone (2002), 'Civil society, social entrepreneurship and economic calculation: towards a political economy of the philanthropic enterprise', working paper No. 8, Fairfax County, Virginia: The Philanthropic Enterprise.

Bornstein, D. (2004), *How to Change the World: Social Entrepreneurs and the Power of New Ideas*, Oxford: Oxford University Press.

Borzaga, C. and J. Defourny (eds) (2001), *The Emergence of Social Enterprise*, London: Routledge.

Borzaga, C. and R. Spear (eds) (2004), *Trends and Challenges for Co-operatives and Social Enterprises in Developed and Transition Countries*, Trento, Italy: Fondazione Cariplo.

Brinckerhoff, P. (2000), *Social Entrepreneurship: The Art of Mission-Based Venture Development*, New York: John Wiley and Sons.

Brouard, F. and S. Larivet (2009), 'Social entrepreneurship: definitions and boundaries', Paper presented at the ANSER–ARES 2009 Conference, Carleton University, Ottawa, 27–29 May.

Christie, M. and B. Honig (2006), 'Social entrepreneurship: new research findings', *Journal of World Business*, **41**(1), 1–5.

Dees, J.G. (1998), 'Enterprising nonprofits', *Harvard Business Review*, **76**(1), 54–66.

Dees, J.G. (2001), 'The meaning of "social entrepreneurship"', conceptual note, Duke University: The Fuqua School of Business.

Defourny, J. (2001), 'Introduction: from third sector to social enterprise', in C. Borzaga and J. Defourny (eds), *The Emergence of Social Enterprise*, London: Routledge, pp. 1–28.

Evers, A., and J.L. Laville (2004), *The Third Sector in Europe*, Cheltenham, UK and Northampton, MA, USA: Edward Elgar.

Freeman, R.E. (1984), *Strategic Management: A Stakeholder Approach*, Boston: Pitman Publishing.

Fulton, K. and G. Dees (2006), 'The past, present, and future of Social Entrepreneurship – A conversation with Greg Dees', Duke University: Fuqua School of Business, available at: http://www.caseatduke.org/documents/deesinterview.pdf, accessed 19 December 2006.

Gaudiani, C. (2004), *The Greater Good: How Philanthropy Drives the American Economy and Can Save Capitalism*, New York: Owl Books.

Hibbert, S., G. Hogg and T. Quinn (2005), 'Social entrepreneurship: understanding consumer motives for buying The Big Issue', *Journal of Consumer Behavior*, **4**(1), 159–72.

Jenkins, H. (2006), 'Small business champions for corporate social responsibility', *Journal of Business Ethics*, **67**(3), 241–56.

Lohmann, R. (2007), 'Charity, philanthropy, public service, or enterprise: what are the big questions of nonprofit management today?', *Public Administration Review*, **67**(3), 437–44.

Mair, J. and I. Martí (2006), 'Social entrepreneurship research: a source of explanation, prediction and delight', *Journal of World Business*, **41**(1), 36–44.

Margolis, J. and J. Walsh (2003), 'Misery loves companies: rethinking social initiatives by business', *Administrative Science Quarterly*, **48**(2), 268–305.

Matlay, H. (2005), 'Researching entrepreneurship and education, Part 1: what is entrepreneurship and does it matter?', *Education and Training*, **47**(8/9), 665–77.

Matlay, H. (2006), 'Researching entrepreneurship and education, Part 2: what is entrepreneurship education and does it matter?', *Education and Training*, **48**(8/9), 704–18.

Matlay, H. (2008), 'The impact of entrepreneurship education on entrepreneurial outcomes', *Journal of Small Business and Enterprise Development*, **15**(2), 382–96.

Matlay, H. (2009), 'Entrepreneurship education in the UK: A critical analysis of stakeholder involvement and expectations', *Journal of Small Business and Enterprise Development*, **16**(2), 355–68.

Nicholls, A. (2006a), 'Introduction' in A. Nicholls (ed.), *Social Entrepreneurship: New Models of Sustainable Social Change*, Oxford: Oxford University Press, pp. 1–35.

Nicholls, A. (2006b), 'Playing the field: a new approach to the meaning of social entrepreneurship', *Social Enterprise Journal*, **2**(1), 1–4.

Ostrom, E. and T. Ahn (eds) (2003), *Foundations of Social Capital*, Cheltenham, UK and Northampton, MA, USA: Edward Elgar.

Perrini, F. (ed.) (2006), *The New Social Entrepreneurship: What Awaits Social Entrepreneurship Ventures?*, Cheltenham, UK and Northampton, MA, USA: Edward Elgar.

Pestoff, V. (1998), *Beyond the Market and State: Social Enterprise and Civil Democracy in a Welfare Society*, Aldershot: Ashgate Publishing.

Porter, M. and M. Kramer (2006), 'Strategy and society: the link between competitive advantage and corporate social responsibility', *Harvard Business Review*, **84**(12), 78–92.

Sharir, M. and M. Lerner (2006), 'Gauging the success of social ventures initiated by individual social entrepreneurs', *Journal of World Business*, **41**(1), 6–20.

Spear, R. (2002), 'National profiles of work integration social enterprises: United Kingdom', Working Paper No. 02/06, EMES European Research Network.

Spear, R. (2006), 'Social entrepreneurship: a different model?', *International Journal of Social Economics*, **33**(5/6), 399–410.

Thompson, J., G. Alvy and A. Lees (2000), 'Social entrepreneurship – a new look at the people and potential', *Management Decision*, **38**(5), 328–38.

# Index

Tracey, P. 36, 44
training 69–70
  coaching 266, 268
transborder cooperation 139–40
  case study of Upper Rhine Valley
    131–5
    complexity of cross-border
      cooperation 135–6
    need for additional boundary
      spanners 137
    competitive advantage and
      transborder regional
      development 130–31
    importance for European
      integration 125–6
transition economies 74
trends
  social entrepreneurship and 15–16,
    82–3
trust 160
Tse, Karen 95
Tyson, L. 110

unemployment 60
  reduction programmes 63
United Kingdom
  Department for Trade and Industry
    (DTI) 65
    definition of social enterprise 35
  entrepreneurial environment in 25
  not-for-profit organizations in 147
  social entrepreneurship in 29, 61, 64,
    65–7, 70, 71
  welfare system 15
United Nations Development
  Programme (UNDP) 74
United States of America
  non-profit organizations in 59, 147,
    287, 291
  social entrepreneurship in 23, 29, 57,
    79–80, 110
  social franchising case study 165–6

Valéau, P. 220
value
  economic 275
  social, *see* social value
Van de Ven, A. 128
Van Vuuren, M. 222
Vasakaria, V. 44
Venkataraman, S. 88, 91, 144, 150
Vesper, K.H. 207
Vienney, C. 119
VisionSpring 165–6, 168, 169–70,
  172, 173, 174, 175
voluntary sector 62, 66, 68, 77,
  217
vulnerability 114

Waddock, A.A. 40
Wagner, J.A. 94
Wallace, S.L. 210
Webb, J.W. 207, 224
Weber, Max 67, 309
Weerawardena, J. 45, 49
Weick, K.E. 92
Wei-Skillern, J. 49, 253
welfare systems 15, 60, 61, 63, 144
women entrepreneurs 253
Woods, C. 42, 47
work-integration social enterprise
  (WISE) 70, 80–81, 109, 111,
  114

Xela Accords 195

Yale University Program on
  Non-profit Organizations 59
Yin, R.K. 163
Young, D. 61
Yunus, Muhammad 145, 266, 277

Zahra, S.A. 49, 50, 233
Zietlow, J.T. 289
Zollverein 125